C000050356

AFFECTIVE ECOCRITICISM

Affective Ecocriticism

EMOTION, EMBODIMENT, ENVIRONMENT

Edited by Kyle Bladow and Jennifer Ladino

UNIVERSITY OF NEBRASKA PRESS   LINCOLN AND LONDON

© 2018 by the Board of Regents of
the University of Nebraska

All rights reserved
Manufactured in the United States of America

Library of Congress Cataloging-in-Publication Data
Names: Bladow, Kyle A., 1985– editor. |
Ladino, Jennifer K., editor.
Title: Affective ecocriticsm: emotion, embodiment,
environment / edited by Kyle Bladow and Jennifer Ladino.
Description: Lincoln: University of Nebraska Press,
[2018] | Includes bibliographical references and index.
Identifiers: LCCN 2017049296
ISBN 9781496206794 (cloth: alk. paper)
ISBN 9781496207562 (pbk.: alk. paper)
ISBN 9781496208569 (epub)
ISBN 9781496208576 (mobi)
ISBN 9781496208583
Subjects: LCSH: Climatic changes—Psychological
aspects. | Affect (Psychology) | Ecocriticism.
Classification: LCC BF353.5.C55 A44 2018
| DDC 152.4—dc23 LC record available at
https://lccn.loc.gov/2017049296

Set in Arno by Mikala R. Kolander.
Designed by N. Putens.

CONTENTS

ILLUSTRATIONS

ACKNOWLEDGMENTS

As with many collections, this one evolved from conversations at conferences—in particular, the Association for the Study of Literature and Environment (ASLE) conference in Moscow, Idaho, in 2015. We thank Sylvan Goldberg for being part of our panel "Speaking a Word for Affect: Affective Ecocriticism" (and for inspiring that panel's and this collection's title) and the enthusiastic audience members who attended and posed provocative questions. ASLE continues to be a vibrant and supportive intellectual community, for which the editors are grateful.

We'd also like to thank the two anonymous readers for their careful reviews of the manuscript and thoughtful suggestions for revisions. Their responses shaped this book in important ways. The editorial staff at the University of Nebraska Press has been professional and helpful throughout the process, and we appreciate their energetic support of this project.

Finally, we would like to thank our "dream team" of contributors. This group of authors surpassed all our expectations for promptness of submissions, diligence of revisions, and quality of scholarship. They made this project a pleasure to work on.

AFFECTIVE ECOCRITICISM

Toward an Affective Ecocriticism
Placing Feeling in the Anthropocene

KYLE BLADOW AND JENNIFER LADINO

"The Great Barrier Reef of Australia passed away in 2016 after a long illness. It was 25 million years old." So begins *Outside* magazine's mock "obituary" for the Great Barrier Reef, one of the more recent victims of climate change and its associated impacts.[1] Dismayed scientists were quick to insist that the reef's death was, if not greatly exaggerated, certainly overstated, but not before many readers had read, shared, and responded to the satirical piece with real feelings of grief, despair, anger, and resignation.[2]

Articles like this one, which cast environmental catastrophe in affectively striking terms, are all over the news. A twenty-four-hour news cycle and mobile information technologies at our fingertips increase the speed, frequency, and intensity with which many of us seek out and share news stories. Meanwhile, these same technologies enable corporations to track and manage our affects: emotion recognition startups help tech giants pinpoint the emotional states of individual consumers, while other companies amass composite "moods" using biometric data at sporting events and movie theaters.[3] Affects are at the center of contemporary biopolitics and are more public, more powerful, and more pertinent than ever.

A glance at headlines on any given day, with their reports of high fire danger, record temperatures, climate refugees, melting glaciers, extinct species, and abundant evidence of "global weirding," can be unsettling, alarming, even paralyzing.[4] Some people react to overwhelming data with "psychic numbing" or "compassion fatigue."[5] Others react with a range of emotional forms, such as anxiety, fear, sorrow, and more complicated responses like "climate grief" or other "Anthropocene disorders."[6] Even fairly straightforward emotions like hope are of dubious efficacy. What is clear is that reading the news is never the task of a disembodied mind. As neuroscientists claim with compelling evidence, we process stories with a cognitive apparatus that is not wholly distinct from our bodies, our feelings, and—quite literally—our guts.[7] Our environments too direct how we process information. Indeed, a premise of this book is that place profoundly shapes our emotional lives, from our most banal everyday moods and background feelings to the phenomenon psychologists call "flashbulb memory": that vivid "snapshot" of how we felt and *where we were* when we first read, saw, or heard about an especially shocking event.[8]

As we write this, there is plenty to find shocking. Terrorist attacks seem increasingly commonplace, and nationalism is on the rise in the United States and Europe. The failure of the press and most polls to predict Donald Trump's stunning victory in the 2016 U.S. presidential election—followed by alarming new discourse about "alternative facts" and "fake news"—raises concerns about a posttruth world in which emotional appeal, not reason, wins the day. Emotions are running high. In the United States the Right and Left are more polarized than ever, with strong feelings surfacing, for example, in postelection debates over whether to approach Trump supporters with a "spirit of empathy" or to "shame" them as racist, sexist xenophobes.[9] Fears about national security and anger over neoliberal globalization's failures fuel nationalism on the Far Right, while the Far Left calls for vigilant resistance to the current political order and dedication to inspiring alternatives. Across the political spectrum people are anxious. For environmentally concerned scholars and citizen scholars around the world, a major source of anxiety is the American public's apparent apathy about climate change. While the emergence of the term "climate justice" is a healthy sign, environmental issues played no significant role in the 2016 U.S. election. And while local and state governments and nongovernmental organizations vow to redouble their efforts to curb carbon emissions in response to Trump's decision to abandon the Paris Agreement, that decision nevertheless raises major concerns about the nation's commitment to mitigating the effects of climate change—and about its role in global politics.

Environmental humanities scholars find ourselves faced with important tasks: we must find new, more compelling ways to foreground connections between environmental and social justice, and we must reach across ideological, species, and scalar boundaries to find common ground in this new geologic epoch. A premise of this collection is that affect theory can help with both. Since both climate and social justice activists require altruistic emotions as a foundation for action, a clearer sense of what those emotions are and how they work might reconnect environmental and social justice.[10] Perhaps looking for micro-moments of affective intersection and building from them may be one small way forward in a political atmosphere of bubbles, divides, and seemingly entrenched polarization. If Heather Houser is right that "it is emotion that can carry us from the micro-scale of the individual to the macro-scale of institutions, nations, and the planet," then affect theory can clarify how that scalar transference works.[11]

Reading is one instance in which affect begins at the "micro-scale," and scholarship that draws on cognitive science to account for what happens affectively in readers is an area of growing interest. But reading is a relatively small part of most people's field of daily experience. Besides the ubiquitous news headlines, the many non-narrative affective triggers in our everyday environments—the weather, built spaces, nonhuman animals, and objects with which we inhabit the world—deserve assessment in terms of their emotional impacts. Our book draws on the rich interdisciplinary field of affect theory to identify the emotions that circulate around environmental issues today, to clarify how that circulation works, to acknowledge the powerful role environments themselves play in shaping affective experience, and to identify new affects emerging in our contemporary moment.

Affective Ecocriticism imagines a more *affective*—and consequently, we argue, a more *effective*—ecocriticism, as well as a more environmentally attuned affect studies. Bodies, human and nonhuman, are perhaps the most salient sites at which affect and ecocriticism come together. While affect theorists have tended to prioritize affect within and in relation to bodies and to overlook the environment's role in shaping it, ecocritics have too often neglected the affectivity of human bodies in their eagerness to champion greater attention to the more-than-human world. Still, there is much common ground between the surge of interest in affect—the "affective turn"—and the concurrent "material turn," especially its incarnation as material ecocriticism. Both affect studies and ecocriticism emerged in part as reactions to the poststructuralist focus on discourse and the dogged pursuit of ideology critique. Both approach subjects—emotion or nature—that must be understood as simultaneously material and ideological. And both recuperate terms that had long found themselves on the denigrated side of entrenched Cartesian dualisms: if "emotion" was theoretically suspect before the affective turn, "nature" was just as suspect prior to the emergence of ecocriticism. These points of overlap, as well as the relative simultaneity of these two theoretical turns, signal an opportune moment to conjoin affect theory and ecocritical theory more deliberately.

The "affective turn" has deep roots in Marxist, psychoanalytic, feminist, and queer theory and is understood at least in part as a corrective to a poststructuralist overemphasis on discourse at the expense of embodied experience.[12] Raymond Williams's provocative term "structures of feeling" and Eve Kosofsky Sedgwick and Adam Frank's recuperation of Silvan Tomkins's work on affect are often cited as foundational moments in affect studies. Queer theorists such as Lauren Berlant, Ann Cvetkovich, and Heather Love, among others, have produced important touchstones as well. Patricia Clough and, more recently, Rachel Greenwald Smith have taken up affect in relation to the political economy, attending to the increasingly complex ways markets influence and capitalize on our emotional lives.[13]

The turn to affect has culminated in several strands of affect theory across a spectrum from neuroscience to cultural theory. *The Affect Theory Reader* distinguishes no fewer than eight "affectual orientations" and insists there are "infinitely multiple iterations" affect theory might take.[14] Even so, it's possible to identify "two dominant vectors" in the humanities: "Silvan Tomkins's psychobiology of differential affects" on the one hand and "Gilles Deleuze's

Spinozist ethology of bodily capacities" on the other.[15] Although these vectors "resonate" and at times "interpenetrate" with each other, they are differentiated by the extent to which they see affect as contained in individual bodies.[16] Neuroscientists try to explain how emotions register in people; these scientists, as well as many psychologists—with the notable exception of the late Teresa Brennan—tend to focus on affects as contained within, or at least originating in, a human organism. At the other end of the spectrum, such cultural theorists as Brian Massumi and Kathleen Stewart align their work with a Spinozist definition of affect to conceive of it as "virtual" and "autonomous," co-produced by contingent and shifty assemblages.[17]

Affect theory in this vein understands affect as asignifying, precognitive bodily feeling, an "intensity" or a perpetual state of "becoming."[18] The geographer Ben Anderson concisely defines affect as "the transpersonal or prepersonal intensities that emerge as bodies affect one another."[19] Emotions can be distinguished as consciously interpreted or narrated affects—in Brennan's words, "feelings that have found the right match in words."[20] Massumi differentiates between emotion and affect by arguing that the former is just one possible form—albeit the "most intense (most contracted) expression"—affect can take within a particular body.[21] Because many (but not all) of our contributors are persuaded by these distinctions, we've chosen "affect" as our umbrella term.

However they negotiate the relationship between affect and emotion, affect scholars across the spectrum have seldom been in dialogue with ecocritical theory, though some do allude to the significance of environments in producing affect.[22] Antonio Damasio occasionally gestures toward the ways in which physical places matter in shaping both cognition and emotion.[23] Brennan suggests but doesn't pursue the role of environments in affect transmission when she describes that transmission as "an interaction with other people and an environment."[24] But scientific research cannot fully account for the cultural and political dimensions that environmental humanities scholarship prioritizes. Geographers such as Anderson and Nigel Thrift have contributed some of the most environmentally oriented theories of affect, including reconceiving "atmosphere" as a product of combined environmental, affective, political, and other material forces.

Lauren Berlant, Sianne Ngai, and Sara Ahmed have been especially influential in affect studies informed by feminist, queer, and critical race theory. Although their pathbreaking works are not primarily invested in the role of environment in shaping affect, some of their main theoretical tenets—Berlant's formulation of "cruel optimism," Ngai's focus on "ugly feelings," and Ahmed's description of how affect can "stick" to objects and bodies, as well as her method of connecting individual bodily response to emotion at broader scales—are ripe for reframing in ecological terms, and several of our contributors take these fruitful concepts in new directions. Jane Bennett too has produced important theoretical foundations for our project: *The Enchantment of Modern Life* and the more recent *Vibrant Matter*, a favorite among material ecocritics.[25] Our collection foregrounds the environmental dimensions of affect alluded to in the work of these and other influential affect theorists. *Affective Ecocriticism* more directly examines affect and environment by reconceiving familiar affects in spatial terms, by expanding what counts as an environmental affect, and by identifying new affects that can be understood more clearly through the lens of ecocritical theory.

If the affective turn explores dynamic interactions between and within bodies, then the "material turn" marks the widespread interest across fields in reappraising materiality and embodiment. Diana Coole and Samantha Frost outline this interest by noting materialist developments in ontology, biopolitics, and political economy, which are related in "their emphasis on materialization as a complex, pluralistic, relatively open process" and in their assertions that humans are "thoroughly immersed within materiality's productive contingencies."[26] These shared features (openness, inextricability, contingency) resonate with definitions of affects as embodied capacities—phenomena that arise and circulate as intensities among assemblages. New materialisms and affect theories align, for instance, in examining how biological and chemical factors—such as hormones, volatile organic compounds, omega-3 fats, or lead—condition the affects we experience. Such approaches extend beyond anthropocentrism, insisting that we consider nonhuman actors.

Materialism is not exactly "new" to ecocriticism, though it has taken on greater significance in recent years as new materialist projects develop. Ecocriticism emerged in the 1990s to study the relationship between literature and the natural environment, and it has since expanded to explore a wider range of texts and environments, forging interdisciplinary connections with fields like cultural studies, cinema studies, and animal studies. A number of ecocritics have found affinities with new materialist thought, leading to the development of material ecocriticism, a lively subfield claiming multiple inspirations but perhaps none so prominently as material feminisms, which denote feminist reconsiderations of bodies and materiality occurring after the poststructuralist emphasis on linguistic signification. Throughout her work, and most recently in her book *Exposed*, Stacy Alaimo advocates for analyzing the enmeshment of material and sociocultural phenomena using the insights of feminist scholarship, maintaining that "material feminisms are at the heart of new materialisms."[27] In the influential collection *Material Feminisms* Alaimo and Susan Hekman write, "Women have bodies. . . . We need a way to talk about these bodies and the materiality they inhabit."[28] They also articulate what has since become a hallmark of material ecocriticism: "nature is agentic—it acts, and those actions have consequences for both the human and nonhuman world."[29] Ecocritics, long attentive to the literary and cultural enunciations of ecological thinking, were primed to recognize and elaborate such claims about agentic natures.

Serenella Iovino and Serpil Oppermann, editors of the subsequent volume *Material Ecocriticism*, point out the particular influence of material feminisms in this work. Iovino and Oppermann advocate for the legibility of the more-than-human world as a site of narrativity. Writing that "the world's material phenomena are knots in a vast network of agencies, which can be 'read' and interpreted as forming narratives," they assert that material ecocriticism "is the study of the way material forms . . . intra-act with each other and with the human dimension, producing configurations of meanings and discourses that we can interpret as stories."[30] The emphasis on the meaningfulness of the world and on the ability to "read" it coincides well with attempts to better attend to affect's complexity, including how we "feel" materiality in profound ways. Several of *Material Ecocriticism*'s chapters foreground affect. In her contribution, Catriona Sandilands traces how the poet Sean Borodale's *Bee Journal* entices readers to "become deeply aware of the bees' affective presence in his life, of the way in which he has become part of an emotional bee-human community."[31] Bennett also contributes an essay, in which she merges the affective and the material in her exploration of sympathy as "a material agency, a power of bodies human and non-human, a mode of impersonal connection, attachment, and care that proceeds from below subjectivity into subjectivity."[32] Bennett and Sandilands anticipate what has become a growing priority for material ecocritics: accounting for the ways affective attachments and exchanges infuse a lively material world in which we are deeply embedded alongside other beings.

As our brief sketch of the affective and material-ecocritical turns suggests, affect is ecological "by nature," since it operates at the confluence of environments, texts, and bodies—including nonhuman and inanimate bodies. Affect theory disrupts both discrete notions of embodied selfhood and static notions of environment, encouraging us to trace the trajectories of transcorporeal encounters that are intricate and dynamic. Material ecocriticism likewise foregrounds the unstable and processive nature of all environments and objects; however, unlike much affect theory to date, it takes environments seriously, as agents in generating and shaping affect. Reappraising matter to consider more carefully its agency and vibrancy better equips us to see how it actively participates in the flows and intensities of affect.

Not surprisingly, given these points of convergence, ecocritics have not been silent on the subject of affect. Yi-Fu Tuan's "topophilia" and E. O. Wilson's "biophilia" gained traction in ecocriticism's early phases, offering portable terminology and interdisciplinary perspectives on positive feelings about places (often encapsulated in the phrase "sense of place"). Simon Estok countered these phrases with the introduction of his early and abiding example of ecocritical attention to affect: "ecophobia," the "contempt and fear we feel for the agency of the natural environment."[33] Lawrence Buell wrote of "ecoglobalist affects" in another notable, if underexplored, early reference. Some of ecocriticism's "new voices" are beginning to speak the language of affect theory more fluently. Sarah Ensor's "Spinster Ecology" suggests attending to nonreproductive "figures like the spinster might inspire a queer ecocritical practice attentive to affects customarily considered too weak or quiet to be politically efficacious."[34] Sylvan Goldberg's standout chapter in the collection *New International Voices in Ecocriticism* draws helpfully on Ngai's *Ugly Feelings* to call for increased attention to "a quieter range of affective engagements," including "eco-irritation."[35] We've adopted Goldberg's phrase "affective ecocriticism" as our collection's title.

Exciting new monographs are attending to affect in more sustained ways. In *Ecosickness in Contemporary U.S. Fiction: Environment and Affect*, Houser theorizes what she calls "narrative affect," a provocative if tightly focused way of defining what affect can do and how it works. Alexa Weik von Mossner's *Affective Ecologies: Empathy, Emotion, and Environmental Narrative* explores readers' engagements with environmental narratives, draws on cognitive narratology and neuroscience, and theorizes affect in relation to these fields. Nicole Seymour's award-winning *Strange Natures: Futurity, Empathy, and the Queer Ecological Imagination* and *Bad Environmentalism: Irony and Irreverence in the Ecological Age* bring together affect theory and ecocritical theory along with a third discipline: queer studies. In *Bad Environmentalism*, Seymour's compelling argument for the addition of "bad" affects—such as gaiety, irony, humor, and irreverence—to the repertoire of more familiar environmentalist affects has already influenced our book.

Edited collections have also begun to compile a rich body of work on the relationship between affect and ecology and/or place. Joyce Davidson, Liz Bondi, and Mick Smith's *Emotional Geographies* and Tonya K. Davidson, Ondine Park, and Rob Shields's *Ecologies of Affect: Placing Nostalgia, Desire, and Hope* were among the first to focus primarily on affect in relation to place. Christine Berberich, Neil Campbell, and Robert Hudson's *Affective Landscapes in Literature, Art and Everyday Life: Memory, Place and the Senses* assesses affective landscapes in an impressive range of visual and literary texts, predominantly using cultural studies and an understanding of affect informed by Spinoza, Massumi, and Stewart. Lisa Ottum and Seth T. Reno's *Wordsworth and the Green Romantics: Affect and Ecology in the Nineteenth Century*, like our collection, puts affect theory and ecocriticism into conversation, and we share its premise that "a wide range of affective experiences and literary emotions are potentially 'green.'"[36] Weik von Mossner's *Moving Environments: Affect, Emotion, Ecology, and Film* made strides in bringing together scholarship on affect and environments—as did Adrian Ivakhiv's *Ecologies of the Moving Image: Cinema, Affect, Nature*—within a film studies framework. Our study builds on the excellent scholarship in these texts, and we are fortunate to feature here new work by Seymour, Weik von Mossner, Campbell, and Ottum.

Affective Ecocriticism expands and enriches these conversations in several key ways. First, our authors appraise the affect-environment confluence within new temporal and generic territories. While many of the contributions focus on literature and film of the twentieth and twenty-first centuries, several chapters reach across time, engaging philosophies bearing on affect from Descartes to Wordsworth, from Darwin and Freud to Wendell Berry, offering a depth and a range that contextualize present environmental crises and imagine possible futures. Together the chapters consider an eclectic variety of primary texts, including short-story collections, films, poetry collections, curricular programs, and geopolitical hotbeds like Canada's tar sands. Second, our book moves beyond strictly literary or textual emotions. Our authors coin terms for extratextual affects, including "land affect," "food affect," "queer environmental affect," and "solastalgic distress." Third, we explore and model a wide range of methodological approaches to affect theory. We've deliberately commissioned work by scholars across the spectrum of affect studies, from cognitive science to cultural theory. Several chapters contribute to pressing debates within ecocriticism, affect studies, and narrative theory (among other fields) about empathy, an affective state that is lauded, and often misunderstood, in popular as well as academic discourse.

Affective Ecocriticism takes a broad and at times irreverent approach to traditional environmental affects. Ecocritical theory brings new and neglected affects into the conversation and expands the scales at which affect can be understood to function, from the individual to the Anthropocenic. Our collection seeks to represent the wide range of affects that reflect the complex and frequently conflicted nature of our contemporary lives. We find that what Ngai terms "noncathartic" emotions might be not only more representative of our actual affective lives but also more politically productive, a proposition many of the authors in our collection pursue in a wider range of primary texts, beyond narrative fiction.[37]

Finally, our collection draws attention to the preponderance of new, often "bad" affects emerging or being redefined in the Anthropocene, including despair, resignation, climate grief, and solastalgia, as well as familiar feelings like disappointment and anxiety. Environmentalists and other activists, especially in the United States, have long been derided or dismissed for encouraging asceticism, preaching about simplicity, and delivering jeremiads about the end of the world.[38] Environmentalist killjoys—green kin of Ahmed's feminist killjoys—take center stage in our project.[39] Several of our authors suggest we might recuperate "bad feelings" for environmentalist purposes in our new geologic epoch. *Affective Ecocriticism* approaches emergent affects with a sense of urgency and an accessible style that we hope will speak to readers across a range of disciplinary and geographic locations.

The book's first three chapters model distinct theoretical approaches to affect studies and illustrate different ways of intervening in ecocritical projects. We open with Nicole Merola's provocative formalist analysis of Juliana Spahr's poetry, which sets a tone of "Anthropocene anxiety" that resonates throughout the collection. Merola's chapter invites scholars of affective ecocriticism to "tarry at the juncture of form and affect." Merola draws on scholars of form and affect such as Houser and reaches back to William James's theories of emotion to ask what new affects the Anthropocene inspires and what familiar ones it reworks. Positing Juliana Spahr as one of the most insightful theorists of affect in the Anthropocene, Merola shows how melancholy, anger, and resignation cohere into what she calls "Anthropocene anxiety": a temporally doubled affect of nervousness and unease that is anticipatory, influential in both the present and the future. Ultimately, Merola suggests, living in the Anthropocene might necessitate an "avowal of the eco-unpleasant."

Alexa Weik von Mossner takes a different tack in her chapter, "From Nostalgic Longing to Solastalgic Distress: A Cognitive Approach to *Love in* the *Anthropocene*." Weik von Mossner models, as she argues for, a cognitive ecocritical approach to affect studies—one that accounts for the embodied experience of readers. Drawing on empirical work in embodied cognition, as well as scholarship in cognitive science and affective narratology, Weik von Mossner offers a new reading of the short-story collection *Love in the Anthropocene*. Her chapter reveals not only how love and loss are closely connected in a time of accelerated environmental change but also how readers are cued empathically to imagine, and to feel, both the eco-nostalgic longing that many of the characters feel and a "solastalgic distress" about what is being lost. Her treatment of nostalgia and solastalgia is timely, as global environmental changes demand that broader demographics become more attuned to losses in our environments.

Neil Campbell's "A New Gentleness: Affective Ficto-Regionality" models a third approach to affect studies: affect theory in a cultural studies vein. Inspired by the work of Félix Guattari and aligned with contemporary scholars of affect theory such as Massumi and Stewart, Campbell's chapter teases out the ecological and affective dimensions of Guattari's *The Three Ecologies* and offers an exciting new take on Stewart that champions her treatment of affect as a kind of ecological consciousness. "A New Gentleness" is a theoretical provocation in which Campbell conjoins concepts such as "ficto-regionality," a "prismatic ecology," and "an ecology of paths" in order to foster new intellectual connections. Campbell outlines the theoretical and political potentials for affective ficto-regionality as a catalyst for what he calls (following Guattari) "a new gentleness": a mix of curiosity, wonder, attunement, and ethical responsibility.

The next three chapters explore applications of affect theory in various genres and contexts related to environmental and social justice, including food studies and Indigenous rights. These scholars suggest that a clearer understanding of our affective attachments to land, to our homes, and to human and nonhuman others is essential for justice. Jobb Arnold's chapter, "Feeling the Fires of Climate Change: Land Affect in Canada's Tar Sands," demonstrates the centrality of Indigenous epistemologies and ontologies in the pursuit of scholarship allied to decolonization and environmental justice. Arnold theorizes "land affect" as "a nontechnologically mediated relation inherent in the *potential to feel with the land* that is innervated by free-floating social and ecological energies." Land affect aligns significantly with Indigenous land-based relational ontologies, which guide Arnold's critique of industrial resource extraction. Weaving together diverse theoretical influences, including Glen Coulthard, Giorgio Agamben, and Rey Chow, Arnold advocates for land-based relations (and the land affects they generate) taking priority in sustainability plans.

In "Wendell Berry and the Affective Turn," William Major takes a skeptical look at the increasingly prevalent social and political calls for empathy, and he presses for a more precise accounting of what empathy is as well as how it works, especially in relation to the more-than-human world. Major reminds us that empathy is more than just "compassion" or "understanding"; it is feeling *with* someone, or perhaps with some*thing* else, as opposed to feeling *for* them. Major's insightful analysis of Wendell Berry's National Endowment for the Humanities Jefferson Lecture (2012) examines how empathy is invoked in discourse on new agrarianism in particular, as well as how it operates at local, global, and temporal scales. Like Weik von Mossner, Major draws on cognitive theorists to explore their potential for understandings of human identity as well as for environmental politics and to argue for "empathic realism."

Tom Hertweck's "A Hunger for Words: Food Affects and Embodied Ideology" develops a theory of the phenomenon of "food affect," the affective dimensions of the drive of hunger. Drawing on Silvan Tomkins's work as well as Elspeth Probyn's *Carnal Appetites*, Hertweck conceives of food consumption as an "embodied ideology" and of hunger as an affective oscillation "between metabolic and cultural need." His chapter insists that cultural theorists of affect take food affect seriously in order to better account for the interactions between consumer desires and choices, marketing claims, and the environmental impacts of industrial food systems.

In "Uncanny Homesickness and War: Loss of Affect, Loss of Place, and Reworlding in *Redeployment*" Ryan Hediger gauges the emotional impacts of war on veterans' bodies. Hediger draws on Massumi's broad conception of affect as a "becoming" and Freud's *unheimlich* to theorize homesickness as an uncanny affect resulting in and from wartime environments, a desire for home, and a sense of being sick of and/or sick at home. This chapter reads Phil Klay's 2014 collection of short stories about the war in Iraq, *Redeployment*, to argue that veterans' experiences are often extreme versions of more common responses to geographical mobility, especially forced mobility, in modernity. Veterans' affective states thus register increasingly common feelings of disorientation that must be reckoned with in the Anthropocene. Hediger shows that this affective disorientation has unexpected and potentially positive diagnostic implications, including a greater sensitivity to the hypercapitalist and often alienating environments of everyday life.

The next three chapters investigate how affect informs human understandings of and relationships with nonhuman animals. Robert Azzarello opens this section with "Desiring Species with Darwin and Freud," in which he probes the extent to which desire is speciesist in the works of both writers. Considering the absence of the word "desire" in Darwin and its omnipresence in Freud, Azzarello identifies overlaps between two thinkers often conceptualized as antithetical in their views of desire's relationship to reproduction. Azzarello investigates the ethical dimensions of desire and its potential for crossing species boundaries, in the process updating the insights of Darwin and Freud for scholars of affect and animal studies.

Brian Deyo's "Tragedy, Ecophobia, and Animality in the Anthropocene" argues for increased attention to ecophobia as we grapple with anthropogenic environmental changes. Tracing our anthropocentrism back to origins in the Enlightenment, Deyo recasts ecophobia as a precognitive sense of our animality—our vulnerability, finitude, and mortality. He draws on the works of diverse writers—from Descartes and Montaigne to J. M. Coetzee and Amitav Ghosh—to explore this ecophobic awareness and the ways in which its attendant fears and anxiety manifest in tragic art. In studying tragedy and engaging the affects it helps circulate, Deyo also sees opportunities for humans to renew thinking and feeling through our animality in this new geologic epoch.

In "Futurity without Optimism: Detaching from Anthropocentrism and Grieving Our Fathers in *Beasts of the Southern Wild*," Allyse Knox-Russell calls into question popular affective responses to climate change—notably "resilience"—as potentially reinforcing neoliberal ideology and perpetuating what Lauren Berlant terms "cruel optimism." *Beasts*, Knox-Russell demonstrates, reminds viewers of the disproportionate levels of violence and disruption that people of color face as climate change accelerates, even as the film and its reception warn against romanticizing frontline communities. Exploring how futurity without optimism "can *feel* very different to different viewers," Knox-Russell homes in on the concept of "beastliness" applied to characters in the film. This "derided animality" offers an alternative to resilience and, potentially, "a pathway toward empathy."

The final cluster of essays embraces and reinvigorates the label "environmentalist killjoy" as it tracks some of the ways in which "bad feelings" might be useful for politics and pedagogy in the Anthropocene. These authors queer familiar and noncathartic affects and suggest why even the "bad" ones might be important to cultivate in our present environmental moment, in which the diametrically opposed feelings of hope and despair are too often framed as the only options. Nicole Seymour's contribution, "The Queerness of Environmental Affect," uses a transdisciplinary approach to suggest that camp, irony, humor, and other forms of affective playfulness exist alongside (and often productively complicate) more entrenched environmental affects, such as melancholia, shame, and depression. Seymour theorizes "queer environmental affect" as affective response *to* queer environments; as affective response *within* queer environments; and most broadly as *any* "bad"—as in negative and/or inappropriate—affective response to environments, "be they gay bars or gardens." Seymour makes a compelling case for the centrality of queer theory to an affective ecocriticism, as well as to what she calls "bad environmentalism."

In "Feeling Let Down: Affect, Environmentalism, and the Power of Negative Thinking" Lisa Ottum takes a historical approach to emotions, citing the work of behavioral economists, psychologists, and cultural critics to develop a unique theory of disappointment as a "peculiar temporality" that sparks reflection. Her analysis reveals disappointment as an affect that disorients and "arrests" us, stopping time for a moment in the face of a particular object. What happens, Ottum asks, when the object in question is a landscape? Her chapter focuses on the prevalent (and transhistorical) experience of "touristic disappointment," which she develops by reading

Wordsworth's *The Prelude*, especially its deployment of the picturesque, alongside Geoff Dyer's *White Sands: Experiences from the Outside World*. Ottum's insightful analysis of these texts suggests how disappointment may be useful for contemporary ecocritics.

Next, Graig Uhlin claims that affect's characteristic aspect is environmental insofar as it registers in specific bodies and places but is otherwise hard to capture. Uhlin's chapter, "Feeling Depleted: Ecocinema and the Atmospherics of Affect," explores the "atmospherics of affect" in three recent films (Kelly Reichardt's *Old Joy*, Lars von Trier's *Melancholia*, and Gus Van Sant's *Gerry*), evoking how affects in each film—particularly sorrow, melancholy, and exhaustion—are played out in its formal features and how affect becomes part of a film's atmosphere. Uhlin also examines noncathartic affects, a move that broadens the inquiry of ecocinema scholarship, which often focuses on how spectators' emotional responses lead to catharsis, if not action.

Finally, Sarah Jaquette Ray's chapter—which she describes as partly a "love letter" to her students, many of whom struggle with despair and hope as seemingly the only affective responses to climate change—invokes affect theory to map what she calls the "affective arc" of environmental studies classrooms. "Coming of Age at the End of the World: The Affective Arc of Undergraduate Environmental Studies Curricula" draws on Ray's experiences as director of environmental studies at Humboldt State University to challenge the common perception among ecocritics and environmental justice scholars that our pedagogy must follow an "arc of hope" in order to prevent despair. Instead she encourages teachers to make space for conversations about affect in the classroom and to allow students to dwell in more of the so-called negative emotions, including melancholy. Ray's is an analysis of pedagogy with far-reaching implications, not only for teachers and learners but for anyone trying to understand their complex emotional responses to the Anthropocene.

In the face of crises that seem too big to process emotionally, these essays explore some of the many ways in which affect theory can be a useful tool for developing more nuanced understandings of complicated feelings. The essays collected here move us beyond hope and despair toward a more inclusive, sophisticated "suite of emotions" related to environmental loss and change of all kinds.[40] We must account for our affective lives in more careful terms as we push for a more just, more sustainable world. If affect is unpredictable—a "becoming" with infinite possibilities—then future prospects for research in affect studies are not just exciting but boundless. Whatever directions they take, we suggest these future studies proceed with environments in mind. Surely understanding how affect works—within individuals and between species, as well as in and across various environments, genres, and scales—is a more urgent project than ever.

NOTES

1. Rowan Jacobsen, "Obituary: Great Barrier Reef (25 Million BC–2016)," *Outside*, October 11, 2016, https://www.outsideonline.com/2112086/obituary-great-barrier-reef-25-million-bc-2016.

2. Scientists clarified that a percentage of the reef has actually not succumbed to the bleaching that is its "cause of death." For one response see Sophie Lewis, "The Great Barrier Reef Is Not Actually Dead," CNN, October 14, 2016, http://edition.cnn.com/2016/10/14/us/barrier-reef-obit-trnd/. Still, retweets and Facebook shares and even some news publications promoted the literal version of the story. The *Spokesman-Review*, in Spokane, Washington, even repackaged the story under the misleading title "Great Barrier Reef Pronounced Dead by Scientists." Rich Landers, *Spokesman-Review*, October 13, 2016, http://www.spokesman.com/blogs/outdoors/2016/oct/13/great-barrier-reef-pronounced-dead-scientists/.

3. For one account see Tom Foster, "Ready or Not, Companies Will Soon Be Tracking Your Emotions," *Inc.*, July–August 2016, www.inc.com/magazine/201607/tom-foster/lightwave-monitor-customer-emotions.html.

4. Thomas Friedman, to whom "global weirding" is often attributed, credits Hunter Lovins, of the Rocky Mountain Institute, for the term. Thomas L. Friedman, "The People We Have Been Waiting For," *New York Times*, December 2, 2007, http://www.nytimes.com/2007/12/02/opinion/02friedman.html. On paralysis see Norgaard, *Living in Denial*. While her context is Norway, her analysis is applicable elsewhere.

5. These psychological phenomena are explored in Slovic and Slovic, *Numbers and Nerves*.

6. Laura Schmidt, a graduate student in the University of Utah's environmental humanities program, coined the term "climate grief" and is developing support groups for sufferers. See Sara Peach, "How to Address Climate Grief," *Yale Climate*

Connections, December 5, 2016, http://www.yaleclimateconnections.org/2016/12
/how-to-address-climate-grief/. "Anthropocene disorders" is Timothy Clark's
phrase for how "the mind is suspended, uncertainly, between a sense of rage and
even despair on one side, and a consciousness of the majority perception of such
reactions as disproportionate and imbalanced, on the other." Clark, *Ecocriticism
on the Edge*, 140.

7. See, for instance, Cryan and O'Mahony, "Microbiome-Gut-Brain Axis."

8. See Brown and Kulik, "Flashbulb Memories," for a fuller definition of this
   phenomenon.

9. For an early response to the election, see Michael Lerner, "Stop Shaming Trump
   Supporters," *New York Times*, November 10, 2016, https://www.nytimes.com
   /interactive/projects/cp/opinion/election-night-2016/stop-shaming-trump
   -supporters. Some on the Left still embrace "shame" as an appropriate way of
   calling out and refusing to normalize racism, sexism, and xenophobia.

10. For one study on emotions in public engagement see Roesner, "Risk Commu-
    nication, Public Engagement, and Climate Change."

11. Houser, *Ecosickness*, 223.

12. For an early multidisciplinary overview of the turn to affect see Clough and
    Halley, *Affective Turn*. For a brief overview see Cvetkovich, "Affect."

13. Smith, in *Affect and American Literature in the Age of Neoliberalism*, theorizes dis-
    ruptive and noncathartic "impersonal feelings" as possible ways to circumvent a
    neoliberal economy that co-opts individual emotion. She treats skeptically both
    empathy and the "affective hypothesis"—the assumption that we read in order
    to feel with, or for, fictional characters.

14. Gregg and Seigworth, *Affect Theory Reader*, 4–9.

15. Gregg and Seigworth, *Affect Theory Reader*, 5.

16. Gregg and Seigworth, *Affect Theory Reader*, 6.

17. Stewart's *Ordinary Affects*, while not in explicit dialogue with ecocriticism, includes
    U.S. landscapes in its ethnographic study.

18. Stewart and Massumi trace these terms to Spinoza and Deleuze. Massumi shows
    how the two ends of the affect theory spectrum can come together, as he draws on
    neuroscientific studies in his pathbreaking work on affect, *Parables for the Virtual*.
    See Leys, "Turn to Affect," for an influential critique of Massumi in particular
    and the affective turn more generally.

19. Anderson, "Affective Atmospheres," 78.

20. Brennan, *Transmission of Affect*, 5.

21. Massumi, *Parables for the Virtual*, 35.

22. Debates continue about how to define both terms, and some scholars simply use

emotion and affect as synonyms. This is not the place for an extensive overview. For a helpful parsing of these terms see Ngai, *Ugly Feelings*, 25–27.

23. For instance, even though "the inducers of background emotions are usually internal," for Damasio, they might also be "engendered . . . by the organism's interactions with the environment." Damasio, *Feeling of What Happens*, 52.

24. Brennan, *Transmission of Affect*, 3. The "other environmental factors at work" are outside the scope of her analysis (8). Her work resonates with material ecocriticism's belief that matter is only passive by human standards that perceive objects as not able to "carry out intentions of their own," as lacking "free will or agency" (93–94).

25. While the earlier book deals more explicitly with affect (largely in the Spinozist strand), Bennett rarely engages its potential to register as emotion.

26. Coole and Frost, "Introducing the New Materialisms," 7. Their important collection *New Materialisms* takes a range of approaches to new materialisms across the humanities and social sciences and features essays by Bennett and Ahmed, among others.

27. Alaimo, *Exposed*, 12.

28. Alaimo and Hekman, *Material Feminisms*, 4.

29. Alaimo and Hekman, *Material Feminisms*, 5.

30. Iovino and Oppermann, *Material Ecocriticism*, 1, 7. The term "intra-act" is adopted from Barad, *Meeting the Universe Halfway*.

31. Sandilands, "Pro/Polis," 166.

32. Bennett, "Of Material Sympathies," 250.

33. Estok, "Painful Material Realities," 131. Ecophobia describes "how we respond emotionally and cognitively to what we perceive as environmental threats and as a menacing alienness" (131).

34. Ensor, "Spinster Ecology," 410.

35. Goldberg, "What is it about you . . . that so irritates me?," 57.

36. Ottum and Reno, *Wordsworth and the Green Romantics*, 14.

37. Ngai, *Ugly Feelings*, 6.

38. A *National Review* article dubs Bill McKibben an "environmentalist killjoy" for declaring that ocean acidification and global warming have already effected the end of the earth as we knew it: "Only an environmentalist like McKibben could be a killjoy about the apocalypse itself." Jonah Goldberg, "Inhospitable Earth," *National Review*, July 3, 2013, http://www.nationalreview.com/article/352591/inhospitable-earth-jonah-goldberg.

39. Also the title of Ahmed's blog, the term "feminist killjoy" identifies the process by which, in exposing problems, one becomes identified as their origin or cause.

40. Siperstein, Hall, and LeMenager, *Teaching Climate Change*, 7. This important collection devotes significant space to emotions, including (but not limited to) hope and despair.

BIBLIOGRAPHY

Ahmed, Sara. *The Cultural Politics of Emotion.* New York: Routledge, 2004.

———. "Happy Objects." In *The Affect Theory Reader*, edited by Melissa Gregg and Gregory J. Seigworth, 29–51. Durham: Duke University Press, 2010.

Alaimo, Stacy. *Exposed: Environmental Politics and Pleasures in Posthuman Times.* Minneapolis: University of Minnesota Press, 2016.

Alaimo, Stacy, and Susan Hekman, eds. *Material Feminisms.* Bloomington: Indiana University Press, 2008.

Anderson, Ben. "Affective Atmospheres." *Emotion, Space and Society* 2, no. 2 (2009): 77–81.

Barad, Karen. *Meeting the Universe Halfway: Quantum Physics and the Entanglement of Matter and Meaning.* Durham: Duke University Press, 2008.

Bennett, Jane. *The Enchantment of Modern Life: Attachments, Crossings, and Ethics.* Princeton: Princeton University Press, 2001.

———. "Of Material Sympathies, Paracelsus, and Whitman." In *Material Ecocriticism*, edited by Serenella Iovino and Serpil Oppermann, 239–52. Bloomington: Indiana University Press, 2014.

———. *Vibrant Matter: A Political Ecology of Things.* Durham: Duke University Press, 2010.

Berberich, Christine, Neil Campbell, and Robert Hudson, eds. *Affective Landscapes in Literature, Art and Everyday Life: Memory, Place and the Senses.* London: Routledge, 2015.

Berlant, Lauren. "Cruel Optimism." *differences: A Journal of Feminist Cultural Studies* 17, no. 3 (2006): 20–36.

Bloom, Paul. *Against Empathy: The Case for Rational Compassion.* New York: Ecco Press, 2016.

Brennan, Teresa. *The Transmission of Affect.* Ithaca: Cornell University Press, 2004.

Brown, Roger, and James Kulik. "Flashbulb Memories." *Cognition* 5, no. 1 (1977): 73–99.

Buell, Lawrence. "Ecoglobalist Affects: The Emergence of U.S. Environmental Imagination on a Planetary Scale." In *Shades of the Planet: American Literature as World Literature*, edited by Wai Chee Dimock and Lawrence Buell, 227–48. Princeton: Princeton University Press, 2007.

Chakrabarty, Dipesh. "The Climate of History: Four Theses." *Critical Inquiry* 35, no. 2 (2009): 197–222.

Clark, Timothy. *Ecocriticism on the Edge: The Anthropocene as a Threshold Concept.* London: Bloomsbury, 2015.

Clough, Patricia Ticineto, and Jean Halley, eds. *The Affective Turn: Theorizing the Social*. Durham: Duke University Press, 2007.

Coole, Diana, and Samantha Frost. "Introducing the New Materialisms." In *New Materialisms: Ontology, Agency, and Politics*, edited by Diana Coole and Samantha Frost, 1–43. Durham: Duke University Press, 2010.

Cryan, J. F., and S. M. O'Mahony. "The Microbiome-Gut-Brain Axis: From Bowel to Behavior." *Neurogastroenterol Motil* 23, no. 3 (2011): 187–92.

Cvetkovich, Ann. "Affect." *Keywords for American Cultural Studies*, edited by Bruce Burgett and Glenn Hendler, 13–16. New York: New York University Press, 2014.

Damasio, Antonio. *The Feeling of What Happens: Body and Emotion in the Making of Consciousness*. Orlando FL: Harcourt, 1999.

Davidson, Joyce, Liz Bondi, and Mick Smith, eds. *Emotional Geographies*. Burlington VT: Ashgate, 2005.

Davidson, Tonya K., Ondine Park, and Rob Shields, eds. *Ecologies of Affect: Placing Nostalgia, Desire, and Hope*. Waterloo ON: Wilfred Laurier University Press, 2011.

Ensor, Sarah. "Spinster Ecology: Rachel Carson, Sarah Orne Jewett, and Nonreproductive Futurity." *American Literature* 84, no. 2 (2012): 409–35.

Estok, Simon. *Ecocriticism and Shakespeare: Reading Ecophobia*. New York: Palgrave Macmillan, 2011.

———. "Painful Material Realities, Tragedy, Ecophobia." In *Material Ecocriticism*, edited by Serenella Iovino and Serpil Oppermann, 130–40. Bloomington: Indiana University Press, 2014.

Goldberg, Sylvan. "'What is it about you . . . that so irritates me?' *Northern Exposure*'s Sustainable Feeling." In *New International Voices in Ecocriticism*, edited by Serpil Oppermann, 55–70. Lanham MD: Rowman and Littlefield, 2014.

Gregg, Melissa, and Gregory Seigworth, eds. *The Affect Theory Reader*. Durham: Duke University Press, 2010.

Houser, Heather. *Ecosickness in Contemporary U.S. Fiction: Environment and Affect*. New York: Columbia University Press, 2014.

Iovino, Serenella, and Serpil Oppermann, eds. *Material Ecocriticism*. Bloomington: Indiana University Press, 2014.

Ivakhiv, Adrian. *Ecologies of the Moving Image: Cinema, Affect, Nature*. Waterloo ON: Wilfred Laurier University Press, 2013.

Leys, Ruth. "The Turn to Affect: A Critique." *Critical Inquiry* 37, no. 3 (2001): 434–72.

Love, Heather. *Feeling Backward: Loss and the Politics of Queer History*. Cambridge MA: Harvard University Press, 2009.

Massumi, Brian. *Parables for the Virtual: Movement, Affect, Sensation*. Durham: Duke University Press, 2002.

Ngai, Sianne. *Ugly Feelings*. Cambridge MA: Harvard University Press, 2005.

Norgaard, Kari Marie. *Living in Denial: Climate Change, Emotions, and Everyday Life*. Cambridge MA: MIT Press, 2011.

Oppermann, Serpil. *New International Voices in Ecocriticism*. Lanham MD: Rowman and Littlefield, 2014.

Ottum, Lisa, and Seth T. Reno, eds. *Wordsworth and the Green Romantics: Affect and Ecology in the Nineteenth Century*. Lebanon: University of New Hampshire Press, 2016.

Roesner, Sabine. "Risk Communication, Public Engagement, and Climate Change: A Role for Emotions." *Risk Analysis* 32, no. 6 (2012): 1033–1040.

Sandilands, Catriona. "Pro/Polis: Three Forays into the Political Lives of Bees." In *Material Ecocriticism*, edited by Serenella Iovino and Serpil Oppermann, 157–71. Bloomington: Indiana University Press, 2014.

Sedgwick, Eve Kosofsky, and Adam Frank, eds. *Shame and Its Sisters: A Silvan Tomkins Reader*. Durham: Duke University Press, 1995.

Seymour, Nicole. *Bad Environmentalism: Irony and Irreverence in the Ecological Age*. Minneapolis: University of Minnesota Press, 2018.

———. *Strange Natures: Futurity, Empathy, and the Queer Ecological Imagination*. Urbana: University of Illinois Press, 2013.

Siperstein, Stephen, Shane Hall, and Stephanie LeMenager. *Teaching Climate Change in the Humanities*. New York: Routledge, 2016.

Slovic, Scott, and Paul Slovic. *Numbers and Nerves: Information, Emotion, and Meaning in a World of Data*. Corvallis: Oregon State University Press, 2015.

Smith, Rachel Greenwald. *Affect and American Literature in the Age of Neoliberalism*. Cambridge: Cambridge University Press, 2015.

Solnit, Rebecca. *Hope in the Dark: Untold Histories, Wild Possibilities*. New York: Nation Books, 2004.

Spinoza, Benedict de [Baruch]. "The Ethics." In *A Spinoza Reader: The "Ethics" and Other Works*, edited and translated by Edwin Curley, 85–265. Princeton: Princeton University Press, 1994.

Stewart, Kathleen. *Ordinary Affects*. Durham: Duke University Press, 2007.

Thrift, Nigel. *Non-Representational Theory: Space, Politics, Affect*. New York: Routledge, 2008.

Weik von Mossner, Alexa. *Affective Ecologies: Empathy, Emotion, and Environmental Narrative*. Columbus: Ohio State University Press, 2017.

———. *Moving Environments: Affect, Emotion, Ecology, and Film*. Waterloo ON: Wilfrid Laurier University Press, 2014.

Williams, Raymond. *Marxism and Literature*. Oxford: Oxford University Press, 1977.

PART 1

Theoretical Foundations

"what do we do but keep breathing as best we can this / minute atmosphere"

Juliana Spahr and Anthropocene Anxiety

NICOLE M. MEROLA

In 2005, prior to the commonplace adoption in the environmental humanities of the term "Anthropocene" to describe the advent of a new geological epoch characterized by the legibility of anthropogenic impacts on earth systems, including human and nonhuman forms of inhabitation, Juliana Spahr published *this connection of everyone with lungs: poems.*[1] *this connection* marks a turning point in Spahr's oeuvre: the beginning of a sustained engagement with human entanglement in large-scale ecological, economic, geopolitical, and social systems that percolates throughout her recent work. In *this connection* Spahr excavates her complicity with the U.S. military-industrial complex in a post-9/11 world. In the prose-poem-memoir *The Transformation* (2007) she worries together systems of capital, climate change, colonialism, military-industrialism, politics, social formation, technological mediation, and toxicity. Poems in *well then there now* (2011) fret about biodiversity loss, climate change, consumerism, pollution, and connection to place. The manifesto *#Misanthropocene: 24 Theses* (2014), cowritten with Joshua Clover, spits with anger about uneven economic conditions, relative powerlessness in the face of "the sheer scale of the misanthropocene," and extinctions past, present, and future.[2] And in poems in *That Winter the Wolf Came* (2015) oil culture vexes. Taken together, *this* connection, *The Transformation, well then, #Misanthropocene,* and *That Winter* constellate a set of formal experiments through which Spahr questions, encounters, materializes, and wrestles with the epistemological and onto-logical pressures that accrue to the newly self-reflexive, anxious position into which the Anthropocene interpellates us.[3]

The Anthropocene is fundamentally estranging: what we thought we knew about the continuance of a habitable biosphere for currently evolved creatures has turned out to be a mirage. The knowledge that we have fouled our only form of life support positions humans in an alienated relationship to the earth. We have made the irrevocable shift from "reading 'the great stone book of nature'" to writing it.[4] The pressure the Anthropocene puts on how to conceptualize humans and our relationships to other humans, other nonhumans, and other things also strains how to think about the contours and roles of cultural forms and their work. If the Anthropocene is among other things a period in which linear time and progressive narratives are undercut by effects of the material persistence of things we thought would disappear (carbon emissions, plastics); a period when speeds of biological change (habitat disruption, extinction, monocultures) exceed natural background rates; a period of diminishments in some locations (glacial ice) and augmentations in others (ocean acidification); a period when measuring and rendering technologies like the Keeling Curve, paleo-climatological records, and projections in the Intergovernmental Panel on Climate Change (IPCC) reports force encounters with the recorded and probable consequences of anthropogenic actions; a period when we must find ways to think about things and processes that are too big, nebulous, diffuse, and complicated to easily apprehend or comprehend (climate change, slow violence);[5] a period that simultaneously produces and demands scale confusion;[6] a period when individual and collective human actions exceed the boundaries of the body, the neighborhood, the region, the nation in new and frightening ways;[7] then we need to pose the following questions: What genres, forms, tactics, strategies, and politics are commensurate with this strange period? What new or reworked affects does the Anthropocene spawn? What roles can and should cultural forms take in mediating, capturing, registering, modeling, and experimenting with how to live in Anthropocenically precarious times?[8]

Readers familiar with Anthropocene discourse know that robust debates about the advent of the period abound. Candidates include 13,800 BP (human predation of megafauna and vegetation changes), 11,000–9,000 BP (worldwide domestication of plants and animals), 8,000–5,000 BP (the spread of human agriculture), 1492/1610 (contact between New and Old Worlds/the Orbis Spike), 1769 (James Watt's first patent for improvements to Newcomen's steam engine, a catalyst for the Industrial Revolution), 1945 (the United States' detonation of atomic bombs during World War II), and circa 1950 (the beginning of the Great Acceleration).[9] While the Working Group on the Anthropocene (AWG), citing the dispersion of radioactive elements from nuclear bomb tests and deployments as the probable Golden Spike, has proposed circa 1950 as the official beginning, I find 1492/1610 the most conceptually interesting as a biocultural marker.[10] While evidence in the geological record might not be sufficient for scientists to use 1492/1610 as the official beginning, positioning the Anthropocene as coterminous with New/Old World contact and its index, the Orbis Spike (a low point of atmospheric CO_2, measured in glacial ice and thought to be the result of the rapid population decline of New World peoples due to exposure to disease, war, enslavement, and famine and of contact-driven changes in agricultural practices) usefully elongates the period while also emphasizing these critical elements of the Anthropocene concept absent from earlier start dates: a global scale of irrevocable change, a speed of change distinct from background rates of change, and the establishment of an anthropogenic world-system for exercising power through transporting biological resources (human and nonhuman) across vast distances. These systems are the progenitors of today's global capitalisms.

Within this 1492-to-present Anthropocene period I want to highlight a date I see as crucial for both contextualizing and formulating Anthropocene anxiety, an affect specifically concerned with inaction in the face of and worry about global socioecological change: March 29, 1958. This date marks the first data point on the now iconic Keeling Curve, an ongoing graph of atmospheric CO_2 measurements at the Mauna Loa Observatory.[11] The Keeling Curve and other related scientific technologies that measure, communicate, and/or project the effects of anthropogenic activities serve as key context for Anthropocene anxiety because they play dual, connected roles. They capture and make legible the effects of anthropogenic activity, offering baseline knowledge that underwrites environmental affect. And, when wrapped with electronic and televisual communication systems and the rise of twenty-four-hour punditry, they work as components in the amplification of Anthropocene anxiety and guilt. That is, the more various detrimental trends (in carbon emissions, biodiversity loss, ocean acidification, sea ice loss, etc.) increase, the less we do about arresting those increases, the more anxiety and guilt we feel, the more affective impact the next graph or chart can have, and so on—a classic example of a feedback loop. These capacities for global real-time measuring and future modeling and quick and wide distribution of these charts, graphs, and models, which serve in part to amplify environmental affect, make current forms of environmental feeling qualitatively different than older, more temporally and spatially limited forms.

Scientific measuring technologies and the graphs and charts that synthesize and communicate information are one cultural form for capturing the Anthropocene and understanding some of the catalysts of its affects. Literary forms, which offer another cultural location for Anthropocene capture, can also trap the more embodied and personal forms that scientific technologies sieve; they engage affective registers not conventionally appropriate to scientific forms. A brief example from *this connection*, which serves as both companion and foil to the Keeling Curve in its expression of awareness of anthropogenic activity, signals how Spahr tracks, worries, and materializes the transition from Holocene to Anthropocene frameworks while also figuring the reset to human-nonhuman epistemologies and ontologies the Anthropocene demands. Spahr closes the poem "December 2, 2002" with three couplets occasioned by Space Shuttle Mission STS-113 (*Endeavour*). The end reads as follows: "Beloveds, the shuttle is set to return home and out the window of / the shuttle one can see the earth. // 'How massive the earth is; how minute the atmosphere,' one of / the astronauts notes. // Beloveds, what do we do but keep breathing as best we can this / minute atmosphere?"[12] The affective and conceptual movement across the three couplets, from wonder to anxious awareness of limits, indexes the transition from Holocene to Anthropocene. The first couplet evokes two iconic photographs of earth taken from space, *Earthrise* (1968) and *The Blue Marble* (1972). These images highlight the planet's aesthetic beauty and suggest its exceptional nature. In *Earthrise* the gray surface of the moon fills the frame's foreground, setting off the magnificent colors of an earth that floats in the black void of space. *The Blue Marble* also emphasizes color: the blue Atlantic and Indian Oceans, the white clouds, the reds, tans, and browns of the African continent, the island of Madagascar, and the Arabian Peninsula. Although these photographs fall within the Anthropocene period, they are not Anthropo(s)cenic in nature since they do not record any legible human impact on the planet.[13] They emphasize, rather, the kind of wholeness conveyed by the term Holocene (from the Greek *holos*, meaning whole or entire).[14] The second couplet, which introduces concepts of spatial scale, fragility, and limits, interjects the notion of planetary vulnerability and begins the shift from Holocene to Anthropocene epistemologies. The third couplet completes this conversion, foregrounding both human dependence on the earth and its fragile atmosphere and the resignation of our constrained options: all that is left for us is to "keep breathing as best we can." Through the doubled connotation of "minute," the third couplet also figures temporal scale, the time-limited nature of the earth's atmosphere. By setting off the phrase "minute atmosphere" as its own line and by ending the poem with a question, Spahr concretizes anxieties, implicit here but explicit elsewhere in *this connection* and in her other work, about the impacts of anthropogenic activities on how humans and nonhumans breathe and live. Spahr's focus on respiration here, and on the earth's oxygen-rich atmosphere that enables it, foreshadows a different kind of attention she will pay to breath in "Dynamic Positioning," the poem I consider in depth below.

As environmental humanities scholars continue to mull what to talk about when we talk about the Anthropocene, and as the brief juxtaposition of two kinds of cultural forms above suggests, it is important to tarry at the juncture of form and affect. While form might be commonly understood as mold, or structure, or shape, or essence, I am interested in its agential, performative capacities in the text, in the circuit between text and reader, and in the realm of argumentation. As Ellen Rooney argues, "the extinction of an entire range of modes of formal analysis has eroded our ability to read every genre of text—literary texts, nonliterary texts, aural and visual texts, and the social text itself. The cost is a loss of power for the politicized readings we eagerly seek to project beyond the boundaries of mere texts or disciplines, including readings of cultural forms that are not in any sense literary or (narrowly) linguistic, such as race, the market, the immune system, democracy, virtuality."[15] Although Rooney targets literary and cultural studies scholarship in general when she critiques reading practices that tend toward the thematic, historical, political, theoretical, and contextual at the expense of the formalist, her point pertains also to much environmental humanities work.[16] For Rooney form should be understood as both "the enabling condition and the product of reading," "both theory's/ideology's/history's shadow and the force that permits the text to emerge as ideology's or theory's interlocutor, rather than as its example," and as "the contrariness of the text insofar as it is the moment at which the reading both blocks and engages with any theory."[17] Anahid Nersessian provides another useful angle on form, defining it as an adjustment or an operation that puts experience and representation into a "noteworthy" asymmetrical relationship.[18]

In addition to including the ecological as a category for formalist study, a pivot from the categories Rooney lists, Nersessian's focus on anxiogenic forms also turns us back toward the affect/form interface and into the company of contemporary scholars such as Lauren Berlant, Eugenie Brinkema, Heather Houser, Sianne Ngai, and Rachel Greenwald Smith, with whose work mine converses.[19] Although Brian Massumi's work figures in many affect studies, for my purposes here it is not attentive enough to form.[20] On the relationship between affect and form Massumi and Brinkema occupy opposite ends of the spectrum. For Massumi "affect is unqualified. As such it is not ownable or recognizable and is thus resistant to critique."[21] For Brinkema, on the other hand, affect studies turn nonsensical without attention to form and to the reading practices its analysis demands. One of the trenchant questions Brinkema poses—"What, in other words, would happen to the study of affectivity and form if we were to reintroduce close reading to the study of sensation, not as felt by moved bodies, but as wildly composed in specific cinematic, literary, and critical texts?"—indexes the central importance of the text in her work.[22] Thus for Brinkema the human who encounters the text is less important than the text and what it does formally to compose affects. I think the formal experiments Spahr conducts demand affect studies and reading modes that fasten closer to Brinkema than Massumi but that also, contra Brinkema, position the human reader and body as centrally important to the composition, elicitation, production, and circulation of affect. In this respect Houser's formulation "narrative affect," in which "'affect' designates body-based feelings that arise in response to elicitors as varied as interpersonal and institutional relations, aesthetic experience, ideas, sensations, and material conditions in one's environment" and in which "affects are attached to formal dimensions of texts such as metaphor, plot structure, and character relations," offers a useful pathway.[23] However, as I suggest below, through the formal tactics Spahr employs (many of which occupy a physiological register "below" those engaged by plot structure, character relations, or metaphor) her writing complicates the formulation "narrative affect" by excavating and foregrounding William James's notion of the "bodily sounding-board" as an important lever for thinking and feeling Anthropocene affects.[24]

Since the late aughts critics have paid increasing attention to Spahr's writing, focusing, for instance, on how her writing engages issues in contemporary poetics, manifests networks, and evinces an ecopoetics.[25] While much of the scholarship on Spahr is compelling, to date there has been little attention paid to how her formal and syntactic tactics materialize endemically Anthropocene forms of affect.[26] Spahr worries the same concerns across a range of genres and forms, and she engages a range of Anthropocene affects—including very circumscribed forms of interpersonal hope, dis-ease, distraction, irritation, grief, anger, rage, and "west melancholy."[27] As a result, her work offers an exemplary network for attending to what I call the form/affect/Anthropocene seam. As this list indicates, I position

Spahr as a doyenne of unpleasant ecological feelings working within the context of a pervasiveness in recent U.S. and British literature and films of what some might identify as less salutary ecological affects, in particular, sadness, despair, grief, melancholy, anxiety, fear, resignation. Encouraged by Stephanie LeMenager's reminder that "feeling ecological need not be pleasant," and in alignment with Houser's work on environment and affect, my examination of Spahr's work helps stake the claim for the importance of remaining open to unpleasant ecological feelings, tracking how they show up in contemporary cultural forms, and parsing the consequences of their appearance.[28] These activities, I wager, can help us articulate how to live with "geological changes moving us rapidly away from a certain ingrained normativity, a certain set of expectations about relations among the past, present, and future."[29] To put it more simply, I see avowal of the eco-unpleasant as commensurate with the Anthropocene.

In *The Transformation* Spahr outs her complicated attachment to a cluster of avant-garde poetic practices and forms with the often repeated list "fragmentation, quotation, disruption, disjunction, agrammatical syntax, and so on."[30] Through this list and the multiple ways she deploys it in *The Transformation*, Spahr positions her work as both belonging to and critical of modernist traditions and avant-garde practices.[31] Spahr employs "fragmentation, quotation, disruption, disjunction, agrammatical syntax, and so on" across her oeuvre, and although she certainly does not intend this list as all-encompassing, I think its brevity sells short her inventiveness. In other words I see a more expansive range of formal tactics operative in her work, among them accumulation, acceleration, feedback, fragmentation, indeterminacy, repetition, and suspension. In addition to evoking Spahr's list, which is limited to language practices, mine stages the Anthropocene. That is, the forms and practices I name tug at two registers—poetic and earth systems—calling into encounter radically different temporal, processual, experiential, spatial, and biocultural scales. Fragmentation, for instance, could describe both the way language is arranged on a page and a once-continuous habitat shattered into noncontiguous pieces. Accumulation could describe both the additive logic of a sentence that piles up phrases or the way an argument builds over the course of a text and what greenhouse gases are doing in the atmosphere. Reading in this doubled way (e.g., with habitat fragmentation in mind when organizational, grammatical, or lexical disorder appears) represents one mode of enacting, producing, and residing in the Anthropocene scale confusions that Timothy Clark and Derek Woods diagnose and promote as productive.[32] I propose that it is the doubled forms and practices of accumulation, acceleration, feedback, fragmentation, indeterminacy, repetition, and suspension, which also underwrite her critiques of capitalism, colonialism, and environmental degradation, that enable Spahr to register and produce the specifically Anthropocene malady I call Anthropocene anxiety.

Anxiety, a temporally doubled affect of nervousness and unease that infects both present and future, suffuses Spahr's writing. In "Poem Written after September 11, 2001," for instance, the collective activity of breathing in and out and the connections this activity draws between bodies are, in the post-9/11 landscape, both "lovely" and "doomed."[33] "Poem Written from November 30, 2002 to March 27, 2003," the series that comprises the rest of *this connection*, perpetuates this thematic stress on being doomed, an anxious form, by tracking the various embroiled networks contributing to anxiety. The impossibility of unknitting this Gordian knot of networks underlines the perpetuity of being doomed, which is generated, Spahr suggests, not by any one thing or event or network or node but rather by the very interconnectedness of systems. Formally Spahr repeatedly uses accumulation in both *this connection* and *The Transformation* to mimic and produce doom's affective quality: weight. In some instances the form's amplitude is relatively short. It might be bounded within a sentence or a page or two. In other instances it spans pages.[34] A key element to the anxiogenic affect of this form, whether of short or long duration, is its polymeric nature, the suggestion that the enchainment of words, things, ideas, worries could accumulate endlessly. In "Unnamed Dragonfly Species" anxiety arises, formally, from the conjoining and intercutting of two contradictory forms—an alphabetical list of New York State's endangered, threatened, and special concern species and a quasi narrative constructed from fragments of worry about climate change, extinction, and melting glaciers, among other things—each of which demands a different reading practice. This collision of contrary forms forces the disturbing cognitive operation of ignoring one thread in order to concentrate on the other, an operation that underwrites and reinforces the thematic staging of anxiety and guilt. In an Anthropocenic update of Charles Darwin's "endless forms most beautiful," these examples gesture toward Spahr's facility with proliferating anxious forms.[35] They also function as a contextual and formal framework within which to situate a more recent encoding of socioecological anxiety, the poem "Dynamic Positioning" from *That Winter the Wolf Came*, which responds to the April 20, 2010, explosion of the offshore oil rig *Deepwater Horizon* and the blowout of the Macondo well it was drilling.[36]

In ways more pronounced than in Spahr's earlier work, "Dynamic Positioning" enacts the very embodied nature of affect in a way that emphasizes the often curious absence of the body in many literary affect studies that purport to attend to embodiment. The poem refuses representation of an anxious speaker (in an attempt to use projection or identification as the vector for producing anxiety) and instead (through the visual, aural, and physiological levers its formal techniques spring) directly plays the reader's body into Anthropocene anxiety. In "Dynamic Positioning" Spahr tugs the thread of breath she thematically deploys in other locations to set up a formally produced anxiogenic circuit between author, language, socioecological circumstances, and reader that forces an embodied performance of how anthropogenic activities, accumulated into the Anthropocene, might have an impact on the basic bodily activity of breathing. Through this performative method, which brings experience of possible future socioecological circumstances into the present through the body, "Dynamic Positioning" stages late nineteenth-century ideas about body/environment/affect relationships to craft a crucial literary mode for the Anthropocene.

Spahr's title signals a triple register. At one level "Dynamic Positioning" refers to the computer-controlled system for maintaining a vessel's position and heading by using its propellers and thrusters. In the context of offshore oil drilling dynamic positioning keeps the drilling units in the right place over the well during drilling operations. At this level the title gestures to Spahr's desire to excavate the mundane elements of offshore drilling (what she calls the "common / Vocabulary"), which are invisible to most readers.[37] At another level the phrase identifies the activity of the poem, an attempt to hover both the poet and the readers over the tragedy in order to try to parse the actions that led to the deaths of eleven men; countless injuries, some fatal, to nonhumans; and ongoing detrimental impacts to the socioecologies and economies of the Gulf Coast. At yet another level the title sets up a relay between different forms of control: the technology of dynamic positioning, a synecdoche for resource extraction, and the technologies of poetic meter and stanza. "Dynamic Positioning" records the limits of drilling technology while also experimenting with strict adherence to poetic meter and stanza length. The failures of language forced by this strict metrical and stanzaic adherence underline the possibility of disaster lurking in all resource extraction. Even more striking, however, is that Spahr sets up these failures of drilling and language as metonyms for the ways cruelly optimistic attachments to petrocapitalism keep us tightly sutured to systems that are bound to destroy the habitability of the biosphere.[38] This ironic knowledge, made palpable through form, is a prime source of Anthropocene anxiety.

In a remarkable formal departure Spahr deploys iambic pentameter in the poem. Formal rigidity marks the poem's stanzas as well; each is a couplet. Within these forms, "Dynamic Positioning" encircles the "innovations" that permit offshore drilling, the ocean zones through which the well passes on its 18,360-foot exploratory crawl, the period prior to drilling when "an environmental // Impact and blowout plan declared to be / Not necessary," the period from the beginning of drilling on April 20 through "when the first mayday call was made. // The Deepwater Horizon gutted stem // to stern," and the explosion and its immediate aftermath, which includes a list of the names of the eleven men killed, notice of the poet's televisual consumption of the event, and her indictment of three corporate executives and one government official for "watching."[39] Within the iambic pentameter and couplet forms, Spahr nests other, contradictory sets of forms. The poem is both linear and tentacular, continuous and fragmented. Its temporalities are elastic; some temporal periods are demarcated while others are not, and although the poem's meter stays consistent, its narrative rhythms fluctuate such that within the rigid container of meter the feeling is of being unmoored, dislocated. In its shape, meter, and relentless downward vertical vector—couplet, break, couplet, break, repeat seventy-four more times—the poem resembles the action of drilling. What Spahr prospects in the poem are a hypervisibility trained on the drilling technologies and steps of drilling in the generic (i.e., what would take place at any offshore drilling site); an illumination of the particular actions, inactions, and missteps that led to the disaster; a reckoning, at personal (embodied, kinesthetic) and socioecological registers, of the material consequences of petrocapitalism; and an entanglement of the reader with the affects of anxiety and resignation that accrue to Anthropocene petrocapitalism.

In keeping with this essay's project of reading for how Spahr formalizes different kinds of Anthropocene anxiety, I concentrate on the interplay between her poem's primary shaping forms—meter and stanza length—and the deformation of language and meaning that adherence to these forms forces in the section of the poem that runs from the start of drilling through the mayday call.[40] This section takes literally the injunction "tell the story of This Well"; Spahr concentrates all its energies to detail specific actions and events on the rig and in the well.[41] In contrast to the sections that immediately precede and follow it, where Spahr uses the first-person "I" to indicate her position vis-à-vis petrocapitalism, in this section she deploys a rigorously third-person objective stance to keep the focus on the rig and well. In terms of the concordance of meter, line length, stanza length, the visual nature of the language on the page, and the breath and rhythms of reading, the beginning of this section aligns with all preceding material. For instance, a couplet early in the section reads, "The drill pipe run in hole to eight thousand / And three hundred and sixty seven feet." Both lines fit iambic pentameter without recourse to elision or counterelision. And although syntactically a bit funky, the couplet's visual nature is regular and its meaning clear. These congruities, however, disintegrate at a pace roughly synchronous with the buildup of pressure inside the well. The first difficulty emerges when rig engineers run a test and "partial lab // Results, a circulation pressure that / Did not yet match the modeling results // And yet cement job pumped."[42] The phrase "*did not yet match*" (emphasis added) and the decision to proceed anyway, both of which presume the earth will yield its resources in expected ways, that the reality of drilling will match the modeling, index the technoindustrial hubris that underwrites all offshore drilling. Just as the workers proceed, ensconced within the cocoon of business-as-usual, the regularity of the poem's frameworks here comfortably enfolds this trouble. With the line "Decreased. Drill pipe pressure increased," however, the concordance of the poem's conventions begins to fray and the metric-stanzaic form that has disciplined the reader begins to misinform the aural performance of the poem.[43] Read outside the poem's context, this line has four feet. But within the form meter imposes, its control metonymic for the technology of dynamic positioning, the words "decreased" and "increased" get elongated to three syllables—de-creas-ed and in-creas-ed—in order to satisfy metrical demands. The reverse occurs in the next stanza. In the line "It goes on. Drill pipe pressure. Kill line open," iambic pentameter refuses the extra half foot, compressing the word "pressure" into one syllable, an irony both delicious and terrible.[44] This metrically generated elongation and compression of the pronunciation of language that looks regular on the page is both dislocating and anxiogenic, for what has been expected of and given via the meter-pronunciation contract thus far is no longer upheld.[45] It also anticipates and prepares the reader for the visual irregularities—the deformations of words—and the stuttering of breath, fissuring of meaning at the level of the word, and concomitant ratcheting up of pressure and anxiety that begin in the next stanza with the word "sea- / Water."[46]

"sea- / Water," the first instance of a new form, layered grammatical and lexical enjambment, signals the disintegration of the concordances noted earlier and inaugurates a new regime characterized by a fully realized triumph of meter. In this subsection—where various pumps are started, stopped, and restarted; "drill pipe pressure fluctuates"; mud overflows the line onto the rig floor; gas and other alarms sound; and the rig loses power, shuts down, fails, and twice explodes—Spahr hypercharges the rule of meter such that the relationship between word and meaning unravels and anxiety is pressurized.[47] Words are fractured, like "sea- / Water," across lines within couplets and also, like "open- // Ed," across the break between them.[48] With the exception of "sea- / Water," where the words stand on their own as meaningful, all the other fractured words deform into non-sense, their meaninglessness further emphasized by the futile practice of capitalizing whatever starts each line in an attempt to pry meaning back into the fissured word.[49] Initially Spahr uses lexical enjambment occasion-ally, but as "the volumes of gases, fluids, drill- // Ing mud, seawater, then is steadily in- / Creasing. And it begins again. Or be- // Gins some more," she increases the frequency of use, bookending all of the last twenty lines of this section of the poem except for the final, "when the may-day call was first made," which she end-stops.[50] These visual stutter-steps within words across lines and stanzas correlate with uneven, ragged breathing and reading. The breath-sounds of reading are further emphasized through the use of consonantal echo ("degasser," "pressure," "increasing," "discharging," "hissing," "processes"), via which Spahr forces the reader into a form of becoming-well: the hissing sound the reader makes underlines complic-ity with the well; the emission of sound here relays from body to carbon emissions generated by fossil fuel consumption and back. Spahr also enacts pronounced temporal disjuncture in this subsection. Even as the meter and stanzas tick constantly, and activity, pressure, and anxiety crescendo, time slows in an asymptotic approach to ten o'clock. It takes thirteen couplets to get from noon to nine o'clock and twenty-five to get to "almost" ten. The poem remains "almost at ten o'clock" for nine couplets and then moves to "almost close to ten o' / Clock" for four.[51] The last semidefinitive temporal marker, which is also the end of the section, is "not yet ten / O'clock," the moment of the mayday call.[52] Taken together, all of these formal, syntactic, and lexical tactics move through the body to initiate, accelerate, and amplify a feedback loop of anxiety.

In the section of the poem discussed above, Spahr's connection to William James's work on affect resonates clearly. James first proposes his theory of relationship between perception, body, and affect in the 1884 essay "What Is an Emotion?," in which he suggests that *bodily changes follow directly the perception of the exciting fact, and that our feeling of the same changes as they occur is the emotion.*[53] And although he revises the specific contours of the perception-body-emotion vector in his later work, he retains the emphasis on physiological activity as generative of emotion.[54] What recommends

James's work on emotion for environmental affect studies is the way he positions the body as open to being reverberated by its environment in physiologically fundamental ways; for James emotions are "instances of the way in which peculiarly conformed pieces of the world's furniture will fatally call forth most particular mental and bodily reactions, in advance of, and often in direct opposition to, the verdict of our deliberate reason concerning them."[55] For James "the world's furniture" might be objects, people, experiences, or circumstances. In Spahr's writing from the aughts the "world's furniture" includes language, formal experimentation, and the tools and impacts of anthropogenic activity. In "Dynamic Positioning" she makes visible and rearranges this furniture in order to sound the body into Anthropocene anxiety through the performance of a multiscalar shortness of breath that is a "bodily reverberation" of the explosion of the Macondo well, the well's role as a node in a global network of climate change–inducing petrocapitalism, and future changes to atmospheric composition that will have an impact on future forms of breathing.[56] As per James, then, her poem captures, registers, and produces a form of ragged breathing that is, feels like, and amplifies Anthropocene anxiety.

The visual-lexical-physiological-anxiogenic feedback loop Spahr produces through strict adherence to meter and couplet in this section of the poem is additionally remarkable in the following ways. First, it differs significantly from the sections that immediately precede and follow it in that Spahr suspends explicit critique in favor of chaotic action and its corollary, chaotic feeling. Once the mayday sounds, Spahr releases the tyrannically strict metrical control, frantic pace, and fractured language and the poem subsides back into the concordances that marked its beginning. This subsidence is necessary in part to regain the distance needed to consider the disaster's aftermath, witness the eleven dead, and render judgment, which Spahr shapes through her indictment of petrocorporations and the government and our habit of "watching" our "Relationship to oil / Our oil."[57] Departing from frenzied anxiety also enables Spahr to adjust the pitch back to the lower-level, more gestural form of anxiety that characterizes the poem's beginning. What is perhaps more important, the move coalesces the poem's tone of resignation, to which I will return below.[58] Second, the hyperanxiogenic nature of this section positions the poem as a deft interlocutor for other contemporary theories of anxiety. By formally reengaging the centrality of one of the body's most basic physiological functions, breathing, the poem reminds us of the ways literary texts can operate at levels "beneath" the cognitive functions engaged by the literary techniques that usually interest scholars pursuing literary affect studies.

Additionally, the poem challenges Sianne Ngai's ideas about the gendered nature of anxiety, the comportment of the anxious individual, the scale of anxiety, and its tone, which she defines as "the objective and subjective feeling that our aesthetic encounters inevitably produce" but that cannot be "entirely reducible to a reader's emotional response to a text or reducible to the text's internal representations of feeling."[59] Ngai's account draws from Sigmund Freud, Martin Heidegger, Alfred Hitchcock, and Herman Melville to present anxiety as "an anticipatory structure explicitly linked to a male subject's quest for interpretive agency."[60] For Ngai the spatialization of anxiety takes precedence over its temporality, and its appearance is yoked to the figure of the male intellectual; anxiety is "the male knowledge-seeker's distinctive yet basic state of mind" in the texts she considers.[61] Ultimately for Ngai anxiety offers a "form of dispositioning that paradoxically relocates, reorients, or repositions the [male] subject" in a relation of "'revolutionary uplift'" with respect to "the questions of 'sinking' worlds" and "'horrible interspaces.'"[62] Spahr interrogates this gendered notion of anxiety by un- and/or multigendering her anxious subjects and speakers.[63] The speaker in "Dynamic Positioning" is un-gendered; although we may be inclined to read the gender of the poem's "I" as aligned with Spahr's, nothing in the poem directs this maneuver. The theory of anxiety Spahr forms in "Dynamic Positioning" also pressures Ngai's version in terms of scale and comportment (which orbit each other), as well as tone, which depends in part on the contours of scale and comportment. Ngai's analysis circuits the personal/interpersonal interface and concerns existential crisis rooted in the subject. Although the sociopolitical is important for Ngai and she historicizes the affects she considers, the human subject is the primary matter.

Spahr, in contrast, by performatively using the reader's body as a sounding board to reverberate present and future socioecological circumstances, takes

Ngai's "'sinking' worlds" and "'horrible interspaces'" into the ecological register, embroiling the personal/interpersonal circuit in this larger framework. Spahr worries about the domestic in both its narrowest sense—the body—and in its broadest sense—the affairs of the planet and all its creatures. She reminds us that the existential crises the Anthropocene fashions ping at multiscalar registers, simultaneously personal and cosmological. The tone of anxiety, for Ngai, involves a moody tacking that results in the paradoxical uplifting of the subject. For Spahr, however, anxiety affords no reprieve; commensurate with the entrapment of Anthropocene circumstances, its tone is worried resignation. The last word of "Dynamic Positioning," "watching," inflected by all the forms of inaction that contributed to the *Deepwater Horizon*/Macondo disaster, perfectly encapsulates this worried resignation and designates the grossly limited agency of the anxious position we continue to occupy.[64]

I have attended to Spahr's work from *this connection* to *That Winter* in general and to the poem "Dynamic Positioning" in particular because her formal experiments across and within texts and poems disclose myriad ways environmental anxiety formally emerges in literary texts, because her versions of Anthropocene anxiety offer unique perspectives on theories of anxiety, and because in her attentiveness to locatedness she reminds us that neither the Anthropocene nor Anthropocene anxiety should be understood as universal or ahistorical. Anthropocene anxiety is rather a specifically post-1958 malady that affects Western, industrialized, internet-addicted subjects whose dreaming and waking moments are haunted by Keeling Curves, hockey-stick graphs, IPCC Special Reports on Emissions Scenarios (SRES) and Representative Concentration Pathways (RCPs), and a fatal inability to wean ourselves from petrocapitalism. Anthropocene anxiety, Spahr shows us, is an asymptotic affect; it may be temporally doubled in its simultaneous orientation toward present and future, but it does not ultimately resolve into more "active" affects, what James would call "standard emotions" like anger, fear, or lust.[65] Such "inactivity" might prove challenging for camps within environmental studies that privilege overt activism, but dismissing affective forms like anxiety because of their modes of comportment would be a form of denialism scholars can ill afford.

As noted above, I see the Anthropocene as characterized fundamentally by multiscalar, multiply entangled unpleasant ecological affects. The effects of anthropogenic activity from circa 1950 to the present, or 1769 to the present, or 1492 to the present, or 13,800 BP to the present—take your pick—have compounded into an exceedingly weighty set of circumstances; this is the condition Spahr diagnoses via the word "doomed" in *this connection* and, in "Dynamic Positioning," via both her foregrounding of one way the body reverberates the effects of petrocapitalism and the anxiously resigned position of watching that ends, without closing, the poem. For Spahr this condition of doomed, anxious waiting updates Lauren Berlant's form "cruel optimism" for an Anthropocene socioecological register by foregrounding our entrapment in the very systems that, post–Keeling Curve, we demonstrably know represent our undoing. Berlant defines cruel optimism as a relation that "exists when something you desire is actually an obstacle to your flourishing" and "a relation of attachment to compromised conditions of possibility whose realization is discovered to be *im*possible, sheer fantasy, or *too* possible, and toxic."[66] Berlant elaborates the concept by noting that all forms of attachment, however they feel and whatever the desired object, are optimistic in that they involve "a sustaining inclination to return to the scene of fantasy that enables you to expect that *this* time, nearness to *this* thing will help you or a world to become different in just the right way."[67] What tips optimistic attachment into cruel optimism, however, is "when the object/scene that ignites a sense of possibility actually makes it impossible to attain the expansive transformation for which a person or a people risks striving; and, doubly, it is cruel insofar as the very pleasures of being inside a relation have become sustaining regardless of the content of the relation, such that a person or a world finds itself bound to a situation of profound threat that is, at the same time, profoundly confirming."[68] For someone concerned with carrying capacity and other kinds of environmental limits, the phrase "cruel optimism" reads as synonymous with late capitalism, a system that produces socioecological conditions that are both impossible—that is, impossible to sustain—and all too toxic because they are too possible, that is, too easy to continue. Spahr reinflects cruel optimism for the Anthropocene by exposing the "good-life fantasies" Berlant tracks as not just paradoxical but as fundamentally socioecologically impossible to perpetuate.[69]

Whether foregrounding the grimness of socioecological circumstances in the Anthropocene can fatally short-circuit the reproduction of relations of cruel optimism may be an open question for other environmental writers and thinkers, but for Spahr any circuits that might spark change have always already been disconnected by globalized systems, grown increasingly more powerful and complex since 1492, that we cannot override. This does not mean dispensing with acts of literary resistance, however futile, for these do offer us something important. In answer to questions like Timothy Clark's—"Can [the Anthropocene's] new demands be met by new forms of artistic and cultural innovation[?]"—Spahr's work says, resoundingly, yes, but only if those texts engage affect via form at fundamentally physiological levels.[70] It is not enough, Spahr's work argues, to merely represent or think the affects of the Anthropocene. Rather we have to performatively embody them in ways that materialize our vulnerabilities, whether shared or particular. Spahr's continued formal experiments and her activisms around constructing literary communities help us practice forms of Anthropocene inhabitation. While these activities will not assure survivability, they do operate as critical coping mechanisms that register and compose how we conceptualize and live the Anthropocene, its effects, and its affects.[71]

NOTES

1. Most Anthropocene scholarship tracks the emergence of the term to 2000 and the publication of Crutzen and Stoermer, "Anthropocene.'" They argue in it that we are living in a new geological epoch marked by the "central role of mankind in ecology and geology" (17). See also Lewis and Maslin, "Defining the Anthropocene," for discussion of the Anthropocene term and concept.

2. Clover and Spahr, #Misanthropocene, 4.

3. My use of the pronoun "us" follows Spahr's practice in *this connection* and *The Transformation*, where she uses pronouns like "we," "us," and "they" to various ends but always as clearly located: "we/us" equals Western, industrialized, carbon-emitting people with the "leisure" to worry about things like avant-garde poetic practices and climate change.

4. This sentiment is Bronislaw Szerszynski's. The phrase "the great stone book of nature," quoted in Szerszynski, "End of the End of Nature," 165, comes from the

nineteenth-century geologist David Thomas Ansted, whose attitudes about the relationship between humans and nature Szerszynski employs as emblematic of the Holocene.

5. On slow violence see Nixon, *Slow Violence and the Environmentalism of the Poor*.

6. On the importance of scale see Clark, "Derangements of Scale"; Clark, *Ecocriticism on the Edge*; and Woods, "Scale Critique for the Anthropocene."

7. Serres, *Natural Contract*.

8. For additional engagement with some of these questions see Merola, "Materializing a Geotraumatic and Melancholy Anthropocene"; and Merola, "Mediating Planetary Attachments."

9. BP signifies years before present. For discussion of proposed start dates see, for instance, Clark, *Ecocriticism on the Edge*, 1–3; Lewis and Maslin, "Defining the Anthropocene"; and Smith and Zeder, "Onset of the Anthropocene."

10. See Damian Carrington, "The Anthropocene Epoch: Scientists Declare Dawn of Human-Influenced Age," *The Guardian*, August 29, 2016, https://www.theguardian.com/environment/2016/aug/29/declare-anthropocene-epoch-experts-urge-geological-congress-human-impact-earth, for a summary of the AWG's recommendation, made at the Thirty-Fifth International Geological Congress, August 29, 2016. On 1492/1610 see Lewis and Maslin, "Defining the Anthropocene," 174–75.

11. On March 29, 1958, atmospheric CO_2 measured 313 ppm. For comparison, the monthly average from March 1 to September 1, 2016, was 401.75 ppm. For CO_2 data from periods ranging from hourly, daily, and weekly averages for 1700 to the present and for the last eight hundred thousand years see Scripps Institute of Oceanography, "The Keeling Curve," accessed September 10, 2016, http://scripps.ucsd.edu/programs/keelingcurve/.

12. Spahr, *this connection*, 26.

13. I use Anthropo(s)cenic here to emphasize the aesthetic and ocular. I use Anthropocenic elsewhere as the adjectival form of Anthropocene.

14. For readings of these photographs see Boes, "Beyond Whole Earth"; and Heise, *Sense of Place*, 17–67.

15. Rooney, "Form and Contentment," 35.

16. For this critique see Rooney, "Form and Contentment," 34, 36–37, 38.

17. Rooney, "Form and Contentment," 43.

18. Nersessian, "Two Gardens," 313.

19. Silvan Tomkins's work on emotion, important for Houser and Ngai, functions as deeper background for this chapter.

20. Massumi's texts *Parables for the Virtual* and *Politics of Affect* are the works most regularly cited in affect studies. For a critique of Massumi see Leys, "Turn to Affect."

21. Massumi, *Parables for the Virtual*, 28.

22. Brinkema, *Forms of the Affects*, xvi. For critical assessments of current modes of affect studies see Brinkema, *Forms of the Affects*, xi–xvi; and R. Smith, *Affect and American Literature*, 1–29.

23. Houser, *Ecosickness in Contemporary U.S. Fiction*, 3; see also 1–30.

24. James, "What Is an Emotion?," 202. Houser does identify "sensations" as encircled by "narrative affect," but her focus, given the lengthy and complex novels she assesses, tends toward structures and techniques that engage cognitive faculties more than toward those that engage physiological actions.

25. On poetics see Keller, "'Post-Language Lyric'"; Mayer, "Aggregators"; Milne, "Dearly Beloveds"; and Ronda, "Anthropogenic Poetics." On networks see Ngai, "Network Aesthetics." On ecopoetics see Chisholm, "Juliana Spahr's Ecopoetics"; Chisholm, "On the House That Ecopoetics Builds"; Keller, "'Post-Language Lyric'"; Ronda, "Anthropogenic Poetics"; and Welch, "Entangled Species."

26. In terms of situating Spahr within the Anthropocene, Margaret Ronda's essay "Anthropogenic Poetics" is the exception. Dianne Chisholm thinks about form—the refrain—in "Juliana Spahr's Ecopoetics" but not about affect.

27. Clover and Spahr, *#Misanthropocene*, 4, 5, 6, 7.

28. LeMenager, *Living Oil*, 105; Houser, *Ecosickness in Contemporary U.S. Fiction*.

29. Pinkus, "Search for a Language," 252.

30. Spahr, *Transformation*, 59.

31. For a trenchant critique of how "the government that currently occupied the continent" co-opts these formal tactics see Spahr, *Transformation*, 155.

32. For elaboration of new reading practices the Anthropocene necessitates see Clark, *Ecocriticism on the Edge*.

33. Spahr, *this connection*, 10.

34. See Spahr, *this connection*, 24–25, for an example of short-duration accumulation and Spahr, *Transformation*, 137–64, for an example of long-duration accumulation.

35. Darwin, *On the Origin of Species*, 427.

36. For details of the disaster and its aftermath see "Deepwater Horizon Oil Spill: An Interactive Look at What Happened," *New York Times*, accessed June 15, 2016, http://www.nytimes.com/interactive/us/spill_index.html.

37. Spahr, *That Winter*, 44.

38. I return to cruel optimism, Lauren Berlant's formulation, in my conclusion.

39. Spahr, *That Winter*, 48, 49.

40. Spahr, *That Winter*, 45–48.

41. Spahr, *That Winter*, 45.

42. Spahr, *That Winter*, 45.

43. Spahr, *That Winter*, 46.

44. Spahr, *That Winter*, 46.

45. In prosody the elongation is called counterelision and the compression, elision. Here I use the vernacular to underline the temporal aspect of Spahr's decisions.

46. Spahr, *That Winter*, 46.

47. Spahr, *That Winter*, 46–48 (quote on 47).

48. Spahr, *That Winter*, 46.

49. For some words (e.g., "in- / Creasing") one syllable might make sense in isolation, but for the majority (e.g., "othe- // Ers") the fracture renders both syllables nonsense. For all, regardless of whether discrete syllables make sense or not, meaning at the lexical level is delayed or foreclosed.

50. Spahr, *That Winter*, 48.

51. Spahr, *That Winter*, 47, 48.

52. Spahr, *That Winter*, 48.

53. James, "What Is an Emotion?," 189–90 (original emphasis).

54. See also James, "Physical Basis of Emotion"; and James, *Principles of Psychology*, esp. 442–85. For a contemporary engagement with James's theories see Damasio, *Feeling of What Happens*.

55. James, "What Is an Emotion?," 190.

56. James, "What Is an Emotion?," 192.

57. Spahr, *That Winter*, 49.

58. On tone see Ngai, *Ugly Feelings*, 24–31, 43–49. See also R. Smith, *Affect and American Literature*, 17–18, 58–59.

59. Ngai, *Ugly Feelings*, 30, 29, respectively.

60. Ngai, *Ugly Feelings*, 215.

61. Ngai, *Ugly Feelings*, 247.

62. Ngai, *Ugly Feelings*, 247. For Ngai's full discussion of anxiety see *Ugly Feelings*, 209–47. On anxiety in an environmental frame see Houser, *Ecosickness in Contemporary U.S. Fiction*, 16, 167–216.

63. This is especially true in *The Transformation*, where the referents of Spahr's pronouns are both ambiguous and slippery.

64. Spahr, *That Winter*, 49.

65. James, "What Is an Emotion?," 189.

66. Berlant, *Cruel Optimism*, 1, 24.

67. Berlant, *Cruel Optimism*, 2.

68. Berlant, *Cruel Optimism*, 2.

69. Berlant, *Cruel Optimism*, 2.

70. Clark, *Ecocriticism on the Edge*, 24.

71. Latour, "Attempt at a Compositionist Manifesto."

BIBLIOGRAPHY

Berlant, Lauren. *Cruel Optimism*. Durham: Duke University Press, 2011.

Boes, Tobias. "Beyond Whole Earth: Planetary Mediation and the Anthropocene." *Environmental Humanities* 5, no. 1 (2014): 155–70.

Brinkema, Eugenie. *The Forms of the Affects*. Durham: Duke University Press, 2014.

Chisholm, Dianne. "Juliana Spahr's Ecopoetics: Ecologies and Politics of the Refrain." *Contemporary Literature* 55, no. 1 (2014): 118–47.

———. "On the House That Ecopoetics Builds: Juliana Spahr's 'Eco' Frame." *Textual Practice* 28, no. 4 (2014): 631–53.

Clark, Timothy. "Derangements of Scale." In *Telemorphosis: Theory in the Age of Climate Change*, vol. 1, edited by Tom Cohen, 148–66. Ann Arbor: Open Humanities Press, 2012.

———. *Ecocriticism on the Edge: The Anthropocene as a Threshold Concept*. London: Bloomsbury, 2015.

Clover, Joshua, and Juliana Spahr. *#Misanthropocene: 24 Theses*. Oakland CA: Commune Editions, 2014.

Crutzen, Paul J., and Eugene F. Stoermer. "The 'Anthropocene.'" *IGBP Global Change Newsletter* 41 (2000): 17–18.

Damasio, Antonio. *The Feeling of What Happens: Body and Emotion in the Making of Consciousness*. New York: Harcourt, Brace, 1999.

Darwin, Charles. *On the Origin of Species*. 1859. New York: Penguin, 2009.

Heise, Ursula K. *Sense of Place and Sense of Planet: The Environmental Imagination of the Global*. Oxford: Oxford University Press, 2008.

Houser, Heather. *Ecosickness in Contemporary U.S. Fiction: Environment and Affect*. New York: Columbia University Press, 2014.

James, William. "The Physical Basis of Emotion." *Psychological Review* 1 (1894): 516–29.

———. *The Principles of Psychology*. Vol. 2. New York: Henry Holt, 1890.

———. "What Is an Emotion?" *Mind* 9 (1884): 188–205.

Keller, Lynn. "'Post-Language Lyric': The Example of Juliana Spahr." *Chicago Review* 55, no. 3–4 (2010): 74–83.

Latour, Bruno. "An Attempt at a Compositionist Manifesto." *New Literary History* 41, no. 3 (2010): 471–90.

LeMenager, Stephanie. *Living Oil: Petroleum Culture in the American Century*. Oxford: Oxford University Press, 2014.

Lewis, Simon L., and Mark A. Maslin. "Defining the Anthropocene." *Nature* 519 (2015): 171–80.

Leys, Ruth. "The Turn to Affect: A Critique." *Critical Inquiry* 37, no. 3 (2011): 434–72.

Massumi, Brian. *Parables for the Virtual: Movement, Affect, Sensation*. Durham: Duke University Press, 2002.

―――. *Politics of Affect*. Cambridge: Polity, 2015.

Mayer, Sophie. "Aggregators: RSS (Radically Subversive Syndication) Poetics." *SubStance* 38, no. 2 (2009): 43–62.

Merola, Nicole M. "Materializing a Geotraumatic and Melancholy Anthropocene: Jeanette Winterson's *The Stone Gods*." *minnesota review* 83 (2014): 122–32.

―――. "Mediating Planetary Attachments and Planetary Melancholy: Lars von Trier's *Melancholia*." In *Design, Mediation, and the Posthuman*, edited by Amy Propen, Colbey Emmerson Reid, and Dennis Weiss, 249–67. Lanham MD: Lexington Books, 2014.

Milne, Heather. "Dearly Beloveds: The Politics of Intimacy in Juliana Spahr's *This Connection of Everyone with Lungs*." *Mosaic: A Journal for the Interdisciplinary Study of Literature* 47, no. 2 (2014): 203–18.

Nersessian, Anahid. "Two Gardens: An Experiment in Calamity Form." *Modern Language Quarterly* 74, no. 3 (2013): 307–29.

Ngai, Sianne. "Network Aesthetics: Juliana Spahr's *The Transformation* and Bruno Latour's *Reassembling the Social*." In *American Literature's Aesthetic Dimensions*, edited by Cindy Weinstein and Christopher Looby, 367–92. New York: Columbia University Press, 2012.

―――. *Ugly Feelings*. Cambridge MA: Harvard University Press, 2005.

Nixon, Rob. *Slow Violence and the Environmentalism of the Poor*. Cambridge MA: Harvard University Press, 2013.

Pinkus, Karen. "Search for a Language: Response to Ian Baucom." *Cambridge Journal of Postcolonial Literary Studies* 1, no. 2 (2014): 251–57.

Ronda, Margaret. "Anthropogenic Poetics." *minnesota review* 83 (2014): 102–11.

Rooney, Ellen. "Form and Contentment." In *Reading for Form*, edited by Susan J. Wolfson and Marshall Brown, 25–48. Seattle: University of Washington Press, 2006.

Serres, Michel. *The Natural Contract*. Translated by Elizabeth MacArthur and William Paulson. Ann Arbor: University of Michigan Press, 1995.

Smith, Bruce D., and Melinda A. Zeder. "The Onset of the Anthropocene." *Anthropocene* 4 (December 2013): 8–13.

Smith, Rachel Greenwald. *Affect and American Literature in the Age of Neoliberalism*. Cambridge: Cambridge University Press, 2015.

Spahr, Juliana. *That Winter the Wolf Came*. Oakland CA: Commune Editions, 2015.

―――. *this connection of everyone with lungs: poems*. Berkeley: University California Press, 2005.

―――. *The Transformation*. Berkeley CA: Atelos, 2007.

————. *well then there now*. Jaffrey NH: Black Sparrow Press, 2011.

Szerszynski, Bronislaw. "The End of the End of Nature: The Anthropocene and the Fate of the Human." *Oxford Literary Review* 34, no. 2 (2012): 165–84.

Tomkins, Silvan. *Affect, Imagery, Consciousness*. 4 vols. New York: Springer, 1962–92.

————. *Exploring Affect: The Selected Writings of Silvan S. Tomkins*. Edited by E. Virginia Demos. Cambridge: Cambridge University Press, 1995.

Welch, Tana Jean. "Entangled Species: The Inclusive Posthumanist Ecopoetics of Juliana Spahr." *Journal of Ecocriticism: A New Journal of Nature, Society and Literature* 6, no. 1 (2014): 1–25.

Woods, Derek. "Scale Critique for the Anthropocene." *minnesota review* 83 (2014): 133–42.

2

From Nostalgic Longing to Solastalgic Distress

A Cognitive Approach to *Love in the Anthropocene*

ALEXA WEIK VON MOSSNER

Among human emotions love may be the most thoroughly explored and yet most evasive, not only because it comes in so many different forms and guises but also because it can take very diverse objects. The philosopher Martha Nussbaum defines it as an "intense attachment to things outside the control of our will," and yet she also suggests that love—like all emotions—plays a crucial part in our cognitive appraisals and thus in our rationality.[1] In *Political Emotions* Nussbaum argues that "appropriate sentiments of sympathy and love" not only are crucial in the interpersonal realm but can also help overcome injustice and exploitation by sensitizing us for the pain of more distant human and nonhuman others.[2] Scholars in the environmental humanities have extended the level of analysis even further by exploring forms of emotional attachment that take as their object the environments in which such human and nonhuman others exist. In doing so they have traced topophilia and other forms of place attachment back to processes of evolutionary adaptation, habituation, and social interactions.[3] Cognitive psychologists and social anthropologists such as Kay Milton have also explored the role of biological universals in our emotional relationships to our surroundings. Drawing, like Nussbaum, on the insights of affective science, Milton suggests that primary emotions such as love and affection "operate primarily (though not exclusively) in ecological relations."[4] This builds directly on the neurologist Antonio Damasio's claim in *Descartes' Error* (1994) that "mental phenomena can be fully understood only in the context of an organism's interacting in an environment."[5]

Once we realize that our environment plays a central role not only in how we feel but also in our cognitive understanding of how we feel about that environment, the question that suggests itself is, What happens to our emotions when that environment changes drastically? In their coauthored short-story collection *Love in the Anthropocene* (2015) the environmental philosopher Dale Jamieson and the novelist Bonnie Nadzam explore this question in five science fiction stories framed by an introduction and a coda that offer philosophical meditations on love and the Anthropocene. The notion of the Anthropocene, the authors remind us, marks "the scale and significance of . . . human impacts on the planet," a scale and significance that might be substantial enough to be reflected in the geological record of the earth's crust.[6] Their shared concern about these anthropogenic impacts has driven Jamieson and Nadzam to an unusual collaboration that uses storytelling in order to "invite" readers "to imagine human beings living in worlds of the future that have been remade and are almost entirely managed by human action" and to explore what consequences this may have for "the human heart."[7] Love, the two authors claim, is inseparable from nature in our daily experience because our very bodies and the physical processes involved in emotional attachment are part of nature. This insistence on the embodied nature of our emotions is in keeping with much of the multifaceted scholarship mentioned above, but rather than looking at the past or even the present Jamieson and Nadzam harness the imaginative power of science fiction in order to explore the question of what it might mean for our *future* emotional health if we must live in thoroughly anthropogenic environments.

I argue that the authors' response to this question amounts to the claim that love in the Anthropocene is inevitably tied to environmental change and that this will lead us to develop the "earth-related mental issues" that the philosopher Glenn Albrecht has called *psychoterratic dis-eases*—an umbrella term that bundles ailments such as "ecoanxiety, nature deficit disorder, ecoparalysis, solastalgia, eco-nostalgia and global dread."[8] In my investigation of the emotional structure of *Love in the Anthropocene* I use a cognitive ecocritical approach that draws on insights of affective narratology. The first section presents Patrick Colm Hogan's perceptual account of emotion, which I consider useful for an analysis of the affective dimensions of *Love in the Anthropocene*. The second part of the essay then looks at two stories from that collection—"Flyfishing" and "Zoo"—that illustrate particularly well the narrative strategies used by Jamieson and Nadzam to cue in readers an emotional reaction to both the drastically impoverished environments displayed and the psychoterratic dis-eases that characters have developed in response to them. I argue that while the emotional lives of the characters are often reduced to backward-oriented feelings of eco-nostalgic longing, readers are invited to develop the solastalgic distress that, according to Albrecht, results from the "recognition that the place where one [currently] resides and that one loves is under immediate assault."[9] Defined by Albrecht as a "homesickness one gets when one is still at 'home,'" solastalgia, not love, emerges as the dominant emotion in *Love in the Anthropocene*.[10]

Imagining Fictional Worlds: Literature as Mental Instruction Manuals

Given the rapidly increasing interest in the affective dimensions of ecological thinking and related cultural production, it seems regrettable that to date there have been few attempts to harness the insights of affective and cognitive science for ecocritical investigations. As the psychologists Keith Oatley, Raymond Mar, and Maja Djikic have pointed out, literary scholars and cognitive psychologists tend to view each other's methods with suspicion, with the result that "although [they] might be interested in similar topics such as character and emotion, they tend to take no notice of each other."[11] Oatley, Mar, and Djikic find this intellectual disconnect regrettable since, in carrying out the investigation of how narrative thinking works, "dialogue between the humanities and cognitive science is essential."[12] Biocultural and eco-narratological approaches, as they have been developed in recent years by Nancy Easterlin and Erin James, are among the few that already engage in such dialogues. Easterlin has argued that "knowledge of human perception, cognition, and conceptual articulation is more crucial to ecocriticism than it is to perhaps any other area of contemporary literary studies" precisely because of the field's vested interest in narratives that might be able to change their readers' thinking and feeling about their actual environment.[13] James makes a similar point when she observes that all narrative texts, "even those that do not seem to be interested in the environment in and of itself, offer up virtual environments for their readers to model mentally and inhabit emotionally."[14] What makes the virtual environments of self-consciously environmentalist narratives such as *Love in the Anthropocene* particularly interesting for narratological analysis is that they tend to be informed by what Suzanne Keen has called "a scrupulously visible political interest" and that their authors often deliberately try to guide their readers' emotional responses in ways that may lead to a change of mind and, ideally, to altered attitudes and behaviors.[15]

How exactly we engage with the imaginary world of a narrative has been theorized in several ways. The psychologist Richard Gerrig suggests that it is in part unconscious *mental performance* that involves what he calls readers' "memory traces," but he does not spell out how exactly such a performative act plays out in readers' minds.[16] Other psychologists, including Oatley, have argued that fiction is "a kind of simulation that enables exploration of minds and their interactions in the social world."[17] The cognitive narratologist Patrick Colm Hogan draws on Damasio's clinical research to develop a perceptual account of emotion that understands our engagement with a literary work as "some version of an empathic response" that is triggered by imagined perception.[18] The fact that we are responding to fiction and thus to something that does not actually exist is irrelevant in Hogan's perceptual account. Instead our emotional responses to a literary text are determined by the emotional memories we have retained of previous experiences (real and imagined) and by the *vivacity* of the things we imagine while reading.[19] For a definition of vivacity Hogan looks to Elaine Scarry, who has claimed that it "comes about by reproducing the deep structures of perception."[20] What is simulated in literary reading, argues Scarry, "is not only the sensory outcome (the way something looks or sounds or feels beneath the hands) but the actual structure that gave rise to the perception; that is, the material conditions that made it look, sound, or feel the way it did."[21]

Regardless of how we theorize the process of emotional inhabitation, it is crucial to keep in mind that this inhabitation is often the result of careful planning on the part of the author. Narratologists have likened literary narratives to "instruction manuals" that contain "a set of instructions for mental composition" and invite readers to follow those instructions.[22] The metaphor of the instruction manual is an interesting one because it stresses the active role of the reader as someone who *performs* the narrative, as Gerrig would put it.[23] While such performances by readers will be idiosyncratic to some degree, fueled by their own personal experiences and by their historical and sociocultural contexts, they are nevertheless guided by the words on the page. With this in mind I now turn to *Love in the Anthropocene* and to the ways in which it invites us, like an instruction manual, "to entertain certain imaginings (and not others)."[24] The authorial voice of the book, which is "neither Dale Jamieson's nor Bonnie Nadzam's, but a third voice" that the authors "have jointly created," asks us to imagine future worlds in which people's personal emotional lives and their relationships to human and nonhuman others are severely affected by our pervasive influence on the planet.[25] What interests me is the ways in which the text invites emotional responses to those imaginary future worlds and to the fates of the fictional humans who have to live out their (love) lives in them and, as a result, fall prey to a range of psychoterratic dis-eases.

Psychoterratic Dis-eases in *Love in the Anthropocene*

In their introduction to the collection Jamieson and Nadzam quite literally extend an invitation to readers to simulate in their minds what it would be like to live in environments that are thoroughly anthropogenic and anthropocentric: "We invite you to imagine human beings living in worlds of the future that have been remade and are almost entirely managed by human action: rivers, lakes, oceans, forests and fields are as meticulously planned and technologically maintained by humans as are cities and their systems of transportation and utilities. The weather is profoundly affected by the inadvertent consequences of human action, and by clumsy attempts to correct these perturbations and bring them under intentional human control."[26] The five stories that follow this invitation are all set in environments that are subject to human interference, but—as the authors also make clear here—interference does not equal control. Just like the weather, the personal lives of the stories' protagonists are deeply affected by the inadvertent consequences of human actions and too many clumsy attempts at correction.

Much has been written about the perceptional and imaginative difficulties we experience when trying to make reasonable judgments about the risks associated with climate change, resource depletion, species extinction, and other global ecological processes we associate with the Anthropocene. In his *Reason in a Dark Time* (2014) Jamieson locates the problem in our cognitive makeup, stating that "our failure to prevent or even to respond significantly reflects the impoverishment of our systems of practical reason . . . and the limits of our cognitive and affective abilities."[27] The tragedy of the Anthropocene, it seems, is that humans now "collectively wield a geological force" but at the same time experience difficulties when trying to understand the potential consequences of the risks they are taking because they are too abstract and distant.[28] This is where storytelling comes into play. As Ursula Heise has pointed out, we must pay more "attention to the role that particular metaphors, narrative patterns, or visual representations . . . play in the formation of risk judgements."[29] Reading or watching a fictional story about potential future catastrophes might change our perception of risk as well as the way we feel about it.

Jamieson and Nadzam make clear that the purpose of their little book is exactly that: to influence readers' risk perceptions by inviting them "to consider . . . the path we are already on" through a confrontation with fictional scenarios of life on a future planet earth.[30] The five stories they tell expose their characters' difficulties in connecting emotionally to their immediate environments and to other humans. Whether they take their offspring on a weekend fishing trip, meet a casual lover in some business-related situation, visit a pleasure dome, or take someone they've met over the web to see the last living tigress—the protagonists of *Love in the Anthropocene* all have trouble developing feelings that would be even remotely comparable to the powerful primary emotion that gives the book its title. It is the authors' expressed hope that feeling along with these emotionally deprived characters will lead readers to realize that "what we are losing is substantial and that the Anthropocene will in many ways be a diminished world."[31]

Like other authors of ecodystopian science fiction, Jamieson and Nadzam try to influence their readers' perceptions of their actual, contemporary world by evoking speculative future worlds that are recognizable and at the same time substantially different. Eric Otto reminds us that "estrangement, extrapolation, and a sense of wonder constitute an ecorhetorical strategy for works of fiction and nonfiction whose interests lie in questioning deep-seated cultural paradigms."[32] And so it is unsurprising that the opening story of Love in the Anthropocene, "Flyfishing," uses these typical science fiction devices in order to draw our attention to the difference a generation can make: the difference of several decades of embodied firsthand experience or the lack thereof. "Flyfishing" tells the story of an unnamed father and daughter who go on a fishing trip in the foothills of a mountain range. Like all the stories in the collection, it is a simple and mundane narrative, devoid of spectacular plot turns and told by a detached, omniscient narrative voice. The father hopes that the trip will bring him closer to his estranged teenage daughter and wants to create a special memory for them both. Problems abound, however, from the very beginning. Not only does the daughter repeatedly insist that she is "not eating fish," she also does not see why they must go to the mountains at all since they "could have gone fly-fishing right from [their] living room."[33] The teenager cannot seem to share her father's fascination with the material environment outside the high-speed train window, which looks so entirely different from the one he remembers. "God," he exclaims. "When your mother and I came up here it was just dirt and rocks. None of this was here. No trees, none of those hedges. Not much river to speak of at all. . . . You'd hardly know it was the same country."[34] The daughter remains utterly unimpressed because she knows for a fact that the lush landscape that so excites her father is "not real."[35] What bothers her about the trip is that she is expected to "pretend . . . that it is."[36]

From the start the story evokes the theme of environmental authenticity in relation to the emotional relationships of characters, a theme that comes up in every single story of the book. Despite the father and daughter's shared awareness of the artificiality of the environment, their affective responses are extremely unalike. While for the daughter there is little difference between the virtual landscapes she can experience at home with the help of state-of-the-art entertainment technology and the human-made landscape outside, the father insists that the latter consists of "real grass. Real trees. All growing in the rain and the sunshine."[37] For him this material dimension of the environment warrants a different emotional response. The key difference between father and daughter is the latter's lack of lived, embodied experience. It is the daughter's first time in the area, and she has never been in a "natural" material environment. The father on the other hand has at least two affectively charged memories that are vivid enough in his mind to inflect his reaction to what he directly perceives. Mentally comparing it to the barren environment he experienced during a previous visit to the area with his wife, he is amazed by the green space and the achievement of its designers. It is the second mental comparison, however, that becomes increasingly important for his affective relationship to his present environment: his cherished memory of a nighttime fishing trip on the Pere Marquette River in Michigan that he and his brother once took with their grandfather when they were boys.

According to Hogan, we must consider "three modalities of emotion elicitation" in life as well as in literary analysis: "current perception, recollection, and imagination."[38] These three modalities often operate in conjunction. How we react emotionally to something that we currently perceive in the world we physically inhabit is influenced by our memories of previous embodied experience (both actual and virtual) and our imagination of what *might* happen. How we react emotionally to something imagined tends to be influenced by our memories, and the strength of that reaction can be modified by our perception of our actual environment. And how we feel about our memories is in turn influenced by our current perception, by other memories, and by our imagination. In "Flyfishing" the father's emotional response to the actual environment must therefore be seen in the context of both his painful memory of the dead landscape and the older, more pleasant memory of his childhood fishing trip. The daughter, who can only compare what she perceives to the virtual fly-fishing she has done in their living room, cannot feel what her father feels or share his romantic imagination of what might lie ahead of them.

Once they leave the train and enter the Wild Rivers resort, what was only visual perception through a windowpane becomes full-fledged embodied experience. Earlier an older passenger warned the daughter that she shouldn't "let them bullshit" her about the authenticity of a river that has "no rocks" and in which nobody ever "falls, nobody drowns," suggesting that some important aspects of experience are missing in the human-made creation of Wild Rivers.[39] And indeed, once he is physically present in the river environment, it becomes increasingly difficult for the father to make good on his pledge that he is "going to have a great time no matter what."[40] As much as he tries, he cannot ignore the fact that the beautiful landscape is utterly silent under the sky's "hard and empty blue," that what *looks* like eagles must be holograms or "some new kind of technology," and that the river itself indeed does not contain any rocks but an overabundance of "suicidal" fish waiting to be caught.[41] Nadzam had already demonstrated in her debut novel *Lamb* (2011) that she knows how to ironize the well-tried trope of the American wilderness retreat, and "Flyfishing" similarly plays with its conventions.[42] "Actually be kind of exciting to find a weed," exclaims the father at the sight of the carefully designed grasses, trees, and flowers.[43] But there are no weeds in this anthropogenic environment that guarantees a good catch for paying visitors as they throw their rods on a riverbed that feels "like running track."[44] Despite its material reality, the "wilderness" and the undeniable artificiality of it have a decidedly negative impact on the father's affective experience of it. Suddenly he feels "a weight in his chest, and heat burning behind his eyes."[45] On closer inspection his professed enthusiasm for this re-created piece of nature only thinly disguises his nostalgic longing for a truly authentic Nature that is forever lost because it only exists in a remembered past.

The daughter and father thus suffer from several of the psychoterratic dis-eases that Albrecht considers typical for life in the Anthropocene:

whereas the daughter arguably has a "nature deficit disorder" that leads to ecoparalysis and makes it difficult for her to relate emotionally to her environment or to her father, the father's experience of his surroundings depends on his eco-nostalgia for a bygone time. "As it becomes less possible to distinguish a pure or unspoiled natural world that is separate from humans," writes Jennifer Ladino in *Reclaiming Nostalgia*, "some people long for an imaginary Eden."[46] Edward Casey reminds us that "nostalgia, contrary to what we usually imagine, is not merely a matter of regret for lost times; it is also a pining for lost places, for places we have once been in yet can no longer reenter."[47] The narrator of "Flyfishing" does not explain what exactly causes the weight in the father's chest or the heat that burns behind his eyes, but it is suggested that these moments of heaviness and pain are related to his senseless pining for a lost world. Readers are cued to feel along with the father in such moments, not only because it is his perspective that they share throughout much of the story but also because—unlike the daughter—they, too, have memories of their embodied experience of natural environments. Whereas the daughter is a child of the narrative's speculative future in the sense that she no longer knows what it means to physically experience a natural space that was not created by humans, the character of the father extrapolates readers' extratextual experience into the narrative's imaginary future, suggesting that what they take for granted might no longer be around a few decades from now. The authors seem to hope that empathetically sharing the father's experience will cause readers to feel what Ladino has called "anticipatory nostalgia": a future-oriented form of eco-nostalgia that is based on the anticipation of loss and regret.[48] It may also lead to solastalgic distress as readers come to understand that the environment that, for the fictional future father, is located in an irrecoverable past actually lies somewhere right outside their doorstep, waiting to be saved from destruction.

All the more surprising is the story's somewhat morbid twist. The father's eco-nostalgic attachment to the memory of his childhood fishing trip culminates in the moment when his daughter catches a fish they believe to be real. Suddenly all apathy and ecoparalysis fall away from the girl. Torn between excitement, fear, awe, and disgust, she pulls on the rod:

She didn't think it would be so hard. It was like tearing the hook out through bone.

"I want to put it back."

He laughed. "Squeamish?" Her eyes glittered with tears. He shook his head, met her eyes. "This is part of it."

"I hate it."

"You have to remember that this is what fish are made for. They're hatched and grown up there, and they slide down the river for people like us to catch."

"And eat?"

"And eat."

"But I don't want to eat it."

"It's what they are for. Think of all the good river days that fish had."[49]

As it turns out, the father's nostalgic longing for an intact, authentic wilderness coexists with his anthropocentric belief that fish are made for killing and eating. Lacking empathy for both the fish and his daughter, he seems to enjoy the fact that she feels emotionally overwhelmed by the prospect of killing and eating a real animal. While he is troubled by both the large-scale destruction of the natural environment and the all-too-obvious functionality of the manufactured wilderness of Wild Rivers, the father still embraces speciesism and the belief that nonhuman life forms should be used in ways that benefit humans.[50] Even more ironic, however, is that the strong emotions released by the ritual killing of the supposedly authentic animal allow father and daughter to temporarily bond, bridging the abyss of age and experience that separates them. The story ends with the father's promise that he will build a "real fire" so they can bake the fish with a stick of "real butter" inside, just like they did back in the good old days.[51]

The deep longing for the embodied experience of a presumably authentic nature pervades all the stories collected in *Love in the Anthropocene,* and many of them come with a darkly ironic twist. In the third story of the collection, "Holiday," three female coworkers take a break from their difficult jobs in a refugee camp to visit New Harmony, a domed city that promises an outstanding sensual experience. "Bring your hungry, your traumatized,

your bored, your longing to forget," boasts the advertisement for the pleasure dome, suggesting that the human-created environment will cure all
those uncomfortable and painful emotional states.[52] Readers learn that "it
was as green and vibrant as [one] could have imagined. There were lakes,
gardens, schools, restaurants, shops, museums, and yes, an ocean complete
with a necklace of islands and pounding surf of beginner-, intermediate-
and advanced sized waves dissolving in a white lace of clean sea foam on
golden sands."[53] Once again the narrative voice invites us to imagine an
environment that is lush and vibrant while at the same time emphasizing
the extreme degree of its artificiality. And once again it is suggested that
something important is missing from the sensual experience of such an
environment. Gloria, who is the only American character, cannot enjoy the
artificial pleasures of New Harmony's "nature," and so she leaves the dome
and abandons herself to the barren and scorched landscape outside, taking
readers along for an imaginary experience of an authentic environment
that is deeply hostile to human life. After a few minutes in the sun-beaten
wasteland Gloria is picked up by a patrol worker who equanimously explains
to her that they "get about a dozen a day" of her kind: reckless "nostalgics"
whose overwhelming desire to experience "anything real" leads them to
misjudge the risks involved in physical exposure.[54]

Like the other characters in *Love in the Anthropocene*, Gloria has very
little love in her life, and the authors suggest that these deprived emotional
lives are a direct result of deprived environments. "The Anthropocene,"
they write in the coda of their book, "threatens to give us a narcissist's playground—a nature that is only the extension of ourselves and our desires,
without independent meaning or sustenance. Loving relationships are not
possible in a world that consists only of oneself and one's projections."[55]
This is an extreme position that fails to acknowledge not only the fact
that humans actually *can* fall in love with their own creations but also the
problem of unintended consequences. Against the authors' assertions, the
stories collected in *Love in the Anthropocene* quite effectively demonstrate
that narcissists will find that their playground ends where the unintended
consequences of their own self-centered actions begin. Readers are reminded
of the fact not only when the nameless father in "Flyfishing" pines for a real

fish or when they simulate in their minds Gloria's embodied experience of a landscape that has become lethal because of human agency. Other characters in the collection are similarly confronted with parts of nature that are beyond human control, and it is precisely those parts that arouse feelings in them. These feelings may not be love or other powerful primary emotions, but they demonstrate the characters' capacity to care for things other than themselves. This becomes particularly apparent in the last story of the collection, which echoes the concern with animal authenticity that is also at the heart of "Flyfishing" but brings to the fore an aspect of the Anthropocene that up to this point has loomed in the narrative background: species extinction.

Like most stories in *Love in the Anthropocene*, "Zoo" begins with a human-human encounter that is marked by a flat affect and lack of interpersonal connection. A man and a woman meet for a blind date at a restaurant. From the very first moment, their conversation circles around the man's job, since the woman has learned that he is a caretaker for the world's last female tiger. "I usually wait until the second date to talk about the zoo," says the man while coolly assessing the woman's physical attributes.[56] He clearly is well aware of his asset as he slowly and seemingly begrudgingly gives away some information about Anita, as the tiger is called, giving his interlocutor an instruction manual that allows her to simulate in her mind "what it [is] like" to spend one's days with one of the last specimens of charismatic megafauna.[57] The woman does not seem to care very much for the zookeeper, but she has no trouble empathizing with Anita, considering it "a tragedy" that "there *are* no other tigers for this tiger" and that she must therefore live in solitude.[58] The zookeeper, for his part, can tell that the woman wants "to have one of those conversations he hated."[59] Appalled by what he believes to be a hollow and hypocritical nostalgia for soon-to-be extinct animals, he barks at the woman that it is just "so much easier to cry over a single tiger than the world they used to live in."[60]

As Heise demonstrates in *Imagining Extinction* (2016), affective narrative modes such as elegy and comedy are typical for extinction narratives, though the former is much more frequent than the latter.[61] In "Zoo" the elegiac celebration of the last female tiger is both ridiculed and promoted as an appropriate way of mourning. Empirical evidence in social psychology suggests that it is much easier for us to care for a single suffering individual—be it human or nonhuman—than for a large group of individuals who are under distress.[62] Jamieson and Nadzam's zookeeper is thus correct when he observes that it is easier to cry over a single tiger than over the world it used to live in, but his angry declarations that he "enjoy[s] being human" and that he is "so sick of this kind of [nostalgic] talk" are subverted on the final pages of the story when he invites the woman to visit Anita.[63] Ignoring zoo regulations, he leads the woman into the compound and encourages her to touch the tiger's face: "When the woman put her hand on the tiger, she took a deep jagged inhale and her eyes glistened. Her free hand fluttered to the top of her chest, then over her mouth. 'I didn't expect,' she said, glancing at him. 'My God.'"[64] The embodied encounter with the animal triggers a strong emotional response in the woman, but this time the zookeeper does not react with distancing anger or ridicule. All cynicism and apathy are gone as he wishes that the woman "could have seen her in the trees."[65] But Anita is too old now to haul her massive body up into one of the trees in the compound, and he knows that she won't be with him much longer. After the woman has left, he keeps staring at the tigress, "a little tiredness burning the backs of his eyes," as he utters the last words of the story: "That's my girl."[66]

The burning pain the zookeeper feels as he looks at the soon-to-be-lost love of his life echoes the one felt by the father in "Flyfishing" and by Gloria in "Holiday" as they try to come to terms with the longing for something that is irrevocably gone. There is a difference, however, both in temporality and in affective charge, since Anita is still physically present in those last moments of the story and her keeper is revealed to be truly attached to her despite his claims to the contrary. Some psychoterratic dis-eases, it becomes clear at the end of *Love in the Anthropocene*, are coping mechanisms that shelter us from the existential dread that comes with the realization that humanity is engaged in a planetary experiment that might deprive us of those we love and of the very basis of our existence.

On August 29, 2016, the members of the Working Group on the Anthropocene (AWG) voted to formally designate the current geological epoch as the Anthropocene. At the time of my writing, it is unknown whether the International Geological Congress will follow the AWG's recommendations, but, as Heise has noted, the cultural power of the Anthropocene "resides not in its scientific definition as a geological epoch, but in its capacity to cast the present as a future that has already arrived—one of the quintessential functions of contemporary science fiction."[67] From this perspective it seems quite appropriate that Jamieson and Nadzam turn to science fiction in order to invite readers "to imagine . . . the path we are already on and where it might lead."[68] *Love in the Anthropocene* aligns us with the emotional experience of characters who live in an imaginary future that is marked by the negative consequences of anthropogenic environmental change and who cue us to share their helpless longing for a bygone world—the world in which we currently live.

In conclusion, one question that poses itself is whether such cueing of anticipatory nostalgia will help make a difference on the personal, social, and political level, which clearly is the authors' agenda. Heise reminds us that "stories and images of decline go only so far" when it comes to moving people to action, and she asks whether it is possible to "move beyond mourning, melancholia, and nostalgia to a more affirmative vision of our biological future."[69] Albrecht's classification of eco-nostalgia and solastalgia as psychoterratic dis-eases suggests that they may be viewed as both debilitating *diseases* and productive forms of *unease* that can motivate us to act. Ladino has even argued that in some contexts nostalgic longing "can be a mechanism for social change, a model for ethical relationships, and a motivating force for social and environmental justice."[70] This is in keeping with research in psychology that highlights the motivational power of nostalgia.[71] Such scientific findings seem to warrant the narrative strategies of Jamieson and Nadzam and many other authors who rely on solastalgic distress and anticipatory nostalgia to engage readers in the more-than-human world, but it should not keep us from developing the more forward-looking and more affirmative environmental narratives that Heise calls for.

NOTES

1. Nussbaum, *Political Emotions*, 15.
2. Nussbaum, *Political Emotions*, 3.
3. For ecocritical texts that explore place attachments see, for example, Slovic, *Going Away to Think*; Ladino, *Reclaiming Nostalgia*; and Easterlin, *Biocultural Approach*. For inquiries by geographers see Tuan, *Topophilia*; and Smith et al., *Emotion, Place and Culture*.
4. Milton, *Loving Nature*, 4.
5. Damasio, *Descartes' Error*, xxvii.
6. Jamieson and Nadzam, *Love in the Anthropocene*, 18.
7. Jamieson and Nadzam, *Love in the Anthropocene*, 27.
8. Albrecht, "Tipping Points in the Mind."
9. Albrecht, "'Solastalgia,'" 45.
10. Albrecht, "'Solastalgia,'" 44.
11. Oatley, Mar, and Djikic, "Psychology of Fiction," 235.
12. Oatley, Mar, and Djikic, "Psychology of Fiction," 236.
13. Easterlin, *Biocultural Approach*, 92.
14. James, *Storyworld Accord*, 54.
15. Keen, "Narrative Empathy," 83.
16. Gerrig, "Individual Differences," 42.
17. Oatley, "Fiction," 226.
18. Hogan, *Affective Narratology*, 55.
19. Hogan, *Affective Narratology*, 56.
20. Scarry, *Dreaming by the Book*, 9.
21. Scarry, *Dreaming by the Book*, 9.
22. Caracciolo, "Blind Reading," 83; Scarry, *Dreaming by the Book*, 244.
23. Gerrig, *Experiencing Narrative Worlds*, 12.
24. Caracciolo, "Blind Reading," 83.
25. Jamieson and Nadzam, *Love in the Anthropocene*, 27.
26. Jamieson and Nadzam, *Love in the Anthropocene*, 11–12.
27. Jamieson, *Reason in a Dark Time*, 178. On our cognitive limitations in dealing with climate change see also Marshall, *Don't Even Think about It*.
28. Chakrabarty, "Climate of History," 206.
29. Heise, *Sense of Place and Sense of Planet*, 137.
30. Jamieson and Nadzam, *Love in the Anthropocene*, 14.
31. Jamieson and Nadzam, *Love in the Anthropocene*, 26.
32. Otto, *Green Speculations*, 17.
33. Jamieson and Nadzam, *Love in the Anthropocene*, 32.
34. Jamieson and Nadzam, *Love in the Anthropocene*, 32.

35. Jamieson and Nadzam, *Love in the Anthropocene*, 33.
36. Jamieson and Nadzam, *Love in the Anthropocene*, 34.
37. Jamieson and Nadzam, *Love in the Anthropocene*, 33.
38. Hogan, *Affective Narratology*, 48.
39. Jamieson and Nadzam, *Love in the Anthropocene*, 35.
40. Jamieson and Nadzam, *Love in the Anthropocene*, 35.
41. Jamieson and Nadzam, *Love in the Anthropocene*, 46, 50, 44.
42. Nadzam, *Lamb*. For a discussion of *Lamb* and a more detailed development of the cognitive ecocritical approach see Weik von Mossner, *Affective Ecologies*.
43. Jamieson and Nadzam, *Love in the Anthropocene*, 41.
44. Jamieson and Nadzam, *Love in the Anthropocene*, 44.
45. Jamieson and Nadzam, *Love in the Anthropocene*, 51.
46. Ladino, *Reclaiming Nostalgia*, 164.
47. Casey, *Getting Back into Place*, 37.
48. Ladino, *Reclaiming Nostalgia*, 103. On anticipated nostalgia and loss see also Slovic, *Going Away to Think*, 38.
49. Jamieson and Nadzam, *Love in the Anthropocene*, 53.
50. Speciesism is the idea of assigning value to a being based on species membership alone. In practical contexts it has regularly led to the exclusion of all nonhuman animals from the rights, freedoms, and protections afforded to humans. For in-depth discussions of the issue see Sorenson, *Critical Animal Studies*.
51. Jamieson and Nadzam, *Love in the Anthropocene*, 56, 39.
52. Jamieson and Nadzam, *Love in the Anthropocene*, 107–8.
53. Jamieson and Nadzam, *Love in the Anthropocene*, 108.
54. Jamieson and Nadzam, *Love in the Anthropocene*, 128, 116.
55. Jamieson and Nadzam, *Love in the Anthropocene*, 207.
56. Jamieson and Nadzam, *Love in the Anthropocene*, 170.
57. Jamieson and Nadzam, *Love in the Anthropocene*, 172.
58. Jamieson and Nadzam, *Love in the Anthropocene*, 173.
59. Jamieson and Nadzam, *Love in the Anthropocene*, 174.
60. Jamieson and Nadzam, *Love in the Anthropocene*, 174.
61. Heise, *Imagining Extinction*, 4.
62. Kristof, "Power of One."
63. Jamieson and Nadzam, *Love in the Anthropocene*, 181.
64. Jamieson and Nadzam, *Love in the Anthropocene*, 193.
65. Jamieson and Nadzam, *Love in the Anthropocene*, 193.
66. Jamieson and Nadzam, *Love in the Anthropocene*, 195.
67. Heise, *Imagining Extinction*, 203.
68. Jamieson and Nadzam, *Love in the Anthropocene*, 207.

69. Heise, *Imagining Extinction*, 213.
70. Ladino, *Reclaiming Nostalgia*, 8.
71. While nostalgic experiences tend to occur "in response to negative mood and the discrete affective state of loneliness," explain Tim Wildschut et al., they have been found to bolster social bonds, increase positive self-regard, and generate positive affect. Wildschut et al., "Nostalgia," 975.

BIBLIOGRAPHY

Albrecht, Glenn. "'Solastalgia': A New Concept in Health and Identity." *PAN* 3 (2005): 41–55.

———. "Tipping Points in the Mind: The Drama of Solastalgia and Soliphilia." *TEDx Sydney*, June 2, 2010. https://www.youtube.com/watch?v=-GUGW8rOpLY.

Caracciolo, Marco. "Blind Reading: Toward an Enactivist Theory of the Reader's Imagination." In *Stories and Minds: Cognitive Approaches to Literary Narrative*, edited by Lars Bernaerts, Dirk de Geest, Luc Herman, and Bart Vervaeck, 81–106. Lincoln: University of Nebraska Press, 2013.

Casey, Edward S. *Getting Back into Place: Toward a Renewed Understanding of the Place-World*. Bloomington: Indiana University Press, 2009.

Chakrabarty, Dipesh. "The Climate of History: Four Theses." *Critical Inquiry* 35, no. 2 (2009): 197–222.

Damasio, Antonio. *Descartes' Error: Emotion, Reason, and the Human Brain*. London: Vintage, 1994.

Easterlin, Nancy. *A Biocultural Approach to Literary Theory and Interpretation*. Baltimore: Johns Hopkins University Press, 2012.

Gerrig, Richard J. *Experiencing Narrative Worlds: On the Psychological Activities of Reading*. Boulder CO: Westview Press, 1998.

———. "Individual Differences in Readers' Narrative Experiences." *Scientific Study of Literature* 1, no. 1 (2011): 88–94.

Heise, Ursula K. *Imagining Extinction: The Cultural Meanings of Endangered Species*. Chicago: University of Chicago Press, 2016.

———. *Sense of Place and Sense of Planet: The Environmental Imagination of the Global*. Oxford: Oxford University Press, 2008.

Hogan, Patrick Colm. *Affective Narratology: The Emotional Structure of Stories*. Lincoln: University of Nebraska Press, 2011.

James, Erin. *The Storyworld Accord: Econarratology and Postcolonial Narratives*. Lincoln: University of Nebraska Press, 2015.

Jamieson, Dale. *Reason in a Dark Time: Why the Struggle to Stop Climate Change Failed and What It Means for Our Future*. New York: Oxford University Press, 2014.

Jamieson, Dale, and Bonnie Nadzam. *Love in the Anthropocene.* New York: OR Books, 2015.

Keen, Suzanne. "Narrative Empathy." In *Toward a Cognitive Theory of Narrative Acts,* edited by Frederick Luis Aldama, 61–94. Austin: University of Texas Press, 2010.

Kristof, Nicholas. "The Power of One." In *Numbers and Nerves: Information and Meaning in a World of Data,* edited by Scott Slovic and Paul Slovic, 77–83. Corvallis: Oregon State University Press, 2015.

Ladino, Jennifer K. *Reclaiming Nostalgia: Longing for Nature in American Literature.* Charlottesville: University of Virginia Press, 2012.

Marshall, George. *Don't Even Think about It: Why Our Brains Are Wired to Ignore Climate Change.* New York: Bloomsbury, 2014.

Milton, Kay. 2002. *Loving Nature: Towards an Ecology of Emotion.* New York: Routledge.

Nadzam, Bonnie. *Lamb.* New York: Other Press, 2011.

Nussbaum, Martha. *Political Emotions: Why Love Matters for Justice.* Cambridge MA: Belknap Press of Harvard University Press, 2015.

Oatley, Keith. "Fiction: Simulation of Social Worlds." *Trends in Cognitive Science* 20, no. 8 (2016): 218–28.

Oatley, Keith, Raymond Mar, and Maja Djikic. "The Psychology of Fiction: Present and Future." In *Cognitive Literary Studies: Current Themes and New Directions,* edited by Isabel Jaén and Julien Jacques Simon, 235–49. Austin: University of Texas Press, 2012.

Otto, Eric. *Green Speculations: Science Fiction and Transformative Environmentalism.* Columbus: Ohio State University Press, 2012.

Scarry, Elaine. *Dreaming by the Book.* 1999. Princeton: Princeton University Press, 2001.

Sedikides, Constantine, and Tim Wildschut. "Past Forward: Nostalgia as a Motivational Force." *Trends in Cognitive Science* 20, no. 5 (2016): 319–21.

Slovic, Scott. *Going Away to Think: Engagement, Retreat, and Ecocritical Responsibility.* Reno: University of Nevada Press, 2008.

Smith, Mick, Joyce Davidson, Laura Cameron, and Liz Bondi, eds. *Emotion, Place and Culture.* Farnham, UK: Ashgate, 2009.

Sorenson, John, ed. *Critical Animal Studies: Thinking the Unthinkable.* Toronto: Canadian Scholars' Press, 2014.

Tuan, Yi-Fu. *Topophilia: A Study of Environmental Perception, Attitudes, and Values.* Englewood Cliffs NJ: Prentice Hall, 1974.

Weik von Mossner, Alexa. *Affective Ecologies: Empathy, Emotion, and Environmental Narrative.* Columbus: Ohio State University Press, 2017.

Wildschut, Tim, Constantine Sedikides, Jamie Arndt, and Clay Routledge. "Nostalgia: Content, Triggers, Functions." *Journal of Personality and Social Psychology* 91, no. 5 (2006): 975–93.

3

A New Gentleness
Affective Ficto-Regionality

NEIL CAMPBELL

> Ecology must stop being associated with the image of a small nature-loving minority or with qualified specialists. Ecology in my sense questions the whole of subjectivity and capitalistic power formations, whose sweeping progress cannot be guaranteed to continue.
>
> –Félix Guattari, *The Three Ecologies*

A Generalized Ecology

As the quotation above shows, Félix Guattari had definite and profound views on the state of ecology, wanting to broaden its parameters to include "subjectivity" and "power formations," since, he argued, "the ecological crisis can be traced to a more general crisis of the social, political and existential." He asks, "How do we change mentalities, how do we reinvent social practices that would give back to humanity . . . a sense of responsibility, not only for its own survival but equally for the future of all life on the planet, for animal and vegetable species, likewise for incorporeal species such as music, the arts, cinema, the relation with time, love and compassion for others, the feeling of fusion at the heart of the cosmos?"[1] This coupling of responsibility for the "cosmos" with an expanded ecology including the "incorporeal" and the "corporeal" ideas, affects, and emotions is a fascinating, speculative, and productive route to "trigger creative sparks" and "engender pockets of awareness" through "elaboration and intervention."[2] Through shifting perspectives and deliberately introducing innovative terminology and ways of thinking and writing that challenge established structures and definitions, Guattari generates what he calls "new collective assemblages of enunciation" or "different ways of seeing and of making the world."[3] This "expanded ecological consciousness" rejected "archaizers and folklorists" who for too long had cornered arguments about ecology through a narrow focus on "nature-loving" and "specialism" in favor of new social practices and politics that insisted "issues of a very local nature" were always linked with "the global problems of our era."[4] Guattari believed therefore that ecology had to be this expanded triangulation of "social," "mental," and "environmental"—what he famously termed his "three ecologies."

This chapter explores this "triangulation" in dialogue with my concept of *affective critical regionality* as a way of seeing the local as both charged and dynamic, working critically across the social, mental, and environmental spheres through the active prism of regionality, employing the fictocritical writing of Kathleen Stewart, whose careful attunements follow lines, webs, connections spinning out and thrown together into assemblages of affect as lived "compositionality" rather than a dead specimen, already defined and represented *for us*.[5] To this end the chapter examines how Stewart's fictocriticism combined with her attention to the local or regional allows such productive attunements to emerge. One of fictocriticism's founders, Stephen Muecke, states in his briefest definition of the genre that "it tells a story and makes an argument at the same time," thus blurring the lines between established practices, creating the unsettling "intersection, on the page, of storytelling with philosophical arguments—making the two indistinguishably reliant on each other," and producing, as a consequence of this intersection, "valid fictional contributions to non-fictional debates."[6] Many of these aspects are summed up in Amanda Nettlebeck's words: "Fictocriticism might most usefully be defined as hybridized writing that moves between the poles of fiction ('invention'/'speculation') and criticism ('deduction'/'explication'), of subjectivity ('interiority') and objectivity ('exteriority'). It is writing that brings the 'creative' and the 'critical' together—not simply in the sense of placing them side by side, but in the sense of mutating both, of bringing a spotlight to bear upon the known forms in order to make them say something else."[7]

Such fictocritical approaches enable a nuanced appreciation of the world as "vibrant matter," in Jane Bennett's terms, and can, I believe, aid a reconsideration of Guattari's notion of "generalized ecology" or "ecosophy."[8] Indeed such reflexive strategies might enable us "to think transversally" and so to appreciate "resonances, alliances and feedback loops between various regimes, signifying and non-signifying, human and non-human, natural and cultural, material and representational."[9] Furthermore, Guattari's interest in aesthetics and "mental ecology" and his call for "new ecological practices" confronts capitalism's deleterious effects "in everyday life: individual, domestic, material, neighbourly, creative or one's personal ethics" and pleads for "political regeneration . . . as an ethical, aesthetic, and analytic engagement . . . a new gentleness."[10] Integrated world capitalism operated for Guattari as a process of limitation and control, environmental damage, climate change, and uneven power relations, forming a "sedative discourse," squeezing creative difference into routines of predictability, infantilization, and sameness.[11] Life's potential refrains, in other words, were compromised by this capitalist consensus of consumerism, media blandness, and curtailed values but could be countered by Guattari's forms of dissensus celebrating active difference, "infinite variety," underpinned by a "new gentleness" of affective experience, responsibility, attunement, and mutuality.[12] To reenergize Guattari's ideas, I put them in dialogue with Stewart's "ordinary affects," the title of her second book, in which fictocritical vignettes of place, action, and descriptive detail assemble the inflections and surprises of the everyday as an emergent and sensitive form of ecology, both proximate and engaged in the complex relations of worlding.[13]

To demonstrate these connections, I focus here on how fictocriticism can be closely aligned to Guattari's "ecology of the virtual," which is "as pressing as ecologies of the visible world . . . [and] will not simply attempt to preserve the endangered species of cultural life but equally to engender conditions for the creation and development of unprecedented formations of subjectivity that have never been seen and never felt."[14] The Guattarian subject is therefore, as Gary Genosko makes clear, "an entangled assemblage of many components, a collective (heterogeneous, multiple) articulation of such components before and beyond the individual; the individual is like a transit station for changes, crossings, and switches."[15] Stewart's attention to subjectivity as a "transit station" registers and forms an "idiosyncratic map of connections," visible and "virtual," material and immaterial, tracking events and "forms of attention and attachment" through which a different, expanded ecology emerges.[16] Through her fictocritical engagement this becomes an active *composition* of affective regionality revealed as an assemblage or "bloom space"—"an event that jumps between landscape and bodies of all kinds . . . ambient, and therefore atmospheric. . . . It strikes the senses. It pulls hard matter into alignment with a composition."[17] "One gets to know" such assemblages (regionality is the assemblage here), "not through representation but through affective contamination," argues Guattari, as "hyper-complex compositions" of affects pulsing through the "transit station" akin to the way aesthetics work through and within us as a "block of sensation": "I am no longer as I was before. I am swept away by a becoming other, carried beyond my familiar existential Territories."[18] Utilizing Muecke's work on *and* of fictocriticism as a guide, I show how Stewart realigns anthropology and ecology to tell new stories of place, things, and people, forming regionality as a "praxic opening-out which constitutes the essence of 'eco'-art."[19]

Affective critical regionality is therefore not made from "coherent imprints or effects of something else" imposed and fixing place, nature, and people but rather "lived modalities and a history of social production and uses," "qualities and affects" that are dynamic, in composition—"living forms that generate a zone of connectivity" not because of "what they are" in some already-decided definition or territory but because of "what they do" and how they provoke, project, and vibrate with interrelations and trajectories.[20] Feeling and thinking regionality in this way generates a "prismatic ecology," a "geography of what happens," a "speculative topography of the everyday" captured in the unconventional, affective contamination or "incorporeal ecosystem" of fictocriticism.[21] To *experience* regionality therefore demands both the "energetics" needed to reflect and speculate about the motions of its changing nature while simultaneously carrying the weight of its role as a "carapace of spent and living forms."[22] Affective critical regionality is thus always ecological since it preserves and activates, holds onto and lets go, contains and edges; it *worlds*.

Fictocriticism

Stewart's "work is an experiment that writes from the intensities in things. It asks what potential modes of knowing, relating or attending to things are already being lived in ordinary rhythms, labors, and the sensory materiality of forms of attunement to worlds."[23] Learning from Martin Heidegger's "The Thing," an essay to which she often refers, Stewart's approach is "attending to what is near" in order to appreciate how things "stand forth" through their relations with the world.[24] Rejecting narrow acts of "mere information," representation, or scientific, universal definitions, Heidegger enacted a deep *opening up* of the apparently inert thing, like a simple jug, to its fullest "round dance" with the world, standing forth as a relational process of interconnections, "gathering in" and outpouring, being of a source, a process, *and* a becoming: "The thing," as he puts it, "things," and "Thinging gathers."[25] An object becomes activated through attention and attunement to its various relations with the world, its "gatherings" themselves dynamic, vibrant, and multiple. "The world presences by worlding"; that is, we come to experience the world not through representations of it but rather through the actions, reactions, and relations between those processes that compose it.[26] As Muecke explains, "As long as history has Man central stage and things (animate, inanimate, natural) as a support act, the kinds of continuities and necessary dependencies among them will be obscured."[27] Through attention to the overlooked small things, our careful attunement to their different, often contrary, active relations, flows, and surprising presences, we are drawn "nearer" to the multiple processes that constitute the world or Guattari's "ecology."

Nature is not separate and distinct from other processes but rather part of the relational flux of things, an elaborate, entangled meshwork of lines, forces, thoughts, dreams and elements, corporeal and incorporeal "species." Muecke's fictocriticism has influenced Stewart's writing, explaining how, in a similar fashion, "things" take on a life or a "career," as he calls it, as a "composition" both material and "more fanciful," becoming "hybrid . . . packaged into a network of relations that move the object around and give it life—vibrancy, as Jane Bennett would say of the 'political ecology of things'—particularly in relation to those human beings who are connected with such commodities."[28]

Bennett, influenced by Deleuze and Guattari in her call for "vibrant matter" tracked through the "liveliness of its relations" with other forces and objects, explains Guattari's three ecologies as "a more ecological sustainable relationship with nonhuman nature."[29] Bennett's work develops Guattari's stated vision of "new micropolitical and microsocial practices, new solidarities, a new gentleness, together with new aesthetic and new analytic practices."[30] This is achieved, recalling Heidegger's jug, through commingling relations of human and nonhuman, distant and near, trammelled together to the point that "the environment is actually inside human bodies and minds [like] unruly relatives to whom you are inextricably bound and with whom you will engage over a lifetime, like it or not."[31] So, with Stewart in mind, "when we couple criticism to fiction, to the imaginative, we seek rather to perform a kind of ethics by asking, *what can that thing do that it couldn't do before? What can that sentence say?* And in consideration of these things, *how has my place in the world shifted?*"[32] New forms of writing bring these types of questions to life on the page because "fictocriticism is concerned with our linguistic-discursive and especially textual practices of being in the world."[33]

One of Muecke's essays, for example, traces the relational histories of coal and ivory through their use, cultural meaning, economic value, or the associated "magic of the stories spun about [them]," as if precisely showing "what they do" and how this affects our relative positions in the world: "I have highlighted ivory and given it a career, which is to say a *kind of life*. In being *alert* to the forces at work in real time in shaping this life, one *notices* different kinds of *agency*, which lead me to endorse the idea of objects being animated . . . in every relationship that gives them function, meaning and affect."[34] Objects are not secondary or dead matter since they "vibrate" through multiple relations with other material and immaterial forces along complex "lines of affect," following "trajectories . . . transformations and connections."[35] Muecke tracks ivory's relations, its "composition," from the butchered elephant and slavery, through ornate artworks, billiard balls, jewelry, and piano keys to its "decomposition" through its banning and cultural decline through the affective challenges of outrage, compassion, and moral righteousness. Thus "a more-than-human vision of the world" emerges, an ecological narrative without the "conceit, so common in phenomenology, that reality comes into being through human interpretation of it."[36]

This attention to relational networks of forces working across life, from the very smallest, overlooked thing to the larger contextual frameworks (Guattari's micropolitical and microsocial practices) typifies both Stewart's and Bennett's drive to register the *liveliness* of matter through, as Muecke notes, the *affective*. For, as Deleuze and Guattari put it, "We know nothing about a body until we know what it can do . . . what its affects are, how they can or cannot enter into composition with other affects, with the affects of another body."[37] Muecke wants a different kind of writing following "various lifelines, its political trajectories, its liveliness" and bringing together relational networks or assemblages, incorporating the "technological, the economic, the political, the social and the natural and the affective in the one text," one that would "be interdisciplinary, but also novelistic," something like Bennett's "onto-story," capable of conveying that "everything is, in a sense, alive."[38]

Similarly Guattari felt that "mental ecosophy" would enable different views to emerge, challenging reductionist, established, prejudicial attitudes to human/nonhuman relations (integrated world capitalism) and offering instead ways of working that would "be more like those of an artist," because, as Genosko explains, "ecosophic activism 'resembles' the work of artists in extracting details that serve as path-breakers for subjective development and as guidance in responsibly negotiating refrains."[39]

Variously called "paraliterature," "philosophical fiction," or "autoethnography," fictocriticism is primarily dialogical: "The *ficto*-side of fictocriticism follows the twists and turns of animated language as it finds new pathways. The *-criticism* part comes in the risky leap of taking the story to a different 'world.'"[40] Muecke sees fictocriticism as "not . . . an inflammatory critique, but a cooler one that proceeds by way of tracing the relations between things, that decomposes these relations in such a way that decision-making processes are slowed down (rather than rushing to the usual conclusions via the usual transcendent concepts). Combine inventive storytelling with a more cautious analysis, then, in a poetry that decomposes and recomposes things in their lively relations."[41] Refusing to explain, judge, or summarize, fictocriticism is "experimental" in the sense implied by Stewart: "Not a judgment. Committed not to demystification and uncovered truths that support a well-known picture of the world but to speculation, curiosity and the concrete, it tries to provoke attention to the forces that come into view as habit or shock, resonance or impact."[42] Influenced by working with Michael Taussig at the University of Michigan, her readings within *écriture féminine* and poststructuralism, and with her admiration for writers like Muecke, Donna Haraway, and Alphonso Lingis, Stewart's mix of self-reflexivity, recitation, storytelling, and critique owes much to their approaches. Stewart's *ficto-regionality*, as I term it, contains the ghostly traces of other voices, reinforcing Anna Gibbs's assertion that "fictocriticism is a 'haunted writing': traced by numerous voices which work now in unison, at other times in counterpoint, and at others still against each other, in deliberate discord."[43] Like Muecke, Stewart's acute attunement to things, events, and ordinary affects gradually evolves toward a complex and poetic expression of ecological relations as a compositional, fluid, and dynamic assemblage of *regionality*. At the heart of such fictocriticism is a desire "to keep thought on the move" by not, as much fiction does, "finishing itself off" but instead by finding the critical edge of self-reflection allowing it to reach out beyond the "human scale" and refusing to be hemmed in by commodification.[44] Fictocriticism "will surprise" and experiment with "ways of being in the world, with forms of subjectivity," but as a "process of thought or a way of knowing" rather than any fixed and presupposed framework: "It follows leads, sidesteps, and delays, and it piles things up, creating layers on layers, in an effort to drag things into view, to follow trajectories in motion, and to scope out the shape and shadows and traces of assemblages that solidify and grow entrenched, perhaps doing real damage or holding real hope, and then dissipate, morph, rot, or give way to something new."[45] Stewart's storied arguments therefore express regionality as a complex assemblage of human and nonhuman relations, intersections, and "bloom spaces," an edgy compositionality of things, circulations, sensations, and events that "encompasses not only what has been actualized but also the possibilities of plenitude and the threat of depletion."[46] Through such reimagining of place-person relations, ficto-regionality, with its strong pull to affectivity through eddies of descriptive detail, functions like "a magnet burdened with impressions, a matter of drawing lines that *set off* reveries and *produce* palpable edges."[47] Suddenly, through the "ficto" appreciation of experience and impressionistic intensities, a whole energized meshwork of potential links and relations is opened up, "set off," and "produced," in the processual sense of regionality being explored. Like Guattari's three ecologies, Stewart produces "a mixed media composite of matter and thought-feelings" registering "the energetic life of an emergent object that exists as meaning, matter, and potentiality in objects, scenes, situations, social formations, laws, and figures."[48] Guattari himself argued his "new ecosophy" would have to be "at once applied and theoretical, ethico-political and aesthetic . . . a multi-faceted movement . . . that will simultaneously *analyse* and *produce* subjectivity . . . that completely exceeds the limits of individualization, stagnation, identificatory closure, and will instead *open itself up* on all sides."[49]

These words spell out fictocriticism as a toolkit for new ecological writing, or what Muecke called "stories, then, but also forms of analysis," permitting Stewart to register the multiple, dialogical nature of regionality without falling into the nostalgic trap of looking back to an origin of things or to an imposition of prescribed values.[50] As she has said, "Forms, to me, are social material. My claim is always that these are compositions that are happening and ones that I'm doing. I'm interested in what something is, what is going on, and where it is going."[51] Thus fictocriticism's hauntedness creates a layering of the text without repeating an already established structure of thought or ideology such as submissive modes of authority or established values and attitudes. For Gibbs, this is "the necessity of haunted writing: to move from citation, the kind of repetition you have when reference is deference to disciplinary authority, to recitation—the performance of repetition, a repetition of repetition in order not to reproduce identity, but to try instead to engender new differences."[52] Rather than "deference to disciplinary authority," Stewart's writing omits theoretical frames: "I just embed the theory in whatever it is I'm writing," leaving its traces in brief asides, which the reader then *actively* engages with (or not), following lines of flight, "trajectory" or suggestion (or not), "not to reproduce identity" or place as a finished thing, but to spark instead new differences and relations out of the lived experience of the writing and where it points us.[53] Such a processual and active approach frees up "descriptive eddies that wonder what the object of analysis might be, to create a speculative attunement that . . . aspires to align with the commonplace labours of becoming sentient to whatever is happening."[54] Or as Guattari put it, echoing fictocriticism, "Process . . . strives to capture existence in the very act of its constitution, definition, and deterritorialization."[55]

Stewart explains her rejection of standard critical writing for a form imbued with "curiosity and responsibility that attempts to approach the diverging practices, materialities, and events that comprise an object of analysis."[56] In the friction her writing creates she gathers up and follows, delves into and deflects so that the "ficto" and the "critical" emerge as provocative, projective elements entangled and questioning of the "objects" under discussion. Hence her essay "New England Red" becomes a multistrand, "prismatic ecology" through which we see a range of refracted histories, objects, refrains, and imaginings of "redness" in the region of New England, while "Road Registers" explores "roadness" accumulated as a "live composition" revealing "the lines of force and prismatic potentialities of the road" in a "series of snapshots shot through with . . . rhythms, tones, and spatio-temporal orientations."[57] To return to the contribution this type of work might make ecologically is to understand how, as Guattari reminds us, one must not separate human and nonhuman, micro or macro, body, earth, and world, for as Stewart explains, "each element thrown together into a form of the road has precise and shifting histories, generative forms, divergent social functions, and qualities that link it to countless other elements and partial assemblages."[58]

Crucially her affective ficto-regionality "tries to mimic felt impacts and half-known effects as if the writing were itself a form of life" that "leaps," performing not like a "trusted guide" helping the reader link objects seamlessly to meanings or to represent the world reassuringly, but rather provocatively and "more-than-representationally," "caught in the powerful tension between what can be known and told and what remains obscure or unspeakable but is nonetheless real." Consequently her writing throbs with critical questions: "What is going on? . . . What forces are becoming sensate as forms, styles, desires, and practices? . . . How are people quite literally charged up by the sheer surge of things in the making? What does cultural poesis look like?"[59] "Road Registers" assembles roadness as an "ontological contact zone" or "worlding" through which generative events are described: "elderly, handicapped, and minority bodies" like "a world held apart" because they do not drive cars; Kerouac's *On the Road* "folding world into word . . . a perpetual variation . . . an audience yet to come"; New Hampshire remembered as "walks, drives, gatherings, natural disasters, or shopping trips . . . a thing made up of our itineraries shuttling back and forth across its surface"; a body by a freeway in Medellin in a story told by Michael Taussig, or Las Vegas car culture.[60] Together, as one reads and responds to the essay, an ecology emerges through her attention to the "regionality" of the road as a "composition scored into matter . . . charged with potentiality." Her writing actively creates a "world" made up of force lines that "propel," "spread," and "diverge" so that we become drawn into its production "like a musical score" through which the road is layered in myth, history, aesthetics, hard practicality, economics, and aspiration, becoming a "creative geography . . . of effects and affects," an assemblage of regionality bringing together much of this chapter's expanded ecology capable of jumping "from matter to metaphor, structure to fantasy, dull repetition to virtuality" aligned with a new gentleness of curiosity and responsibility, "wondering and worlding." This process serves to "displace and flatten conceptual hierarchies" between the "big (important) and small (off-register, invisible)" so that distance is reduced in favor of the intricacies and nuances of the everyday, which nonetheless always relates to wider narratives, like the road itself as a "national macadam of living form . . . matter touching dreamworlds." To return to Guattari's ecosophy, Stewart's road registers an assemblage in which "matter and thought are not opposed" but mix to form "the energetic life of an emergent object that exists as meaning, matter, and potentiality," like a complex, shifting, and composing ecology.[61]

An Ecology of Paths

Stewart's attention to "ordinary affects" assembles what Guattari would term "existential territories": the road, "New England," a suburban street, Vermont, a life—"strands of cohabitation with the things of the world," which can be "precarious, finite, finitized, singular, singularized, capable of bifurcating into stratified and deathly repetitions or of opening up processually" through something "almost imperceptible," which, from its smallness, might spring "enormous repercussions."[62] Guattari's ecological vision insisted upon opening up potentially circumscribed existential territories onto "a constellation of Universes," just as Stewart's often small-scale environments, such as the road or a house, are connected to wider forces and patterns: "the contours of the landscape, the rocks the glaciers left, the climate, the layers of determination laid down by histories, the leftovers of everything that has happened."[63] In a series of examples Guattari too explains how the small, minor, or overlooked can work to such ends: "a rock loosed by frost balanced on a singular point of the mountain-side, the little spark which kindles the great forest, the little word which sets forth the world a-fighting."[64] From the minuscule to the "Universes" of possibility, these trigger "thresholds" or an "interface between sensible finitude . . . and the trans-sensible infinitude," making possible "incorporeal domains of entities" where "nuclei of eternity lodged between instants."[65] In Stewart's terms, Guattari "outlined a theory of the affective as a state of potential, intensity, and vitality," and her work translates this into language that "tracks the pulses of things as they cross each other, come together, fragment, and recombine in some new surge," creating a "cartography of what happens here"—"something atmospheric distributed across a geography of elements that swell . . . that produces worlds out of thin air."[66]

Guattari's "analytic cartographies . . . extend beyond existential Territories," like affective critical regionality extends beyond regionalism, "as in painting or literature" with their capacity to "evolve and innovate . . . open up new futures, without their authors having prior recourse to assured theoretical principles." Just as some forms of regionalism are nostalgic and romanticized, Guattari is quick to point out that "it would be absurd to want to return to the past in order to reconstruct former ways of living," since in extending and unsettling old existential territories (like regions) "nature cannot be separated from culture" because to comprehend "the interactions between ecosystems" and understand that there are three ecological registers, one must "learn to think 'transversally.'" Guattari opposed closure and stasis in his work and saw subjectivity as a creative work-in-progress, assembling itself through its relations and contacts with others and the world (other existential territories, Universes, and the Cosmos). Thus transversality promotes greater sensitivity, like new gentleness, working across and between the three ecologies and their "interfaces," nonreductively as "a logic of intensities . . . concerned only with the movement and intensity of evolutive processes." Guattari's eco-logic captures process as opposed to rigid systems, structures, or frames, presenting "existence in the very act of its constitution, definition and deterritorialization . . . processual lines of flight."[67] However, as I have shown, fictocriticism performs a similar process, refusing, as Stewart puts it, to use theory to "beat its objects into submission to its dreamy arguments" and to instead "approach its object slowly and enigmatically" through "descriptive detour or a lyrical evocation . . . attuning to it as a thing of promise and contact . . . things coming into form."[68] Similarly, ecological consciousness is about "becoming sentient to a world's bodies, rhythms, ways of being," tracking worlds *of all kinds* forming and deforming, "both abstract and concrete, actual and unfolding," through writing that "tries to mimic felt impacts and half-known effects as if the writing itself were a form of life."[69]

So, like Muecke's affective histories of coal and ivory, Stewart will follow the itineraries of "New England Red" along what she calls an "ecology of paths" tracing "redness" along "lines of contact [that] radiate out in a prismatic structure of etchings and refrains," "sparking from tree to blood to paint to skin to photograph" as a "cartography of color." In so doing, her approach records how "energies distribute across a field of subjects-objects-bodies-trajectories-affects," starting from Sarah Messer's *Red House*

(2005): "Before the highway, the oil slick, the outflow pipe; before the blizzard, the sea monster, the Girl Scout camp; before the nudist colony and flower farm; before the tidal wave broke the river's mouth."[70] Here Stewart challenges "regional prejudice," finding in the Red House a "compositional node" or "prismatic structure" through which matter produces a "worlding landscape" radiating energies, stories, memories, hauntings, affects like light through a prism stretching, connecting, and creating still further new lines, moving outward toward something like Guattari's "constellation of Universes." Rather than rely on ready-made representations and established categories "metastasized into circulation" by repetition and habit, Stewart's ecology of paths, her affective ficto-regionality active in "Road Registers," "prompts curiosity and care about the potentialities in things that happen." Curiosity *and* care are vital elements in any ecological vision, recalling Guattari's comment at the opening of this chapter that ecology struggles to "give back to humanity . . . a sense of responsibility, not only for its own survival but equally for the future of all life on the planet, for animal and vegetable species." To see and feel the potential in all things, as relations, energies, and interconnected destinies, demands the type of new gentleness ever present in Guattari's three ecologies and played out in Stewart's "cultural poesis" of curiosity and care following multiple, entangled lines, like "a tendril of practices and sensibilities gathered into an energetics of form" producing "affinities, accidental admixtures, and refrains on which people and things travelled . . . worlded."[71]

Guattari's desire too was to interrupt the self-perpetuating "turning in circles" defining so much established institutional thought and practice with tangled lines of difference presenting the political possibilities of ecology and regionality as an energized sense of care—a "new gentleness"—of responsibility, attunement, and mutuality. "Ways should be found," he writes, "to enable the singular, the exceptional, the rare, to coexist with a State structure that is the least burdensome possible" but one that will always have to be cognizant of the small-scale and the local, or what he terms "multiple molecular revolutions."[72]

An example Guattari gives is of the kitchen at the La Borde psychiatric clinic functioning as an affective "territory" or, for my purposes, like a region "close[d] in on itself... the site of stereotyped attitudes and behavior, where everyone mechanically carries out their little refrain." Like one of Stewart's vignettes of the ordinary, this territory/region "can also come to life, trigger an existential agglomeration, a drive machine ... a little opera scene: in it people talk, dance and play with all kinds of instruments, with water and fire, dough and dustbins, relations of prestige and submission." Suddenly the kitchen shifts from repetitive behaviors within the ordinary to something that sparks, spawning different relations like a "resource of ambience, of contextual subjectivity . . . indexed to the degree of openness."[73] Thus territory/region is "more than" it first appears, becoming, like Stewart's "live composition," a layered "ecology of potentiality" that might "find itself in direct contact with Universes of alterity" beyond its "existential entrapment"—"a story in which there is always something more to be said."[74]

Like regionality, Guattari's "existential territorialities" are always "partial and yet open to the most diverse fields of alterity" (such as La Borde's kitchen) so that even "the most autistic enclosure," like the most inward-looking, nostalgic, conservative region, "can be in direct contact with ambient social constellations . . . historical complexes and cosmic aporias" that challenge, extend, and stretch it beyond itself. Of course this maps onto Guattari's expansive sense of "the future of all life," which requires "different ways of seeing and of making the world," emphasizing new modes of understanding relating to the everyday, the small-scale, and the minor as consistent building blocks to wider perceptions and actions in the world. From the local to the global, from self to other, finite to infinite, subject to object, across all possible "bodies," affective critical regionality similarly functions to "reinvent social practices that would give back to humanity . . . a sense of responsibility" with "love and compassion for others" and "the feeling of fusion at the heart of the cosmos." Of course this is political, insisting upon a "new type of social practice better suited *both* to issues of a very local nature and to the global problems of our era," gathering up and producing "assemblages of enunciation" reflecting "the singularity of a situation."[75] In other words, politics produced from "multiple micropolitical registers" and affects providing "ways of connecting, to others and to other situations," offering "our angle of participation in processes larger than ourselves," resonate back to Stewart's "ordinary affects" and a "new gentleness."[76]

For Guattari this is exemplified in the work of writers, artists, and poets whose efforts foreground this contestation over the "question of subjectivity" aligning with his tri-ecosophical vision. Subjectivity is therefore no more a "natural given . . . than air or water," and so artists must engage in the narrowest *and* widest of struggles: "How do we produce it, capture it, enrich it, and permanently reinvent it in a way that renders it compatible with Universes of mutant value?" This too is the progressive, active, and potential function of affective critical regionality and its firm belief that "the world can be rebuilt from other Universes of value and . . . other existential Territories should be constructed towards this end."[77] As the geographer David Matless explains, "Movements make the region, furnishing rather than diminishing geographic particularity. Never complete, always refurbished, regional identity cannot help but be provisional; provision denoting not only tentativeness, but sustenance."[78] Through Guattari's leaps of language and concept there emerges this exact sense of the "provisional" applied to a rethinking of regionalism as regionality, as well as ecology, being both tentative, precarious, and vulnerable *and* simultaneously productive and sustaining.

In one last poetic example, Guattari expresses this sense of provisionality as a resource emerging through our interactions with place and our capacity for creative change and the formation of "new constellations" triggered by the "refrain-making of the sensible world": "What sometimes minuscule details does the perception of a child walking down the dismal passageways of a social housing estate fasten on to? How, starting from a distressing seriality, does he succeed in consummating his discovery of a world of magical haloes?"[79] From the distressing seriality and repetition of ordinary experience a world of magical haloes might emerge—worlds born of immanence, not transcendence, not from life as it should be but from life as it is. Or, to return to Stewart, this invokes the capacities of affective ficto-regionality not as "social construction—but the moment itself when an assemblage of discontinuous yet mapped elements throws itself together into something" that, even if repetitive, "leaves a residue like a track or a habit . . . a composition—a poesis—and one that literally can't be seen as a simple repository of systemic effects imposed on an innocent world but has to be traced through the generative modalities of impulses, daydreams, ways of relating, distractions, strategies, failures, encounters, and worldings of all kinds."[80] What Stewart performs in her fictocriticism then is an "ecology of paths," veering and tracking, leaping and following, delving into and scoring the surface of things, because her ficto-regionality is, as she says, "a hinge. Or a necessary detour. Or a phenomenal cartography that reaches a point of expressivity: a queer performativity of flighty infrastructures, an energetics of attention, a comagnetizing of things."[81]

> Every scene I can spy has tendrils stretching into things I can barely, or not quite, imagine.... The world is still tentative, charged, overwhelming and alive. This is not a good thing or a bad thing. It is not my view that things are going well but they *are* going.... Ordinary affect is a surging, a rubbing, a connection of some kind that has an impact. It's transpersonal or prepersonal—not about one person's feelings becoming another's but about bodies literally affecting one another and generating intensities. Human bodies, discursive bodies, bodies of thought, bodies of water.[82]

Here curiosity and care extend into a new political and ecological consciousness, to Guattari's "new gentleness," which Muecke sees as fictocriticism's purpose, propelling the reader "gently but firmly on a journey whose signposts sometimes express feelings, sometimes ways of knowing. So *that's* how you got there, the reader sighs at the end, I never thought you'd make it!"[83] Indeed Bennett conveys the impact of Guattari, Muecke, and Stewart together in a powerful, final ecological vision, suggesting that the "new gentleness" of ficto-regionality outlined in this chapter might "chasten my fantasies of human mastery, highlight the common materiality of all that is, expose a wider distribution of agency, and reshape the self and its interests."[84]

1. Guattari, *Chaosmosis*, 119–20.
2. Guattari, *Chaosmosis*, 120.
3. Guattari, *Chaosmosis*, 120.
4. Guattari, *Three Ecologies*, 52; Guattari, *Chaosmosis*, 122, 121.
5. See Campbell, *Affective Critical Regionality*; Stewart, "Regionality," 277.
6. Muecke, *Joe in the Andamans*, 113; Haas, *Ficto/Critical Strategies*, 11, 14.
7. Nettlebeck, "Notes towards an Introduction," 4.
8. Bennett, *Vibrant Matter*, 43.
9. Herzogenrath, *Deleuze/Guattari and Ecology*, 5.
10. Guattari, *Three Ecologies*, 50; Guattari, *Chaosmosis*, 91–92.
11. Guattari, *Three Ecologies*, 41.
12. Guattari, *Three Ecologies*, 47, 50, 38.
13. Stewart, *Ordinary Affects*.
14. Guattari, *Chaosmosis*, 91.
15. Genosko, "Subjectivity and Art in Guattari's *The Three Ecologies*," 106.
16. Stewart, *Ordinary Affects*, 4–5.
17. Stewart, "Regionality," 275.
18. Guattari, *Chaosmosis*, 92–93.
19. Guattari, *Three Ecologies*, 53.
20. Stewart, "Regionality," 279.
21. Stewart, "Regionality," 281, 283; Guattari, *Chaosmosis*, 94. See Tsing, *Mushroom at the End of the World*, and her discussion of "contamination as collaboration": "We are contaminated by our encounters; they change who we are as we make way for others" (27). Tsing is an example of ecological ficto-regionality employing "curiosity" (6) as she follows the matsutake mushroom's stories as "an open-ended assemblage" "making worlds" (viii, 58).
22. Stewart, "Regionality," 284.
23. Stewart, official web page.
24. Heidegger, *Poetry, Language, Thought*, 166.
25. Heidegger, *Poetry, Language, Thought*, 174.
26. Heidegger, *Poetry, Language, Thought*, 179.
27. Muecke, *Joe in the Andamans*, 40
28. Muecke, "Composition and Decomposition of Commodities," 2.
29. Bennett, *Vibrant Matter*, 113.
30. Guattari, *Three Ecologies*, 51.
31. Bennett, *Vibrant Matter*, 116.
32. Muecke, *Joe in the Andamans*, 15.
33. Haas, *Ficto/Critical Strategies*, 32.

34. Muecke, "Composition and Decomposition of Commodities," 5, 9 (emphasis added).
35. Muecke, "Composition and Decomposition of Commodities," 6.
36. Muecke, "Composition and Decomposition of Commodities," 6, 14.
37. Deleuze and Guattari, *Thousand Plateaus*, 257.
38. Muecke, "Composition and Decomposition of Commodities," 6, 8; Bennett, *Vibrant Matter*, 117.
39. Guattari, *Three Ecologies*, 35; Genosko, "Subjectivity and Art in Guattari's *The Three Ecologies*," 110.
40. Muecke, *Mother's Day Protest*, xii.
41. Muecke, "Composition and Decomposition of Commodities," 10.
42. Stewart, *Ordinary Affects*, 1.
43. Gibbs, "Fictocriticism, Affect, Mimesis," n.p.
44. Muecke, *Joe in the Andamans*, 15.
45. Muecke, *Joe in the Andamans*, 15; Stewart, "Cultural Poesis" 1028.
46. Stewart, "Regionality," 277; Stewart, "Weak Theory in an Unfinished World," 80.
47. Stewart, "Road Registers," 560 (emphasis added).
48. Stewart, "Road Registers," 560.
49. Guattari, *Three Ecologies*, 68 (emphasis added).
50. Muecke, "Composition and Decomposition of Commodities," 10.
51. Stewart quoted in Pittman, "Interview with Kathleen Stewart," n.p.
52. Gibbs, "Fictocriticism, Affect, Mimesis," n.p.
53. Stewart quoted in Pittman, "Interview with Kathleen Stewart," n.p.
54. Stewart, "Achievement of a Life, a List, a Line," 32.
55. Guattari, *Three Ecologies*, 44.
56. Stewart, "Road Registers," 550.
57. Stewart, "Road Registers," 550.
58. Stewart, "Road Registers," 551.
59. Stewart, "Cultural Poesis," 1016, 1028; Stewart, *Ordinary Affects*, 5; Stewart, "Cultural Poesis," 1028.
60. Stewart, "Road Registers," 556–57.
61. Stewart, "Road Registers," 549–50, 550, 551, 553, 560.
62. Stewart, "Achievement of a Life, a List, a Line," 33; Guattari, *Three Ecologies*, 53, 10.
63. Guattari, *Chaosmosis*, 17; Stewart, "Regionality," 278.
64. Guattari, *Three Ecologies*, 11.
65. Guattari, *Chaosmosis*, 111, 17.
66. Stewart, "Cultural Poesis," 1028, 1041; Stewart, "Regionality," 276.
67. Guattari, *Three Ecologies*, 40, 41, 43, 28, 42, 43, 44.
68. Stewart, "Regionality," 284.

69. Stewart, "Cultural Poesis," 1028.
70. Stewart, "New England Red," 19, 23; Messer, *Red House*, 1.
71. Stewart, "New England Red," 20, 24.
72. Guattari, *Three Ecologies*, 51; Guattari, *Chaosmosis*, 21.
73. Guattari, *Three Ecologies*, 69.
74. Stewart, "New England Red," 32; *Chaosmosis*, 95, 70; Stewart, *Space on the Side of the Road*, 7.
75. Guattari, *Chaosmosis*, 118, 120, 121 (emphasis added).
76. Guattari, *Chaosmosis*, 128; Massumi, *Politics of Affect*, 6.
77. Guattari, *Chaosmosis*, 135, 134.
78. Matless, *In the Nature of Landscape*, 219.
79. Guattari, *Schizoanalytic Cartographies*, 209.
80. Stewart, "Weak Theory in an Unfinished World," 73.
81. Stewart, "New England Red," 29.
82. Stewart, *Ordinary Affects*, 128.
83. Muecke, *Joe in the Andamans*, 16.
84. Bennett, *Vibrant Matter*, 122.

BIBLIOGRAPHY

Bennett, Jane. *Vibrant Matter: A Political Ecology of Things*. Durham: Duke University Press, 2010.

Campbell, Neil. *Affective Critical Regionality*. London: Rowman and Littlefield International, 2016.

Deleuze, Gilles, and Guattari, Félix. *A Thousand Plateaus: Capitalism and Schizophrenia*. 1980. London: Athlone, 1996.

Genosko, Gary. "Subjectivity and Art in Guattari's *The Three Ecologies*." In *Deleuze/Guattari and Ecology*, edited by Bernd Herzogenrath, 102–15. Basingstoke: Palgrave Macmillan, 2009.

Gibbs, Anna. "Fictocriticism, Affect, Mimesis: Engendering Differences." *TEXT* 9, no. 1 (April 2005). http://www.griffith.edu.au/school/art/text/.

Guattari, Félix. *Chaosmosis: An Ethico-Aesthetic Paradigm*. Sydney: Power Publications, 1995.

———. *Schizoanalytic Cartographies*. London: Bloomsbury, 2013.

———. *The Three Ecologies*. London: Athlone, 2000.

Haas, Gerrit. *Ficto/Critical Strategies Subverting Textual Practices of Meaning, Other, and Self-Formation*. Bielefeld: Transcript Verlag, 2017.

Heidegger, Martin. *Poetry, Language, Thought*. New York: Harper Colophon, 1971.

Herzogenrath, Bernd, ed. *Deleuze/Guattari and Ecology*. Basingstoke: Palgrave Macmillan, 2009.

Massumi, Brian. *Politics of Affect*. Cambridge: Polity, 2015.

Matless, David. *In the Nature of Landscape: Cultural Geography of the Norfolk Broads*. Oxford: Wiley Blackwell, 2014.

Messer, Sarah. *Red House: Being a Mostly Accurate Account of New England's Oldest Continuously Lived-In House*. New York: Viking, 2005.

Muecke, Stephen. "The Composition and Decomposition of Commodities: The Colonial Careers of Coal and Ivory." In "Writing Creates Ecology and Ecology Creates Writing," edited by Martin Harrison, Deborah Bird Rose, Lorraine Shannon and Kim Satchell. Special issue, *TEXT* 20, no. 1 (2013). http://www.textjournal.com .au/speciss/issue20/Muecke.pdf.

————. *Joe in the Andamans and Other Fictocritical Stories*. Sydney: Local Consumption, 2008.

————. *The Mother's Day Protest and Other Fictocritical Writings*. London: Rowman and Littlefield International, 2016.

Nettlebeck, Amanda. "Notes towards an Introduction." In *The Space Between: Australian Women Writing Fictocriticism*. Crawley: University of Western Australia Press, 1998.

Pittman, Alex. "An Interview with Kathleen Stewart." *Orature* 1 (September 2012–May 2013). http://performance.tisch.nyu.edu/object/OratureVolI.html.

Stewart, Kathleen. "The Achievement of a Life, a List, a Line." In *The Social Life of Achievement*, edited by N. J. Long and H. L. Moore, 31–42. New York: Berghahn Books, 2013.

————. "Cultural Poesis: The Generativity of Emergent Things." In *The SAGE Handbook of Qualitative Research*, edited by N. Denzin and Y. S. Lincoln, 1027–42. 3rd ed. London: SAGE, 2005.

————. "New England Red." In *Non-Representational Methodologies*, edited by Philip Vannini, 19–33. London: Routledge, 2015.

————. Official web page. Accessed October 8, 2016. https://liberalarts.utexas.edu /anthropology/faculty/kcs.

————. *Ordinary Affects*. Durham: Duke University Press, 2007.

————. "Regionality." *Geographical Review* 103, no. 2 (April 2013): 275–84.

————. "Road Registers." *Cultural Geographies* 21, no. 4 (2014): 549–63.

————. *A Space on the Side of the Road: Cultural Poetics in an "Other" America*. Princeton: Princeton University Press, 1996.

————. "Weak Theory in an Unfinished World." *Journal of Folklore Research* 45, no. 1 (2008): 71–82.

————. "Worlding Refrains." In *The Affect Theory Reader*, edited by Melissa Gregg and Gregory J. Seigworth, 339–53. Durham: Duke University Press, 2010.

Tsing, Anna Lowenhaupt. *The Mushroom at the End of the World: On the Possibility of Life in Capitalist Ruins*. Princeton: Princeton University Press, 2015.

PART 2

Affective Attachments

Land, Bodies, Justice

4

Feeling the Fires of Climate Change

Land Affect in Canada's Tar Sands

JOBB ARNOLD

In the spring of 2016 large swaths of the Canadian tar sands region were engulfed by a giant forest fire that destroyed significant parts of the Alberta oil town of Fort McMurray. Unusually hot temperatures and little rain allowed the fire to spread quickly and with extreme intensity, burning over a million acres of boreal forests and displacing nearly one hundred thousand people, many of whom were workers employed at major industrial tar sands extraction sites.[1] As the fires raged on, waves of emotionally charged stories flooded across Canada's national news media and received attention globally. Cell phone videos taken by fleeing residents were uploaded to social media and went viral, circulating harrowing scenes of escape through walls of fire as raging flames threatened to swallow the few existing roadways to safety.

News reports on the wildfires immediately surged through all levels of Canadian media. For decades mainstream media narratives have dominated coverage of the tar sands, presenting the projects as the economic engine of Canada and framing their continued expansion as both a necessity and an inevitability. These well-financed narratives have recently faced major opposition from a large coalition of grassroots actors led by Indigenous peoples and supported, in part, through environmental NGOs that offer a very different narrative about the tar sands. Buoyed by the global scientific consensus on the relationship between extreme fossil-fuel extraction and the growing impacts of climate change, these alternative narratives have become effective at demonstrating to Canadians that the tar sands are not only a reckless industry dependent on environmental destruction but a real economic liability.

These media narratives, both for and against the tar sands, have helped to powerfully establish what Sara Ahmed calls "affective economies."[2] As emotionally charged stories, images, films, and news reports—both good and ill—about the tar sands move across the skin of Canada's imagined communities, they do the work of defining and aligning Canadians into camps for and against the tar sands.[3] The 2016 wildfires temporarily punctured the surface-level affective economies that have sustained these Canadian climate discourses. The surge of affective intensity generated by the fires disrupted national social alignments, creating a situation in which both sides of the tar sands antagonism needed to reframe what was happening in order to respond to a new and unprecedented reality. Panicked residents of Fort McMurray were suddenly faced with an unstoppable force feeding off the energy of an ecosystem that they could no longer ignore or compartmentalize. During the fires the power of the land became not only visible, it became acutely felt.

As an oil town, Fort McMurray owes its current modes of existence to the vast hydrocarbon energy deposits located in the region. Many of the people who work in the industry have very little meaningful connection to the surrounding lands themselves outside of the extractive process. As a result, the energy inherent in the land itself is seldom experienced in any way other than through modes of extraction determined and paid for by industry.[4] The 2016 blaze demonstrated how the power of the land can cut through discourse and upend even the most advanced modern industrial contrivances. This presencing of land-based energy, and the ways it is transmitted to humans, provides the starting point for an exploration of land affect.

Land Affect

This essay explores the particular meanings of the Fort McMurray fire—and extreme weather events more generally—through the speculative concept of *land affect*. I use the term "land affect" to refer to nontechnologically mediated experiences of affective energy that cause people *to feel with the land*. Intense experiences of land affect—such as an encroaching forest fire—mobilize and transmit latent ecological energies, innervating the connective tissues that exist between interdependent webs of human and other-than-human life. Although land affect is always already present, it is seldom registered in modern human awareness until the power of the land is mobilized and brought to bear upon embodied subjectivities.

My thinking around land affect draws heavily upon Deborah Gould's analysis of affect and social mobilization in her remarkable study of *Act Up!*, one of the first queer-led responses to the early days of the 1980s AIDS epidemic. Gould describes affect as

> Nonconscious and un-named, but nevertheless registered, experiences of bodily energy and intensity that arise in response to stimuli imping-ing on the body. These experiences are registered in that the organism senses the impingement and the bodily effects, but nonconscious in that this sensing is outside of the individual's awareness and is of intensities that are inchoate and as yet inarticulable . . . affect [is] unbound: it has no fixed object, no prior aim; rather it is unattached, free-floating, mobile energy.[5]

Gould's definition of affect provides a useful basis for thinking about the different ways that a "free-floating, mobile energy" relates to, and is embodied in, other-than-human relations and how these interdependencies interact in dynamic and changing ecologies such as the tar sands. Additionally, Gould's reading of affect can be usefully developed in ways that resonate with the worldviews of many of Canada's diverse Indigenous peoples.[6] Indigenous elders, scholars, and cultural practitioners such as Vine Deloria have provided extensive discussions of the place-based ontologies that have traditionally grounded their people, quite literally, in the land.[7]

Land affect is the direct experience of mobilized free-floating ecological energies, registered unconsciously and sometimes consciously in human affective states. Following Gould's approach to affect, I use the term "land affect" to refer to the experiential intensities of lived realities in relation to ecological forces (e.g., fire, flood, wind) that are primarily "nonconscious, noncognitive, nonlinguistic, noncoherent, nonrational, and unpredetermined."[8] I conceptualize the transmission of land affect as operating analogously to the process of synaptic transmission that occurs during neuronal firing in the human brain. Neural synaptic transmission occurs when electrical energy in the brain is converted into chemical energy so it can move across the synaptic cleft (the space between neurons). When the chemical signal reaches a receptor neuron on the other side of the cleft, the energy is converted back into an electrical form, enabling the energetic flows of information to continue through established neural circuits and also to form new connections through the process of innervation.[9]

As discussed in more detail below, the ability to feel with the land is epistemologically important in the worldviews of many Indigenous peoples as well as other land-based and ecologically attuned cultural groupings. Such land-based ontologies are often defined by cultural practices that stem from an implicit understanding of land affect as it exists in the ordinary affects of day-to-day life.[10] For many people who live in modern industrialized urban societies like Canada, such land-based-ways of knowing have been dimmed. However, even for people disconnected from the land, intense experiences of land affect cannot be ignored when they directly impinge upon one's bodily senses. In this sense land affect works to innervate physiological pathways of reception; that is, it facilitates the growth of nervelike connectivity between people and the land, transmitting powerful affective energies that can flow through multiple possible trajectories, or even create new connective pathways.[11]

Land affect is not bound by individual bodies but is registered as fleeting experiential and relational sensations grounded in land-based, embodied ways-of-being and knowing that exist between human and other-than-human agents.[12] In this chapter I argue that a grounded conception of land affect provides an often overlooked counterpoint to the sorts of affective economies described by Sara Ahmed that place an emphasis on the "surfacing of individual and collective bodies through the way in which emotions circulate between bodies and signs."[13] In Ahmed's analysis, the surface-level circulation of affect occurs primarily through digitally mediated discourses.

I am seeking to advance land affect as a more grounded description of how affect functions to constitute the ontological, epistemological, normative, and political dimension of life in an earth being transformed by climate change. This aim resonates with recent work exploring "emotional geographies" conceived "as relational flows, fluxes or currents, in-between people and places rather than 'things' or 'objects' to be studied or measured."[14]

The Affective Impasse of the Canadian Tar Sands

The ecological destruction caused by the Fort McMurray fires was quickly converted in the mainstream media into primarily a story of human suffering and economic loss but also the unity and resilience of the residents of Fort McMurray. The national scope of the tar sands projects was again revealed through the country-wide outpouring of compassion, including material and financial aid, for the people displaced and left destitute by the fire. Campaigns with names like "Fort McMurray Strong" sprang up to raise relief funds, all the while fusing the nationalistic narratives of Canadian industry with stories of community perseverance.

In many of the counternarratives, stories of personal tragedy emerging from Fort McMurray were also quickly interpreted as evidence that the proverbial chickens of anthropogenic climate change had come home to roost. The world's largest industrial project, and Canada's single biggest emitter of greenhouse gases, was burning because of environmental conditions created by climate change.[15] These narratives were quick to label the fires as clear and highly ironic evidence of the perils of extreme fossil fuel extraction, using the opportunity to redouble calls for the government to stop expansion and scale back the projects.

What was clear in both narratives, albeit presented in very different fashion, was that in Fort McMurray, as in so many other climate-affected sites around the world, the distinction between natural and social disasters had collapsed.[16] As the narratives about the fires circulated through the media, they mobilized a great deal of affective force, albeit in very different directions, confirming Gould's view of affect as unpredetermined, free-floating energy that can take on different forms. These reactions to the fires serve to underscore the seemingly intractable influence that the tar sands industry had on Canadian society, producing a state of affairs that can be described as an affective "impasse."

Lauren Berlant describes an impasse as "a time of dithering from which someone or some situation cannot move forward."[17] Such stasis can be seen as preventing a needed change; however, the holding pattern implied by an impasse can also seem like a best-case scenario in times of great upheaval. As Berlant puts it, "When many of the traditional infrastructures for reproducing life are . . . crumbling at a threatening pace . . . living in an impasse would be an aspiration."[18] Such is Canada's affective impasse when it comes to the tar sands. Although the Canadian government enthusiastically endorsed the 2015 Paris Agreement, they are incapable of ending their support for industries that are damaging to Indigenous ways of life, ecologically unsustainable, and contribute to global warming. Canada has opted to remain in a holding pattern, hoping to escape the worst impacts of climate change while continuing to profit from the expansion of even more tar sands projects.

Ordinary Affects in the Tar Sands

Many Canadians have friends and family members who are employed in sectors directly or peripherally related to the tar sands projects. The 2016 fire struck a nerve for Canadians across the country, not only because it drew attention to the ecological disaster of the tar sands but also because it signaled further decline in an industry already cutting jobs and languishing amid falling oil prices. The fire revealed just how entangled Canada has become with the tar sands industry, heightening the national sense of uneasiness and ambivalence.

Known colloquially as "Fort McMoney," the tar sands region has long been a destination for skilled and unskilled laborers from cities and towns across Canada. Many Canadians have turned to the tar sands to as way to make it through hard economic times. This has been particularly true in communities where local industries have collapsed, leaving people desperate for well-paying jobs. This needs-based pattern of economic migration to the tar sands can clearly be seen among people from Atlantic Canada, who regularly leave home to find work "out west" in the oil industry. This pattern of out-migration was solidified in the early 1990s after a moratorium was placed on the cod fishing industry, after extreme overfishing led to the collapse of a once renewable resource.[19] The large out-of-province work force in the tar sands has contributed to Fort McMurray's reputation as a hub for transient workers with no connection, or accountability, to the place itself. Even people with more permanent jobs in the industry project their hopes and desires to faraway places, either to their homes and families across the country or to the exciting vacation destinations and luxuries goods that they can afford to purchase.[20]

The tar sands industry also plays a central role in Canada's ongoing nation-building process, a process centered on the dominant role of white nationals, people Sunera Thobani describes as "exalted subjects."[21] Relative to Canada's privileged white settler community, immigrants—particularly migrant workers and refugees—are treated as suppliants and are offered conditional inclusion in return for their complete loyalty and unflagging productivity within the nation. Unlike immigrants who can be selectively included or excluded, Indigenous people's claims to the land and their demands for recognition as sovereign peoples presents a fundamental challenge to the colonial fiction of Canada.[22] For this reason, Thobani argues that Indigenous people will continue to be marked for extinction by the Canadian state, through one means or another. These differenti-ated statuses permeate and sustain the affective economies of Canada's multiculturalist discourse that is ostensibly meant to balance Indigenous and migrants' rights claims against the "real" and legitimate interests of white-settler Canada.[23]

The territories along the Athabasca River valley, where Fort McMurray is located, have a long history of Indigenous habitation, land-based subsis-tence, and river-based trade. Following the heavy industrialization of the region, many Indigenous peoples have been compelled, out of necessity and an absence of alternatives, to participate in the tar sands industry. Still, despite the economic disincentives to do so, many other Indigenous peoples continue to actively oppose the systematic violence being done to the land, which goes hand-in-hand with the annihilation of their culture.[24] Amid the widespread news coverage of the fires, there was surprisingly little attention paid to the impacts on the local Indigenous peoples. This omission is consistent with the fact that Indigenous peoples have largely been excluded from the mainstream economic-ecological discourses that fuel national affective economies around the tar sands projects. However, the affective experience of ontological destruction is something Indigenous communities have been forced to live with for years as they have been subjected to a process of slow industrial genocide.[25]

Viewing climate disasters like the Fort McMurray fires through the lens of land-based Indigenous values powerfully decenters the mainstream environmental and economic thinking that sustains Canada's contemporary colonial discourse. Indigenous-led resistance to cumulatively destructive systems like the tar sands provides critical insights into the ontological stakes and motivations that are associated with land affect in the tar sands region. Indigenous ways of knowing (epistemologies) and being (ontologies) provide a drastically different view of the world, opening up a very different range of possibilities for feeling with the land in an epoch defined by the effects of climate change.

The prospect that humans might be able to become more attuned to land affect in the era of climate change opens up some hopeful possibilities.[26] What would it mean for non-Indigenous peoples to find new and authentic ways of aligning their energies behind, and in support of, Indigenous led eco-cultural change? As mentioned above, I understand land affect as being deeply connected to the intellectual and political histories and traditions of Indigenous peoples whose values and practices have long centered on land-based relational ontologies.[27] From this perspective, becoming attuned to, and aligned with, traditional Indigenous wisdom and politics is an affective task more than an intellectual one. If true, such an assessment would seem to corroborate some key insights emerging from the field of affect studies. As Deborah Gould argues, "The most important contribution of the emotional turn is that it introduces a different ontology, a different conception of social reality, into the study of social movements and other forms of contentious politics."[28]

Land-Based Ontologies: Destruction or Resurgence

In its 2015 final report the Truth and Reconciliation Commission (TRC) of Canada stated that Canada implemented policies of physical, cultural, and spiritual destruction carried out against Indigenous peoples that constituted genocide.[29] Despite the importance of national gestures such as the TRC, the processes of settler colonialism are to a large extent still ongoing and normalized within Canadian society.[30] These colonial processes continue to displace Indigenous peoples from their lands so that industrial developments can proceed unimpeded.[31] The destruction of Indigenous bodies is also closely linked with the destruction of Indigenous lands. As "Native peoples [particularly Native women] have become marked as inherently violable," explains Andrea Smith, "their lands and territories have become marked as violable as well."[32]

National sacrifice zones are an example of such systemic violations. In the name of national interest, the sovereign power of the state can be used to impose "states of exception" upon the land, removing all obstacles to limitless extraction while exempting industry from any form of accountability. Once sacrifice zones are established, the land can be transformed into what I have described as *bare nature*, a condition of regulated ecological precarity that makes it possible for lands to be stripped of all life-value and reduced to the most basic and singular unit of energy—oil.[33] These inherently violent practices constitute elements of what Andrew Woolford has described as ontological destruction. Woolford writes, "It is a disservice to force Aboriginal experiences of ecological destruction into a framework that acknowledges only the subsistence value of land to a group, even if this move might initially appear to advance their justice claims by clearly locating land and wildlife destruction within the terms of the [UN Convention on Genocide]. To fully acknowledge the Aboriginal experience of attempted destruction, we need to understand land and environment not simply as means of sustaining group life, but as key components of group life."[34]

In addition to recognizing the "land and environment" as components of group life, affective forces are also central to constituting and sustaining particular ecological relationships that animate and provide coherence to group life. For example, Rob Shields has demonstrated how modes of cultural reproduction in the tar sands have given rise to the particular affects that make day-to-day life in places like Fort McMurray possible. The production of the strange normality of an oil town functions to sustain the affective disjuncture between the material realities of tar sands extraction and the capacity to relate to, or feel with the land. "Reduced to its energy capacity the supplementarity of values in the landscape—nature as beauty, for example, or as a complex ecosystem, including other forms of animate life—is repressed.... This exclusion deprives bare nature of participation in semiotic systems which give meaning except as a point of contrast to the spaces of everyday life."[35] When the land is stripped bare of its energy, land affect is negated, subtracted by an industrial apparatus of ontological destruction.

In the documentary *The Land of Oil and Water* Warren Cariou, a Métis scholar and artist whose ancestral territories overlap with the Athabasca tar sands region, further elaborates the processes of affective and ecological negation by interrogating the process of stripping *overburden* from lands designated to become sacrifice zones.[36] Overburden, in the language of the tar sands industry, refers to the surface layers of boreal forest, the muskeg and organic materials that lie atop the bitumen-rich sands themselves. Once tar sand industrial expansions are approved, the process of stripping away the sedimented layers of ecosystem begins, including removing the peoples and cultures that are part of these interdependent systems. Cariou's work captures the deep foreboding and ambivalence felt by people living through various phases of tar sands project expansion. The stories they tell convey the deeply troubled experience of land affect in a sacrifice zone. Cariou's documentary project is an act of witnessing as the stories and cultures that constitute the affective ontologies of these places continue to be stripped away like the rich ecological complexity of the boreal landscape.

As I write this, there is a resurgence of land-based cultural values and practices in Indigenous communities, particularly among the youth, that is reshaping Canadian political discourse.[37] Indigenous political mobilization itself entails, among other things, proactive cultural reclamation informed by traditional ways of knowing that are put into action through land-based practices and ceremonies. These constitute, in Gould's language, powerful, ecologically attuned affective ontologies. Glen Coulthard, a Dené scholar whose own territories have been impacted by extractive industries, also describes his people's worldview as one grounded in land-based relations with ethical guidelines:

> In the Weledeh dialect of Dogrib (which is my community's language) ... "land" ... is translated in relational terms as that which encompasses not only the land ... but also people and animals, rocks and trees, lakes and rivers, and so on. Seen in this light, we are as much a part of the land as any other element. Furthermore, within this system of relations human beings are not the only constituent believed to embody spirit or agency. Ethically, this meant that humans hold certain obligations to the land, animals, plants, and lakes in much the same way that we hold obligations to other people.[38]

Coulthard's depiction of land-based ontologies, when coupled with Gould's understanding of free-floating affective energy, suggest a dynamic scape across which land affect is capable of mobilizing, intensifying, and transforming relationships within ecosystems.

Affective ontologies do work to decenter the primacy of anthropocentric ontologies by shifting the focus away from the isolated human and toward the rising and falling of affective intensities that shape different modes of meaning making and ways of inhabiting particular spaces.[39] For Gould, affective ontologies open up a conceptual space that has "been difficult to inhabit in light of the important claims of the cultural and linguistic turns about the centrality of linguistic meaning-making practices in social life."[40] The grounded political power of many contemporary Indigenous movements readily points to ongoing revitalization of traditional languages as a crucial part of reconnecting to the power of the land and the inherent legal and cultural ways of life.[41]

Land Affect: Now You See It, Now You Don't

Sara Ahmed's conception of affective economies emphasizes the "crucial role that emotions play ... in the 'surfacing' of individual and collective bodies through the ways in which emotions circulate between bodies and signs."[42] As discussed above, the circulation of emotionally charged narratives related to the tar sands has done a great deal of work in aligning Canadians into camps that vehemently oppose the projects against those that vigorously support them.[43] These affective economies play an important role in sustaining the day-to-day operations of the tar sands by mobilizing the labor force needed to meet industrial needs.[44] Given the nature of these polarizing and emotionally charged differences, why has there been so little substantive change when it comes to the ability of the tar sands industry to maintain a viable part of Canada?

Gould suggests that "affect actually may be one of the most important sources of political inaction."[45] Indeed this seems to ring true when we consider that, despite surfacing the idea of the tar sands persistently at the level of Canadian discourse, this has not translated into any significant concrete, land-based challenges to the tar sands operations themselves. What was significant about the 2016 fires was that the affective intensity made it impossible to retreat to the usual narrative positions that lend coherence and stability to the established affective economies. The intense burst of affect generated by the fires exceeded the existing affective alignments.

As tar sands workers fled Fort McMurray panicked by the fires of climate change, their ordeal blurred into a tangle of land-based realities and online narratives that punctured the veneer of existing affective economies. Land affect had made itself felt. Feeling with the land became an inescapable reality that people could not look away from; they could only flee or be consumed. This sense of inescapability was transmitted through the personal accounts of dread, danger, incoherence and loss. This affective puncture temporarily exposed an affective reality of the tar sands that had been beyond the emotional reach of most people up until that point. The calamity brought home the reality of climate change and the power of unbounded ecological energies in ways that no aerial images of tailings ponds or online graphics depicting the relative economic and environmental impact of the tar sands industry ever could.

This apparent chasm between "surface-level" mediated online affective economies and "grounded" land affect can be explored further through a phenomenon that Rey Chow describes as *transmedial capture*.[46] The explosion of digital communication technologies has initiated a period of unprecedented mediation, hybridization, and augmentation of the human condition. The availability of media has allowed people to become viewers of an endless number of experiences—from sex and war to trekking in remote forests or viewing sea life at the bottom of the ocean. This mediated proximity allows people to disconnect from the affective intensity of place-based realities, stifling our ability to emotionally "know" what these experiences actually entail. Such affective disconnection maintains a form of colonial unknowing that facilitates the extractive processes of colonial capitalism by insisting on an arelational approach to a world.[47]

"The mediatization of reflexivity," Chow argues, has created an epistemic conundrum in which "thought can no longer proceed without mediatization and yet mediatization cannot be trusted; an obsessive-compulsive dependency on media technologies now goes hand in hand with what comes across as a frigid human environment."[48] As circulating affective intensities do the work of discursive alignment, we have become captured in a net of affective threads that have no "real" source. This epistemic conundrum is yet another indication of our disconnection from land-based ways of knowing; our collective ignorance in this regard has grave implications when it comes to anticipating and responding to devastating climate-change related events.

The phenomenon of transmedial capture is readily observable in the mediated and aestheticized representations of the tar sands projects. For example, Peter Mettler's film *Petropolis: Aerial Perspectives on the Alberta Tar Sands* is a purposively reflexive meditation on the scale of the tar sands that can only be grasped from the air.[49] *Petropolis* mobilizes an uneasy and muted affect through long pans across boreal forest, open pit mines, sulfur pyramids, separation facilities, and tailings ponds. Accompanied by a capacious and droning electronic soundtrack absent of any dialogue, *Petropolis* lays bare the arelational character of the tar sands, denying the viewer any sustained emotional engagement with land-based realities. These cinematic devices demonstrate an "aesthetics of subtraction" that "magnif[ies] the reasoning of modernist mediatized reflexivity in general."[50] We see these things happening, we know them intellectually, but we cannot feel it. We're captured in a mediated state of affective unknowing.

The transmedial capture occurring in the tar sands has produced a "frigid human environment" where free-floating affective energy is captured, processed, and streamlined in ways that accommodate the flows of bitumen. Rob Shields characterizes the captured, stockpiled life-energy in the tar sands in terms of what Heidegger called "standing reserve" (*Bestand*).[51] For Shields, standing reserve in the tar sands "encompasses many aspects of the exploitation of both nature and of people. *Bestand* is what stands by, awaiting to be called upon, released, transformed and distributed. It doesn't even have the appearance of an object any longer (de Beistegui 2005:110). It is a pure commodity, merely available or set out as a stockpile on hand."[52]

Through a complex set of social, economic, and technical processes, tar sands operations convert the inherent potential of land-based ontological systems into nonrelational ecological standing reserve. Affective economies sustain the conditions needed for the industrial status quo to continue. Meanwhile, the closest most Canadians ever get to the tar sands is through seeing images of vast destruction or the rising and falling numbers in their stock portfolio. Given such stark and bifurcated realities, what role might affective ontologies and land affect have in moving beyond the affective impasse of the tar sands?

Mediated Reflexivity or Land-Based Relationality

The Fort McMurray wildfires of 2016 were characterized by an intense eruption of land affect that punctured the mediated affective economies of Canadian discourse. This intensity was not sustained. Tar sands operations resumed and the stories of fear, displacement, and loss have largely been subsumed into the preexisting Canadian affective economies. As Gould suggests, "affect is bursting with potential . . . giving it a quantity of intensity, and thus force, that prepares the organism to respond to that which is impinging on it, but in no predetermined direction."[53]

The fires demonstrate two modalities of land affect. The first emphasizes the autonomy of land affect when it manifests with the extreme intensity of a wildfire or other extreme weather events. Experiencing the extreme intensity of land affect dispels our anthropocentric notions of control reminding us that we, as humans, cannot escape our own ecological interdependence—it might well be the death of us. Secondly, it seems that land affect is something to which humans can become more attuned through land-based learning.[54] Fostering empathic relationships with places might entail humans learning to connect and engage as co-participants in emerging land relations and affective ontologies.[55]

Unlike the epistemological conundrums that characterize mediated reflexivity, land-based learning entails embodied experiences that actively engage with, relate to, and feel with the mobile energies of land affect. One way of imagining such practices can be found in the creative thinking of artists like Robert Smithson. For Smithson, engagement with the land involves physical presence and energetic alignments through which "the earth's surface and the figments of the mind" disintegrate, creating "sedimentations of the mind" in the form of "earth projects" that become, at least temporarily, part of the affective ontologies of particular land.[56] To put it another way, connecting to land affect seems to involve the recovery of the possibility for relational encounters through which we can feel ourselves as existing within broader affective ecologies.

Indigenous values and practices have long been contextualized within land-based, energetic systems that require humans to align themselves based on the spiritual forces and flows that inhabit particular places. Such ordinary affective relations to the land came before colonial regimes of power sought to accumulate and control these energies. As Indigenous-led movements gain momentum in Canada and elsewhere, they are resurfacing forms of affective value and power in ways that elude and oppose the colonial-capitalist industrial bottom line.

Life forces that have the capacity to innervate and sustain diverse affective ontologies are at stake in the current struggles against the tar sands. The power of land affect is perhaps most visibly present in the growing number of land-based, Indigenous-led movements that are demonstrating ways-of-being in the world that are not opposed but aligned with the land. As much of the world begins to reel with the impacts of climate change, these affective ontologies are resonating and being amplified in many different ways, showing us what kind of change we must make on a region-by-region basis. As Kwagiulth scholar Sarah Hunt puts it, "The future of Indigenous rights and political struggles depend[s] on the ability of Indigenous knowledge to retain its active, mobile, relational nature rather than the fixity it is given in colonial law, stuck at the point of contact with colonizers."[57]

Political inaction has been facilitated by mediated affective economies of capture and apathy in the face of destruction. Land-based relational ontologies embody and practically channel affective intensities into political resurgence. As Glen Coulthard indicates, "Indigenous struggles against capitalist imperialism [are] best understood as a struggle oriented around the question of *land*—struggles not only *for* land, but also deeply *informed* by what the land as a mode of reciprocal *relationship* (which is itself informed by placed-based practices and associated forms of knowledge) ought to teach us about living our lives in relation to one another and our surroundings in a respectful, nondominating and nonexploitative way."[58]

The continued emergence of land-based relational affective ontologies holds the promise of creating communities that are resilient because of their sensitivity and responsivity to changing ecological and climatic conditions. Refusal to engage and adapt with land affect through a humbled and long-term process of embodied learning will leave communities less prepared to cope when land affect comes raging in upon them, either as a wildfire or some other shapeshifting form of climate change disaster.

NOTES

1. Sarah Boon, "Northern Alberta Wildfires," *Science Borealis* (blog), July 18, 2016, www.blog.scienceborealis.ca/northern-alberta-wildfires/.
2. Ahmed, "Affective Economies."
3. Ahmed, "Skin of the Community."
4. Scott, *Seeing Like a State.*
5. Gould, *Moving Politics*, 19–20.
6. For an early discussion on other-than-human relations see Hallowell, "Ojibwa Ontology, Behavior, and World View."
7. Deloria, *God Is Red.* Indigenous peoples have expressed concern that Western scholars are beginning to deploy ecological thinking without recognizing that similar understandings have long been foundational for many Indigenous

worldviews and that their appropriation extends colonial forms of power. See, for instance, Todd, "Indigenous Feminist's Take."

8. Gould, *Moving Politics*, 23.
9. Bear, Connors, and Paradiso, *Neuroscience*.
10. Stewart, *Ordinary Affects*, 37–38.
11. The extent to which affect is registered through conscious awareness is a debated topic. For instance, Ruth Leys suggests that "what fundamentally binds together the new affect theorists and the neuroscientists is their shared *anti-intentionalism*. ... The result is that action and behavior are held to be determined by affective dispositions that are independent of consciousness and the mind's control." Leys, "Turn to Affect," 443.
12. For more detailed discussion of other affective ecologies see T. Davidson, *Ecologies of Affect*.
13. Ahmed, "Affective Economies," 117.
14. J. Davidson, Bondi, and Smith, "Introduction," 3.
15. For example, see Elizabeth Kolbert, "Fort McMurray and the Fires of Climate Change," *New Yorker*, May 5, 2016, www.newyorker.com/news/daily-comment /fort-mcmurray-and-the-fires-of-climate-change.
16. Welzer, *Climate Wars*.
17. Berlant, *Cruel Optimism*, 4.
18. Berlant, *Cruel Optimism*, 4.
19. This moratorium was finally enacted after years of overfishing led to the collapse of the cod population. Hiller, *Second Promised Land*.
20. Dorrow and Dogu, "Spatial Distribution of Hope."
21. Thobani, *Exalted Subjects*.
22. Coulthard, *Red Skins, White Masks*.
23. Day, *Multiculturalism and the History of Canadian Diversity*.
24. In the ecocide-genocide nexus "indigenous peoples fighting to retain or regain their lands . . . are fighting for their life as distinct peoples since, for them, their spirituality and cultural vitality [are] based in and on and with their lands." Crook and Short, "Marx, Lemkin and the Genocide-Ecocide Nexus," 313.
25. See Huseman and Short, "'Slow Industrial Genocide.'"
26. Lifton, *Climate Swerve*.
27. Hunt, "Ontologies of Indigeneity."
28. Gould, *Moving Politics*, 18–19.
29. Truth and Reconciliation Commission of Canada, *Truth and Reconciliation Commission of Canada: Calls to Action*, 2015, www.trc.ca/websites/trcinstitution/File /2015/Findings/Calls_to_Action_English2.pdf.
30. Wolfe, "Settler Colonialism and the Elimination of the Native."

31. Patzer, "Residential School Harm."
32. Smith, *Conquest*, 55.
33. Arnold, "Bare Nature."
34. Woolford, "Ontological Destruction," 89.
35. Shields, "Feral," 211.
36. Cariou, *Land of Oil and Water.*
37. Saul, *Comeback.*
38. Coulthard, *Red Skins, White Masks*, 61.
39. Thrift, "Intensities of Feeling."
40. Gould, *Moving Politics*, 23.
41. McAdam (Sausewahum), *Nationhood Interrupted.*
42. Ahmed, "Affective Economies," 117.
43. See Levant, *Ethical Oil.*
44. Cresswell, Dorow, and Roseman, "Putting Mobility Theory to Work."
45. Gould, *Moving Politics*, 26.
46. Chow, *Entanglements.*
47. Vimalassery, Pegues, and Goldstein, "On Colonial Unknowing."
48. Chow, *Entanglements*, 26, 29.
49. Mettler, *Petropolis.*
50. Chow, *Entanglements*, 29.
51. Shields, "Bare Nature."
52. Shields, "Feral Suburbs," 8.
53. Gould, *Moving Politics*, 23.
54. These two affective modes correspond to findings from contemporary neuro-science, which argues that there are two cognitive systems for thinking: fast and slow. Kahneman, *Thinking, Fast and Slow.*
55. Basso, *Wisdom Sits in Places.*
56. Robert Smithson, "A Sedimentation of the Mind: Earth Projects," *Artforum* 7 (September 1968), reprinted in Smithson, *Robert Smithson*, 82.
57. Hunt, "Ontologies of Indigeneity," 30.
58. Coulthard, *Red Skins, White Masks*, 60.

BIBLIOGRAPHY

Ahmed, Sara. "Affective Economies." *Social Text* 22, no. 2 (2004): 117–39.

———. "The Skin of the Community: Affect and Boundary Formation." In *Revolt, Affect, Collectivity: The Unstable Boundaries of Kristeva's Polis*, edited by Tina Chanter and Ewa Płonowska Ziarek, 95–112. Albany: State University of New York Press, 2005.

Arnold, Jobb D. "Bare Nature and the Genocide-Ecocide Nexus—The Conditions of General Threat and the Hope of Cultural Adaptation: The Case of Canada's Tar Sands." *Space and Culture* (November 2017): 1–15.

Basso, Keith M. *Wisdom Sits in Places: Landscape and Language among the Western Apache*. Albuquerque: University of New Mexico Press, 1996.

Bear, Mark F., Barry W. Connors, and Michael A. Paradiso. *Neuroscience: Exploring the Brain*. 2nd ed. Baltimore: Lippincott Williams & Wilkins, 2001.

Berlant, Lauren. *Cruel Optimism*. Durham: Duke University Press, 2011.

Cariou, Warren, dir. *The Land of Oil and Water*. Winnipeg MB: Aboriginal Peoples Television Network, 2012. DVD.

Chow, Rey. *Entanglements, or Transmedial Thinking about Capture*. Durham: Duke University Press, 2012.

———. "When Reflexivity Becomes Porn: Mutations of a Modernist Theoretical Practice." In *Entanglements, or Transmedial Thinking about Capture*, 13–30. Durham: Duke University Press, 2012.

Coulthard, Glen. *Red Skins, White Masks: Rejecting the Colonial Politics of Recognition*. Minneapolis: University of Minnesota Press, 2014.

Cresswell, Tim, Sara Dorow, and Sharon Roseman. "Putting Mobility Theory to Work: Conceptualizing Employment-Related Geographical Mobility." *Environment and Planning A* 48, no. 9 (2016): 1787–1803.

Crook, Martin, and Damien Short. "Marx, Lemkin and the Genocide-Ecocide Nexus." *International Journal of Human Rights* 18, no. 3 (2014): 298–319.

Davidson, Joyce, Liz Bondi, and Mick Smith. "Introduction: Geography's Emotional Turn." In *Emotional Geographies*, edited by Joyce Davidson, Liz Bondi, and Mick Smith, 1–18. Burlington VT: Ashgate, 2005.

Davidson, Tonya K., Ondine Park, and Rob Shields, eds. *Ecologies of Affect: Placing Nostalgia, Desire and Hope*. Waterloo ON: Wilfred Laurier University Press, 2011.

Day, Richard J. F. *Multiculturalism and the History of Canadian Diversity*. Toronto: University of Toronto Press, 2000.

Deloria, Vine, Jr. *God Is Red: A Native View of Religion*. Golden CO: Fulcrum Publishing, 1973.

Dorow, Sara, and Goze Dogu. "The Spatial Distribution of Hope in and beyond Fort McMurray." In *Ecologies of Affect: Placing Nostalgia, Desire and Hope*, edited by Tonya Davidson, Odine Park, and Rob Shields, 271–93. Waterloo ON: Wilfred Laurier University Press, 2011.

Gould, Deborah B. *Moving Politics: Emotion and ACT UP's Fight against AIDS*. Chicago: University of Chicago Press, 2009.

Hallowell, A. Irving. "Ojibwa Ontology, Behavior, and World View." In *Contributions to Anthropology: Selected Papers of A. Irving Hallowell*, 357–90. Chicago: University of Chicago Press, 1976.

Hiller, Harry H. *Second Promised Land: Migration to Alberta and the Transformation of Canadian Society*. Montreal: McGill-Queen's University Press, 2009.

Hunt, Sarah. "Ontologies of Indigeneity: The Politics of Embodying a Concept." *Cultural Geographies* 21, no. 1 (2014): 27–32.

Huseman, Jennifer, and Damian Short. "'A Slow Industrial Genocide': Tar Sands and the Indigenous Peoples of Northern Alberta." *International Journal of Human Rights* 16, no. 1 (2012): 216–37.

Kahneman, Daniel. *Thinking, Fast and Slow*. New York: Macmillan, 2011.

Levant, Ezra. *Ethical Oil: The Case for Canada's Oil Sands*. Toronto: McClelland and Stewart, 2010.

Leys, Ruth. "The Turn to Affect: A Critique." *Critical Inquiry* 37 (Spring 2011): 434–72.

Lifton, Robert Jay. *The Climate Swerve: Reflections on Mind, Hope and Survival*. New York: New Press, 2017.

McAdam, Sylvia (Sausewahum). *Nationhood Interrupted: Revitalizing nêhiyaw Legal Systems*. Toronto: Purich, 2015.

Mettler, Peter, dir. *Petropolis: Aerial Perspectives on the Alberta Tar Sands*. 2010. Toronto: Mongrel Media, 2014. DVD.

Patzer, Jeremy. "Residential School Harm and Colonial Dispossession: What's the Connection?" In *Colonial Genocide in Indigenous North America*, edited by Andrew Woolford, Jeff Benvenuto, and Alex L. Hinton, 166–85. Durham: Duke University Press, 2014.

Saul, John Ralston. *The Comeback: How Aboriginals Are Reclaiming Power and Influence*. New York: Penguin, 2015.

Scott, James C. *Seeing Like a State: How Certain Schemes to Improve the Human Condition Have Failed*. New Haven: Yale University Press, 1998.

Shields, Rob. "Bare Nature." Paper presented at the Canadian Association of Geographers conference, Vancouver BC, June 2015.

———. "Feral Suburbs: Cultural Topologies of Social Reproduction, Fort McMurray, Canada." *International Journal of Cultural Studies* 15, no. 3 (2012): 205–15.

Smith, Andrea. *Conquest: Sexual Violence and American Indian Genocide*. San Francisco: South End Press, 2005.

Smithson, Robert. *Robert Smithson: Collected Writings*. Berkeley: University of California Press, 1996.

Stewart, Kathleen. *Ordinary Affects*. Durham: Duke University Press, 2007.

Thobani, Sunera. *Exalted Subjects: Studies in the Making of Race and Nation in Canada*. Toronto: University of Toronto Press, 2007.

Thrift, Nigel. "Intensities of Feeling: Towards a Spatial Politics of Affect." *Geografiska Annaler* 86, no. 1 (2004): 57–78.

Todd, Zoe. "An Indigenous Feminist's Take on the Ontological Turn: 'Ontology' Is

Just Another Word for Colonialism." *Journal of Historical Sociology* 29 (March 2016): 4–22.

Vimalassery, Manu, Juliana Hu Pegues, and Alyosha Goldstein. "On Colonial Unknowing." *Theory and Event* 19, no. 4 (2016).

Welzer, Harald. *Climate Wars: Why People Will Be Killed in the 21st Century*. London: Polity Press, 2012.

Wolfe, Patrick. "Settler Colonialism and the Elimination of the Native." *Journal of Genocide Research* 8, no. 4 (2006): 387–409.

Woolford, Andrew. "Ontological Destruction: Genocide and Canadian Aboriginal Peoples." *Genocide Studies and Prevention* 4 (2009): 81–97.

5

Wendell Berry and the Affective Turn

WILLIAM MAJOR

Empathy: A Cruel Zeitgeist

Is this really the Age of Empathy?[1] I often wonder whether the widespread anxiety over affective scarcity in the public sphere, expressed most often by President Barack Obama's frequent allusions to our collective empathy deficit, is more an indication of what we hope empathy will do—repair, ameliorate, amend, if not revolutionize human relations—than a critically reflective understanding of what it is.[2] Widespread calls for a general empathic renewal or affective restoration imply a hope for a rapprochement between who we are and who we can be and further hint at a tear in the collective social fabric that only an empathic suturing can mend. For many this need appears especially acute after the presidential election of 2016, which by many accounts was evidence of such a shortfall. With a renewed sense of vigor if not outrage in the public sphere after the election of Donald Trump, however, it will be instructive to note the extent to which empathy maintains its hold on the discourse of renewal or whether other affective states are routinely invoked in an attempt to clarify where we may have gone awry—and where we might go from here.

The empathic and affective turn that permeates general cultural discourse, academic conferences, and special journal issues, that occupies the research agendas of cultural anthropologists, primatologists, philosophers, and cognitive scientists—to name a few—originates, in part, in a sense of loss.[3] Lauren Berlant notes such loss is always built into the hope that accompanies affective relationships, hope that is "cruel" because it marks the "condition of maintaining an attachment to a problematic object *in advance* of its loss," a dynamic that in reality concerns the inability to let go of the object because that would concretize loss before the fact: "one makes affective bargains about the costliness of one's attachments, usually unconscious ones, most of which keep one in proximity to the scene of desire or attrition." It is difficult to give up on what Berlant calls our "cluster of desires" without succumbing, as it were, to despair, even when we suspect that those desires will never fulfill their object.[4] Empathy as an imagined ideal or as a practical relationship with an object offers one such promise, even as it inscribes a moment of loss.

The empathy zeitgeist barely registers the too-much of emotive and cognitive connections, the cost, as Berlant notes, that I take is always getting paid even as the zeitgeist structures further emotional debt. Empathy is never satisfied; it is also never *de trop*. If I am skeptical over the political role of empathy—at least as it is understood as a social or political panacea—it is only to circumscribe the uses to which it can be put and thereby condense its power.[5] This essay considers what empathy is for when applied to two diverging but nevertheless interrelated fields, the local and the global, and specifically explores its deployment within the writer and farmer Wendell Berry's articulation of a new agrarianism, itself an environmental practice whose focus is relentlessly local and affective. In doing so it also addresses whether local connections can have wider political efficacy and conversely whether a more global, cosmopolitan vision undermines empathy's presumptive political value. In the final section of this essay I explore a related matter: that the empathic experience, in highlighting the instability of embodiment, challenges commonplace assumptions about the solidity of individualism and selfhood. Gregory J. Seigworth and Melissa Gregg, for instance, explain that during certain affective experiences "thought is itself a body" in "perpetual *becoming*": "with affect, a body is as much outside itself as in itself—webbed in its relations—until ultimately such firm distinctions cease to matter."[6] The point here is that as much as we need the self—and

I believe we do—that self is both here and there, and this too is part of empathy's promise as well as its cruelty. In this way empathic experiences highlight the porous nature of consciousness, being, and identity: a shaky ground indeed on which to build an effective affective politics. This essay finally asks whether the affective power of local connections such as those recommended by Berry can be the foundation for an "empathic realism" in which objects of affection and empathy do not forever disappoint, are not forever cruel.

Wendell Berry's Affective Ethic and the Problem of Scale

In 2012 Wendell Berry, the writer known for his work in the new agrarianism, was awarded the Jefferson Medal from the National Endowment for the Humanities and gave that year's Jefferson Lecture in the Humanities, "It All Turns on Affection." The lecture, published in the book that shares its name (2012), capitalizes on many of the ideas that have characterized Berry's work over the decades: family, care, marriage, fidelity, and place. As to the last, one of the reasons Berry's oeuvre has had relatively more popular than academic appeal has to do with his consistent evocation of "place" as the basis of an ethical economy. Berry's articulation of the local as the nucleus of beneficent land use is often strategically coupled to a definition of economy that hinges upon limitation. I use the word *economy* advisedly here, if only out of respect for Berry's employment of the term as describing a careful domestic practice inevitably fixed by local limits and ideal cultural practices. For Berry right use begins at home not as environmentalism but as *oikos* and *nomos*: good home management. He writes, "I am nominating economy for an equal standing among the arts and humanities. I mean, not economics, but economy, the making of the human household upon the earth: the *arts* of adapting kindly the many human households to the earth's many ecosystems and human neighborhoods."[7] Economy is here allied with practices within a circumscribed geographical sphere in which limitation is fundamental to an ethic of care.

Early in his lecture Berry invokes a syllogism in which imagination, sympathy, and affection create an ideal vision for a local ethical economic system:

For humans to have a responsible relationship to the world, they must imagine their place in it. To have a place, to live and belong in a place, to live from a place without destroying it, we must imagine it. By imagination we see it illuminated by its own unique character and by our love for it. By imagination we recognize with sympathy the fellow members, human and nonhuman, with whom we share our place. By that local experience we see the need to grant a sort of preemptive sympathy to all the fellow members, the neighbors, with whom we share the world. As imagination enables sympathy, sympathy enables affection. And in affection we find the possibility of a neighborly, kind, and conserving economy.[8]

Imagination, here a local phenomenon, serves as foundation for an economy of kindness that exceeds abstraction, as in its typical usage, *the economy*. In this way, Berry insists, imagination transcends mere "'dreaming up,'" as it is both a figurative and literal seeing of others through "'the mind's eye,'" an invocation of presence that replicates cognitive empathic positioning—putting yourself in someone's shoes, so to speak. Transitive imaginative connection is always of and for something or someone else, an essential and valuable projection of one's sympathetic vision into the being of another ("its own unique character"). Berry's economics are moreover achieved through acts of startling recognition and affective transference: grounded by "contact, [by] tangible connection," imagination becomes a "visionary force."[9] In other words, a conserving ethical economy hinges upon an affective practice presumed by a porous and synthetic imagination.

Although Berry suggests imagination leads to a "preemptive sympathy," we can more properly understand Berry's syllogism as trading on a deeper affective connection: empathy, a *feeling and seeing into the other* (from the German, *Einfühlung*, originally used to denote one's feeling *into* art objects), here theorized as a moral force from which an ethical economy springs. Sympathy and empathy are thus distinct categories of feeling and emotion only insofar as the former lacks the profundity of shared experience that categorizes the multidirectional attachments of the latter. Berry's slide from imagination to sympathy to affection therefore seeks to narrow the space between subject and object in order to nullify the distance upon which the economy of alienation depends. In maintaining a semblance of this distance, sympathy hardly does justice to the presence of the other within a self (or within the moral imagination) whose ethical practices are always circumscribed by such presence. Remember that Berry first asks that we imagine our place in the local world. An affective economy—or an economy of affection—thrives within the limitations set by an imagination whose sphere is relentlessly local and limited.

But empathy is not so easily willed, much less easily achieved. In fact much of the critical literature on empathy focuses on the difficulties of having an empathic response to so-called "out groups." These groups can be racial or gendered others, for instance; they are often people or places proximally removed through time (*the future* is a problem for those interested in climate change) and by space (geographical distance). However, for the "cultural thinker" Roman Krznaric—general empathy provocateur and founder of England's empathy museum —these limitations can be overcome and the empathic impulse nurtured by enhancing real and imaginative contact in the present. Want to get someone in the West interested in climate change in a visceral way? Have her go to India and experience massive flooding firsthand or even better experience her own house being flooded so she can understand what it's like when the waters rise.[10] For Krznaric and the psychologist Jamil Zaki, empathy—while not without emotional and financial cost—has boundless potential to overcome many of the barriers mentioned above (time, space) through acts of will or choice. For instance, Zaki's interests are in what he calls a "motivated view of empathy" in which empathy can be chosen depending on the subject's degree of motivation. Empathy, he argues, can often "align" with people's "values."[11] Accordingly, for both Krznaric and Zaki, empathy's moral field is theorized as both large and associated with the obligation and willingness to act—in other words, it always raises questions of practical ethics. When we *choose* to empathize with "out" groups, we are linked to a deeper and larger sense of moral responsibility that now includes those who may have once been outside the "natural" scope of empathic concern.

There are some curious parallels between Zaki and Krznaric's vision of empathic connection across time and space and Berry's place-based agrarian economics. Early in his lecture Berry introduces the figure of James B. Duke, whose monopolistic practices as head of the American Tobacco Company in the late nineteenth and early twentieth century led to lives of catastrophic penury for tobacco farmers across the South. For Berry, Duke stands as the paragon of an impersonal industrialist logic, one lacking any real affective connection to the farmers or their land. I use the term "impersonal" here because it signifies in part the difficulty in applying affective relations to a large-scale industrial and agricultural system that would seem to abjure them. In Berry's estimation Duke is not so much emblematic of a man devoid of all moral consideration as he is the embodiment of a mode of savagery in which morality and economics are incompatible. After coming upon a statue of Duke on a visit to Duke University, Berry writes, "On one side of his pedestal is the legend: INDUSTRIALIST. On the other side is another single word: PHILANTHROPIST. The man thus commemorated seemed to me terrifyingly ignorant, even terrifyingly innocent, of the connection between his industry and his philanthropy. But I did know the connection. I felt it instantly and physically. The connection was my grandparents and thousands of others more or less like them. If you can appropriate for little or nothing the work and hope of enough such farmers, then you may dispense the grand charity of 'philanthropy.'"[12] Paradoxically the distance between the monopolistic American Tobacco Company and the farmers now *transcends* space and time and becomes present in a moment of imaginative connection between Berry and his ancestors and their community. What does it mean that Berry can feel something for a time and a place now a century in the past so that it seems imminent? "I felt it instantly and physically."[13] Is he "choosing empathy," as Zaki might argue? What does it mean that Berry appears to enact Krznaric's idea that we can in fact invoke an empathic response (albeit diluted) without a more proximate encounter with the object that precipitates it?

The problem with industrialism is in part one of scale. For those such as Krznaric, if not President Obama, empathy addresses the issue of scale by nullifying it—as if by fiat—through acts of imaginative connectivity that annul time and space. Although this seems to be the case in the above passage, Berry's antipathy for James B. Duke in reality manifests itself in the now, less through personal animus than through contact with an immediate, ruinous agricultural and economic landscape mirroring that of 1907, when Berry's grandfather returned from a tobacco auction in Louisville "'without a dime.'"[14] While Berry holds Duke to account for his role in undermining his family's farm and their economic well-being, he understands that Duke is everywhere *now*, alive and present today. He is a figure in the family narrative, sure, but what is more important is that he represents a global story that usurps local affections by separating us from a responsible economy. To suggest that Duke is merely a historical personage is to miss his representative standing as that which still mediates material and affective life, which for Berry is most prominently seen in denuded rural landscapes, topsoil loss, and rural despair. What would interrupt the industrial model, the alienation of people from affection and a just economy? Contact, a scaling down of industrial capitalism, and a scaling up of local affections.

Just as empathy is first a personal, local, and in-group phenomenon (despite cruelly optimistic hopes otherwise), so for Berry is a place-based ethical economy. He therefore lauds recent efforts that seek to connect cities with surrounding land-use communities, efforts that "rest exactly upon the recognition of human limits and the necessity of human scale. [Their] purpose, to the extent possible, is to bring producers and consumers, causes and effects, back within the bounds of neighborhood, which is to say the effective reach of imagination, sympathy, affection, and all else—including enough food—that neighborhood implies. An economy genuinely local and neighborly offers to localities a measure of security they cannot derive from a national or a global economy controlled by people who, by principle, have no local commitment."[15] The moment of recognition across time and space initiated by his encounter with the statue of Duke is here figured as an argument in which local affection mitigates the impersonal force of industrial destruction. This is an economics of the imagination, Berry avers, that thrives only under presence since affection and imagination are primarily limited and interpersonal. Like empathy itself, these qualities are prejudicial, small, imperfect, and often parochial, but they are here construed as revolutionary virtues in a disquieting global world. And yet the "discounting of affection" over which Duke and the last century's industrial ethos presided and fostered remains all too real today.[16]

One wonders whether the attempt to widen the affective economy—articulated at the global scale by President Obama and Roman Krznaric and at the local by Berry and other regionalists—paradoxically creates an opening for the impersonal forces of global capital that precipitates the moral crisis of the imagination Berry identifies as the wellspring of our violent economic lives. For globalists and regionalists alike, the affective/empathic economy is imagined as a substitute for structural economic changes that might challenge the industrial ethos (if they challenge such ethos at all). For Berry in particular, however, local connections are imagined as so strong that they could undermine capital's indifference to morality and ethics, even taking into account his caveat that local economies have been, and often continue to be, plenty destructive. For Krznaric and Obama connection operates as an addition to the regnant economic order—a mere softening, if you will—and certainly not revolutionary. I would only say here that there is upscaling and there is upscaling. Berry's vision, notably (and notoriously) partial, does not seek a global empire of affect as a solution to environmental and economic crises, while the grander politics of empathy partake of a liberal logic (if not economic liberalism) that arguably reproduces that which it seeks to ameliorate. An ever-widening empathic and affective domain—which I suggest is a feeble response to the depredations of capitalism or, as Berry would say, "industrialism"—may make us *feel* better, but its fragility hardly carries the force of revolutionary political transformation. This domain is cruelly optimistic.

Other Ethical Considerations: The Self Is Someone Else

Berry's focus on the small as necessary for affective ties is homologous to a range of neurocognitive research telling us that empathy is more apt to occur when it registers locally. In other words, scale and empathy and ethics are inseparable. What is more, Berry's faith in limitation as an ethical obligation highlights a lively debate over how empathic arousal may in fact give the lie to self/other differentiation. By this I mean that the representative

ideology of autonomous identity and selfhood, dependent as it is on separation and delineation, undergoes a kind of epistemological crisis during
empathic arousal (which is also an imaginative or ethical arousal in Berry's
metaphysics). I see Berry's place-based economy as an attempt to come to
terms with what it means to imaginatively identify with another—in this
case with both human and nonhuman—and as such it dramatizes how a
heuristics of identity plays out "on the ground," so to speak. In discounting
large-scale industrial economic practices and improbable emotive connections, Berry's localism speaks the transitive language of self/other making
that is perpetually in flux but is also ideally ever present. To be sure, the
ambiguity inherent in a borderless affective economy calls for a practice
in which *limitation* governs material economic behavior (earlier I noted
this as the problem of scale). For an effective affective economy to flourish,
therefore, that limitation arrives in robust local associations whereby the
imagination is contained by the ties that inspire it. With too much possibility—as is the case in an industrial economy—affection ceases to govern
and imagination is severed from its object. The infinite global economy
separates the self from its affective ties and undermines the imaginative
connections grounded by sympathy, empathy, and love.

Without question Berry's affective economy—indeed *any* ethics
grounded in empathy—raises other issues about the propriety of a total
connection, especially when such connection may confuse empathizers
with their object. In emphasizing clear distinctions between empathic
identification and emotional *contagion*, for example, the philosophy professor Amy Coplan argues that the latter is an "immature" process that
lacks the imaginative component important to empathic experience.[17] For
Coplan, empathy always maintains proper distance between self and other;
"differentiation" is a necessary component of this dynamic.[18] In this way
Coplan stresses cognitive empathic attachments over emotive contagion
to create a firm distinction between what we can ostensibly control (cognition) and what we apparently can't (contagion). As to the latter Coplan
notes that contagion fails the empathy test because it does not retain the
figure of a differentiated self. "The presence of self-other differentiation in
empathy has a number of important effects," she argues. "First, it prevents

empathy-induced experiences from motivating the empathizer to act as though she is actually having the target's experiences. Second, it enables the empathizer to have her own separate experiences while simultaneously empathizing. Third, it enables the empathizer to observe the boundaries of the other as well as his- or herself and to respect the singularity of the other's experience as well as his or her own."[19] Coplan's differentiation-in-empathy maintains the integrity of the subject and object, especially as an ethics that respects the other. I would say only that such differentiation, while allowing for subjectivity only partially affected by emotional contagion, conceivably overvalues the very "separation" emotional empathy by definition undermines. I do not mean to split hairs, but the "loss" of self that differentiation precludes also *presumes* that self as the ground of this loss. More important for our purposes, these demarcations also open spaces between self and other that are too easily filled by a scaling up of industrial logic. The farther we reside from the object of our empathy— the more it is not "us," as it were—the more difficult it is to imagine. It's not without importance that Berry's affective economy operates in this gray area: "There is in fact no distinction between the fate of the land and the fate of the people. When one is abused, the other suffers."[20] On balance the boundary between self and other that Coplan notes is an ethical imperative—"empathizing with another does not entail that I take myself to be identical to another"—seems to me a good deal more permeable during emotive connection than her analysis suggests.[21] I bring up this tension between autonomy and loss only to dramatize in part the anxiety that hinges upon retaining boundaries that affective desires destabilize, perhaps to foreclose upon "cruelty" that inevitably follows.

The neuroscientist Antonio R. Damasio's work on the structure of consciousness is salient to this self-other discussion and, by extension, to the question of scale upon which Berry's economy in part depends. Damasio argues that "consciousness, as we commonly think of it, from its basic levels to its most complex, is the unified mental pattern that brings together the object and the self."[22] Distinctions between empathizer and object dissolve in the embodiment that characterizes the moment of feeling—which is also the moment of consciousness for Damasio—and help structure the self. One might say that the self is inevitably other. Consciousness is here likened to a process, a "feeling of a feeling," as Damasio says, one in which "the organism is involved in relating to some object, and ... the object in the relation is causing a change in the organism."[23] Damasio's consciousness-as-embodiment contrasts with the differentiation-in-empathy that Coplan locates as intrinsic to a proper understanding of a "mature" empathic experience. I think Berry's affective economics is closer to Damasio's embodiment than it is Coplan's differentiation. This is only to say that for Berry we have to pay attention to the abstractions of people from each other and from land, if only because the degradations inherent to large-scale agricultural capitalism depend upon them. As he notes, the further our economic practices are removed from the land, the more likely we are to engage in abusive practices through what he calls our "increasing abstraction and unconsciousness of our connection to our economic sources in the land, the land-communities, and the land-use economies."[24] The scaling up of industrial and agricultural capitalism consequently depends upon rigid boundaries, the dissociation of self from other and, one might say, from self—as if economic life were something distinct from basic cognitive/emotive mechanisms inherent to being human.[25]

The uncertainty through which the subject imagines the other through empathy is the place of ethics. Accordingly, in imagining, one does have to be careful about foreclosing on experiences and possibilities that can often range widely outside of our own. To put the matter differently, the compulsion toward ethics that I (and Berry) believe is inherent to cognitive and emotive empathy may make of you a mere satellite in my orbit. This explains in part Coplan's wariness over emotional contagion, and it is also why Suzanne Keen reminds us that empathizers ought to be cautious when reducing to universals those experiences that may mark deep cultural differences. As well, one must be ever present to the potential to silence a "subject who may or may not be empowered to speak for herself, to correct misconceptions about her feelings, and to refuse the pitying gaze."[26] With Coplan's and Keen's reservations and Paul Bloom's skepticism firmly in mind, I would say that in comparison with large-scale agricultural and industrial mechanisms of violence, the disparate turn toward empathy and affection on the part of President Obama and Wendell Berry offers a strategic alternative to the blandishments of a global ethic that by definition cannot imagine such connections.

It is difficult to say where affection begins and ends; indeed if "it all turns on affection," as Berry maintains, arriving at "it" through affection or sympathy or empathy is really an acknowledgment that ethics is always elsewhere. For Berry such an ethics understands first that living the local is one sure way to realize a truth that is always outside of itself. When it comes to affective economies, scale matters. If you wish to grasp "it," affection and imagination can take you part way while also highlighting the impossibility of ever knowing "it" in full immanence. Incarnation is both here and there, inside and outside—part of the self elsewhere. The big vision, the grand theory, the macroscopic approach provide *certainty*, but for Berry it is certainty bereft of feeling, bereft of attachment, and it thrives in the safety of distance. Apologists for global empathy invoke arenas of affection too easily imagined by other global materialisms, such as agricultural industrialism, such as war, whose affective ties are about as trustworthy as those of James B. Duke. Is it not curious therefore that our former "empathy president" deported more "illegal" immigrants than any president before him? President Obama would seem to have had a rather "cruel" attachment to what for him resided in the realm of ideas rather than in the imagination—as a clever rhetorical note operating as realpolitik rather than as a guiding ethical principle. Perhaps he didn't "feel" it. At this scale an affective ethics is only as good as what it may cost politically, and it doesn't even have to answer to lines of affection that must be traversed, experienced, and felt.

Finally, one might say that Berry's scene of "optimism," to invoke Berlant, is equally "cruel," that his investments in the local and in the place in which imagination and affection thrive have disappointment built into them. I would essentially agree with this assessment as long as we understand, too, that this very disenchantment is also and ever registered and enacted within a global industrial marketplace perpetually *divested* from the affection so important to local economic ties. Berlant puts it best: "The object that you thought would bring happiness becomes an object that deteriorates the conditions for happiness. But its presence represents *the possibility of happiness as such.* And so losing the bad object might be deemed worse than being destroyed by it. That's a relation of cruel optimism."[27] But if we also figure the place of optimism less as a scene of happiness or unhappiness and more as one that "unblocks" and separates us from optimistic fantasies—pulls the film from our eyes in a kind of "realism" that does not misrecognize our attachments[28]—then possibly we can embed ourselves in it, abjuring fantastic, global articulations of empathy whose tenuous bonds inevitably disappoint. I am not convinced at the last that affection and empathy move us toward altruistic or prosocial behavior as Obama suggests, nor do I find the empathic affections of the local as kindly as Berry intimates. However, if we are to invest ourselves in a politics in part dependent upon affection and imagination—and if we are prepared to face the cruelty that follows disappointments without recourse to grand imaginary objects of affection—we may find that local ties offer some modicum of resistance to the allurements of the global that may always exceed our grasp.

NOTES

1. The reference is to the primatologist Frans de Waal's *The Age of Empathy*. Responding to those who flirt with a discredited social Darwinist agenda, de Waal observes that "anyone looking for [a] rationale of how to structure society should realize that this [survival of the fittest] is only half the truth. It misses by a mile the intensely social nature of our species. Empathy is part of our evolution, and not just a recent part, but also an innate, age-old capacity. Relying on automated sensitivities to faces, bodies, and voices, humans empathize from day one" (205). De Waal is not without his critics, however. For instance, see Silk, "Fellow Feeling."

2. President Obama's repeated references to empathy formed a theme of his presidency, culminating (notoriously for conservatives) in his observation that empathy ought to be a principal characteristic of U.S. Supreme Court justices. In 2006 candidate Obama suggested that the country suffered from an "empathy deficit," as Patrick Healy reported in "Obama Meets Party Donors in NY," *New York Times*, December 5, 2006, http://www.nytimes.com/2006/12/05/us/politics/05obama.html. Like most deficits, this one has apparently been growing. President Obama's comments to the novelist Marilynne Robinson, as featured in the *New York Review of Books* in late 2015, recall his earlier musings on empathy and politics, though here he applies affective connection to the importance of fiction in humanizing us—another pervasive idea that sounds intuitive but isn't

entirely supported by evidence. Obama and Robinson, "Conversation in Iowa" (parts I and II). See Keen, *Empathy and the Novel*, for a thorough study of the relationship between empathy, literature, and prosocial action.

3. Patricia Clough calls the "affective turn" both a reaction to the "limitations of poststructuralism and deconstruction" and, what is more important, another important manifestation of the "subject's discontinuity with itself, a discontinuity of the subject's conscious experience with the non-intentionality of emotion and affect." Clough, "Affective Turn," 206. Clough further points to the importance of the body's "dynamism" and its ability for "self-organization" as elemental to the affective turn (207). Alternatively Ruth Leys understands the "affective turn" as based, in part, on recent advances in the "neurosciences of emotion" and their effects on a variety of disciplines. Her essay examines debates surrounding the "non-intentionalist" and "intentionalist" affective accounts in the sciences and social sciences over several decades. See Clough, "Affective Turn," 206–25; and Leys, "Turn to Affect," 434–72.

4. Berlant, "Cruel Optimism," 94 (original emphasis).

5. Initial drafts of this essay were composed prior to the publication of Paul Bloom's *Against Empathy: The Case for Rational Compassion*. I am aware of Bloom's several articles supporting a politics in which empathy plays at best a minor role in the public sphere.

6. Seigworth and Gregg, "Inventory of Shimmers," 3 (original emphasis).

7. Berry, *It All Turns on Affection*, 37 (original emphasis).

8. Berry, *It All Turns on Affection*, 14.

9. Berry, *It All Turns on Affection*, 14.

10. This appears to be what happened to Jenna Meredith in 2007 in the United Kingdom. As Krznaric reports, after her own home was flooded she visited Orissa, India, where residents had also experienced severe flooding and lost everything. "Jenna was overwhelmed by her face-to-face meeting with the villagers in Orissa," Krznaric writes. Roman Krznaric, "Empathy and Climate Change: Proposals for a Revolution in Human Relationships," 1, http://www.romankrznaric.com/wp-content/uploads/2011/12/Empathy%20and%20Climate%20Change%20Krznaric.pdf. Krznaric suggests that such experiences are important if we in the West are to "generate empathy on a large scale" and "bring about major social change." "Tackling climate change," he writes, "requires nothing less than a revolution of the empathic imagination" (2).

11. Zaki, "Choosing Empathy."

12. Berry, *It All Turns on Affection*, 13.

13. Berry, *It All Turns on Affection*, 13.

14. Berry, *It All Turns on Affection*, 10.

15. Berry, *It All Turns on Affection*, 30–31.
16. Berry, *It All Turns on Affection*, 32.
17. Coplan, "Empathic Engagement with Narrative Fictions," 145.
18. Coplan, "Empathic Engagement with Narrative Fictions," 144.
19. Coplan, "Empathic Engagement with Narrative Fictions," 144.
20. Berry, *It All Turns on Affection*, 18.
21. Coplan, "Empathic Engagement with Narrative Fictions," 144.
22. Damasio, *Feeling of What Happens*, 11.
23. Damasio, *Feeling of What Happens*, 133.
24. Berry, *It All Turns on Affection*, 23.
25. Religious life may offer another interesting parallel to Berry's affective economics and Damasio's melding of subject and object. The social psychologist Jonathan Haidt notes that "religious experiences often involve decreased activity in brain areas that maintain maps of the self's boundaries and position, consistent with widespread reports that mystical experiences involve feelings of merging with God or the universe." Haidt, "New Synthesis in Moral Psychology," 1001.
26. Keen, *Empathy and the Novel*, 162.
27. Berlant, "On Her Book *Cruel Optimism*" (original emphasis).
28. Berlant, "On Her Book *Cruel Optimism*."

BIBLIOGRAPHY

Berlant, Lauren. "Cruel Optimism." In *The Affect Theory Reader*, edited by Melissa Gregg and Gregory J. Seigworth, 93–117. Durham: Duke University Press, 2010.

———. "On Her Book *Cruel Optimism*." *Rorotoko*, June 5, 2012. http://rorotoko.com/interview/20120605_berlant_lauren_on_cruel_optimism/.

Berry, Wendell. *It All Turns on Affection: The Jefferson Lecture and Other Essays*. Berkeley CA: Counterpoint, 2012.

Bloom, Paul. *Against Empathy: The Case for Rational Compassion*. New York: Ecco, 2016.

Clough, Patricia T. "The Affective Turn: Political Economy, Biomedia, and Bodies." In *The Affect Theory Reader*, edited by Melissa Gregg and Gregory J. Seigworth, 206–25. Durham: Duke University Press, 2010.

Coplan, Amy. "Empathic Engagement with Narrative Fictions." *Journal of Aesthetics and Art Criticism* 62, no. 2 (Spring 2004): 141–52.

Damasio, Antonio R. *The Feeling of What Happens: Body and Emotion in the Making of Consciousness*. New York: Mariner, 2000.

de Waal, Frans. *The Age of Empathy: Nature's Lessons for a Kinder Society*. New York: Three Rivers, 2010.

Haidt, Jonathan. "The New Synthesis in Moral Psychology." *Science* 316, no. 5827 (May 18, 2007): 998–1002.

Keen, Suzanne. *Empathy and the Novel*. New York: Oxford University Press, 2010.

Leys, Ruth. "The Turn to Affect: A Critique." *Critical Inquiry* 37 (Spring 2011): 434–72.

Obama, Barack, and Marilynne Robinson. "A Conversation in Iowa [part I]." *New York Review of Books* 62, no. 17 (November 5, 2015): 4, 6, 8.

———. "A Conversation in Iowa [part II]." *New York Review of Books* 62, no. 18 (November 19, 2015): 6, 8.

Seigworth, Gregory J., and Melissa Gregg. "An Inventory of Shimmers." In *The Affect Theory Reader*, edited by Melissa Gregg and Gregory J. Seigworth, 1–25. Durham: Duke University Press, 2010.

Silk, Joan. "Fellow Feeling." Review of *The Age of Empathy: Nature's Lessons for a Kinder Society*, by Frans de Waal. *American Scientist*, March–April 2010. http://www.americanscientist.org/bookshelf/pub/fellow-feeling.

Zaki, Jamil. "Choosing Empathy: A Conversation with Jamil Zaki." *The Edge*, October 20, 2015. https://www.edge.org/conversation/jamil_zaki-choosing-empathy.

6

A Hunger for Words
Food Affects and Embodied Ideology

TOM HERTWECK

Ecocriticism has always had a kinship with food studies. After all—with certain rare exceptions—humans must get their food from the nonhuman world, and so food culture has maintained good relations with the (agri)cultural experience of turning resources into the energy of human progress. And yet the linkages between these two areas of concern remain diffuse, food studies always being welcomed but never quite fitting neatly within the realm of ecocriticism proper, owing in large part to ecocritique's text-based criticism and food studies' highly anthropological and sociological foci.[1]

The recent expansion and application of affect theory from psychology into cultural studies poses a compelling way to interrogate more meaningfully our so-called gut ecocritical instincts about food. At the same time, food affect in general has been little studied.[2] The taking up of both inquiries simultaneously, however, suggests not only how tightly imbricated these two ideas are but also the extent to which becoming attuned to the affect of food choices can illuminate affect studies and ecocriticism. In this chapter I present a theory of affective eating that understands food as *embodied ideology*. This model takes seriously the drive that is hunger as established by Silvan Tomkins, the foundational psychological affect theorist. Simultaneously it reorients our thinking about contemporary forms of eating under the regime of multinational capitalism that confounds and dissipates the naturalized hunger drive and instead places emphasis on the discursive reality of food that precedes the act of eating in the marketplace. As we focus on the manufactured (and affective) discourses of foods rather than some nonspecific or mystically external notion of foods themselves, the environmental implications are difficult to ignore: in the space between feeling and market rationality, eaters engage the use of resources in better and worse ways based on what their previous experience tells them about products and through the intervention of texts that force them to audit the very information that differentiates one product from another. In this fraught way foods' textual representation becomes the battleground where producers fight the inelastic demand of hunger to spur further consumption, the result of which is a host of negative environmental effects—produced from seemingly positive affects.

Embodied Ideology

While a full delineation of affect as an embodied ideology is not possible in a work of this length, it is nonetheless possible to sketch the idea's boundaries in brief so as to explain its import to ecocriticism. To that end, food's production of affect as an embodied ideology emerges from a two-part process. First, it understands food as different from its usual presentation as a material form of sustenance or a symbolic repository and instead as a merger of both notions that is ultimately mediated by food's discursive reality in the marketplace. Second, it understands that the process of food consumption—in both market and bodily terms—is an act that proceeds from physiological hunger (as a baseline) that responds to the webs of affective discourses used to compel the subject to eat.[3]

THE DISCURSIVE REALITY OF FOOD

Food is difficult to rethink for precisely the same reasons it should be so appealing to ecocritics: it takes something external to the subject and literally transforms it through the mechanism of digestion into a part of the body and powers the subject's life and thinking. In short it brings the world inside and makes it a part of us. This is why any discussion of food can turn contentious, because to be implicated in acts of "bad" eating risks marking the bad eater as a bad person. Not just energy transfers here, but also a morality—as the old aphorism goes, we are what we eat.[4] This commitment to metaphysics explicitly and implicitly surrounds us every time we take a bite throughout the day, every day. Given the insistent necessity and regularity of eating, however, it seems grievously unfair to expect every single eater to be conscious and deliberative in regard to every single ethical, philosophical, economic, social, or nutritional position to which they are committing themselves.

At the same time, given the experience of eating in the modern world, with its esoteric processed foods and the unavoidable systems of advertising and delivery, such a conscious commitment is also impossible to make. Humans cannot sense without aid of scientific instruments the contents of processed foods, so commodity paratext—all the systems of writing, data, and other food labeling that mark how a food should be used and what qualities it has—takes the place of our sensory abilities. Moreover many processed foods do not present the characteristic of "edibility," making commodity paratext required to signal that the thing contained by packaging is indeed food. (Consider the Twinkie: had you never had one described via packaging images and text, would you eat it? Many who have still won't eat them, claiming they aren't food.) Furthermore, as global systems of food provisioning have access to a greater variety of foodstuffs than at any other point in history, supermarkets receive from around the world and display exotic foods (processed, as well as unfamiliar whole foods), some so curious that only their contextual appearance in a grocery store would mark them as foods to consumers of a particular region. Our general wealth of food options in the industrialized world is also a source of great frustration to everyday eaters.

Such a problem is not unknown. The food writer Michael Pollan explored this issue anecdotally in his best-selling *Omnivore's Dilemma: A Natural History of Four Meals* (2006). As Pollan explains, humans, by virtue of their omnivorous—if not to say promiscuous—eating capabilities, require an apparatus to help aid in the daily struggle to eat to wellness and also not poison ourselves. Pollan writes, "Our culture codifies the rules of wise eating in an elaborate structure of taboos, rituals, recipes, manners, and culinary traditions that keep us from having to reenact the omnivore's dilemma at every meal."[5] Unlike, say, koalas, which eat only eucalyptus leaves all day long and do not seek out other options, humans pass down information (in more distant history) in story or (lately) construct buildings to demarcate that which is good to eat. Of greater interest to Pollan, however, are the more recent technological innovations in eating that have arisen as a result of modern industrialized food production, which covers over pesticide-ridden farms with cartoon renderings of happy farmers toiling near red barns, transforms traditional staple foods into unrecognizable shapes and fortifies them with extracted and abstracted nutrients, and commits untold ethical crimes against workers and animals, slaughtered in the millions via automation, all in an attempt to increase consumption and profit.

The story is all too familiar to any reader already interested in thinking about what they eat. Pollan spends the majority of his book worrying somewhat emptily over the relative "goodness" of the meals he describes.[6] However, the literary-critical point that can be gleaned implicitly from the work is important: food today is the sum of the language and textual apparatuses we construct not only to help us remember what is simply edible but to consider more carefully whether or not we are eating well. One of the examples Pollan uses in many of his public lectures, the "cereal straw," little resembles anything we would have recognized as a food even a decade ago. As a technological advance, though, it is a marvel, transforming cheap cereal grains into a brightly colored, milk-solid-lined gimmick in order to charge more for staple ingredients because they are now "value-added" products. The point here is not that such a development is a mass deception—though much of it is, as Pollan and numerous food writers have pointed out—but rather that *all* food today is attached to a complex system of signification that constitutes food's reality. Would one know a cereal straw was a food, or how it should be used, or why one should even care, without its commodity paratext? Likely not. Such is the era in which we live now. This paratextual presence, from simple words and phrases to entire narrative marketing campaigns, necessarily engages affective energies.

In *First as Tragedy, Then as Farce*, the cultural theorist Slavoj Žižek's analysis of "cultural capitalism"—the practice he describes as augmenting banal consumer choices with the purchase of social good beyond the price of the commodity itself—illustrates well this increased attention to the discursive reality of foods by describing the common experience of choosing an organic apple in the grocery store. He writes, "Who really believes that half-rotten and overpriced 'organic' apples are really healthier than the non-organic varieties? The point is that, in buying them, we are not merely buying and consuming, we are simultaneously doing something meaningful, showing our capacity for care and our global awareness, participating in a collective project."[7] Žižek asserts rightly that capitalism now contains the cost of some form of altruism in the prices of commodities themselves as an attempt to ameliorate now-widespread knowledge of and guilt over the ills global capitalism wreaks. What is just as striking and that is left merely implied is that the value of "organic" in an apple, while having a material footprint and a specific history of production, is to the consumer an entirely discursive reality. People cannot taste "organic" or in any other way sense the presence of one kind of pesticide or fertilizer on their own: organic and conventional apples are for all intents and purposes interchangeable in the marketplace, and it is simply the label and our belief that labels are true that create a critical difference between them for the consumer. Language determines the commodity's reality.[8] For the consumer wanting information about ingredients (e.g., gluten, animal products) or productive means (e.g., pesticides, fair trade), the intervention of text is essential. And while a critic might suggest that market forces vis-à-vis advertising are themselves responsible for the very choices that complicate our lives—that the complications of food labeling create food capitalism's hegemony—this terrain of textual presence is the reality of supermarket shopping today: the grocery store is a discursive textual archive in which we all dwell.

THE HUNGER DRIVE AND AFFECTIVE AMPLIFICATION

The affective implications contained in Žižek's microanalysis are made even clearer in a public lecture based on his book. In that lecture he remarks on the connection between discursive reality and affective appeals to one's hunger without explicitly calling it affectivity. Ever the proponent of psychoanalytic thought, he implores his listeners, "Look deep into yourself. I don't think you really believe you think those apples are really any better. I claim that we are cynics there, we are skeptics. But you know, it makes you *feel warm*. I am doing something for our Mother Earth, I'm doing something for our planet."[9] Irrespective of whether we believe in the value of organic commodities over conventional ones, it is certainly the case that dominant discourses about foods dictate organic is a good—moral, environmental, nutritional—choice, and therefore selecting it provides an affective charge we metaphorically understand as warmth. As a result, we begin to see how Žižek illustrates food choice operating in affective terms. Hunger, a universal human experience, presents itself affectively and needily. We then enter into the market where our choices rather than the foods themselves have the potential to provide happiness as much or even more than sating the bodily need to eat.

The trouble with taking food this way is that hunger itself is not an affect but rather a drive—a state of affairs that goes some way toward explaining why precious little work has been done on food affects. At the same time, the casting of food into affective networks of bodily thought is possible and necessary for cultural studies in order to help us understand the individual's experience of choosing foods that have become mediated by their discursive realities. This, as we will see later, has even more important implications for ecocritical cultural studies. More immediately, hunger needs to be cast as an energetic force in and among the affects from which cultural work can proceed.

Hunger is quite obviously a feeling. We palpably register its pangs; more than this, we have a robust, intuitive, almost diagnostic knowledge of how to read others' emotional states as resulting from hunger. The recent proliferation of the portmanteau *hangry*, which describes the emotional state of some people's experience of low blood sugar, for example, perfectly illustrates the merger of the physiological-metabolic drive for calories (hunger) and affective response that attends it (anger/rage). As such, it should come as no surprise that in his foundational work on affects, the four-volume *Affect Imagery Consciousness*, Silvan Tomkins addresses this curious reality head on, as well as in an implied threaded narrative in which food seems to act almost as a living character in humans' affective realities.[10] Tomkins is quite clear, however, that hunger is not to be counted among the nine affects he defines but is rather a *drive*, which he explains is low-level biological information, most frequently about the movement of materials in and out of the body. At the same time, however, the relationship between drives and affects is less clear than this conceptual separation would seem. "The drive system is," Tomkins writes,

> secondary to the affect system. Much of the motivational power of the drive system is borrowed from the affect system, which is ordinarily activated concurrently as an amplifier for the drive signal. The affect system is, however, capable of masking or even inhibiting the drive signal and of being activated independently of the drive system by a broad spectrum of stimuli, learned and unlearned.... [The affect] system is the primary provider of blueprints for cognition, decision and action. The human being's ability to duplicate and reproduce himself is guaranteed not only by a responsiveness to drive signals but by a responsiveness to whatever circumstances activate positive and negative affect.[11]

This schema upends what had been until then the traditional orientation of drives as the primary motivational force in humans. Instead Tomkins, rather than reversing the order of operation, expresses drive's motivational power precisely in terms of affect: "the biological drives have motivational impact only when amplified by the affective system."[12] This conjoined emotional motivation usually involves taking some sort of action; in hunger terms this almost always results in consumption for satiation (pleasure) of diminishing the negative drive-affect machinery, which will become central to the environmental impacts discussed below.

Both of these systems, merged with our individual personal histories—which one might reasonably call learning—constitute the realm of emotion. Accordingly, affectivity establishes the central activity-based element of our experience with the world and orients our ability to want to choose among and between foods. The point of departure for the cultural theorist of affect is the degree of separation between drive and affect. First, drives are innate and are not learned; one does not learn to be hungry. Second, drives are abstract and nonspecific; hunger, properly speaking, is a signal to eat but does not say what or even very clearly how much. The affects fill this separation by being the learned, expressive response to choices. To the extent that emotional knowledge catalogs personal history about one's feelings, we can begin to parse the ways that individuals and even whole societies become habituated to certain cultures of food feeling. In this view history as such no longer provides the sole metaphysical inertia as to why certain peoples eat what they eat. Affect's bodily knowledge does. Pushing this thought further, then, we can begin to see an expression of food affect that emerges as ideological. Hunger in this more robust, affective way oscillates between metabolic and cultural need, pulling both needs together within it. Consider the colloquial ways of speaking about food that show how we learn and unlearn food desire all the time: "Beer is an acquired taste," "Eat this—it's good for you," "Only poor people eat that crap," "Black people love watermelon and fried chicken," and so on. Each time one speaks about food, the speaker disciplines others' behavior and reaffirms one's own sense that what he or she does and does not eat is right and good. Plainly, as these examples show, not all this knowledge is objectively true, helpful, or nonracist. However, each emerges over time as bodily (not absolutely) true, from "gut instincts" that are a mixture of acquired discourses from reliable or dubious sources and from our own hard-wired sense of what foods we love and disdain.

Taken together as affective and responding to the discursive reality of food culture, hunger in our contemporary moment is far more richly social and mediated an experience than the stimulus-response-action circuitry that Tomkins would hold steady in order to explain affects themselves. If anything, the internal stimulus of food affect only reopens the omnivore's dilemma. After all, as Tomkins's disciple Donald Nathanson describes in the prologue to Tomkins's work, "Affect is motivating but never localizing; the experience of affect tells us only that something needs our attention. Other systems must be engaged in order to decide what must be done and how."[13] Eaters after the advent of processed and globalized foods must constantly negotiate not only the discursive apparatuses of commodity paratext that proclaim what a food is and how it should be used but also a variety of competing public and specialist discourses from nutrition ("lower your cholesterol"), environmentalism ("buy organic"), social justice ("buy fair-trade products"), food safety ("be sure it's pasteurized"), to simple economy ("save when you buy in bulk").[14] Instead it is through and among cultural mechanisms—the "other systems," which include rational and nonrational thought—that food affect is directed or manufactured.

Food Affect and Consumption

What food-and-affect work exists uses to some extent this discursive ideological conditioning as a way to interrogate eating's bodily knowledge that, while not always factually true, nonetheless conditions what and how we eat. In the most sustained engagement, Elspeth Probyn's *Carnal Appetites*, the use of affect instantiates a foundational metaphoric-energetic relation between how we talk about and represent food, especially food that rises to culinary art, to establish and trouble relations between sexes, races, nationality, and identity. An excellent introduction to the possibilities of food affect, Probyn's work uses affect as a mode of representational consolidation, a strategy that allows for psychoanalytic readings of numerous cultural texts. Likewise, Ben Highmore uses our sense of taste as a metaphor for reading broad-based social aesthetics, suggesting that cultural intermingling and gatekeeping happen in scenes of "sensual pedagogy," which can be literal meals or simply discourses that legitimate cultural values.[15] Lauren Berlant's discussion of obesity in *Cruel Optimism* seemingly extends this position as it describes how post–Cold War America sought to increase consumption in developed nations while simultaneously creating a cultural-value narrative that labeled the overweight as morally bad in order to consolidate state control and undermine individual sovereignty.[16] What unites these forms of affective cultural criticism—not to mention those of other important affect theorists such as Sara Ahmed and Brian Massumi, though to a lesser extent—is the simultaneous connectivity with and distancing from the literal body. These theorists rightly affirm that the body is a site that requires acknowledgment of its propensities but from which they depart to return to more familiar symptomatic-ideological critique. In this manner they use affect more as a propulsive for questioning how ideological positions are maintained and directed through largely metaphoric transference of the affects. There is nothing wrong with such an approach, especially inasmuch as it aligns more cleanly with established disciplinary practices in critical theory, and the work of such an approach pays off immensely. At the same time, however, there are other critics who double down on the body's affective potentialities. The work of scholars such as Sianne Ngai and the late Teresa Brennan has taken a more thoroughgoing basis for their affective-ideological critique.

Ngai's major works exemplify the kind of criticism one can expect within the more bodily inflected perspective I advocate. Her *Ugly Feelings*, which accounts for the philosophical position of negative-affective experiences of modern life, not only includes passing mentions of food (the experience of disgust in Nella Larsen's novel *Quicksand* that ties the feeling to racial conflict, for example) but also lays groundwork for reconfiguring our notions of "bad feeling" as an essential and undervalued component of desire. Even more pointedly, though, Ngai's assertion of the value of her intellectual labors in *Our Aesthetic Categories* sounds a clarion call for reaffirming the body/conceptual unity of food affectivity when she summarizes her objects of study as "the circulation of information, the consumption of commodities, and the becoming-labor of performance."[17] Each of these aspects constitutes a part of the domain of food's appearance, organization, and narration under capital, as (respectively) competing discourses about what one should eat, the material foods themselves in marketplaces, and the assertion of a certain identity or value system manifest when making choices. Add to this the bodily drive of hunger that many of her own wholly aesthetic objects of study do not invoke, and one sees the emergence of new intellectual terrain. The invitation the work extends to increase the number of categories would fit well within a food studies frame, with *tasty*, *healthy*, and *gross* as merely the most obvious initial candidates. Ngai's focus on the aesthetic artifacts of the culture industry would do much to extend the work of cultural criticism but while also calling attention to these artifacts within the cultures of feeling that make them potent, energetic points of convergence for food's bodily work. At the same time, reassessing or transcending the aesthete's incessant focus on beauty, Ngai nonetheless opens a space for the contemporary commonality of food as a banal object of contemplation, as well as economic and bodily consumption.

Perhaps unsurprisingly one suspects that lurking around the edges of the more cultural-ideological affect theorists is an understandable affect-determinism phobia. However, Brennan's *Transmission of Affect* proves to be an important and often overlooked work that establishes the foundational play of the affects without devolving into human determinism. *Transmission* systematizes an affective critique that is a true "resurrection of the body" in theory, and it requires thinking of bodies as collective producers of affect that do not rigidly produce *meaning* in isolation but instead aid in the production of *consciousness*, a term that entails a great deal more than simple awareness and something more like a holistic "logic of life."[18] Brennan's Lacanian-Marxist approach approves of chaos (liveliness) over regulatory regimes, while also taking seriously the way in which bodies are themselves regulated and how they variously empower and interrupt thought. By tracking hormones, pheromones and olfaction, and maternal effects, as well as cataloging an immense cache of scientific literature on other forms of "bodily knowledge," Brennan expresses a holistic model of the affects that name their cultural roles in changing human biology, the opposite of the accepted neo-Darwinian view held by more strictly genetic thinkers. Introducing her new paradigm, she writes, "What is at stake with the notion of the transmission of affect is precisely the opposite of the sociobiological claim that the biological *determines* the social. What is at stake is rather the means by which social interaction shapes biology."[19]

Ecocritics should be particularly sympathetic to this position. After all, they are well aware of the inherent (productive) messiness that makes up so much of ecological science, and they labor under the assumption that bodies exist, matter, and are governed by complex systems that we do not yet fully understand and that those systems are subject to external stimuli ranging from beauty, to chemicals that bioaccumulate, to nonhuman animals that share the planet with us. This chaotic rendering of life coincides with Brennan's view of the affects and Ngai's interventions into the cultures they produce—and also makes sense in the supermarket. As many who attempt to study the desires manifest in human shopping point out, the "unmanageable consumer" is not nearly as controllable as global producers would like to think.[20] Not only does unmanageability make sense in the context of Brennan's argument about the affects and horde of examples Ngai catalogs, but it also obtains by avoiding food consumption determinism. Because of the increasing complexity (variety) and abstraction (processing and innovation) of the food marketplace, consumers are less controllable than ever and more subject to their individual needs and whims.

Focusing on the body more directly proposes an initial focus on positive affects, as those affects are the ones that spur consumption. The promise of happiness—consolidated from the promises of politics, nutrition, kinship care, long life, novelty, and so on, suggested by foods' paratext—is so common as to need little explanation: any food enjoins you to be happy. A more deeply embodied variant of Sara Ahmed's cultural "happiness duty," however, the desire for happiness emanates from the internal, as much as if not more than from the cultural external.[21] Just look at any baby being offered different foods, or consider a rat in a study: food preferences correlate with pleasure and can be isolated and replicated.[22] More strangely, pleasure's inverse (disgust) can become a transmuted source of pleasure. Current "gross-out culture" transforms disgust into a form of enjoyment, from the superlative flavors of Tear Jerkers sour gum or Scandinavian salt licorices, to the hottest of ghost peppers, to gag-inducing fermented foods consumed in something like gastrointestinal feats of strength—not to mention the increasing numbers of spectators of and entrants into food-eating competitions like the Nathan's Hot Dog Eating Contest, held every Fourth of July.[23] Food commodities are moved off shelves for the affective work we expect them to do, as well as for the affective needs they can drum up that need servicing. Only white-package generics avoid this, but even they become part of a pride-affective narrative of thrift. The fact that they are becoming increasingly difficult to find in grocery stores shows how important developing overt affective energy is for contemporary consumption.

The primary mechanism for producing food commodity affects is the one with which I began this chapter and that symptomatically aggregates food affect's embodied ideology: food commodity paratext. Not only do commodities signal the usual abstract ideological discourses through language, but they also determine their place in the market and within the consumer's felt identity. As the computational linguist Dan Jurafsky has pointed out, language signals, among other things, levels of distinction (à la Bourdieu) for which specific discursive moves—lists of ingredients a potato chip does *not* contain, for example—can rationalize increased costs by engaging an eater's class or desire for worldly change in the same way Žižek describes. This parallels and shifts the focus of Massumi's explicitly affective linguistics-based theory of the virtual. In this case the comparison is more than simply suggestive when Massumi writes, "As vitally as food, a life feeds on habits, memories, and tropisms."[24] Jurafsky's work therefore suggests the possibility of a "virtual hunger" presented by menus, advertising, and packaging that the chaotic, specific, and ir/rational subject's responses to affect can cajole into a literal hunger (agential desire) for justice, nostalgia, community, freedom, weight loss, and the like. Moreover, as a number of studies have pointed out, the synesthetic capacities of the brain in processing language and images have the ability to create hunger, even in the absence of any actual food or metabolic need.[25] As anyone who has ever listened in hungry envy to the detailed description of someone else's better dessert knows, rhapsodic language can muster a curious feeling of hunger despite one's lack of any actual need for more sugar.

But a potentially more striking feature of food affect, one on which food producers regularly capitalize, is the extent to which food itself can become implicated in producing its own desire. In this case some food ingredients have such a powerful force on affective-neurological systems that they can turn the natural (bodily) desire for food on its head and rewire body chemistry. Unlike when a person exhibits gluttony (usually figured as a moral wrong knowingly indulged), the presence in foods of certain chemicals—such as monosodium glutamate (MSG, only the most notorious example)—short-circuits the brain's ability to feel full. Meanwhile the taste-enhancing properties are so strong that they entice the eater to keep eating. Add to that the trinity of salt, fat, and sugar that compose traditional "comfort foods," and one can see how products like Doritos flavored tortilla chips, as food writers like Michael Moss have detailed, are purposely built to be consumed almost mindlessly, that is, consumed without the help of neurological hunger inputs (drive) and solely affectively.[26] If anything, this idea of "tastiness" is precisely the same sort of aesthetic category that Ngai's work establishes as essential to affect studies. Foods live and die in the marketplace by their ability to establish tastiness, since consumers are generally unable to sample products in the supermarket. Conversely tastiness looms over foods designated as healthful by describing to the reader-eater that the sacrifice in taste is worth it (by omission of taste language in exchange for full-throated health-benefit claims) or that the food performs some sort of miracle by being both healthful *and* tasty ("tastes great, less filling!" or "all the flavor but half the fat!"). Within this complex economy of images, text, neural overload, and latent physiological hunger, we see the ways that food affect can be manipulated through any number of channels to spur consumption that is separate from the body's usual mechanisms of hunger valuation. But the mistake would be to begin to mark such forms of consumption as "unnatural" because this would presume that at some point in human history there was a moment of naturalized hunger affect. Such gimmicks sell diet programs and cookbooks, and these (Paleo, the Maker's Diet, etc.) are rife with affective ideological power. Our moment is dominated by multinational grocery capitalism, and under this regime the manipulation of food affect to the ends of increased consumption is the generalized state of affairs as it is now: overconsumption.

Overconsumption has become generalized alongside the industrial development of food affect for commoditized foods. The telling detail is the concurrent development of a psychological diagnosis for food addiction, in which one's use of food to modify brain chemistry to trigger the release of dopamine, the neurotransmitter associated with pleasure, mirrors the use of other addictives. Despite being described by the psychological community in the 1950s, food addiction has only lately become a diagnosable condition in the recently revised *Diagnostic and Statistical Manual of Mental Disorders* (*DSM-5*), an unsurprising turn of events in this era of insistent consumption.[27] Any food with high potential for generating cravings (chocolate, cheese, etc.) can possess well-known addictive qualities. So strong is the power of some of these foods to rewire and overwhelm the brain that research indicates the same neural pathways for pleasure triggered by these foods are those used by morphine and its analogs, and interest in food can be affected by opiate blockers like naloxone.[28] In short, food addiction is an affective disorder inasmuch as the food addict becomes fixated on producing the affective experience provided by eating, as a part of the hunger experience but also distinct from it. What the understanding of food affect's work on all psyches and not just those who fall into overconsumption in a pathological way begins to suggest, however, is that we are all to one degree or another open to becoming addicts to food such that we are all subject to the intensification of food affect as a result of food's marketplace, that we are all eating our feelings. Simply put, affective overconsumption leads to the overuse of the land, materials, labor, and energy along the entire chain of production and as such marks food culture—and especially value-added processed foods that necessarily rely on paratext—to be an affective environmental problem.[29]

This is a familiar Marxist argument, to be sure, in that food production in our world serves to produce still more consumption. And, to be sure, the idea of eating more simply in ways that avoid resource-intensive agricultural and production is difficult to imagine now that the Pandora's box of processed food has been opened. But the twist of affectivity's inclusion is that it places some of the burden of such rapid, incessant consumption squarely—bodily—within the eater, not in abstract moral terms but in the sense that eaters themselves are responsible for attending to the mangled affective terms of their hunger desire. Responsibility, however, is not the same thing as blame. If anything, food affect provides a starting point for rethinking our entire relationship with food. Based on the research of how our bodily hunger is manipulable by industry as well as our own responses to affects that are and are not our own, food affect is a new addition that locates an actual conduit between market and consumer, between foods and our hunger desire. That conduit proceeds directly through conceptual issues about hunger that should not be ignored.[30] Nor should such issues—via agriculture and industrial processing—be ignored as there are increasingly important environmental questions regarding pesticide use, food sovereignty, resource extraction, the consolidation of power in making food choices (which are always land-based choices as well), good values for energy consumption in the raising and processing of food commodities, our ethical relationships with nonhuman animals and their uses in and as foods, and more, to say nothing of the extent to which food choices in the industrialized world ripple out into less-sovereign communities in the developing world. Being able to take account of the contentious and too frequently unexamined emotional matrices of thought that guide our deliberation on such a subject will be more than essential.

A single essay on food affect could never say all there is to say about the idea. Nonetheless, it is possible to see from even this brief outline that affective discourses of food commodities make possible the circulation and maintenance of food's political economy. And inasmuch as the affects that amplify (aid and abet) responses to food's discursive reality spur material metabolic need, we begin to see how food shows us affect as an embodied form of ideology, differentiating it from traditional, entirely external forms of ideology that cultural theorists spend considerable time tracking. Food affect thus describes tidily its dual character. On the one hand we understand through affect theory why food takes such a central place under late capitalism in that food's unknowable and imperceptible character is mediated by individual negotiations with competing (in ultimately market-based terms) discourses about foods and the subject's desire to address drive-affective signals. Affects urge us toward feeding our bodies, but also our sense of self, our communities, and our own moral calculus. On the other hand we understand through food that affect theory can richly inform everyday—in fact seemingly banal—aspects of our culture, affirming and strengthening the argument of affective-cultural theorists that the discursive realities of ideology are housed within bodies that have needs that institutions (from official state offices and discourses to food packaging and folkways) are constantly attempting to understand through language. Along these lines, food affect's existence as an embodied ideology challenges the notion that ideology is only ever imposed through external mechanisms, or, conversely, our base desires give rise to restrictively deterministic forms of existence. It should be comforting and empowering that it is neither and both of these cases and that continued critical explorations of the reproduction of culture will be necessary to reassess shifting power dynamics that tell us what is good to eat and why.

Indeed once we attune ourselves to this enmeshed notion of embodied ideology as a way of seeing food affect the ecocritical implications become clear. Rather than insist upon merely meliorist changes to intractable regimes over which individuals have little power, we can better understand the mechanisms by which people listen to their stomachs as they reach for their wallet and vote with their dollars for commoditized forms of resource use. More than the old truism—which is frequently used as a term for things we have largely given up on—that capitalism produces its consumers' desire (environmental damage be damned), theorizing food affect in this way allows us to recognize how our bodies indeed produce true desires—not rational, not irrational, but nonrational—but that those desires engage, conflict, and assess forms of knowledge that recirculate within the body's affective mechanisms and return again also bodily true. In other words the point is not to blame someone who loves, say, strawberries—arguably the most resource intensive, pesticide laden, and migrant-labor exploitative mainstream agricultural commodity—for their bad environmentalism and social injustice. Environmental thought has for too long wasted unnecessary energy chastising behaviors that *feel* right. Instead, affective environmental politics could include the habit of acknowledging the Pandoran desire made possible by global markets—say, the relatively recent development of having strawberries in grocery stores all year—and casting a valued counternarrative that thinks through the consumer's desire and the discourses that produce it. We might respect the fact that the affective payoff of wanting and eating a strawberry is a very real thing. Once that thing exists, it can't be taken back; it effervesces in a body that is separate from systems of marketing and advertising, while also being caned onward by forces of capital that exploit such truths in order to consolidate wealth in the hands of people seeking to control markets. Somewhere between the truth of the body and the injunctions of the culture industry, the devil of embodied ideology worth exorcising is in the details.

1. Happily of course this has been changing. And admittedly agricultural history fills this gap to a degree; however, given the various institutional cosmogenies and scholarly organizations for food studies (anthropology, sociology, history, and the Association for the Study of Food and Society, founded in 1985), ecocriticism (English—especially American literature, and the Association for the Study of Literature and Environment, 1992), and agricultural history (history proper, and the Agricultural History Society, 1919), one can see no real need to interlope lest one consciously heed the recent calls for increasing interdisciplinarity.

2. Elspeth Probyn's excellent *Carnal Appetites* is the sole book-length treatment; Ben Highmore's fine contribution to the *Affect Theory Reader* and Lauren Berlant's parallel discussion of obesity in *Cruel Optimism* are the exceptions that prove the rule.

3. Although I would distance myself from the omnibus critical position that goes by the name of speculative realism/object-oriented ontology/new materialism that might attend this because of its often haphazard (though not in every case) deployment, the view I espouse here nonetheless shares a number of affinities with the best of the good work, including Jane Bennett's useful discussion of food and materiality in *Vibrant Matter*, particularly her view that food is a "self-altering, dissipative materiality" that "enters into what we become" and that is "operative in the moods, cognitive dispositions, and moral sensibilities" (51). Such a position is surely affective and eschews the mysticism (she calls it "soul" [xvii]) I also seek to avoid.

4. It is obligatory that one of the earliest modern works of literary gastronomy, Jean Anthelme Brillat-Savarin's *Physiologie du goût, ou Méditations de gastronomie transcendante* [The physiology of taste, or transcendental gastronomy] (1826) instantiates this line of thinking explicitly when it says, "Dis-moi ce que tu manges: je te dirai ce que tu es" (viii) [Tell me what you eat: I will tell you who you are], as well as connecting food culture to cultures of feeling. As we shall see, the telling—that is, discourse—is central to this kind of understanding.

5. Pollan, *Omnivore's Dilemma*, 4.

6. There is a bourgeois air to the work, though his books and public speaking since are far more egalitarian.

7. Žižek, *First as Tragedy*, 54.

8. Such a vision of reality contains numerous complications, as in the widespread practice of organic farmers off-selling entire lots of organic produce that are then sold as conventional due to market fluctuations (usually an oversupply of organic produce as more farmers attempt to enter the market, as in the case of British organic lamb nearly a decade ago). In these cases where the organic label is not

present, some consumers would actively avoid what is in actuality an organic product. The commodity paratext makes a real-world difference.

9. Žižek, "First as Tragedy."

10. Tomkins's threaded food narrative is ripe for lengthy discussion all on its own, especially inasmuch as it begins to feed the diagnostic power of his later script theory. For the purposes of this essay I focus primarily on the explanation of the drive-affect relationship in the first volume of his work (note that the collected work's page numbers are sequential and so do not require complicated volume/page citations). Simply put, the experience of reading food and responding to the hunger drive and amplified affective impulses is not an individual or social dysfunction (except in the most cynical terms) but rather the common experience of eating today.

11. Tomkins, *Affect Imagery Consciousness*, 13.

12. Tomkins, *Affect Imagery Consciousness*, 4.

13. Nathanson, prologue, xiii.

14. One might even argue that the human species never did learn to negotiate that rocky terrain of competing discourses; even Tomkins mentions in passing the ancient Hebrews' learned affective responses were based in part on food-safety mechanisms to avoid cross-contamination (described in the tradition as purity) and largely as a way of building cultural intimacy. Tomkins, *Affect Imagery Consciousness*, 417. But even this taboo (which Muslims also respect and is similar to the taboo on beef among Hindus) has been reconsidered along materialist lines that say such taboos, necessary on an ecological basis, then became cultural-affective prohibitions. Harris, "Abominable Pig."

15. Highmore, "Bitter after Taste," 134.

16. Berlant, *Cruel Optimism*, 106–14.

17. Ngai, *Our Aesthetic Categories*, 233.

18. Brennan, *Transmission of Affect*, 159, 158.

19. Brennan, *Transmission of Affect*, 74.

20. Gabriel and Lang, *Unmanageable Consumer*.

21. Ahmed, *Promise of Happiness*, 7.

22. Tomkins, *Affect Imagery Consciousness*, 37. Bodily signals about pleasure and food can also change while eating; Tomkins cites research that shows how rats given multiple foods will hierarchically eat of the foods in order of preference without exhausting any of them. In human terms, one can eat dessert first, tire of it, and still want to move on to a delicious salad.

23. Hot dogs are of course the processed food par excellence, adding to the short-circuiting of our usual hunger desire: conventional wisdom says no one really

ought to eat them, especially in quantity, but they nonetheless are an American summertime staple. That the Nathan's contest has the appearance of sport (authenticated by ESPN's broadcast) does little to temper the specter of disgust that surrounds it, given the all-but-guaranteed vomiting into the provided (and branded) buckets. On competitive eating see Fagone, *Horsemen of the Esophagus*.

24. Massumi, *Parables for the Virtual*, 205.

25. See González et al., "Reading *Cinnamon* Activates Olfactory Brain Regions"; and Elder and Krishna, "Effects of Advertising Copy on Sensory Thoughts and Perceived Taste."

26. Moss's *Salt Sugar Fat* is a treasure trove of clinical sources on the mind-body chemistry of processed foods and, despite his more pessimistic view in regard to food-consumption determinism (he thinks we are more or less duped), worth exploring for its evidentiary basis. On the legal wrangling that makes and keeps many of these forms of consumption legal see Nestle, *Food Politics*.

27. Theron Randolph first described the dysfunction in 1956 in "The Descriptive Features of Food Addiction," so official diagnostic canonization took nearly sixty years, a time period that would make it concurrent with the rise of postmodern food culture. Food addiction is therefore easily figured an affective disorder in much the same way Brennan reconceives chronic fatigue syndrome, for example, as an affective disorder (see Brennan, *Transmission of Affect*, 45–50). For one example of the addictive mechanism, see Lennerz et al., "Effects of Dietary Glycemic Index." Even the call by those such as Hebebrand et al., in "Eating Addiction' Rather than 'Food Addiction,'" to rename the disorder makes sense in these terms, because it is not the food alone that is materially the cause of the fixation but the mix of affective charges one gets from the act of consumption in which taste plays a part.

28. Drewnowski et al., "Naloxone." In a study of female binge eaters naloxone reduced intake of foods high in fat and sugar.

29. A clarification: it would be easy to misunderstand the obesity epidemic as a result of this affective machinery and attempt to call its presumed overconsumption an environmental problem. However, recent research into obesity and body weight suggests that there are a number of confounding physiological and emotional factors that are not yet fully understood. For a popular aggregate overview see Glassner, *Gospel of Food*, 177–49; on the notion of "naturalized" body weight and shape see Fothergill et al., "Persistent Metabolic Adaptation."

30. Hunger also undermines cognitive-intellectual work and so has serious real-world implications. One ten-month study of eight Israeli parole judges found that a petitioner was up to six times more likely to be paroled if their hearing followed (rather than preceded) one of two scheduled meal breaks, revealing the

capricious nature of the complex affective networks (anger, disgust, etc.) required for rational sympathy that are confounded by the hunger drive. Danziger, Levav, and Avnaim-Pesso, "Extraneous Factors."

BIBLIOGRAPHY

Ahmed, Sara. *The Promise of Happiness*. Durham: Duke University Press, 2010.

Bennett, Jane. *Vibrant Matter: A Political Ecology of Things*. Durham: Duke University Press, 2009.

Berlant, Lauren. *Cruel Optimism*. Durham: Duke University Press, 2011.

Brennan, Teresa. *The Transmission of Affect*. Ithaca: Cornell University Press, 2004.

Brillat-Savarin, Jean Anthelme. *Physiologie du goût, ou Méditations de gastronomie transcendante*. Paris: A. Sautelet, 1826.

Danziger, Shai, Jonathan Levav, and Liora Avnaim-Pesso. "Extraneous Factors in Judicial Decisions." *Proceedings of the National Academy of Sciences* 108, no. 17 (April 26, 2011): 6889–92.

Drewnowski, A., D. D. Krahn, M. A. Demitrack, K. Nairn, and B. A. Gosnell. "Naloxone, an Opiate Blocker, Reduces the Consumption of Sweet High-Fat Foods in Obese and Lean Female Binge Eaters." *American Journal of Clinical Nutrition* 61, no. 6 (June 1995): 1206–12.

Elder, Ryan S., and Aradhna Krishna. "The Effects of Advertising Copy on Sensory Thoughts and Perceived Taste." *Journal of Consumer Research* 36, no. 5 (2010): 748–56.

Fagone, Jason. *Horsemen of the Esophagus: Competitive Eating and the Big Fat American Dream*. New York: Crown, 2006.

Fothergill, Erin, Juen Guo, Lilian Howard, Jennifer C. Kerns, Nicolas D. Knuth, Robert Brychta, Kong Y. Chen, Monica C. Skarulis, Mary Walter, Peter J. Walter, and Kevin D. Hall. "Persistent Metabolic Adaptation 6 Years after *The Biggest Loser* Competition." *Obesity* 24, no. 8 (May 2, 2016): 1612–19. http://onlinelibrary.wiley .com/doi/10.1002/oby.21538/full.

Gabriel, Yiannis, and Tim Lang. *The Unmanageable Consumer*. 3rd ed. Los Angeles: SAGE, 2015.

Glassner, Barry. *The Gospel of Food: Everything You Think You Know about Food Is Wrong*. New York: Ecco, 2007.

González, Julio, Alfonso Barros-Loscertales, Friedemann Pulvermüller, Vanessa Meseguer, Ana Sanjuán, Vicente Belloch, and César Ávila. "Reading *Cinnamon* Activates Olfactory Brain Regions." *NeuroImage* 32, no. 2 (August 15, 2006): 906–12.

Harris, Marvin. "The Abominable Pig." In *Food and Culture: A Reader*, edited by Carole Counihan and Penny Van Esterik, 54–66. 2nd ed. New York: Routledge, 2008.

Hebebrand, Johannes, Özgür Albayrak, Roger Adan, Jochen Antel, Carlos Dieguez,

Johannes de Jong, Gareth Leng, John Menzies, Julian G. Mercer, Michelle Murphy, Geoffrey van der Plasse, and Suzanne L. Dickson. "'Eating Addiction' Rather Than 'Food Addiction' Better Captures Addictive-Like Eating Behavior." *Neuroscience and Biobehavioral Reviews* 47 (November 2014): 295–306.

Highmore, Ben. "Bitter after Taste: Affect, Food, and Social Aesthetics." In *The Affect Theory Reader*, edited by Melissa Gregg and Gregory J. Seigworth, 118–37. Durham: Duke University Press, 2010.

Lennerz, Belinda S., David C. Alsop, Laura M. Holsen, Emily Stern, Rafael Rojas, Cara B. Ebbeling, Jill M. Goldstein, and David S. Ludwig. "Effects of Dietary Glycemic Index on Brain Regions Related to Reward and Craving in Men." *American Journal of Clinical Nutrition* 98, no. 3 (September 2013): 641–47.

Massumi, Brian. *Parables for the Virtual: Movement, Affect, Sensation.* Durham: Duke University Press, 2002.

Moss, Michael. *Salt Sugar Fat: How the Food Giants Hooked Us.* New York: Random House, 2013.

Nathanson, Donald. Prologue to *Affect Imagery Consciousness: The Complete Edition,* by Silvan Tomkins, xi–xxvi. New York: Silvan Tomkins Institute/Springer, 2008.

Nestle, Marion. *Food Politics: How the Food Industry Influences Nutrition and Health.* 2nd ed. Berkeley: University of California Press, 2013.

Ngai, Sianne. *Our Aesthetic Categories: Zany, Cute, Interesting.* Cambridge MA: Harvard University Press, 2012.

————. *Ugly Feelings.* Cambridge MA: Harvard University Press, 2005.

Pollan, Michael. *The Omnivore's Dilemma: A Natural History of Four Meals.* New York: Penguin, 2006.

Probyn, Elspeth. *Carnal Appetites: Foodsexidentities.* New York: Routledge, 2000.

Randolph, Theron G. "The Descriptive Features of Food Addiction." *Quarterly Journal of Studies on Alcohol* 17, no. 2 (June 1956): 198–224.

Tomkins, Silvan S. *Affect Imagery Consciousness: The Complete Edition.* New York: Silvan Tomkins Institute/Springer, 2008.

Žižek, Slavoj. *First as Tragedy, Then as Farce.* New York: Verso, 2009.

————. "First as Tragedy, Then as Farce." YouTube video, posted by "TheRSA," March 10, 2010. https://youtu.be/cvakA-DF6Hc.

7

Uncanny Homesickness and War

Loss of Affect, Loss of Place, and Reworlding in *Redeployment*

RYAN HEDIGER

It is widely acknowledged but perhaps insufficiently appreciated that ecocriticism can be used to study any environment: "wilderness," urban, riparian, arctic, and in this essay, wartime. Yet ecocritics have not sufficiently studied the environments and ecologies of war, despite their massive importance in terms of impacts both on the planet and on human cultures and histories. The term "environment," especially in the context of war, refers not only to nonhuman places but to ones created largely by humans, who thus deeply inform places' spirit, mood, feel. Wartime environments are indeed often dominated by human-created affectivity. In writing this, I have in mind affect in the broad sense, the one drawn from Spinoza and applied in much contemporary writing on the subject. Brian Massumi, in his book of interviews and discussion, *Politics of Affect*, defines this sense of affect as "a kind of potential," as "an 'ability to affect or be affected.'"[1] This second definition, which Massumi draws directly from Spinoza, involves a radical openness, what Massumi calls a "vagueness," a "boundary condition," "a threshold of potential."[2] This condition is often uncomfortable.

In warfare this openness is both the problem and, horribly enough, the reality to exploit. In war a person is uncommonly exposed to harm, and a combatant uses that openness and vulnerability in others to harm or injure them and thereby influence larger events (which are also in a boundary condition, susceptible to change). That scenario is at the ugly heart of war. In this way the circumstance of warfare is a particularly instructive test case of environmental affectivity, because it is so exaggerated and so intense. Indeed, warfare risks unmooring soldier and civilian alike from their senses of meaning and belonging. In "War and Representation," Fredric Jameson argues that war always has the potential to cause "an utter transmogrification of the familiar into the alien, the *heimlich* into the *unheimlich*, in which the home village—the known world, the real, and the everyday—is transformed into a place of unimaginable horror."[3] The *heimlich*, or the "homely," becomes the "unhomely"; it becomes, in the common translation of *unheimlich*, uncanny.[4] This feeling of uncanniness is often perceived or expressed as a longing for home, for the familiar, mixed with a dizzying sense that the familiar is gone, even that it never was the way we remember it. I am calling this ambivalent affect "homesickness," meaning to evoke both the desire for home and the sense of being sick of home, sick at home, when home proves alien and uncanny. In this way "homesickness" combines both "nostalgia" and "solastalgia," the latter being Glenn Albrecht's term for the pain one feels when a familiar place is being radically changed.[5] This chapter focuses on such feelings as they appear in the short-story collection *Redeployment* (2014) by Phil Klay, a veteran of the Iraq war. Klay traces with great subtlety the challenges of returning home to an uncanny sense of place and sense of self, with a psyche still engaged in the shocks of war elsewhere.

Of course one too-frequent response to these challenges for veterans is suicide, a grim summary of the destruction of their feelings of identity and belonging. However, in this chapter I argue that the state of being unmoored from the familiar is also potentially deeply instructive, even useful. As an affective state, a "threshold of potential," and a "change in capacity," this homesickness opens new potential ways of being.[6] Veterans of war bring home not only traumatic memories and emotional injuries but also radically new perspectives on life and meaning. Doing justice to veterans' experiences, and experience more generally, requires recognizing both of these realities. Inhabiting a new state of affectivity resistant to easy cognitive accounting, veterans denaturalize the familiar environment of contemporary life and perhaps especially of consumer capitalism. Their experiences produce a kind of estrangement effect akin to the response Bertolt Brecht sought from art.[7]

This constructive potential is of foremost importance to veterans themselves as they work to find footing in life after combat, to make their experiences useful, and to reworld themselves, never an easy task. But it is also important relative to questions of affect and environment more generally. The extreme affective openness of soldiers, often to the point of suffering, demonstrates how our perceptions of environment are very much culturally and historically conditioned and that they can be estranged, for good or ill. Particularly in the age of the Anthropocene, as familiar and beloved places are affected by climate change and rendered foreign, we can make a virtue of necessity by engaging the strangeness as an opportunity to recast forms of living. In making this case I do not mean we should go in pursuit of traumas per se nor—of course—that war is inherently good. I also do not mean to excuse the excessive militarism that is a crucial problem. However, trauma is a feature of life, and in particular it is a consequence of war. So as long as humans continue to wage wars we are obliged to find ways to learn from experiences in them. At bottom this argument includes the hope that we might also learn how to stop waging war.[8]

My approach in this chapter borrows from the introduction to *Ecologies of Affect: Placing Nostalgia, Desire, and Hope*. There the book's editors, Tonya K. Davidson, Ondine Park, and Rob Shields, consonant with Massumi's thinking on affect, point out that "ecologies are always in a state of emergence, hovering on the verge of unpredictability."[9] This is so, they note, even though ecologies are "grounded" and "decidedly concrete and determined."[10] When the notion of ecology has been used to anchor overly simple human feelings of permanence and stability, the idea of ecology has been poorly served. Real ecologies resist this simplification. As Massumi underscores, affect theory likewise understands "change as primary, and sees the regularities of life as temporary barrier islands of stability in stormy seas."[11] In war, change is shocking, abrupt, violent. Similarly, in the Anthropocene human beings are learning this truth of instability in a novel and profound way. After all, the Anthropocene names the radical and unpredictable changes wrought on the planet by humans.[12] But it is an error to think that only global changes produce such effects. As I argue in this chapter, many environments, scrutinized carefully, prove unpredictable and alienating. Those of war are exemplary.

Although warfare is commonly understood to exemplify the awful power of humans, agency in war, especially modern war, when studied closely becomes fuzzy and complex. Often war is far less an activity displaying control than it is an undertaking of rapid and haphazard improvisation in which weapons, buildings, materials, and other people become desperately sought affordances and tools. In war we rely even more clearly and profoundly on other people and on the nonhuman objects and places where we perform our ostensibly independent human actions.

War therefore clearly dramatizes something else that Massumi's affect theory underscores about subjectivity more generally: that "we are never alone," since "affects in Spinoza's definition are basically ways of connecting, to others and to other situations. They are our angle of participation in processes larger than ourselves. With intensified affect comes a stronger sense of embeddedness in a larger field of life—a heightened sense of belonging, with other people and to other places."[13] Although Massumi does not accent this fact here, his final clause marks how a robust theory of affect is profoundly ecological, revealing that what we are and what we can do results to a significant degree from the environment in which we live. We are our places to a significant degree. Similarly, despite seeming to affirm the power of human action, war, along with its powerful undertow of confusion and disorientation, noted above, reveals the more complex reality of agency. This fact may explain why cultures work so hard to narrate war experiences as meaningful and patriotic—precisely because the experiences are so threatening to familiar forms of understanding, especially, argues Sebastian Junger, for a community not engaged as a whole in war.[14] From the perspective of affect theory, however, this uncertainty is potentially "empowering—once you realize that it gives you a margin of manoeuvrability."[15]

In many other traumas, due to weather, catastrophe, or the like, human communities have often been radically—if often temporarily—reconfigured, reworlded in positive ways. Rebecca Solnit writes about such cases in her book *A Paradise Built in Hell,* in which she shows how prosocial, procommunity behaviors often develop in times of trauma, despite sensationalist media reports to the contrary.[16] Sebastian Junger has subsequently made similar arguments in *Tribe: On Homecoming and Belonging.* He suggests, "One way to determine what is missing in day-to-day American life may be to examine what behaviors spontaneously arise when that life is disrupted."[17] He notes, like Solnit, that "communities that have been devastated by natural or man-made disasters almost never lapse into chaos or disorder; if anything, they become more just, more egalitarian, and more deliberately fair to individuals." That is true, he observes, of New Orleans after Hurricane Katrina.[18]

Junger also cites the example of World War II, noting that in anticipation of the conflict, English authorities worried that social decencies would collapse: "So poor was their opinion of the populace—particularly the working-class people of East London—that emergency planners were reluctant to even build public bomb shelters because they worried people would move into them and simply never move out. Economic production would plummet." However, Junger asserts, "Nothing could have been further from the truth." During the Blitz, Germany's fifty-seven-day bombing of London, the British showed remarkable fortitude and resolution. "Conduct was so good in the shelters," he notes, "that volunteers never even had to summon the police to maintain order."[19]

Indeed, surprisingly, not only was there little "mass hysteria," there was little "individual psychosis."[20] Further, "psychiatrists watched in puzzlement as long-standing patients saw their symptoms subside during the period of intense air raids."[21] Junger points out that this improving mental health was a general trend, that suicide rates dropped during European wars beyond World War II, as did rates of depression. Psychologists worked to understand this counterintuitive reality. One of them, H. A. Lyons, quoted by Junger, argues that "when people are actively engaged in a cause their lives have more purpose ... with a resulting improvement in mental health."[22] In the passage quoted by Junger, Lyons concludes that "people will feel better psychologically if they have more involvement with their community."[23]

In our frenetic contemporary lives community involvement is too often neglected. War changes that. Indeed war is harmful partly because it forces people to step outside their ordinary lives, and in this strangely de-cultured or alter-cultured space, they can—they must—perceive life anew. Ironically this homesickness can *enable* perception of the slow violence that tends to escape notice because it is so familiar: the relentless forms of individuation, specialization, and isolation of capitalist economies like that of the United States. To call such war-borne perceptions potentially useful does not equal calling war itself good or desirable any more than insisting we can learn from a car accident means we should pursue more car accidents. Instead the point is to show what we can learn from the conditions of war and from similar traumas that reopen settled cultural states. In trauma human activity is reframed and reprioritized, and the possibility of new forms of life, new affective states, emerges. This conception of affect is consistent with Massumi's definition, borrowed from Spinoza: a change in affect as a "change in capacity."[24]

Questions of trauma are tricky to navigate because of their paradoxical character. Many veterans, for instance, define their lives by their experiences in war despite or even because those experiences were trying. Veterans often tell and retell their prized war stories (certainly this is not true for every veteran). Other experiences of trauma often function similarly, becoming touchstone events in people's lives.[25] In his book *Deep Survival* Laurence Gonzales details a range of such stories and often returns to the refrain he presents regarding Nick Williams's near-death experience after getting lost on skis: it left him with "a rare and precious knowledge of the world."[26] Those experiences are notable and traumatizing often precisely because they are strikingly different and difficult to assimilate.

Folding such outlier experiences into a functional subjectivity requires studying and learning from the difficult events, testifying to them, and self-consciously bearing witness to them, rather than repressing them. In her analysis of literature of trauma Kalí Tal even goes so far as to argue that "bearing witness is an aggressive act. It is born out of a refusal to bow to outside pressure to revise or to repress experience, a decision to embrace conflict rather than conformity, to endure a lifetime of anger and pain rather than to submit to the seductive pull of revision and repression. Its goal is change."[27] This change can go beyond merely ending the conditions that caused the trauma; it can involve using the unsettling insights possessed by survivors of trauma to change culture for the better more generally.

For Junger a big part of veterans' shock in returning from war derives from the dysfunctional character of much of mass society in the United States. One of his central points is that a "modern soldier returning from war . . . goes from the kind of close-knit group that humans evolved for, back into a society where most people work outside the home, children are educated by strangers, families are isolated from wider communities, and personal gain almost completely eclipses collective good." Junger concludes this paragraph, "Whatever the technological advances of modern society—and they're nearly miraculous—the individualized lifestyles that those technologies spawn seem to be deeply brutalizing to the human spirit."[28] For Junger, then, even though war exposes humans to ferocious traumas, it also has the potential to teach us about what he regards as more fundamental human values—the need to belong, to feel real purpose in our actions, and so on. (I would add that clearly such lessons can also be learned outside of war.) In this way, the affect of uncanny homesickness, the sense of disorientation felt by soldiers, is not necessarily a condition to "cure." Instead, it can be seen as a form of insight about problems in the environments of contemporary American culture, a type of cosmopolitan perspective.

Such efforts are thematized in Klay's *Redeployment*. He opens the collection in reverse chronological fashion, by underscoring how difficult it is for soldiers to return home to civilian life. This eponymous first story, "Redeployment," emphasizes the unassimilated condition of war experience. What the soldiers see, hear, and do during war is so raw, so visceral, so strange, and so all-encompassing that, as Klay writes, "you don't think about it. You're thinking about who's in that house, what's he armed with, how's he gonna kill you, your buddies. You're going block by block, fighting with rifles good to 550 meters, and you're killing people at five in a concrete box." In the next paragraph Klay explains, "The thinking comes later, when they give you the time. See, it's not a straight shot back, from war to the Jacksonville mall. When our deployment was up, they put us on TQ, this logistics base out in the desert, let us decompress a bit." The challenge of reintegration is due not just to the horrors and the intensity of war experience, but to its unsorted and unprocessed character. Klay insists on the difficulty of making sense of events, noting, for instance, "The problem is, your thoughts don't come out in any kind of straight order. You don't think, Oh, I did A, then B, then C, then D. You try to think about home, then you're in the torture house. You see the body parts in the locker and the retarded guy in the cage. He squawked like a chicken. His head was shrunk down to a coconut."[29]

The extreme nature of these sense experiences makes them more difficult to digest and assimilate, but all experience is similar in this way, if in less exaggerated form. A basic model of experience goes this way: first arrives the sense of a change in environment, the affect of the encounter; then we attach emotional responses to our affective experiences; and finally we impose on experiences a narrative and a kind of cognitive order. Massumi underscores that the first stage of affect is more pregnant with various potentials than the consequent emotion and conscious thought, which tend to reduce and foreclose the possibilities present in the first moment.[30] But those possibilities are not absolutely open, according to Massumi, because the experiencing body "has a past that follows it." He notes that this "past includes what we think of as subjective elements, such as habits, acquired skills, inclinations, desires, even willings, all of which come in patterns of repetition." Moving forward in time, "there's a reactivation of the past in passage towards a changed future."[31] So Klay, encountering these shocking experiences in the environment of war, feels the impact of his own carried past, and then his new wartime experiences become part of the new self, which then has its own impact on future experiences. In this sense experience itself involves a kind of homesickness, one in which the novel encounters and their possibilities for offering new practices and perspectives thereby call into question our carried sense of self. Who we are is relativized by the novel experiences and environments (and vice versa).

Our ideas of subjectivity are therefore a kind of homesickness, ideas of self rooted in past experiences.

Warfare forces soldiers into such new perspectives. This process happens in surprising ways, as Klay testifies in the story "Prayer in the Furnace," written in the voice of a Marine chaplain in Iraq. In this powerful narrative, the soldier Ramiro Rodriguez comes to the chaplain to discuss what his company is doing, such as breaking with the standard rules of engagement, killing civilians indiscriminately, and more. Rodriguez is particularly afflicted by the loss of his friend and comrade at arms, Denton Tsakhia Fujita, when one of their troubling strategies goes wrong. The soldiers in this company had inadvertently developed a method of drawing Iraqi fire: one soldier would strip to his underwear, climb on the roof of the building where they were positioned, and yell taunts at the Iraqis to encourage them to attack. The Iraqis would fire, and the Marines could then counterattack with ostensible justification.

On the occasion that Fujita, by way of rock-paper-scissors, was required to perform this taunting, however, the Iraqis adjusted their techniques. Instead of firing clumsily at the Americans, as they had done in the past, Rodriguez explains, they used a sniper whose one precise shot kills Fujita. The Marines' misconduct had backfired horribly. To make matters more upsetting, Fujita had in the past explicitly resisted the technique of provocation: "He didn't like us setting up contact bait. He said it was fucked up. That if it was his neighborhood, he'd take a shot at some asshole on the roof."[32] The situation seemed particularly unjust: not only were the techniques atrocious, but the person who died executing them had criticized them. Fujita had little choice but to go along with his company, despite his reservations, because of the group dynamics of warfare.

Thinking about this series of events, and focused on the death of Fujita, Rodriguez is deeply upset. The events eat at him so much that he takes the unusual step of telling the story to the chaplain and then, further courageously, of telling the chaplain to "tell anybody you want," hoping to make some change in affairs, in leadership.[33] The chaplain tries, talking to several figures of authority, but he is met with indifference. Major Eklund, a person the chaplain thinks may have ears for this issue, admits there is a deeper problem in the whole company, calling them "Our Kill Company," but then says, "But this is a war. A Kill Company's not the worst thing to have."[34]

Klay renders such scenarios effectively, conveying the horror and helplessness of people captured in them, and he underscores, via a journal entry by the chaplain in the story, how these miseries have surprising effects:

> I had at least thought there would be nobility in war. I know it exists. There are so many stories, and some of them have to be true. But I see mostly normal men, trying to do good, beaten down by horror, by their inability to quell their own rages, by their masculine posturing and their so-called hardness, their desire to be tougher, and therefore crueler, than their circumstance.
>
> And yet, I have this sense that this place is holier than back home. Gluttonous, fat, oversexed, overconsuming, materialist home, where we're too lazy to see our own faults. At least here, Rodriguez has the decency to worry about hell.[35]

The chaplain's thoughts recall the collection's opening story, focused on reconciling wartime subjectivity to life at home, in this "gluttonous" existence of shopping malls and easy indifference. That first story's title, "Redeployment," connotes in part how forms of life, affective dispositions resulting from the bizarre environment of warfare, are unavoidably redeployed at home in the United States—indeed, that is precisely what it means for soldiers to come home. They must face the familiar in light of their new selfhood.

To evoke immediately the jarring disorientation of war, the story (and the collection) begins with a set of stunning declarative sentences: "We shot dogs. Not by accident. We did it on purpose, and we called it Operation Scooby. I'm a dog person, so I thought about that a lot."[36] That point is meant to begin to convey, via a specific example and significant understatement ("I thought about that a lot"), the horrors of war, its strangely remote set of standards, and how these standards, like it or not, come home with the soldiers who have had to adopt them. But it gains deeper resonance in application to this specific character, Sergeant Price, who, he says, is "a dog person." In his punchy but tendentious article "The Trauma Hero," however, Roy Scranton reads this opening, particularly the first sentence, as a "comforting moral lie."[37] He continues, "By focusing on how 'We shot dogs,' Klay allows American readers to ignore the unpleasant fact that we shot people." Scranton's critique of Klay strikes me as significantly unfair. For one thing, *Redeployment* includes many examples of injured and killed Iraqis and much *more* concern about this reality.[38] The story "Prayer in the Furnace," discussed above, *centers* on the guilt some soldiers feel about unjustly killed Iraqis and on the steps some soldiers take to prevent more such killing.

Instead of offering a telling reading of Klay, then, Scranton's critique seems, to use one of Scranton's terms of dismissal, to *shoehorn* Klay into the "trauma hero" thesis of Scranton's article.[39] Scranton opens by defining what he calls "the myth of the trauma hero": "The truth of war, the veteran comes to learn, is a truth beyond words, a truth that can only be known by having been there, an unspeakable truth he must bear for society." He then notes that this myth "informs our politics, shapes our news reports, and underwrites our history" and argues that this myth is harmful. This is a compelling idea, but it leads Scranton to some dubious claims. Reading Hemingway, Klay, Tim O'Brien, and others, Scranton seems to want the truth of war to be more accessible. For instance, he discusses O'Brien's claim in "How to Tell a True War Story" that "in war you lose your sense of the definite, hence your sense of truth itself, and therefore it's safe to say that in a true war story nothing is ever absolutely true."[40] Scranton suggests that "for O'Brien, a true war story is about the failure of language to communicate experience altogether, which is an assertion that the soldier's truth is a mystic truth." We should flag Scranton's exaggeration of O'Brien's claim: O'Brien writes that "nothing is ever absolutely true"; Scranton translates this into "the failure of language to communicate experience altogether." That is a serious distortion. Indeed, if O'Brien believed language cannot communicate, why has he written so much?

In the wake of poststructuralist theory and critiques of metaphysics, and in light of affect theory, it is hardly shocking to accept that human beings lack access to absolute truth, particularly in the intense and dramatic scenarios of warfare. Thus, contra Scranton's seeming desire to make war experiences easily interpretable, it makes sense to begin to approach them as Klay does, by thinking about one concrete scenario in the stateside environment that focuses a veteran's reflections on her or his disorienting war experience: a relationship with a dog. In "Redeployment" we learn more about the importance and representative function of dogs for Price as he negotiates the steps of homecoming with his fellow soldiers, flying back to North America, then busing from their arrival position to Camp Lejeune, where friends and family await. On this nighttime bus ride Price thinks, "Looking out, I sort of knew where I was, but I didn't feel home. I figured I'd be home when I kissed my wife and pet my dog."[41]

This ordinary sentence underscores how ideas of "home" live partly in our human and animal companions, but the sentence is powerful here precisely because it becomes uncanny in this story. We already know this soldier has had to learn to kill dogs, has had to rewire his humanity to engage the seeming exigencies of war. Why did they shoot dogs? To prevent them from drinking human blood. Klay writes, "First time was instinct. [...] And that's the last straw, I guess, and then it's open season on dogs." After a paragraph break, he goes on to the passage quoted above: "At the time, you don't think about it. You're thinking about who's in that house, what's he armed with, how's he gonna kill you, your buddies." In effect, coming home to his dog now has a drastically different meaning, requiring that he relive the selfhood he had developed in Iraq, comparing it to stateside life.

A further twist in this story turns upon the fact that when he returns home, Price finds that the family dog, Vicar, is ill and lives in constant pain: "It looked like it hurt him to do everything, wag his tail, eat his chow. Walk. Sit. And when he'd vomit, which was every other day, he'd hack like he was choking, revving up for a good twenty seconds before anything came out."[42] Klay toggles back and forth in the story between the somewhat ordinary narrative of dealing with this increasingly infirm dog at home and the disorienting experience of being a homecoming veteran of war. As part of this effort of intertwining the accounts, Klay notes Price's physical confusion in giving up his rifle. The gun had become so much a part of his sense of his body that, having turned it in, Price admits, "I didn't know where to rest my hands. First I put them in my pockets, then I took them out and crossed my arms, and then I just let them hang, useless, at my sides."[43] He is unsettled in his own person, homesick in his body-as-home.

The return home to his relationship with his partner, Cheryl, is similar. Price notes, "All deployment, I'd slept on the ground or on canvas cots. I'd worn body armor and kept a rifle slung across my body. I hadn't felt anything like her in seven months. It was almost like I'd forgotten how she felt, or never really known it."[44] This final point—"never really known it"—emphasizes how inhabiting a new realm of affectivity, learning a new form of selfhood, not only renders the familiar strange, uncanny; it offers new information, new insights. I am arguing for the potential value of these insights, but I recognize that they are also challenging and even damaging. While a bullet or an IED produces fast violence, inhabiting a war zone damages, or at least changes, soldiers' sensibility and subjectivity in less obvious or immediate ways, sometimes effecting a kind of slow violence, in Rob Nixon's sense.[45]

Reentry into civilian life requires a reworlding, a conscious and deliberate effort, often by refocusing on basic tasks. Thus, after greeting Cheryl for the first time, Price thinks how glad he is to drive home: "It gave me something to focus on. Go down this street, turn the wheel, go down another. One step at a time. You can get through anything one step at a time."[46] The effort can be frustrating, and many soldiers feel as Sergeant Price admits to feeling: "And glad as I was to be in the States, and even though I hated the past seven months and the only thing that kept me going was the Marines I served with and the thought of coming home, I started feeling like I wanted to go back. Because fuck all this."[47]

One reason for this counterintuitive but common sentiment for veterans is that, as Junger writes, "part of the trauma of war seems to be giving it up," testifying to how radically it transforms people. He quotes veterans and others who miss the "extreme brotherhood," "the unity" resulting from war's exigencies.[48] In Klay's story, rejecting "all this" is refusing America's shopping malls, baseball games, and more; it means rejecting ordinary life, all of which seems both banal and terrifying. Klay writes, for instance, of Price and his wife going shopping in Wilmington: "Last time you walked down a city street, your Marine on point went down the side of the road, checking ahead and scanning the roofs across from him. The Marine behind him checks the windows on the top levels of the buildings, the Marine behind him gets the windows a little lower, and so on."[49] That affective contextualizing renders uncanny the next, otherwise ordinary sentences about shopping:

> In Wilmington, you don't have a squad, you don't have a battle buddy, you don't even have a weapon. You startle ten times checking for it and it's not there. You're safe, so your alertness should be at white [low level], but it's not.
>
> Instead, you're stuck in an American Eagle Outfitters. Your wife gives you some clothes to try on and you walk into the tiny dressing room. You close the door, and you don't want to open it again.
>
> Outside, there're people walking around by windows like it's no big deal. People who have no idea where Fallujah is, where three members of your platoon died. People who've spent their whole lives at white.[50]

This passage hinges on how different affective dispositions radically shift perceptions of our surroundings, our environment. Thus the second and third paragraphs begin with ordinary declarative sentences that ring oddly here, estranging normal life. The default affective disposition of capitalist America is denaturalized and instead proves significantly dependent on context, not universal, not inevitable.

Price, cursing "all this," signals the challenges of reintegration, challenges testified to most dramatically at other moments in the collection when he discusses the problem of veterans' suicides.[51] But—and here again is this chapter's central intervention—the rejection of "all this" also shows that developing a new affectivity in war provides a distinct, informative perspective on ordinary life. Although it is difficult to unlearn what you learn in the environment of war, that is not an entirely bad thing. The understandings and even the skills developed there remain about the person as a kind of affect, a kind of potential. The powerful sense of solidarity with others, the value of purpose, the exposure of consumerism as blasé—all these perceptions resemble other cultural critiques, making possible surprising solidarities with veterans and others.

However, little of this wider potential appears in Klay's stories. They remain too sharply focused on the immediate time frame around combat. When Klay does show the translation of wartime selfhood into stateside action, it therefore tends to remain suffused with trauma. The dog Vicar provides a somewhat gruesome example. When his pain grows excessive, Price and Cheryl agree it is time to put Vicar out of his misery. Cheryl proposes to "take care of it." Price responds, "You mean you'll pay some asshole a hundred bucks to kill my dog."[52] Thus the opening of the story— "we shot dogs"—comes full circle, and the narrator recognizes that it is his trying task to kill another dog. He thinks, replaying memories of his resistance to killing in Iraq, that "something in me is going to break if I do this. And I thought of Cheryl bringing Vicar to the vet, of some stranger putting his hands on my dog, and I thought, I have to do this." Thus, steeling himself to the undertaking and bearing keenly in mind his training, he thinks, "Got to do it right. Hammer pair to the body. A final well-aimed shot to the head."[53]

The point of this specific technique—rapidly firing three carefully placed rounds—is mercy, however brutal it sounds; it is a killing that happens too quickly for pain. The story ends with the task completed but with a new form of disorientation, as the narrator thinks, "I couldn't remember what I was going to do with the body."[54] Here again we have, as we do throughout the story, synecdoche, part for whole, in which Price's disorientation about what to do with his dog's corpse stands in for his larger disorientation, bearing a subjectivity that knows how to kill quickly and is able to do so. How can that affective disposition be redeployed stateside? This story and the other stories in the collection do not have ready answers. Instead they underscore the importance and the complexity of the question. This is my point here too: that veterans inhabit an affective state full of potential, both harmful and beneficial.

Price's homecoming means not only seeing his home place anew, as if for the first time, in a kind of uncanny homesickness, but also, more concretely, it means using his training to kill, mercifully, one meaningful form of life in his home. The dead dog Vicar is thus sign and example of his homesickness. This homesickness is the result of trauma, surely, but it is also due to the passing of time, to mortality itself. Our unavoidable openness to the lapse of time makes us all homesick in this way, I contend. We do not need war to recognize that we are all exposed to change and death. The lapse of time is central to the unpredictable character of places and ecologies, as noted by Davidson, Park, and Shields. Reality therefore is uncanny. It cannot be fixed in a conceptualization; this is a profoundly ecological sense of the Real. Likewise, every experience, every memory subjects *us* to change, making subjectivity itself a form of longing, nostalgia, homesickness. Although veterans' sense of estrangement is especially intense, I suggest that the frequent appearance of nostalgia throughout human life underscores the homesick structure of subjectivity itself. Our culture's frequent disavowals of nostalgia therefore entail a form of denial about the openness and malleability of selfhood.[55]

Confronting temporality and death this way, both in specific cases and more generally as a condition of life, is a powerful method of reorienting our sense of purpose. If it is true, as Junger claims along with many other critics, that the sense of purposelessness is a disease of modernity, this is partly a consequence of our being insulated from matters of life and death. This is ironic, since modern existence, with its technological warfare, its mechanized animal abattoirs, and its mass species extinctions, is saturated with novel forms of mortality. Veterans, however, have had their insulation from death forcibly removed. The affective openness—the uncanny homesickness—that results has the potential to reorient our communities and our culture.

This is true in ways that extend beyond my space to detail them here. The core idea in this essay is that powerful experiences are uncanny and disorienting—words that commonly carry a negative valence. However, in light of affect theory all experiences, even "negative" ones, offer potential for change. Experience of the uncanny and of homesickness, then, in slightly more neutral terms, has an estrangement effect. In this it resembles the work of much art, which can help us re-perceive ossified realities that seem familiar. These sorts of estrangement effects can be very useful to the environmental humanities as we try to rework our ways of seeing and being in the world. Indeed, much of the canon of environmental humanities work aims to do precisely that, estrange: whether it is Rachel Carson in *Silent Spring* showing what pesticides will do if their use continues unabated, Thoreau looking askance at planet Earth from Mount Ktaadn, or Spike Lee revealing the experiences of many in Katrina in *When the Levees Broke*, another text about homesickness. From these often disconcerting, uncanny positions, we can relearn to perceive our surroundings, and our selves. That is, after all, a central purpose of ecocriticism.

NOTES

1. Massumi, *Politics of Affect*, 11, 48.
2. Massumi, *Politics of Affect*, 2–3.
3. Jameson, "War and Representation," 1538.
4. Freud, "Uncanny," 193.
5. Albrecht, "Solastalgia."
6. Massumi, *Politics of Affect*, 3, 4. In the passages cited Massumi discusses affect generally, not homesickness specifically.
7. Brecht, *Brecht on Theatre*.
8. My argument resembles Naomi Klein's case in *This Changes Everything* that climate change may cause the end of capitalism. While she certainly does not view climate change as a good thing, it, like war in the present argument, can be used to recast our cultural norms.
9. Davidson, Park, and Shields, *Ecologies of Affect*, 6.
10. Davidson, Park, and Shields, *Ecologies of Affect*, 6.
11. Massumi, *Politics of Affect*, viii.
12. Morton, *Dark Ecology*; and Clark, *Ecocriticism on the Edge*, are two of many useful texts on the Anthropocene.
13. Massumi, *Politics of Affect*, 6.
14. Junger, *Tribe*, 96–97.
15. Massumi, *Politics of Affect*, 2.
16. Solnit, *Paradise Built in Hell*.
17. Junger, *Tribe*, 117.
18. Junger, *Tribe*, 44.
19. Junger, *Tribe*, 45–46.
20. Junger, *Tribe*, 47.
21. Junger, *Tribe*, 47.
22. Junger, *Tribe*, 49 (ellipsis in original).
23. Junger, *Tribe*, 49.
24. Massumi, *Politics of Affect*, 4.

25. The power of traumatic experience to reshape perspectives is a theme of much literature and theory about trauma. One prominent example is Holocaust survivor Elie Wiesel's long career of writing and teaching about the Holocaust. He repeatedly insisted on the importance of telling about these events and learning from them culturally. In his book *Tribe* Junger interviews Dr. Rachel Yehuda, director of traumatic stress studies at New York's Mount Sinai Hospital. She tells him, "For most people in combat, their experiences range from the best of times to the worst of times. It's the most important thing someone has ever done." Quoted in Junger, *Tribe*, 81.

26. Gonzales, *Deep Survival*, 142.

27. Tal, *Worlds of Hurt*, 7.

28. Junger, *Tribe*, 93.

29. Klay, *Redeployment*, 1–2.

30. Massumi, *Politics of Affect*, 5.

31. Massumi, *Politics of Affect*, 49.

32. Klay, *Redeployment*, 138.

33. Klay, *Redeployment*, 140.

34. Klay, *Redeployment*, 146.

35. Klay, *Redeployment*, 150–51.

36. Klay, *Redeployment*, 1.

37. Scranton, "Trauma Hero."

38. See, for instance, Klay, *Redeployment*, 84, 172.

39. Scranton criticizes George Packer for "shoehorning" war literature into his argument.

40. O'Brien, "How to Tell a True War Story," 82.

41. Klay, *Redeployment*, 5.

42. Klay, *Redeployment*, 11.

43. Klay, *Redeployment*, 6. See Grosz, *Volatile Bodies*, for a discussion of the difference between the physical body and body image and how this distinction sets up the possibility—or inevitability—of a homesickness in embodiment. When we inhabit ourselves, we are inhabiting an affect, a possibility, a virtual self, as Davidson, Park, and Shields might call it; see their *Ecologies of Affect*, 7.

44. Klay, *Redeployment*, 8.

45. In *Slow Violence and the Environmentalism of the Poor*, Nixon defines slow violence as one "that occurs gradually and out of sight, a violence of delayed destruction that is dispersed across time and space, an attritional violence that is typically not viewed as violence at all" (2).

46. Klay, *Redeployment*, 8.

47. Klay, *Redeployment*, 11.

48. Klay, *Redeployment*, 91–92.

49. Klay, *Redeployment*, 12.

50. Klay, *Redeployment*, 12.

51. See, for instance, Klay, *Redeployment*, 162–67.

52. Klay, *Redeployment*, 13.

53. Klay, *Redeployment*, 15.

54. Klay, *Redeployment*, 16.

55. This argument shares with Jennifer Ladino's *Reclaiming Nostalgia* a belief in the progressive potential of nostalgia and, with Susan J. Matt's *Homesickness*, a skepticism of easy rejections of homesickness.

BIBLIOGRAPHY

Albrecht, Glenn. "'Solastalgia': A New Concept in Health and Identity." *PAN: Philosophy Activism Nature*, no. 3 (2005): 41–55.

Brecht, Bertolt. *Brecht on Theatre: The Development of an Aesthetic.* Translated and edited by John Willett. New York: Hill and Wang, 1957.

Clark, Timothy. *Ecocriticism on the Edge: The Anthropocene as a Threshold Concept.* London: Bloomsbury, 2015.

Davidson, Tonya K., Ondine Park, and Rob Shields, eds. *Ecologies of Affect: Placing Nostalgia, Desire, and Hope.* Waterloo ON: Wilfrid Laurier University Press, 2011.

Freud, Sigmund. "The Uncanny." In *Writings on Art and Literature*, translated and edited by James Strachey, 193–229. Stanford: Stanford University Press, 1997.

Gonzales, Laurence. *Deep Survival: Who Lives, Who Dies, and Why.* New York: Norton, 2003.

Grosz, Elizabeth. *Volatile Bodies: Toward a Corporeal Feminism.* Bloomington: Indiana University Press, 1994.

Jameson, Fredric. "War and Representation." In "War." Special issue, *PMLA* 124, no. 5 (2009): 1532–47.

Junger, Sebastian. *Tribe: On Homecoming and Belonging.* New York: Twelve, 2016.

Klay, Phil. *Redeployment.* New York: Penguin, 2014.

Klein, Naomi. *This Changes Everything: Capitalism versus the Climate.* New York: Simon and Schuster, 2014.

Ladino, Jennifer K. *Reclaiming Nostalgia: Longing for Nature in American Literature.* Charlottesville: University of Virginia Press, 2012.

Massumi, Brian. *Politics of Affect.* Cambridge: Polity, 2015.

Matt, Susan J. *Homesickness: An American History.* Oxford: Oxford University Press, 2011.

Morton, Timothy. *Dark Ecology: For a Logic of Future Coexistence.* New York: Columbia University Press, 2016.

Nixon, Rob. *Slow Violence and the Environmentalism of the Poor*. Cambridge MA: Harvard University Press, 2011.

O'Brien, Tim. "How to Tell a True War Story." *The Things They Carried*, 67–85. 1990. Boston: Mariner, 2009.

Scranton, Roy. "The Trauma Hero: From Wilfred Owen to *Redeployment* and *American Sniper*." *Los Angeles Review of Books*, January 25, 2015. https://lareviewofbooks.org/article/trauma-hero-wilfred-owen-redeployment-american-sniper/.

Solnit, Rebecca. *A Paradise Built in Hell: The Extraordinary Communities That Arise in Disaster*. New York: Viking, 2009.

Tal, Kalí. *Worlds of Hurt: Reading the Literatures of Trauma*. Cambridge: Cambridge University Press, 1996.

PART 3

Animality

Feeling Species and Boundaries

8

Desiring Species with Darwin and Freud

ROBERT AZZARELLO

Ecocritics have been exceptionally attentive to the ways in which a desire for other-than-human species works affectively in the human species. Indeed one can easily recognize the great influence that early concepts like Yi-Fu Tuan's topophilia and E. O. Wilson's biophilia have had on the field in general, as well as on specifically feminist and queer reformulations by Greta Gaard, Catriona Mortimer-Sandilands, Simon Estok, and Nicole Seymour. Although each ecocritic may approach the subject of desire differently, each seems to share the general assumption that desire is profoundly significant for ecocriticism for at least two reasons: first because ecocriticism is fundamentally an ethical project, and second because ethics itself emerges in tandem with desire.

In the general theory ethics comes into being through a mind-bodily desire for the other. When one speaks of an ethical consideration for the other, in other words, one is speaking of a consideration that emerges or filters through desire for that other. For ecocritics this ethical theory should be clear and recognizable in its practical instantiations. Some ecosystems, some species, and even some individuals of a species are valued more or less depending on the valuing subject's desire for them. A desert may be considered an undesirable landscape and would thus seem to lend itself almost naturally to the storage of nuclear waste. Likewise a swamp may be deemed ugly and easily sliced up by canals and pipelines if it is lucky or completely drained and developed if it is not. Lions, tigers, and bears may be regarded as sexy species and thus granted a whole different range of ethical consideration than their nonmammalian, less sexy cousins. Even some individuals of a conventionally devalued species—a baby rat, for example—may escape the poison for at least a day or two. These examples illustrate the general theory of ethics and desire that I take to be axiomatic: that ethics emerges in tandem with desire. To deny the phenomenon of desire is to deny a fundamental aspect of how ethical considerations and inconsiderations are negotiated.

Although this general ethical theory may be simple to state and evidentiary cases may quickly come to mind, ethics and desire are complicated phenomena both independently and in relation to each other. Neither should be conceived through easy formulas. Ethics and desire always encompass attraction and revulsion, inclination and disavowal, as well as the often-puzzling bond between the two. In this chapter I extend this line of thinking and propose that there is also much at stake, ethically speaking, in how one conceptualizes desire in the first place. If ecocritics have been exceptionally attentive to the ways in which a desire for other-than-human species works affectively in the human species, they also ought to be attentive to the ways in which the concept works to create a boundary between species that can properly be called desiring and those that cannot, as well as the differentiated ethical value afforded by that distinction. I want to explore, in other words, not only desire as a complex human affect in relating to other species but also the way desire itself is figured as a species-specific capacity. At the most basic level I claim that the way one conceptualizes the desiring capacity or incapacity of an other-than-human species influences the way one ethically considers that species. In order to substantiate this claim I address the following questions: What does desire mean for Darwin and then for Freud? How do they understand the capacity to desire across species lines? And what ethical quandaries result?

Darwin

The question of desire in Darwin is tricky for a number of reasons. To start, the word "desire" itself appears very infrequently in his own published texts. In his long meditations on the sexual lives of animals, for example, Darwin chooses not the phrase "sexual desire" but "sexual selection" to describe what occurs during courtship and mating. Unlike the nebulous or speculative term "desire," the term "selection" provides Darwin with a lexicon that is more concrete and quantifiable. The creature either selects or it does not, and this fact may or may not have anything to do with what we call desire. So first, one must contend with Darwin's own strategic avoidance of the term. When the term "desire" does surface, it either seems tangential or Darwin intends for it to mean simply a desire to select or be selected. Desire for Darwin may thus be conceived in the most elementary of ways: the object of the Darwinian creature's desire is procreative sex, plain and simple. All instincts, habits, and behavior follow from there. Even the desire to survive in Darwin may be read as an effect of a more basic desire to procreate. So second, one must contend with Darwin's own figuration of desire as simple *telos* rather than as complex affect.

In such a situation it is not surprising that the great discourses on desire and its vicissitudes—its ontology, multiple meanings, various objects, epistemological problems, and so on—have not been associated with Darwin but instead with someone like Freud. While there are good reasons why Darwin's and Freud's reputations have developed in such different ways, the two have more in common than is usually acknowledged. "The theories of Darwin," Freud writes in his 1925 autobiography, "strongly attracted me, for they held out hopes of an extraordinary advance in our understanding of the world."[1] Without Darwin there would be no Freud, but to recognize their connection ecocritics must read around Darwin's own avoidance of the term "desire," as well as the strict reductionism with which he is often associated.

For Darwin desire works in two ways: in the affective theory (an analysis of how individuals of a species respond to their worlds) and in the evolutionary theory itself (an analysis of how species change over time by means of natural and sexual selection). Investigating desire in these two ways will help bring into focus the fundamental insights with which Freud will eventually grapple, but it will also help expand the ecocritical work of Gaard, Mortimer-Sandilands, Estok, and Seymour that I referenced above. These writers share the general assumption—and I think they are right—that ethics comes into being through a mind-bodily desire for the other, but I would like to propose that there is also much at stake, ethically speaking, in how one conceptualizes desire in the first place.

In a chapter of *The Descent of Man* called "Mental Powers," Darwin in 1871 lays the groundwork for his affective theory by making an unequivocal claim about the relative capacities of human and other-than-human animals. "My object," Darwin proclaims, "is to show that there is no fundamental difference between man and the higher mammals in their mental faculties."[2] His aim in *Descent*, as it was the next year in *The Expression of the Emotions in Man and Animals*, was to think about similarity rather than difference between human and other forms of life. "Darwin's strategy," Elizabeth Grosz writes, is to repeat that "whatever characteristic we may regard as a defining one [of the human species] may be found in a less developed form elsewhere in the animal kingdom."[3] Indeed Darwin is always critical of strict categorical differentiation and peppers his arguments in *Descent* with incisive comments like this one: "if man had not been his own classifier, he would never have thought of founding a separate order for his own reception."[4] There is a pithy funniness here to be sure, but the statement also reveals something more profound about Darwin's scientific method. It reveals an essential hermeneutics of suspicion, an essential distrust of the static structure of the Linnaean classificatory system he inherits, that informs the very basis for his thought. "Our classifications," Darwin asserts, "will come to be, as far as they can be so made, genealogies."[5]

Darwin's shift from classifications to genealogies is necessary for his larger project. Once he makes an argument about generally similar "mental powers," he can then make an argument about more specific affective capacities. Speaking of the "lower animals" in *Expression of the Emotions*, Darwin writes, "Terror acts in the same manner on them as on us, causing the muscles to tremble, the heart to palpitate, the sphincters to be relaxed, and the hair to stand on end. Suspicion, the offspring of fear, is eminently characteristic of most wild animals."[6] Note the kind of evidence Darwin uses here to make his claim; his reasoning will not be metaphysical. The expression of terror is concrete and verifiable, presenting itself in the muscles, the heart, the sphincter, and the hair. One does not have to perform any logical gymnastics to recognize that the *expression* of emotion verifies the *existence* of emotion.

In this vein Darwin continues: "Man and the higher animals, especially the Primates, [...] have the same senses, intuitions, and sensations—similar passions, affections, and emotions, even the more complex ones, such as jealousy, suspicion, emulation, gratitude, and magnanimity; they practice deceit and are revengeful; they are sometimes susceptible to ridicule, and even have a sense of humor; they feel wonder and curiosity; they possess the same faculties of imitation, attention, deliberation, choice, memory, imagination, the association of ideas, and reason, though in very different degrees."[7] This rich list of shared capacities begs the inevitable question about where to draw the line. After Darwin, one of the main lines that is supposed to separate human from other animals has been the capacity to speak. But Darwin does not subscribe to that position fully. Like other capacities, the capacity to speak and respond through articulate language can be observed in other-than-human life "though in very different degrees." Throughout *Expression of the Emotions*, Darwin suggests that human and other animals share a fundamental desire to communicate, a fundamental desire to express desire through bodily gesture, facial expressions, and vocal sounds even if those sounds are more guttural than linguistic, originating more in the throat than on the tongue.

Interestingly it is the capacity to blush that Darwin identifies as most unique to the human species, including the capacity to speak, ethically deliberate, and even believe in a god. He writes, "Blushing is the most peculiar and the most human of all expressions. Monkeys redden from passion, but it would require an overwhelming amount of evidence to make us believe that any animal could blush."[8] Why does Darwin draw the line here? "It is not the simple act of reflecting on our own appearance," Darwin explains, "but the thinking what others think of us, which excites a blush."[9] Darwin seems to be saying that while other animals do possess self-consciousness, those forms of life are bereft of what we would today call "theory of mind," or the capacity, present in various degrees even within our own species, to imagine the diverse cognitive attributes of mind in an other.

To have "theory of mind" is not just to have the capacity to be aware of oneself, nor is it just to have the capacity to detect the judgment of others and thus to experience something like shame. Darwin asserts that habit is formed in social creatures in large part through the individual's attention to the approbation or disapprobation of other members in the group. To have "theory of mind" is to understand that the other may have the same complicated and often contradictory desires that oneself has, and therefore the judgment of others cannot be taken at face value. In other words, since the approbation of the other may be in fact disguised disapprobation and vice versa, one begins to develop a hermeneutics of suspicion for the other. But it gets worse. One also begins to recognize that one's own hermeneutics of suspicion is equally present in the other. Not only am I suspicious of you and seek to detect your hidden motives or desires, but I understand that you are equally suspicious of me and seek to detect my own. The blush seems to leak out of this situation in which I know that you know that I know something, but we are not going to say anything about it. Within this complicated drama of hiding desire, the blush appears unexpectedly and against the will. Hence the blush is often accompanied by an attempt to conceal the blush with a subsequent bodily motion: a turning away, say, or a blocking of the face with the hand.

The capacity to blush notwithstanding, Darwin is extremely generous in giving affective capacities, as well as multifaceted desire, to other-than-human animals. "Every one has seen how jealous a dog is of his master's affection," Darwin writes in *Expression of the Emotions*, "if lavished on any other creature; and I have observed the same fact with monkeys. This shows that animals not only love, but have desire to be loved."[10] Darwin's openness in giving other-than-human animals the capacity to desire in multiple ways, however, seems to butt heads with conventional wisdom in psychoanalysis and even, ironically, some strains of neo-Darwinism. Desire in both of these quarters has tended to be *specified*—or rather, speciesfied—as a unique capacity of the human species. Psychoanalysis has been complicit in that specification almost by definition. Indeed as a hermeneutics of the psyche (the *psukhē*, or soul) that fetishizes talking, psychoanalysis almost begins its project with species differentiation and casts desire as a complex affect, one that is much too complex for those creatures outside the realm of humanity to experience.

Psychoanalysis after Freud, however, cannot be held solely responsible for what should be understood as a "speciesist" approach to desire. Ironically some neo-Darwinists, many of whom keep a comfortable distance from Freud, are also complicit in thinking about desire in this way. In order to possess desire, a creature must possess a certain kind of consciousness—a certain "kind of mind," in Daniel Dennett's terms—that is capable of reflecting upon its own desire. A creature, in other words, must possess something like a metaconsciousness capable of metadesire that is distinct from instincts, drives, or mindless teleological urges. In his landmark 1962 study called "What Are Affects?" Silvan Tomkins likewise echoes this approach and begins with the following: "All animals 'want' but only man concerns himself with the nature of his own wants."[11] To provide a theory of affect, it seems, Tomkins must first assert a difference in kind between human and other animals, between want and metawant. What is refreshing about Darwin's approach to desire—to Tomkinsian "want"—is that it does not take the human/other dualism as its starting point. Darwin is writing outside of that hard split, and his ethical approach to the many species surrounding him grows out of that conceptualization.

If desire is a significant part of Darwin's affective theory, it is equally so for the evolutionary theory itself. In 1859, in a key moment of *On the Origin of Species*, Darwin writes, "Nothing is easier than to admit in words the truth of the universal struggle for life, or more difficult—at least I have found it so—than constantly to bear this conclusion in mind. Yet, unless it be thoroughly engrained in the mind, I am convinced that the whole economy of nature, with every fact on distribution, rarity, abundance, extinction, and variation, will be dimly seen or quite misunderstood."[12] As many critics have noted, Darwin's *Origin of Species* is not really about the origin of species at all nor is it even about speciation exactly, or locating the precise moment when species *A* evolves into species *B*. Instead it is about discovering and describing the force behind past and always-present changes in "the whole economy of nature." Darwin's question is very complex, but his answer, at least in this passage, is simple. Darwin claims that "the universal struggle for life" is the force behind every instance of "distribution, rarity, abundance, extinction, and variation" of life on planet Earth.

In some sense Darwin is being quintessentially Darwinian here and presents his theory in what will become the most recognizable form. But how does desire fit into this scientific weltanschauung? For Darwin the thing that an individual of a species primarily desires is to go on being an individual of a species. The object, as it were, of desire is to survive as a desiring subject. The additional desires that Darwin traces in the affective theory—to love and be loved, for example, or to communicate—are layered on top of this even more foundational one. But figuring desire in this way departs profoundly from the standard in both evolutionary and psychoanalytical thought where desire is figured as fundamentally oriented toward an external object. For Darwin, in order to understand life one must first recognize a desire that has no specific object at all, save itself. This conceptualization, however, should not be understood as a variety of simple egotism or narcissism in the traditional sense. Although Darwin rarely mentions the history of philosophy, the way he conceptualizes desire as fundamentally a kind of self-desire seems to bear close relation to the notion of *conatus*. In his 1677 work on *Ethics*, for example, Spinoza contributes to the long history of this particular—and peculiar—notion by arguing that the essence of all beings, organic and inorganic alike, is a striving to persevere in its own being. A being is essentially a desire to go on being a being.

To desire to go on being a being, however, does not in itself explain evolutionary change. To strive to persevere in one's own being does not in itself explain speciation. For Darwin there will always be checks and balances, obstacles and disappointments, and a whole lot of death. There will always be, in other words, natural selection. Darwin's theory of natural selection, then, should be understood as a rejoinder to a primary desire to go on being a being, a rejoinder to the philosophical notion of *conatus*. If for Darwin there is a universal desire for life on the one hand, there will also be a natural selection on the other. Hence there is the struggle for life that ensures that a desire for life cannot go on unchecked. Each and every form of life as we know them today—from the most impressive megafauna to the tiniest microbe—and their interactions with each other, "the whole economy of nature," has been enabled, has come to be, through persistent biological crises on scales both large and small.

Of course Darwin does not explain the evolution of species by means of natural selection alone. Sexual selection, too, figures prominently in his theory of how forms of life change over time. In fact by the time Darwin publishes *Descent of Man* in 1871, the theory of sexual selection that at first seems to supplement natural selection in *Origin of Species* actually seems to have supplanted it. The competition within the species for the opportunity to mate takes priority over the competition between species for the opportunity to survive. In this way species come to be not only through environmental—that is, extraspecific factors—but through intraspecific ones as well. In the classic theory Darwin tracks the myriad ways in which the males of the species compete to attract the attention of the female who will do the selecting. Think of Darwin's long descriptions of the plumage of birds, especially of peacocks: the desire to attract changes the bodily form and behavior of the desiring species. This change is not immediate, of course, but happens instead over generations as variations are selected and survive.

For Darwin the concept of desire is integral to the evolution of species in terms of both natural selection and sexual selection. What a species is, its ontology, may be understood as an internal network of desire. Today this relationship between desire and species may even be more apparent when most biology textbooks have adopted Ernst Mayr's definition of species. First formulated in 1942 (but with precedents in *Descent of Man*), Mayr famously defined a species as a grouping of life that is capable of interbreeding, a definition that suggests a species desires itself and through that desire consolidates itself as a species. Ecocritics may find fault here for this theory's problematic reductiveness, as narrowing the *Lebenswelt* into its procreative aim. But Darwin nonetheless makes an important move in unequivocally giving other-than-human species the capacity to desire. Contra E. O. Wilson, in other words, biophilia will not be a unique capacity of the human species. The concept of desiring species instead will be infinitely more complicated, multifaceted, and expressive than many ecocritics imagine it to be.

Freud

The question of desire in Freud is tricky, as it was in Darwin, but for a different reason. If the word "desire" appears infrequently in Darwin, readers will encounter the complete opposite in Freud. Indeed it is no exaggeration to claim that Freud is singularly obsessed with desire as the psychological concept par excellence. For this reason it is difficult to find a stable definition or consistent conceptualization of desire throughout his long and prolific career. Freud also uses diverse terminology to describe the phenomenon of desire; "wishes," "wants," "instincts," and "drives" all form part of the vocabulary. Despite this trickiness, I want to claim that Freud adopts the basic story about desire implicit in Darwin and opens it up to infinite complication. In his 1915 paper "Instincts and Their Vicissitudes," for example, Freud identifies the same two groups of "primal instincts" that Darwin organized his entire theory around: "the *ego*, or *self-preservative*, instincts [self-desire] and the *sexual* instincts [desire for the other]."[13] Freud adopts Darwin's primary insights and adds layer upon layer upon them; he dramatizes the exceptions at almost every turn. In this way Freud does not turn away from Darwin's thought; he intensifies it.

In 1905 Freud famously argues in *Three Essays on the Theory of Sexuality* against the "popular opinion" that human sexual desire is "absent in childhood," that it begins at puberty, and that its sole aim is copulation between two oppositely sexed individuals of the human species.[14] Against this backdrop, Freud instead makes two sweeping assertions. The first is that children, like other-than-human animals, are "polymorphously perverse" because the objects of their desire, as well as their own erogenous zones, are unrestricted by decorum and appropriateness.[15] The second is that puberty is indeed significant in the sexual development of the human individual, but it is not as simple as "the normal picture" would lead us to believe. In one of the key passages Freud writes, "The normal sexual aim is regarded as being the union of the genitals in the act known as copulation, which leads to a release of the sexual tension and a temporary extinction of the sexual instinct—a satisfaction analogous to the sating of hunger. But even in the most normal sexual process we may detect rudiments which, if they had developed, would have led to the deviations described as 'perversions.'"[16] By "rudiments" Freud means all the behaviors that occur outside "the union of the genitals," such as looking, touching, kissing, sucking, stroking, and so on. Because there exist forms of desire outside the ostensible norm even in the most normal of circumstances, Freud instructs his audience to "loosen the bond that exists in our thoughts between instinct and object."[17] When psychoanalysts think of sexual desire, Freud insists, they ought not imagine a simple story of male and female genitals coming together, orgasm, and the production of offspring.

At first glance Freud in *Three Essays* seems to break fundamentally with Darwin, but only if Darwin is read as a reproductive essentialist and Freud as the opposite. In *Three Essays* Freud argues that puberty is the key moment in the life of the individual when "the sexual instinct is now subordinated to the reproductive function."[18] With the maturity of sperm and egg during puberty, in other words, the majority of human bodies come under a different kind of pressure than their original polymorphous perversity. But claiming that the sexual instinct is "subordinated" to reproduction during puberty does not mean that sexual desire is fully or even strongly controlled by it. Subordination for Freud will always also imply insubordination. For this reason Freud writes, "Sex is a biological fact which, although it is of extraordinary importance in mental life, is hard to grasp psychologically."[19] This difficulty arises because sexual desires are overdetermined, they consist of multiple aims and objects that are often in conflict, and they operate on various conscious and unconscious levels of the mind.

Freud is most famous for these kinds of contributions to a psychoanalysis of the individual, but he also asks profound questions about the evolution of the human species. He seeks to uncover the processes not only by which the human person makes its way from birth through life and into death but also by which the human species evolves from nature to culture, from animality to civilization. In 1927 in *The Future of an Illusion* Freud presents his approach to this statement: "the principal task of civilization [Kultur], its actual raison d'être, is to defend us against nature."[20] Two years later, while writing *Civilization and Its Discontents*, Freud repeats his crucial definition: "the word 'civilization' describes the whole sum of the achievements and regulations which distinguish our lives from those of our animal ancestors and which serve two purposes—namely to protect men against nature and to adjust their mutual relations."[21] In presenting the dyad in this way, in choosing classifications over genealogies, Freud departs radically from his predecessor. Unlike Freud, Darwin would argue that human and other-than-human social creatures have culture—and indeed civilization—if the measure of that phenomenon is a species's effectiveness in protecting itself against extraspecific forces ("nature") and in adjusting its intraspecific ones (its "mutual relations").

Freud conceptualizes this fundamental difference, the break between the human and all other species, as a moment locatable in evolutionary history and open to psychoanalytical explanation. Freud approaches this moment in two main ways. The first comes in 1913 with *Totem and Taboo*, Freud's most deliberate engagement with Darwin, in which he imagines a "primal horde" of humans living in the wild. It is a family, with the males competing for control over their female sexual objects. For Freud civilization arises at the moment when the brothers, full of incestuous desire, ban together and kill their tyrannical father. The figurative guide into this moment of patricide of course is the myth of Oedipus, which Freud infuses with evolutionary significance. The primal killing—and indeed eating—of the father, enacted once and then repeated over and over again in actual and ceremonial form, has a number of profound effects: the prohibition against incest and familial murder, the origin of totemic religion, and the social organization of the family, with all its rules and regulations that will become the prototype for civilization writ large.[22]

The second—and perhaps more plausible—psychoanalytical explanation of the origin of civilization comes in 1929 with *Civilization and Its Discontents*. "The diminution of the olfactory stimuli," Freud writes, "seems itself to be a consequence of man's raising himself from the ground, of his assumption of an upright gait; this made his genitals, which were previously concealed, visible and in need of protection, and so provoked feelings of shame in him."[23]

Unlike in *Totem and Taboo*, civilization originates here the moment the human species begins to walk upright. This new posture leads to the desire to conceal desire, to shame, to "organic repression" and the "renunciation of instinct."[24] The ultimate outcome of this new posture is the mark of civilized animality: permanent ambivalence cum gnawing discontent. But there is good news. Through the process of sublimation the Freudian human "endeavors to find substitutes—substitute objects and substitute acts—in place of the prohibited ones."[25] All of these substitutes make up the realm of what is properly called cultural.

Freud's claims in *Totem and Taboo* and *Civilization and Its Discontents* beg many questions about the author's logic and historical accuracy, but the two books nonetheless have many lessons to teach. *Totem* is primarily an analysis of species differentiation, but it is also a meditation on species interaction. The totem animal for Freud reveals a human desire for other species, a fundamental biophilia, but Freud makes clear that the animal's value is primarily utilitarian, springing as it does from its usefulness in expressing complex psychological structures, wishes, and fantasies that remain largely hidden in conscious life. Further, like the actual father that is, in Freud's vision of the primal horde, killed and eaten, missed and mourned, the totem animal is filled with ambivalence. Think of Rat Man, Wolf Man, and Little Hans. Each of these characters maintains an uneasy relation to the other-than-human species with which they are so intimately attached. But there is an ethical problem with this picture. Freud is able to give other-than-human species strictly utilitarian value by making two moves: first, by setting up an essential and unbridgeable gap in kind (rather than degree) between human and all other life-forms and, second, by denying or at least diminishing the capacity of other-than-human life-forms to desire and repress desire. These two moves here are as remarkably unDarwinian as they are ethically questionable.

Freud's most haunting theory, and real departure from Darwin, though, is mapped out in 1920 in one of his most controversial texts, *Beyond the Pleasure Principle*, which argues that the ultimate aim of all life is not to live but to die. Freud writes, "If we are to take it as a truth that knows no exception that everything living dies for internal reasons—becomes inorganic once again—then we shall be compelled to say that *the aim of all life is death*."[26] For Darwin, the threats to the survival of the individual always come from the outside; it is the external world that ultimately does the creature in. The predator, the chance change in climate, the contagious disease, the accidental fall: all these unfortunate events bear into and come to inhabit the individual in deadly ways from the outside. For Freud in 1920 the propulsion into death does not come from the external world alone; there will be an internal mechanism that intrinsically generates the death of the individual. The struggle is not simply or unilaterally between the being and the world but within the being itself. How does Freud reach this conclusion? There is first the historical context of the text; he is writing in the aftermath of World War I, an event in the history of *Homo sapiens* during which a resident violence in the species most awfully turned back in upon itself, all the while hinting that it would do so again very soon. This historical context should not be ignored, but there is also something within the internal logic of his whole lifework that leads him to this conclusion almost inevitably.

Freud begins the book by summarizing what he means by the pleasure principle (*Lustprinzips*). "In the theory of psychoanalysis," he writes, "we have no hesitation in assuming that the course taken by mental events is automatically regulated by the pleasure principle . . . that is, with an avoidance of unpleasure or a production of pleasure."[27] But Freud asks if there is another principle at work in mental life beyond this principle. He is not asking, though, about the reality principle, which he had already described in his 1911 paper "Formulations on the Two Principles of Mental Functioning." He is not asking about a temporary postponement of satisfaction to meet a present exigency in exchange for an even greater satisfaction in the long run. He is asking instead about a desire for unpleasure (*Unlust*) that is enacted and reenacted during the course of a human lifetime. This kind of compulsion to repeat, Freud argues, is "more primitive, more elementary, more instinctual than the pleasure principle which it overrides."[28]

Freud's question about what he will eventually call the death instinct stems from his vision of the very first life-forms on this planet. "The elementary living entity," Freud writes, "would from its very beginning have had no wish to change; if conditions remained the same, it would do no more than constantly repeat the same course of life."[29] This vision of elementary species leads Freud to redefine the concept of instinct as "*an urge inherent in organic life to restore an earlier state of things* which the living entity has been obliged to abandon under the pressure of external disturbing forces."[30] This "inertia," these "conservative instincts which impel towards repetition," however, must be considered in conjunction with "others which push forward towards progress and the production of new forms."[31]

Freud concludes that self-preservative instincts are "component instincts whose function it is to assure that the organism shall follow its own path to death, and to ward off any possible ways of returning to inorganic existence other than those which are immanent in the organism itself."[32] By extending the capacity to desire across species lines, Freud is following in Darwin's footsteps. By including a kind of death wish in that desire, however, Freud seems to write against the Darwinian grain. But it bears repeating, especially in the face of vast anthropogenic extinction all across the planet, that Freud makes a significant qualification in his claim. Life-forms do not desire death simply and without condition. They desire to die in their own way. The ethical imperative here may be to support the material conditions necessary for human and other-than-human species not only to do their own living but also to do their own dying without interference.

Ecocritics have used the concepts of topophilia and biophilia to highlight the human desire for places and other-than-human species, and these concepts have become indispensable for their ethical project. But ecocritics ought not imagine these philias as naming straightforward human desires, nor ought they consider them exclusive to the human species. Indeed one way to diminish the human's ethical responsibility toward the other is to diminish that other's desiring capacity. Darwin and Freud seem to resist this move and give other-than-human species a complex affective life. For them the desire between and among species is the result of complex structures of ecological and evolutionary history that are simultaneously preservative and destructive, erotogenic and thanatogenic, in nature. An affectively grounded ecocriticism would do well in tracking exactly how this drama of desiring species plays out in life and literature.

NOTES

1. Freud, *Autobiographical Study*, 4.
2. Darwin, *Descent of Man*, 86.
3. Grosz, *Nick of Time*, 61.
4. Darwin, *Descent of Man*, 176.
5. Darwin, *Origin of Species*, 172.
6. Darwin, *Expression of the Emotions*, 90.
7. Darwin, *Expression of the Emotions*, 100.
8. Darwin, *Expression of the Emotions*, 286.
9. Darwin, *Expression of the Emotions*, 300.
10. Darwin, *Expression of the Emotions*, 92.
11. Tomkins, "*What Are Affects?*," 33.
12. Darwin, *Origin of Species*, 108.
13. Freud, "Instincts and Their Vicissitudes," in *The Freud Reader*, 568.
14. Freud, *Three Essays*, in *The Freud Reader*, 240.
15. Freud, *Three Essays*, in *The Freud Reader*, 268.
16. Freud, *Three Essays*, in *The Freud Reader*, 247.
17. Freud, *Three Essays*, in *The Freud Reader*, 246.
18. Freud, *Three Essays*, in *The Freud Reader*, 279.
19. Freud, *Civilization and Its Discontents*, 61.
20. Freud, *Future of an Illusion*, 19.
21. Freud, *Civilization and Its Discontents*, 42.
22. Freud, *Totem and Taboo*, 176.
23. Freud, *Civilization and Its Discontents*, 54.
24. Freud, *Civilization and Its Discontents*, 52.
25. Freud, *Civilization and Its Discontents*, 39.
26. Freud, *Beyond the Pleasure Principle*, 45–46.
27. Freud, *Beyond the Pleasure Principle*, 3.
28. Freud, *Beyond the Pleasure Principle*, 25.
29. Freud, *Beyond the Pleasure Principle*, 46.
30. Freud, *Beyond the Pleasure Principle*, 43 (original emphasis).
31. Freud, *Beyond the Pleasure Principle*, 43–44.
32. Freud, *Beyond the Pleasure Principle*, 47.

BIBLIOGRAPHY

Darwin, Charles. *Darwin: A Norton Critical Edition*. Edited by Philip Appleman. 3rd ed. New York: Norton, 2001.

———. *The Descent of Man*. 1871. New York: Penguin, 2004.

———. *The Expression of the Emotions in Man and Animals*. 1872. New York: Penguin, 2009.

———. *On the Origin of Species*. 1859. In *Darwin: A Norton Critical Edition*. Edited by Philip Appleman. 3rd ed. New York: Norton, 2001.

Dennett, Daniel. *Kinds of Minds: Toward an Understanding of Consciousness*. New York: Basic, 1996.

Estok, Simon. *Ecocriticism and Shakespeare: Reading Ecophobia*. New York: Palgrave, 2011.

Freud, Sigmund. *An Autobiographical Study*. 1925. In *The Freud Reader*. Edited by Peter Gay. Translated by James Strachey. New York: Norton, 1989.

———. *Beyond the Pleasure Principle*. 1920. Translated by James Strachey. New York: Norton, 1989.

———. *Civilization and Its Discontents*. 1929. Translated by James Strachey. New York: Norton, 1989.

———. *The Freud Reader*. Edited by Peter Gay. Translated by James Strachey. New York: Norton, 1989.

———. *The Future of an Illusion*. 1927. Translated by James Strachey. New York: Norton, 1989.

———. *Totem and Taboo*. 1913. Translated by James Strachey. New York: Norton, 1989.

Gaard, Greta. "Toward a Queer Ecofeminism." *Hypatia: A Journal of Feminist Philosophy* 12, no. 1 (1997): 114–37.

Grosz, Elizabeth. *The Nick of Time: Politics, Evolution, and the Untimely*. Durham: Duke University Press, 2004.

Mortimer-Sandilands, Catriona. "Desiring Nature, Queering Ethics: Adventures in Erotogenic Environments." *Environmental Ethics* 23, no. 1 (2001): 169–88.

Seymour, Nicole. *Strange Natures: Futurity, Empathy, and the Queer Ecological Imagination*. Urbana: University of Illinois Press, 2013.

Spinoza, Benedict de [Baruch]. *Ethics*. 1677. Translated by Edwin Curley. New York: Penguin, 1996.

Tomkins, Silvan. "What Are Affects?" In *Shame and Its Sisters: A Silvan Tomkins Reader*. Edited by Eve Kosofsky Sedgwick and Adam Frank, 33–74. Durham: Duke University Press, 1995.

Wilson, E. O. *Biophilia: The Human Bond with Other Species*. Cambridge MA: Harvard University Press, 1984.

9

Tragedy, Ecophobia, and Animality in the Anthropocene

BRIAN DEYO

Two summers ago I was struggling with ideas for a paper on the phenomenon and concept of ecophobia, which I later presented in 2015 at ASLE's biennial conference. Operating on the assumption that ecophobia referred to a dynamic set of primal "negative" affects set in motion by nature's unpredictability, I began to speculate on the extent to which anthropocentric cultures work to modulate their intensity. My intuition was that received anthropocentric ideas concerning human beings' status, position, role, and agency vis-à-vis the nonhuman world somehow aided the repression of a primordial awareness of our animality. If indeed anthropocentric cultures are somehow motivated by ecophobia, I concluded that the sense of mastery over nature they produce amounted to a kind of ecological blindness. Recent work in the environmental humanities, however, has helped to lay a foundation for grappling with these problems. Ecocriticism and animal/animality studies are bound together by a preoccupation with the nonhuman world's capacity to problematize anthropocentric habits of seeing. And as human agriculture, industry, and technology become more intimately enmeshed with natural systems, it does indeed appear as though many are waking up to a new sense of themselves in relation to the planet, what Timothy Morton describes as a large and deep "ontological shift in human awareness."[1] In the interest of facilitating and enhancing the upgrade in ontological awareness Morton describes, I contend that an indwelling with tragedy may productively lend itself to this end.

In the course of this chapter I attempt to illustrate how tragedy, like the Anthropocene, engenders an array of affects that in turn unsettle what Val Plumwood refers to as the master model of human identity.[2] As she states, it is "a model of domination and transcendence of nature, in which freedom and virtue are construed in terms of control over, and distance from, the sphere of nature, necessity, and the feminine."[3] In the first section I offer a critical reading of selected scenes from Shakespeare's *King Lear* to illustrate how and why Lear's reversal of fortune and subsequent exposure to the natural world mobilizes a primordial awareness of the human estate. Insofar as Lear becomes subject to affects that belie the logics of anthropocentrism, his imagination is thereby opened to the ethical necessity of recognizing his animality. In the next section I briefly attend to the ways in which the structures of tragic drama correlate with the deeply felt ruptures in time produced by sudden irruptions of environmental change, thereby suggesting how and why such change antagonizes the human imaginary. Afterward I theoretically coordinate the concept of animality with eco-phobia. In pursuing this end I offer a critical reading of selected passages from René Descartes's *Discourse on Method*. The primary aim of my reading is to illuminate how and why Descartes's impassioned insistence on a rigorous ontological distinction between humans and animals is driven by the repression of anxieties concerning human animality, finitude, and mortality. My reading of Descartes lays the groundwork for a very brief consideration of Michel de Montaigne's "An Apology for Raymond Sebond." Montaigne's postulation that awareness of our animal frailty motivates hubristic fantasies of transcendence may lend at least a modest measure of insight into the dynamics of ecophobia. Although our understanding of ecophobia has lately become more nuanced, the role it may play in relation to culture—and, by implication, subject-formation—remains unclear. To the end of greater clarity on these matters I employ the psychological theories of Ernest Becker to suggest that ecophobia may play a more prominent role in the shaping of culture than commonly thought. This chapter concludes by underscoring why recognition of the lives of animals in conjunction with our own animality is indispensable to the creation of ecological sensibilities and ethical orientations that are adequate to the demands of the Anthropocene.

I begin by citing lines from Shakespeare's *King Lear*. Not long after Lear is ousted from his throne, he is per force exposed to the elements. He takes leave of the Fool, asking that he seek shelter from a raging tempest, after which he kneels and prays. The following lines unfold the logic of his prayer, which takes the form of an impassioned meditation on ethical responsibility:

> Poor naked wretches, wheresoe'er you are,
> That bide the pelting of this pitiless storm,
> How shall your houseless heads and unfed sides,
> Your looped and windowed raggedness, defend you
> From seasons such as these? O, I have ta'en
> Too little care of this. Take physic, pomp,
> Expose thyself to feel what wretches feel,
> That thou mayst shake the superflux to them
> And show the heavens more just.[4]

Lear is shaken to the quick by the storm's ferocity, and his meditation evinces the stirring up of a kind of primordial, affectively charged awareness of the human animal's vulnerable position relative to the elements. Not long before Lear's exposure to the storm he is largely insulated from the volatilities of the natural world. For the bulk of his life Lear's self-conception is contingent upon what he possesses: his kingdom, including his daughters, his faithful subjects, as well as the land. When he is abruptly divested of his authority by Goneril and Regan, the bulwarks of his identity begin to fracture. Dispossessed of proprietary privilege and his material possessions, Lear loses his self-possession, not to mention the conceit of mastery over others his accustomed position warrants. As Simon Estok observes, Lear's loss of control over his daughters—and by extension the space over which he reigns—is tantamount to a "dispossession of masculine identity."[5] Although the trauma of losing his social and political identity is undoubtedly acute, Lear's subsequent immersion in natural horror is calamitous. His encounters with the violent extremes of the storm progressively inflame his awareness of the "unaccommodated man"—the "bare, forked animal" of his most aggrieved, lucid, and intense imagining.[6] The extreme power of the storm resists Lear's powers of intellectual conception: its "thought-executing fires" remorselessly prey upon the mind, so that later on his "wits begin to turn."[7] As Estok states, "Quite apart from the graphic horror of blood and death in the play are the horrors of ontological unfixing and loss that nature poses."[8]

And yet the "pitiless storm" seems to open a wound in his psyche that likely preconditions his resolve to attend more seriously to the problem of human suffering: "O, I have ta'en / Too little care of this."[9] He is guided by the impetus to "take physic," to purge everything in himself that would deaden his latent capacity for fellow feeling.[10] This feeling for the horrors nature visits on sentient beings catalyzes Lear's willingness to expose himself to suffering in its myriad forms. Grandstanding or not, his vow to "feel what wretches feel" is telling and instructive for the contemporary moment, especially "during seasons such as these."[11]

Perhaps most instructive is the degree to which the agency of nonhuman forces strenuously impinges upon Lear's bodily sensorium, thereby generating affects—anxiety, terror, and fear—that push his thinking into novel and unanticipated directions. One is profoundly affected by Lear's metamorphosis at the hands of the storm, which can be said to authorize negative affects, yes, but it also engenders positive affects, such as pity, even love. In *King Lear* the elements conspire to challenge notions of nature as a moral, providential order, providing the reader with a harrowing glimpse of the primordial character of the cosmos. However mortifying this may be to countenance, Shakespeare's tragic vision has the advantage of artfully insinuating the demanding responsibilities such a world confers. And it may be the case that the tragic vision Shakespeare offers is just the sort of "physic" we need, now more than ever.[12]

Wai Chee Dimock indicates that tragedy's employment of radical and abrupt reversals of fortune conveys to its audience a "peculiar structure of time": "In the blink of an eye, the world is thrown off keel. Everything that once anchored it, everything once taken for granted, is irretrievably lost."[13] Are we not all occasionally—if not more and more frequently—subject to this sense of temporal disruption, this sense of undeserved harm that confounds expectations of how life on Earth ought to proceed? As Dimock suggests, tragedy reveals a "world beyond human calculation," one in which our cognitive powers may seem exceedingly lame.[14] Furthermore, as she states, "Greek tragedy has always been inhabited by forces both human and nonhuman," and it is typically "the latter that triumphs, that imposes upon the world maximum damage in minimum time."[15] In light of climate-related catastrophes such as Hurricane Katrina—events that tightly follow the narrative logics of Greek tragedy—Dimock urges that we take heed of what the ancient tragedians had to say about the precarity of the human estate: "in the twentieth century, no warning needs to be heard more urgently."[16]

And yet the tragic vision offered up by the Greeks, as moderns, tends to run contrary to experience. Environmental phenomena like climate change confound culturally ingrained assumptions that the nonhuman world is eternally amenable to human projects. William Connolly aptly sums up the dangers of our contemporary condition: "We are, as it were, under water in the grip of a hungry crocodile at the onset of its death roll. Moreover we are surrounded by many who fail or refuse—for reasons rooted in conceptions of science, religious faith, or economic activity—to be *moved* by the situation."[17]

And what's standing in the way of our capacity to be moved? I think Connolly hits the mark when he states that it is rooted in our inveterate allegiance to the order of the concept. As the legatees of Judeo-Christian traditions of thought and the Enlightenment, we are beholden to conceptions of the human that psychologically protect us from the very real impingements of nonhuman forces. To recognize what environmental crisis demands from us—to see ourselves in strenuously ecological terms—is a very tall order indeed. To seriously countenance the ecological basis of our being would mean to be prepared to lose—and perhaps passionately reject—received conceptions of the human's place in nature, the very structures of thought that, according to Cary Wolfe, have "anchored the ontological hierarchy of human and animal in the philosophical tradition."[18]

Human beings have arguably always been at odds with the fact of their animal nature. And it is precisely this ambivalent awareness of our animality that I wish to coordinate with the concept of ecophobia, which Estok succinctly defines as "contempt for the natural world."[19] Estok also claims that ecophobia is part of a "definable and recognizable discourse."[20] As he insists, one of the most obvious instantiations of ecophobic discourse can be found in the book of Genesis, a "constitutional moment" in the history of the West that "gives Man (a man, actually: Adam) divine authority to control everything that lives."[21] I agree that the idea of a providential natural order militates against anxieties concerning nature's unpredictability. But I also think there's something else afoot. Ecophobia is arguably also about control over human self-conception, and I suspect it has a lot to do with control over the fear of death—a fear that is closely related to awareness of our animality.

Ecophobia is most destructive when it's most pervasive and historically entrenched. When it becomes normalized, it's that much more difficult to acknowledge and redress, which is why I begin my analysis of ecophobia by turning to the European philosophical Enlightenment, a historical moment in which conceptual distinctions between humans and nature become increasingly rigid. Given that we are the legatees of the philosophical culture of the Enlightenment—in conjunction with the fact that contemporary environmental attitudes and practices are in so many ways consonant with this culture—I believe it's imperative to speculatively attend to the psychological dynamics that perhaps motivate its most hallowed ideas in the first place. By analyzing selected fragments of René Descartes's *Discourse on Method* and *The Passions of the Soul*, I contend that the rationalist philosophy he propounds and espouses inadvertently suggests an underlying anxiety about the status and authority he claims for humanity. Granting that so much of Descartes's philosophical account of the human agrees with contemporary forms of anthropocentrism, it may be fruitful to offer the hypothesis that ecophobia unwittingly drives his thinking, sometimes threatening to disable its coherence.

In the *Discourse on Method* Descartes synthesizes an array of anthropocentric presuppositions that support his epistemology. His first presupposition operates as a conceptual lynchpin for those that follow in its wake: the existence of God. After positing the logical grounds for deducing the existence of God, Descartes proceeds to define "that part of us which is distinct from the body," the part of our "nature [that] distinctively consists in thinking."[22] He establishes a rigorous distinction between human and animal, supposing "God to have created a rational soul, and to have annexed it to [the] body" of humans.[23] Concerning the reason behind the grafting of a rational soul onto an animal body, Descartes concludes that the power of thought equips humans with the capacity to apprehend "certain laws established in nature by God."[24] Upon considering the "concatenation of these laws," he observes that physical reality is amenable to the operations of reason.[25] By supposing a seemly congruence between nature and the mind's powers of apprehension, Descartes enthuses that our collective capacity for reason may help us to "arrive at knowledge highly useful in life."[26] By ascertaining "some general notions respecting physics," he maintains it is thereby possible to know "the force and action of fire, water, air, the stars, and the heavens, and all the other bodies that surround us."[27] Equipped with such knowledge, he proclaims we may "thus render ourselves the lords and possessors of nature."[28] Reason is thus defined as a salvific power, the proper use of which may enable humans to "enjoy without any trouble the fruits of the earth, and all its comforts."[29]

Descartes programmatically exalts reason, indeed exactly to the extent that he derogates the body and the passions, which he conceptually coordinates with animal life. With the advantage of hindsight, his conceptual inflation of human power—in conjunction with the reduction of the non-human to a passive, infinitely malleable assemblage of things—seems more than a touch hubristic. It's as though he's articulating the emergence of an instrumentalist mentality that, given enough sway and time, unwittingly produces the material conditions for its own destruction—the very reversal of fortune that we are currently experiencing at the hands of the Anthropocene.

Estok has convincingly argued for the merits of analyzing tragedy in light of environmental crisis. As he states, one of the abiding concerns of tragedy is the vexed, highly charged question of agency, especially with respect to the human animal's powers in relation to nature. Tragedy has an uncanny power of reminding us that "nature does not take notice of perceived privileges human beings regard as their right."[30] He continues, "The creeping fear in tragedy is that Shakespeare's Lear is right and that 'man's life is cheap as beasts.'"[31] And maybe Shakespeare's insight into the human condition sums up the affective power of tragedy. Indeed the best tragedies tend to reveal that, despite protestations to the contrary, we are all ultimately subject to a fate in common with our animal cousins—a fate that, especially in the context of the Anthropocene, we ignore at our peril. And if one takes a close look at Descartes's *Discourse on Method*, one indeed catches the philosopher on the verge of Lear's insight. One is inclined to submit that his discourse on the glories of reason and God may be driven, as it were, *away* from an awareness of our vulnerable, mortal, inescapably animal condition. Granting this, is it not reasonable to speculatively attend to whether the Enlightenment discourse of reason is, at least in some critical measure, symptomatically blind to our animality? Can we think of anthropocentrism as a historically entrenched cultural system that shields us from the kind of radical self-knowledge tragedy artfully enacts? And does anthropocentrism not reveal itself to be driven by an irrational desire for mastery and control that is itself driven in some way by ecophobia? The fear and hatred of that which is beyond our full mastery and control, including death? As Estok cannily suggests, "Ecophobia is all about frustrated agency."[32]

As I've argued above, the *Discourse on Method* is strenuously preoccupied with the question of human agency vis-à-vis nature. However, there are moments in the text whereby Descartes's confidence in human exceptionalism is ostensibly shaken. After describing the "reasonable soul," effectively demonstrating that it "could by no means be educed from the power of matter . . . but that it must be expressly created" by God, he is careful to impugn the judgment of those who might be inclined to doubt the truth of his propositions:

> After the error of those who deny the existence of God . . . there is none that is more powerful in leading feeble minds astray from the straight

path of virtue than the supposition that the soul of brutes is of the same nature with our own; and consequently that after this life we have nothing to hope for or fear, more than flies or ants; in place of which, when we know how far they differ we much better comprehend the reasons which establish that the soul is of a nature wholly independent of the body, and that consequently it is not liable to die with the latter; and, finally, because no other causes are observed capable of destroying it, we are naturally led thence to judge that it is immortal.[33]

One clearly sees that the establishment of absolute ontological difference between the human and the animal—and, by implication, nature—is paramount. The logical integrity of his argument on human supremacy depends on the existence of a munificent God and a providential order predisposed to rational mastery and control. To think otherwise would utterly confound the putative rationality of his system: a system of abstract philosophical ideas (conjoined with equally abstract theological presuppositions) that constitutes a rationale for human ascendancy. Rather suggestive is Descartes's formulation that, next to the error of atheism, "there is none that is more powerful in leading feeble minds astray from the straight path of virtue" than the supposition that the nature of humans is one and the same as that of the beasts.[34]

Whence the origin of this notorious "error" in judgment? In Descartes's rhetorical formulations error is equated with unreason, which is to say the realm of the body, of affect—or, in the language of Enlightenment philosophical discourse, the passions. Given the alluring psychological comforts of Descartes's system, one is given to wonder why one would be swayed by its atheistic alternative. Might the origin of this error have anything to do with the passion of sympathy? Sympathy with animals—not with animals as abstract ideas but the sort of sympathy that is grounded in the human body's intuitive sense of kinship? A shared, affectively charged sense of creaturely vulnerability, finitude, and mortality? A sense, moreover, of creaturely interdependence that connects us to a world that sustains life and yet mysteriously, with no apparent good reason, can imperil and destroy it? A sense of the tragic?

One is given to wonder whether the rationality of Descartes's system is driven by a dark, ecophobic core that is at virulent odds with ecological awareness. To cognize ourselves as ecological beings requires a measure of affective attunement to what it is to be a sentient, vulnerable, and, perhaps most agonizingly, mortal animal. Interestingly enough Descartes's aversion to the passions is exceptionally transparent in *The Passions of the Soul*. For instance, in Article 147 he discusses the "intellectual Joy" one derives from the right use of reason, which is described as a kind of mastery over sense-impressions, not to mention the affects they may generate.[35] In Article 148, "That the exercise of virtue is a supreme remedy for the Passions," he goes on to state,

> Now, inasmuch as these inner excitations affect us more intimately and consequently have much more power over us than the passions from which they differ but which are found in them, it is certain that, provided our soul always has what it takes to be content, it needs only to follow virtue diligently. For anyone who has lived in such a way that his conscience cannot reproach him for ever having failed to do anything he judged best ... derives a satisfaction with such power to make him happy that the most vigorous assaults of the Passions never have enough power to disturb the tranquility of the soul.[36]

Descartes thus assumes that the subject, fully equipped with rational knowledge of the passions, can regulate them in accordance with a rather disembodied notion of happiness or what he refers to as the "tranquility of the soul."[37]

This account of the virtuous soul stands in stark contrast with J. M. Coetzee's articulation of the soul in *Elizabeth Costello*. Contra Descartes's restrictive identification of the soul with the powers of reason, Costello claims, "'To be full of being is to live as a body-soul. One name for that experience is joy.'"[38] She continues: "'To thinking, cogitation, I oppose fullness, the sensation of being [...] a heavily affective sensation—of being a body with limbs that have extension in space, of being alive to the world. This fullness contrasts starkly with Descartes' key state, which has an empty feel to it: the feel of a pea rattling around in a shell.'"[39]

By Costello's reasoning Descartes's virtuous soul is happy only insofar as it renders itself impervious to any sort of affective disturbance whatsoever. What is more, the indifference to suffering that Cartesian virtue requires would also demand a reflexive deadening of the senses, not to mention the affects they engender. Hence what Descartes proffers as the acme of human achievement—the masterful triumph of the intellect over the contingencies of mere animal pleasure and pain—Costello implicitly describes as the denial of the very basis of one's humanity.

As Coetzee's recent forays into the lives of animals suggest, anthropocentric systems of thought have a way of alienating us, not only from nonhuman animals but from a visceral, deeply felt sense of our own animality. Commenting on Coetzee's *The Lives of Animals*, Cora Diamond refers to the "awareness we each have of being a living body."[40] Coupled with this awareness is a sense of "exposure," a "bodily sense of vulnerability to death, sheer animal vulnerability."[41] To be able to acknowledge such vulnerability, she remarks, is deeply "wounding."[42] And it is precisely this fraught, affective awareness of our animal being that the Cartesian virtue of reason incapacitates. Inasmuch as one follows virtue in the strict Cartesian sense, one is opting out of the tragic sense of life that, for Coetzee, would seem to be the affective basis of human sociality—what we might call love—a keen sense of responsibility and care for our animal cousins, not to mention the planet on which we depend and that we share. The virtue of disciplining the body—affect, sense, sensation—via a prescriptively restricted *concept* of reason assuredly grants one a considerable degree of power. But this power sounds a lot like the power of sublime indifference—an isolating and lonely power indeed. And it is perhaps worth noting that the origins of the word *virtue* can be traced back to the Latin *vir*, or "Man," signifying notions of virility and valor.

Ironically, if one considers Descartes's anxious reference, cited earlier, to the unsettling power driving the so-called erroneous supposition that the soul of "Man" is akin to the souls of the beasts—from which one might be led to infer our ontological equivalence in a world bereft of divine significance—then the "straight path of virtue" he recommends looks quite lame.[43] For Descartes, to deviate from the supposition that humans are fundamentally

superior to animals signifies an abnegation of the form of reason he dog-
matically prescribes, and to be drawn away from the claims of reason is to
be troubled by mere passion, which perhaps explains his dismissal of those
who are prey to doubts on the question of human exceptionalism: only a
"feeble mind" would refute the anthropocentric logic of his discourse.[44]
However, one wonders whether Descartes isn't projecting his own fears
and anxieties onto his imagined opponents. After all, if one were to reject
a philosophy that posits the existence of a god that implanted a rational
soul in humans for the purpose of exploiting a material universe designed
with them in mind, and if one were to balk at the idea that humans have
immortal souls—thus evincing the fortitude to entertain the utter finality
of death—it seems that, instead of suffering from a deficit of reason, this
person would be in robust possession of it: that is, if we're talking about
reason as a mental faculty that has the capacity to "see . . . feelingly," unbi-
ased by the taint of parochial self-concern.[45]

For Descartes, however, feeling is relegated to a mere complex of physiological forces resisting the authority that reason, by rights, ought to institute.
He's quite keen to delegitimate the ethical authority and agency of passion:
rather than an ennobling power, it is a power that enfeebles, conjuring
notions of human finitude. Descartes's contemporary, Spinoza, marshals
a similar attack on the potential ethical agency of affect: "human infirmity
in moderating and checking the emotions I name bondage: for, when man
is a prey to his emotions, he is not his own master, but lies at the mercy of
fortune."[46] One discerns a peculiar anxiety with respect to affect's capacity
to disrupt the order of reason in both philosophers. Inasmuch as one is
prey to the force of affect, it's as though one is witlessly subsumed in the
physical laws of nature. And, like Descartes, Spinoza is especially chary of
our natural susceptibility to feel compassion for animals: "It is plain that
the law against the slaughtering of animals is founded rather on vain and
womanish pity than sound reason. The rational quest of what is useful to
us further teaches us the necessity of associating ourselves with our fellow-
men, but not with the beasts, or things, whose nature is wholly different
than our own."[47] The energy with which animals and the world of things
are banished from the province of reason—coupled with the sometimes

strident and derisory attitude toward the life of passion—is telling. For one, it reinforces the logocentrism that is widely recognized as a hallmark of the Enlightenment—a cultural tendency that, as Amitav Ghosh explains, has become profoundly entrenched in the last several centuries. Commenting on this tendency, he equates it with the insularity of modernity, a situation whereby humans have increasingly scant "company" with the nonhuman: a "dwindling world" in which we have become immured in our "own abstractions."[48] Again, this cordoning off of the nonhuman from the human, abetted as it is by a habitual predilection for abstraction, arguably betokens a critical measure of fear and anxiety—and not only with respect to the nonhuman but with the agency and authority of affect.

Why, one might ask, do these philosophers so adamantly insist on keeping animals at bay from the realms of human sociality and thought? To answer this question Luc Ferry maintains that "we need a phenomenology of the enigmatic nature of animals and of the contradictory sentiments it evokes in us."[49] Ferry wonders whether the philosophical humanism inaugurated by the Enlightenment isn't somehow "zoophobic" at its core.[50] And as Cary Wolfe has suggested, a concerted intellectual and affective engagement with animal life reveals that, for humans, animals are in possession of an uncanny set of powers, what we may generally define as the agency to "unsettle the very foundations of what we call 'the human.'"[51] Indeed, as Cora Diamond has intimated, precisely to the extent that animals reflect back to us our own animality—our vulnerability, finitude, and mortality—they may also generate the need to protect ourselves via a process of affective deadening, a process that is facilitated by abstraction. As she says, "Our concepts, our ordinary life with our concepts, pass by"—or "deflect"—the "difficulty" that animals present to consciousness.[52]

In "An Apology for Raymond Sebond" Montaigne reflects at length on this difficulty. In the process he speculates on the affective dynamics behind anthropocentrism: "The most vulnerable and frail of all creatures is man, and at the same time the most arrogant. He feels and sees himself lodged here, amid the mire and dung of the world, nailed and riveted to the worst, the deadest, and the most stagnant part of the universe, on the lowest story of the house and farthest from the vault of heaven . . . and in his imagination he goes planting himself above the circle of the moon, and bringing the sky down beneath his feet."[53] Montaigne coordinates our visceral, perhaps unconscious feeling for our animal condition with anthropocentric systems of thought, implying that the gravity and inexplicable mystery of our being—in conjunction with an awareness of our natural frailty—somehow *drive* the pretense of transcendent, godlike power over the planet. Thus Montaigne sees human hubris as a consequence of our precognitive awareness of our animality.

Montaigne's line of thinking, which posits transcendental fantasies of the human as a function of primordial insecurity, suggestively resonates with the psychological theories of Ernest Becker. For Becker, if humans are at all unique in the animal kingdom, it's largely on account of our subjection to what he aptly terms an "existential paradox," the "condition of individuality within finitude."[54] As he states, "Man has a symbolic identity that brings him sharply out of nature. He is a symbolic self, a creature with a name, a life history."[55] For Becker the singularly immense power of consciousness tragically lends itself to a fundamental misapprehension of our nature—the sense that we are somehow "small gods," both "out of nature" and above it. And yet we often find ourselves perforce in thrall to a contradictory sense that we are "hopelessly in it."[56] For Becker this sense of a fundamental duality at the heart of our nature is ameliorated by the mechanism of culture. In short, culture is produced by the unaccountable weirdness of the paradox Becker explores. The strangeness of being human—of feeling marked out by consciousness as special, *and* food for worms nonetheless—produces what he calls "natural narcissism."[57] Combine this with a "basic need for self-esteem," and what you get is a "creature who has to feel himself an object of primary value: first in the universe, representing in himself all of life."[58] In order to feel as though you are "number one," you need culture: you need philosophy, religion, stories, myths, the very means by which, as Becker suggests, human beings posit themselves within a universe of purpose and meaning.[59] For Becker, human systems of signification and meaning facilitate the repression of primary affects that signal creaturely awareness and its kissing cousin, death anxiety: in other words, culture is conceived as both an effect of ecophobia *and* its most reliable soporific.

Inasmuch as anthropocentric cultures work to blunt ecological awareness, it's crucial, on both political and ethical grounds, to develop an array of strategies, aesthetic and otherwise, to inculcate critical reflection on their psychological appeal. As I suggested much earlier, the philosophical vision of human fate that tragedy offers may provide an invaluable impetus for thinking on what it might mean to live—and live well—in the Anthropocene. Pedagogically speaking, we might productively utilize this ancient cultural technology to inspire critical reflection on our own culturally mediated desires for cosmic reassurance. Like the Anthropocene, tragedy powerfully compels engagement with our animal, vulnerable, limited, and mortal condition. Additionally, inasmuch as it dramatizes the complexity, dynamism, and sheer impersonality of the nonhuman cosmos—what the Greeks personified as the gods or a "higher law"—a robust engagement with this genre of storytelling may help to motivate and produce a new range of ecological sensibilities: sensibilities that derive sustenance and strength from feelings of wonder and awe, humility and respect—and perhaps even gratitude for the material, ecological basis of our being. As Amitav Ghosh states, "It is impossible to see any way out of [environmental] crisis without an acceptance of limits and limitations, and this in turn, is, I think, intimately related to the idea of the sacred, however one may wish to conceive it."[60] According to Ghosh, our capacity to reconceive the sacred is crucially contingent upon our species' willingness to "rediscover [its] kinship with other beings," which also means figuring out how we might collectively redress the "predatory hubris" that has produced what he calls "the great derangement"—a tragic, impoverished, and impoverishing state of affairs whereby humans have become progressively insulated from the nonhuman in the course of modernity.[61] Finally, inasmuch as tragedy encourages a collective recognition of our shared, mortal condition with our animal cousins, it may enliven our capacities for sympathy and love, thereby honoring the evolutionary heritage with which our species is so richly endowed.

NOTES

1. Morton, *Hyperobjects*, 100–101.
2. Plumwood, *Feminism and the Mastery of Nature*, 23.
3. Plumwood, *Feminism and the Mastery of Nature*, 23.
4. Shakespeare, *King Lear*, 3.4.28–36 (references are to act, scene, and line).
5. Estok, *Ecocriticism and Shakespeare*, 21.
6. Shakespeare, *King Lear*, 3.4.105–6.
7. Shakespeare, *King Lear*, 3.2.4, 68.
8. Estok, *Ecocriticism and Shakespeare*, 23.
9. Shakespeare, *King Lear*, 3.4.29–33.
10. Shakespeare, *King Lear*, 3.4.33.
11. Shakespeare, *King Lear*, 3.4.32.
12. Shakespeare, *King Lear*, 3.4.33.
13. Dimock, "After Troy," 66.
14. Dimock, "After Troy," 68.
15. Dimock, "After Troy," 80.
16. Dimock, "After Troy," 80.
17. Connolly, *Fragility of Things*, 11.
18. Wolfe, *Before the Law*, 63–64.
19. Estok, "Theorizing in a Space of Ambivalent Openness," 204.
20. Estok, "Theorizing in a Space of Ambivalent Openness," 204.
21. Estok, *Ecocriticism and Shakespeare*, 5.
22. Descartes, *Discourse on Method*, 73.
23. Descartes, *Discourse on Method*, 73.
24. Descartes, *Discourse on Method*, 69.
25. Descartes, *Discourse on Method*, 69.
26. Descartes, *Discourse on Method*, 84.
27. Descartes, *Discourse on Method*, 84.
28. Descartes, *Discourse on Method*, 84.
29. Descartes, *Discourse on Method*, 84.
30. Estok, "Ecocriticism in an Age of Terror," 3.
31. Estok, "Ecocriticism in an Age of Terror," 3.
32. Estok, "Ecocriticism in an Age of Terror," 4.
33. Descartes, *Discourse on Method*, 82.
34. Descartes, *Discourse on Method*, 82.
35. Descartes, *Passions of the Soul*, 100.
36. Descartes, *Passions of the Soul*, 101.
37. Descartes, *Passions of the Soul*, 101.
38. Coetzee, *Elizabeth Costello*, 77–78.

39. Coetzee, *Elizabeth Costello*, 78.
40. Diamond, "Difficulty of Reality," 74.
41. Diamond, "Difficulty of Reality,"74.
42. Diamond, "Difficulty of Reality,"74.
43. Descartes, *Discourse on Method*, 82.
44. Descartes, *Discourse on Method*, 82.
45. Shakespeare, *King Lear*, 4.6.145.
46. Spinoza, *Ethics*, 321.
47. Spinoza, *Ethics*, 347.
48. Ghosh, *Great Derangement*, 84.
49. Ferry, "Neither Man nor Stone," 148.
50. Ferry, "Neither Man nor Stone," 150.
51. Wolfe, *Before the Law*, 3.
52. Diamond, "Difficulty of Reality," 59.
53. Montaigne, *Complete Works*, 331.
54. Becker, *Denial of Death*, 26.
55. Becker, *Denial of Death*, 26.
56. Becker, *Denial of Death*, 26.
57. Becker, *Denial of Death*, 3.
58. Becker, *Denial of Death*, 3.
59. Becker, *Denial of Death*, 3.
60. Ghosh, *Great Derangement*, 161.
61. Ghosh, *Great Derangement*, 162, 56.

BIBLIOGRAPHY

Becker, Ernest. *The Denial of Death*. New York: Free Press, 1997.
Coetzee, J. M. *Elizabeth Costello*. New York: Penguin, 2003.
Connolly, William E. *The Fragility of Things: Self-Organizing Processes, Neoliberal Fantasies, and Democratic Activism*. Durham: Duke University Press, 2013.
Descartes, René. *Discourse on Method*. In *The Rationalists*, translated by John Veitch. New York: Anchor, 1974.
———. *The Passions of the Soul*. Translated by Stephen H. Voss. Indianapolis: Hackett, 1989.
Diamond, Cora. "The Difficulty of Reality and the Difficulty of Philosophy." In *Philosophy and Animal Life*, by Stanley Cavell, Cora Diamond, John McDowell, Ian Hacking, and Cary Wolfe, 43–90. New York: Columbia University Press, 2008.
Dimock, Wai Chee. "After Troy: Homer, Euripides, Total War." In *Rethinking Tragedy*, edited by Rita Felski, 66–81. Baltimore: Johns Hopkins University Press, 2008.

Estok, Simon. *Ecocriticism and Shakespeare: Reading Ecophobia.* New York: Palgrave Macmillan, 2011.

———. "Ecocriticism in an Age of Terror." CLCWeb: *Comparative Literature and Culture* 15, no. 1 (2013): 1–9. http://dx.doi.org/10.7771/1481–4374.2182.

———. "Theorizing in a Space of Ambivalent Openness: Ecocriticism and Ecophobia." *Interdisciplinary Studies in Literature and Environment* 16, no. 2 (2009): 203–25.

Ferry, Luc. "Neither Man nor Stone." In *Animal Philosophy*, edited by Peter Atterton and Matthew Calarco, 147–56. New York: Continuum, 2006.

Ghosh, Amitav. *The Great Derangement: Climate Change and the Unthinkable.* Chicago: University of Chicago Press, 2016.

Montaigne, Michel de. *The Complete Works of Montaigne: Essays, Travel Journals, Letters.* Translated by Donald M. Frame. Stanford: Stanford University Press, 1958.

Morton, Timothy. *Hyperobjects: Philosophy and Ecology after the End of the World.* Minneapolis: University of Minnesota Press, 2013.

Plumwood, Val. *Feminism and the Mastery of Nature.* London: Routledge, 1993.

Shakespeare, William. *King Lear.* Edited by R. A. Foakes. Arden Shakespeare, 3rd ser. London: Thomson Learning, 2003.

Spinoza, Benedictus de [Baruch]. *The Ethics.* In *The Rationalists*, translated by George Montgomery. New York: Anchor, 1974.

Wolfe, Cary. *Before the Law: Humans and Other Animals in a Biopolitical Frame.* Chicago: University of Chicago Press, 2013.

10

Futurity without Optimism

Detaching from Anthropocentrism and Grieving Our Fathers in *Beasts of the Southern Wild*

ALLYSE KNOX-RUSSELL

The bravest thing is to take this first step: Get real. Face the truth and let it sink in. . . . The landscape you will find yourself in, once you allow this realization to take hold, is a different one. Despair lives there, along with helplessness and anger, fear and disorientation, undoubtedly also unspeakable sadness. You are likely to come to recognize that this is a new time. The time before was one in which we insisted and relied on hope, on better tomorrows, in the United States on the "American Dream." Now, we have to accept that "better tomorrows" may not come. It is akin to accepting one's own mortality, maybe a doctor's prognosis of one's impending death, but on a much grander scale.
—Susanne C. Moser, "Getting Real about It"

In an article written for an environmental leadership reference handbook, the geographer and environmental consultant Susanne Moser calls for environmental leaders, above all, to grieve, to become comfortable with working through their own grief so that they can help others with theirs. Mourning might seem a reasonable response to the need to face any trauma, but the time of climate change and species extinction in which humanity currently finds itself erects unique temporal obstacles for grief work as it is usually practiced. To be precise, the temporality of the loss presented by climate change—not something that occurs at once and can be placed in the past, but something like a permanent condition of the past, present, and future—places strain on common understandings of mourning and grief work. How can we grieve that which hasn't yet been lost, a loss that furthermore comes through a complex set of interactions between human behavior and the earth's atmosphere that cannot be easily clarified or explained?

Moreover, our current environmental crisis has so far affected and will continue to disproportionately affect what Judith Butler has called "devalued and ungrievable lives."[1] These lives include both those of plant and animal bodies lost to extinction as well as racialized human lives like those who are losing their homes in the Pacific Islands, those who have experienced climate-intensified storms like Hurricane Katrina, and those who will most likely be forced to flee their homes in the Ganges River delta. Unfortunately, due to prevailing beliefs about what lives are considered worthy of grief (and thus worthy of value), climate change threatens to become a crisis borne overwhelmingly by the poor and nonhuman, while the privileged— those considered most fully "human"—protect themselves at the expense of abandoning the rest.

A question then emerges: How do we grieve, or encourage others to grieve, that which does not fit into normative conceptions of the "grievable," particularly when our unwillingness to acknowledge loss may be the greatest obstacle we face in advocating for social change?

One response might be to attend to exactly what Moser calls on environmental leaders to "accept" in this chapter's epigraph. Here we find a "grief" that concerns itself with cherished ideas as much as material lives. While other sections of her article stress the nonhuman, in this paragraph the coral reefs, the Arctic mammals, drop away in favor of a focus on letting go of "hope," "better tomorrows," and "the 'American Dream'"—in other words, what many Americans consider the future good life they aspire to reach.[2] Unfortunately, the motivating but often environmentally destructive ideals that make up the "American Dream"—ideals that so disregard the health of the nonhuman that it has brought the planetary ecosystem to the brink of collapse—are not necessarily easy to relinquish. In *Cruel*

Optimism Lauren Berlant highlights the difficulty, and at times impossibility, of detaching from these aspirations. Nevertheless it is becoming increasingly crucial that we *do* detach from our fantasies of "better tomorrows," fantasies that are in fact oil-driven fever dreams that are in actuality "an obstacle to [our] flourishing."[3]

In this chapter I seek to explore whether it may be possible for art, particularly film, to provide us with models that enact this process of detachment from current ideas of futurity and the human-centric "good life." Specifically I analyze a possible instance of such a model in the 2012 film *Beasts of the Southern Wild*. In order to fully sketch out my argument, though, I must first consider the risks of investing in film and its generic conventions in working through imminent future crises like climate change. As I discuss in the next section, the structure of conventional linear narrative—still the predominant style of most popular and even much independent film—may hinder the evocation of a grief that can foster audience action rather than complacence.

Narrative and Affective Containment

In her article "Haunting from the Future: Psychic Life in the Wake of Nuclear Necropolitics," Gabriele Schwab summarizes Derrida's "No Apocalypse, Not Now," in service to her concern with what she calls the "nuclear imaginary."[4] Both she and Derrida are concerned with narrative containment of the future danger presented by the nuclear threat. For Derrida, a too-literal imagining of the cause of our anxiety only makes a narrative's audience feel a sense of mastery over what they fear. While Derrida was specifically responding to his own cultural moment and the danger posed by nuclear weaponry, a similar containment manifests in twenty-first-century climate disaster films like *The Day After Tomorrow* or *Interstellar*. These films follow a traditional linear plot line wherein the problem of global environmental collapse, represented through the emergence of a singular or contained series of spectacular events, is overcome by the end of the film. Such stories may affirm the ever-abundant resilience and ingenuity of humanity, but viewers are also sent the message that they have no reason to worry or take meaningful action. They are comforted, rather than spurred into action.

I would further suggest, building on my prior invocation of Berlant, that what is surfacing in films like these is a manifestation of the neoliberal optimistic orientation so memorably highlighted in *Cruel Optimism* but also analyzed at length in what has become almost a subfield of academic writing unto itself.[5] In the case of these climate containment films, optimism functions to meet the psychic need to cope with environmental change through an attachment to romantic notions of unassailable human and technological progress. When the major conflict of the film—the climate disaster—is overcome at its conclusion, climate change is narratively transformed into an obstacle that serves only to urge humanity onward to ever greater heights. Like the "fort-da" game of Freud's grandson, climate containment films enact the destruction of our planet in order to recuperate the power of humanity through its ability to ultimately save it, forgetting that after the destruction rescue might no longer be possible.[6] Thus climate denialism, when expressed through film genre, manifests as an attempt to exert mastery in a time of profound anxiety.

Interestingly Derrida includes in "No Apocalypse, Not Now" a recommendation of another narrative method—experimental work like that of Joyce and Beckett, which, in Schwab's paraphrasing, is "evocative rather than referential and performative rather than conclusive, thus radically undercutting any of the familiar thrills and consolations of an apocalyptic imaginary."[7] Through allegorical displacement, then, a narrative can potentially avoid linear and temporal containment of a future threat. The contemporary climate fiction film that may best fit Derrida's suggestion is Benh Zeitlin's *Beasts of the Southern Wild* (2012). Drawing heavily upon magical realist and expressionist elements, the film retells the events of a storm that may or may not be Hurricane Katrina, as seen through the eyes of a young African American girl named Hushpuppy, who by the end of the film loses both her father and most of her coastal community, called the "Bathtub."

The setting is never specifically articulated in terms of either time or place, and only implicitly does the film reference Katrina—in its inclusion of levees, shots of the shores of Louisiana and actual Katrina wreckage, clear depictions of Louisiana culture (e.g., eating gator meat), and a sequence set in a "shelter" bearing some resemblance to the Superdome.[8] At the

Map of the Bathtub, showing the fictional Isle de Charles Doucet, inspired by the real Isle de Jean Charles, Louisiana. Film still from Zeitlin, *Beasts of the Southern Wild*, via https://film-grab.com/2013/01/05/beasts-of-the-southern-wild/.

same time, since an onscreen map's depiction of the levee dystopically covers what seems to be the entire Louisiana coast—not by any means a contemporary reality—the film's setting seems better attributed to the future than 2005 (fig. 1). Thus the film's uncertain temporality and choice of Katrina as allegory (rather than explicit subject) seem to break the pattern of linear climate fiction plots. In fact I would like to suggest that *Beasts* eludes audience mastery of the climate change threat. I furthermore believe it provides a possible model for both detaching from and grieving for the loss of the world viewers currently inhabit, clearing the way for improvising new ways of living that can meet the environmental challenges they will begin to face—with some important caveats, however.

Many critics and academics at the time of the film's release also saw it as the arrival of a much-needed alternative version of a climate fiction film. Nicholas Mirzoeff called it "perhaps the first film to create a means to visualize climate resistance" and to offer "a way to begin to imagine wild alternatives to governmentality."[9] The *New York Times* critic A. O. Scott felt "a blast of sheer, improbable joy."[10] As the fall of 2012 closed in, however, several scholars and online bloggers, led by bell hooks and followed soon after by Christina Sharpe and Jayna Brown, writing for the *Social Text* blog, began to critique the film's troubling treatment of race.[11] hooks in particular emphasized the possible eroticization of Hushpuppy's small and vulnerable body, and Brown and Sharpe, in slightly different ways, saw Hushpuppy's blackness as the very condition enabling Scott's "blast of . . . joy." Sharpe asks "how else could incipient sexual and other violence, the violence of extreme poverty, flooding, the violence of a six-year-old girl child living alone in her own ramshackle house with no mother or father, be inspiring and not tragic? How does a little black girl child orphaned and abandoned become a vision for climate resistance for so many people who watched the film?"[12]

Perhaps surprisingly, I approach this analysis of *Beasts of the Southern Wild* agreeing far more with hooks, Sharpe, and Brown than with Mirzoeff and Scott. In fact I believe that Scott's joy is in part built on his inability to see Hushpuppy's life and that of her father as grievable. There is something incredibly unjust in laying the burden of climate resistance and resilience on the back of an impoverished and now parentless black child who has already lost so much in her short life. However, I will argue that this injustice is part of what makes *Beasts of the Southern Wild* a prescient, important film about our present and future. In fact I find within it a representation of a *futurity without optimism*—that is, a futurity cleared of fantasies projected from the (patriarchal, anthropocentric) past and thus a futurity radically open to difference and change. Significantly, though, this is a futurity that leaves the Hushpuppys of the world with a terrible burden as much as a gift.

Fixing the Family, Fixing the Universe

In a relatively underanalyzed chapter from *Cruel Optimism* Berlant discusses two films by the Dardenne brothers, *La promesse* (1996) and *Rosetta* (1999), which, similar to *Beasts of the Southern Wild*, feature a fraught relationship between a parent and child as they struggle to survive in conditions of contemporary precarity. Like Hushpuppy, the children in these films undergo attempts to forge better lives for themselves, attempts that in all three cases fail. Berlant's chief interest in the Dardennes' films is to demonstrate the children's persistent optimism in forms of sociality that have already proven to them their unreliability, the fact that "some children reproduce the forms of the bad life insofar as they are rooted in the family."[13] Unlike the children in the Dardenne brothers' films, though, Hushpuppy seems to be able to successfully detach from the "bad life" as enacted through the sometimes loving, often neglectful figure of her father. The question of course is why she is able to do so when others—including her father—are not.

To understand why Hushpuppy is able to act differently from her father, and furthermore in order to see that she does act differently by the end of film, one must first interrogate what is meant by the "beastliness" drawn to our attention by the film's title. Indeed by naming his film what he did, Zeitlin explicitly invites his audience to identify both the humans and the animals onscreen as "beasts," and for some critics, including Sharpe, this has problematically perpetuated stereotypical associations between African Americans and animals, as well as furthered social Darwinist discourses of survival through strength and brutality. These critics have seen the film's depiction of "beastliness" as reproductive, rather than disruptive, of historical relations of power. Toward the beginning of the film Hushpuppy's ideas of beastliness and strength, as communicated via voice-over, are ideas that she's clearly learned from her father. These messages are characteristically masculine—don't be a pussy, don't cry, don't have mercy. In perhaps the most famous scene of the film, Wink interrupts a lesson Hushpuppy is receiving about the "proper" way to eat a crab by yelling at her to "beast it," which he violently demonstrates by tearing the crab's limbs off rather than gently breaking them.[14] Hushpuppy struggles at first but then succeeds at "beasting," culminating with her climbing onto the table to stand with her father, roaring in triumph. Following from her father's teachings, to be a "beast," in Hushpuppy's mind, is a positive identity but one that is founded on and restricted to ideas of strength and dominance. On the basis of these episodes alone, the penultimate scene of Beasts, in which Hushpuppy comes face to face with a gigantic wild aurochs, seems an unqualified celebration of her ability to become "the man" after her father's death, in that she can survive through the practice of a brutal and dominant "naturalness" that her precarious life supposedly requires.

However, such readings also elide the way these ideas of beastliness are consistently undercut throughout the film—by other characters' tenderness, by Hushpuppy's own attentiveness and craving for gentleness and care. A major narrative motif is Hushpuppy's repeated attempts to "listen" to other animals she believes speak in code—animals that include crabs, fish, livestock, and a sick woman on a hospital bed. These attempts often accompany voice-overs that expound upon the fabric of the universe and Hushpuppy's place within it. In these moments of narration, Hushpuppy articulates a fundamentally ecological conception of parts fitting together rather than an ideology of competition and violence (although in fear or anger she sometimes expresses the latter). At one point her fierce village teacher and local wisewoman, while working to heal one of the other Bathtub children, tells Hushpuppy and her friends that the "best thing I can teach you is to care for people smaller and sweeter than you."[15] Indeed the turning point of the film arguably comes when Hushpuppy, overcome with anger at her father, punches him in the stomach to the accompaniment of a distant crack of lightning and reacts immediately with horror at the result of her own aggression, as he falls to the ground in pain. It turns out, despite Wink's attempts to convince her otherwise, that Hushpuppy's father—and by extension her universe—may be far more vulnerable than she thought and thus in need of her tenderness. In fact as the film progresses Hushpuppy begins to work through the tension produced by these contradicting ideas of proper relationship with others, as channeled through her ideas of beastliness: dominance or care, independence or interdependence.

Nicole Seymour, in *Strange Natures*, describes a similar phenomenon in her reading of the transgender novels *Stone Butch Blues*, *No Telephone to Heaven*, and *Cereus Blooms at Night*. In each she finds that "in grappling with their . . . [normatively ascribed] status as less-than-human," the transgender characters "begin to forge strong bonds with the non-human."[16] Ironically the discriminatory logic that classifies transgender people as somehow nonhuman leads to their ability to reclaim that identity and relate to plant and animal life in the novels. In the case of the Bathtub residents we might read their embrace of their beastliness as a defiant response to their exclusion from the social and the human, as represented by the world inside the levee. The adults teach Hushpuppy to identify in that derided animality a pathway toward empathy, and thus she is able to seek and make a connection with the aurochs she so feared in the earlier parts of the film.

As the film continues and the fabric of Hushpuppy's current world unravels, beginning with the onset of her father's illness and progressing with the storm that drowns the Bathtub, a herd of gigantic ancient aurochs rises from beneath the melting Antarctic ice and initiates a journey north. Meanwhile Hushpuppy, thinking she has "broken" the world by hurting her father, sets out on a search for her long-lost mother. The aim of her journey is to repair her universe through the repair of her family, retrieving the mother she has only heretofore fantasized into existence with an old jersey fitted onto a chair. She partially succeeds in this endeavor when she finds in a floating strip club's kitchen a woman cooking gator meat; this woman bears an uncanny similarity to the mother she has dreamed of. As Hushpuppy dances in her maybe-mother's arms, she realizes that when the woman says she can only take care of herself, Hushpuppy has not found the fix she seeks. While the search for her mother was Hushpuppy's attempt to sustain her world through the reconstitution of her family, she learns instead that she must take care of her dying father herself and take up her position in the new world as a parentless child. "Sometimes," she says, "you can break something so bad that it can't get put back together."[17] With this comment she loses her optimism for her "fix," but that loss and concomitant acceptance of the loss of her father and his world set the stage for her improvisation of new forms of sociality beyond the human in the scenes that follow.

Indeed as she returns to her father with a box of leftover gator meat, Hushpuppy and her friends become stalked by the aurochs, who begin to chase them. While the girls who have accompanied her on her journey run in fear, Hushpuppy turns instead to face the aurochs. At the end of a pier the camera closes in on the encounter between Hushpuppy and the head of the pack. Hushpuppy looks at the animal with a determined, confident

Hushpuppy and the aurochs. Film still from Zeitlin, *Beasts of the Southern Wild*, via https://film-grab.com/2013/01/05/beasts-of-the-southern-wild/.

gaze (fig. 2). The aurochs meets her confrontation with a bow to the knee that is repeated by the rest of the animals. At this move, curiously, Hushpuppy smiles and states inquisitively, "You're my friend, sort of," but after a pause she adds forcefully, "I gotta take care of mine."[18]

It is this final confrontation and strangely contradictory bit of dialogue that encapsulates Hushpuppy's detachment from the violent forms of dominant anthropocentrism taught to her by her father, as well as from the ambivalent rather than hopeful relation she has established with the aurochs. If Hushpuppy was following the rules of her father, she might have sought to dominate the aurochs in some way, to kill them or to scare them away, but instead she establishes a brief, necessary, respectful moment of relation, before she leaves to care for the man who has become weaker than she—her father, to whom she feeds her imagined mother's fried gator on his death bed. The moment between Hushpuppy and the aurochs is not a depiction of utopian harmony or hopeful reconciliation between human and animal; it is a meeting between two wary individuals who can respect

Hushpuppy and the last residents of the Bathtub, with the Gulf of Mexico on both sides. Film still from Zeitlin, *Beasts of the Southern Wild*, via https://film-grab.com /2013/01/05/beasts-of-the-southern-wild/.

their mutual implication in each other's lives but may or may not meet again. It is a fleeting connection, a relation left ambivalently open rather than predetermined by optimistic fantasy. Without her family, Hushpuppy arguably enters a world full of such relations.

The final shot, of Hushpuppy and the remaining Bathtub clan marching forward on a small strip of land licked by waves on both sides, symbolizes both the hope and danger this unprecedented world holds (figs. 3 and 4). These last images are certainly not the manifestation of unqualified joy and resilience many critics saw in the film. Indeed the concluding shot of *Beasts of the Southern Wild* captures in exemplary fashion, even more so than Hushpuppy's encounter with the aurochs, what a futurity without optimism might look like—survivors, shed of all previous attachments, managing to move forward into a future they recognize as uncertain, knowing they could be deluged at any moment by the waters that surround them but still open to those aurochs that may appear along their way, that have not yet proven themselves friend or foe.

The closing shot, with the Bathtub's survivors on their spit of land—futurity without optimism. Film still from Zeitlin, *Beasts of the Southern Wild*, via https://film-grab.com/2013/01/05/beasts-of-the-southern-wild/.

Affective Response and the Climate Resilience of Black and Indigenous Bodies

Thus this concept of "futurity without optimism," to which I have briefly alluded, is fundamentally double-sided. On the one hand Hushpuppy is able to detach from a set of nonfunctioning attitudes toward the nonhuman Other in order to improvise an encounter of human-animal relationality that allows her survival. On the other, this improvisation is only facilitated by the failure of her attempts at familial repair, her inability to "fix" the universe through normative human forms of sociality. She is consequently able to escape the reproduction of the heteronormative family as the ultimate ideal of human kinship and civil society, but the reality remains that her family is a *particular* family. The particularity of that family within an American cultural context, in which race is a highly salient identity marker for both an individual and a character, means that Hushpuppy's radical new futurity comes at the cost of the *black* family—which significantly changes the affective impact on actual viewing audiences.

In other words Hushpuppy's specific "futurity without optimism" can *feel* very different to different viewers, in part because of its enactment via a small black female body (however wonderfully played by Quvenzhané Wallis). Adrian Ivakhiv, in a brilliant theorization of the different factors that make up a spectator's affective response to a film, specifies "exo-referentiality" as one of three primary influences. "Exo-referentiality" comprises a viewer's outside "ideological" or "theoretical frameworks," and divergence among outside emotional or intellectual commitments can produce incredibly divergent responses to a film.[19]

For example, in my initial reading of the film, a reading that drew on my own feminist, queer, and environmentally minded "exo-references," Hushpuppy's father, Wink, is the Bathtub's chief representative of dominance and violence toward other creatures, as well as of "cruel optimism" itself. Wink's masculinity leads him not only to certain beliefs about nature and strength that push him to believe that he must teach his daughter to refuse any tendency toward gentleness but also to block his daughter from the knowledge of his own growing weakness. Wink is a man who cannot accept his own death and the death of the Bathtub and thus by extension the death of his world and Hushpuppy's. Any question from Hushpuppy about his health early in the film is met with anger. When the residents of the Bathtub are taken to a shelter inside the levee after the storm, he refuses any medical help and attempts to abandon Hushpuppy with the state as he orchestrates an escape back to the Bathtub. Clinging to the past and refusing to admit any vulnerability, Wink is akin to a climate denier— unable to accept the change in the environment around him and the loss that that entails. Thus his death, for Hushpuppy and the audience, is not just the death of a father but of a set of harmful, clearly self-destructive and nonfunctioning approaches to the world that Hushpuppy has already begun to question throughout the film. If Wink represents the attempt to cling to forms of human sociality that no longer function, Hushpuppy represents the ability to move beyond those now archaic forms, walking into an insecure future without the need to exert mastery over it or the other creatures that will live there alongside her.

Yet, from another standpoint, which I have come to incorporate into my reading, Hushpuppy's insecurity is completely consistent with the historical erasure of black kinship structures that, as Hortense Spillers has forcefully argued, is one of the constitutive violences of the American racial system.[20] In this light the loss of Hushpuppy's mother, father, and community may rid her of the problematic historical attitudes toward the nonhuman as performed by her father, but they also rob her of the same kind of community and cultural resources that African American children have been denied for centuries. Thus the differences between (largely white) critics' initial affective responses to Beasts and the far more critical and even horrified ones on the part of many scholars of color may be more easily explained by one's ability to see this theft of community and family as the theft it is—whether or not it helps Hushpuppy to improvise new human-animal relations at the film's conclusion.

So Hushpuppy finds the strength and capacity to forge unprecedented relations with the aurochs, but it comes at the cost of community and family—specifically the black family. Importantly Hushpuppy's racial identity means that many viewers will approach the film with race in mind, consciously or not, with concurrently divergent valuations of the "grievability" of her family. The reality of this viewing context undercuts the ability for audiences to see Hushpuppy's story as a model for letting go of their own attachments, grieving their own "fathers." Unfortunately the erasure of Hushpuppy's family may play into white fantasies of racial progress, the slate of the past wiped clean as a black female child leads us into a "better" future.

In a densely researched GLQ article on Beasts of the Southern Wild, Tavia Nyong'o unearths the ways Beasts draws on American traditions of racialized erasure, in his case by positing impoverished and racialized bodies as both abstract symbols and real-life enemies of white ideals of environmental conservation. Drawing on Andil Gosine, Nyong'o links the "creation of 'wildlife preserves' and national parks across the colonized world . . . predicated on the removal of their human, reproductive presence: the areas' indigenous populations" to the emergence of Hushpuppy's human-wild encounter on unacknowledged indigenous lands.[21] Beyond the fact that the film's American setting means that it implicitly takes place on colonized territory, Zeitlin has named Isle de Jean Charles, Louisiana, as inspiration for his vision of the Bathtub community. While the Bathtub in the film is inhabited by what appears to be a mix of black and white individuals, Isle de Jean Charles is in actuality primarily inhabited by members of the Choctaw and Houma tribal communities.[22] In other words Zeitlin based his *Beasts* on the experiences of a real indigenous community but then chose to make the film without any explicit reference to indigeneity or indigenous characters. For Nyong'o such an exclusion is not a mistake, as "it is the engulfment of native sovereignty that renders the resultant wildness recuperable for white fantasies of surrogation, adoption, and transplantation."[23] With Native people living there, the land cannot in a U.S. cultural imaginary become an enactment of a recognizably multicultural or progressive future. Thus *Beasts* may enact a dream of sustainable nonanthropocentric futurity, but it still does so through the use of a black female child as symbol and indigenous land as forgotten foundation. It may be nonanthropocentric, but it is not decolonial.

To push this point further Nyong'o traces the source of the film's aurochs to the world's first recorded anthropogenic extinction in the forests of seventeenth-century Poland. The subject of royal decrees seeking to protect the aurochs even at the expense of villagers' hunger or livelihood, the aurochs's story connects even more tightly to Nyong'o's point about white discourses of "wildness." The aurochs, a European mammal, is fundamentally a "sign of the return of the European repressed," one that is "reenact[ing] the European colonization of the New World in bovine form."[24] With this in mind, it becomes even more disturbing that the aurochs must somehow haunt the dreams of an African American child living on Louisiana's endangered coastline.

There remains a terrible verisimilitude in this haunting, disturbing though it is, in that there are and will be more Hushpuppys forced to mourn their families and communities if climate change continues apace with no major political changes to address it.[25] In the end this mirroring of our political reality may be the most convincing reason to consider the underside, and not simply the exciting possibilities, of Hushpuppy's "futurity without optimism." Those living in the path of rising ocean waters are disproportionately the world's poor, and the Indian state has already built a fence to keep out Bangladeshi climate refugees.[26] As I write, indigenous communities living on the coastlines, north and south, of the United States face imminent engulfment. Unfortunately the European repressed, in the form of carbon emissions and increasing global temperatures, has come to confront everyone, most especially those who are nonwhite, poor, and with the least amounts of power. Acting as if that reality is otherwise will only hamper the ability of those who have disproportionately unleashed those emissions—those with the most wealth and privilege to burn both literally and metaphorically—to perceive that they, too, must make difficult choices rather than rely on Others to do it for them.

Furthermore the emergent neoliberal ideology of "resilience," so present in many reviews of *Beasts*, may be part of what underlies the inability of the privileged to care about the basic needs of the present and future Hushpuppys who will be tasked with the responsibility of encountering the worst losses of climate change. The political theorists Brad Evans and Julian Reid contend in *Resilient Life: The Art of Living Dangerously* that urging "resilience" as a tool of survival under neoliberal power is detrimental to developing effective resistance to contemporary structures of power. In fact a valorization of resilience is in Evans's and Reid's minds an implicit acceptance of the new state of things—insecurity, vulnerability, crisis.[27] Similarly Dian Million details how settler colonial nations like Canada, the United States, and Australia, though they have embraced the need to "heal" the past traumas of the indigenous people living in their lands, often actually end up charging those peoples with creating their own healing and affective management systems. These settler colonial states meanwhile fail to take responsibility as perpetrators of these "past" traumas and thus continue to perpetrate them, while blaming indigenous peoples for failing to "heal" themselves.[28]

Thus Hushpuppy, though coded African American rather than Native, could be taken as an incredibly frightening example of someone who in fact brilliantly fulfills the requirements of the ideal neoliberal subject, one who affectively manages herself so well that trauma after trauma can continue to be exacted upon her without need for restitution. "Resilience," then, can work to justify the abandonment of vulnerable peoples who must now fend for themselves, no matter the greater resources of those most responsible for the problems they encounter.

Detaching from anthropocentrism and improvising new forms of relationality is a task for everyone, but that does not justify relying on the Hushpuppys of the world to bear the brunt of the difficult choices that must be made and risks that must be taken. Despite *Beasts of the Southern Wild*'s innovative formal avoidance of climate change containment and mastery, as well as its nonanthropocentric ending, the burden of familial and cultural loss and the need to develop respectful approaches to engagement with the nonhuman falls upon the shoulders of a child both black and poor. While it may be tempting to rejoice in the film's powerful portrait of her resilience, its emulation of the reality of our climate change politics—in which the poorest lose the most, despite benefiting the least from the technologies that have perpetrated their loss—should give us all pause. In addition to offering us a promising model of human-animal relationality, then, *Beasts of the Southern Wild* also enacts a "futurity without optimism" in the most tragic sense, in that the film depicts the unnecessarily imperiled futures that await the world's most vulnerable, as we all move into an unprecedented new universe.

NOTES

1. Butler, *Frames of War*, 22.
2. Moser, "Getting Real about It," 904.
3. Berlant, *Cruel Optimism*, 1.
4. Schwab, "Haunting from the Future," 87.
5. See in particular Ahmed, *Promise of Happiness*; and Povinelli, *Economies of Abandonment*.
6. Freud, *Beyond the Pleasure Principle*. Of course Melanie Klein would later take this up in her discussions of aggression and repair, which have deeply influenced the work of Berlant used prominently in this chapter.
7. Schwab, "Haunting from the Future," 91.
8. Of course Zeitlin makes explicit reference to Katrina and Louisiana in promotional materials for the film; see Rachel Arons, "Mythical Bayou's All-Too-Real Peril: The Making of 'Beasts of the Southern Wild,'" *New York Times*, June 8, 2012, http://www.nytimes.com/2012/06/10/movies/the-making-of-beasts-of

-the-southern-wild.html. But a viewer coming into the film with no knowledge of this artistic inspiration must only read the clues the film gives, which are left vague—and I would suggest purposely so to invoke a "mythic" feel.

9. Mirzoeff, "Becoming Wild."
10. A. O. Scott, "She's the Man of This Swamp," *New York Times*, June 26, 2012, http://www.nytimes.com/2012/06/27/movies/beasts-of-the-southern-wild-directed-by-benh-zeitlin.html.
11. hooks, "No Love in the Wild"; Sharpe, "*Beasts* I"; Brown, "*Beasts* II."
12. Sharpe, "*Beasts* I."
13. Berlant, *Cruel Optimism*, 188.
14. Zeitlin, *Beasts of the Southern Wild*.
15. Zeitlin, *Beasts of the Southern Wild*.
16. Seymour, *Strange Natures*, 30.
17. Zeitlin, *Beasts of the Southern Wild*.
18. Zeitlin, *Beasts of the Southern Wild*.
19. Ivakhiv, "What Can a Film Do?," 190.
20. Spillers, "Mama's Baby, Papa's Maybe."
21. Nyong'o, "Little Monsters," 261–62. See also Gosine, "Non-White Reproduction and Same-Sex Eroticism."
22. Arons, "Mythical Bayou's All-Too-Real Peril." This community has made national news by receiving $48 million from the U.S. government to resettle off the island, thus becoming the nation's first "climate refugees." See Coral Davenport and Campbell Robertson, "Resettling the First American 'Climate Refugees,'" *New York Times*, May 3, 2016, https://www.nytimes.com/2016/05/03/us/resettling-the-first-american-climate-refugees.html; and Hansen, "Biloxi-Chitimacha-Choctaw."
23. Nyong'o, "Little Monsters," 264.
24. Nyong'o, "Little Monsters," 265.
25. And, as this chapter goes to press, those major political changes seem even further away than when this sentence was first written, as the current U.S. president, Donald Trump, pulls the United States out of the Paris climate accords.
26. Carney, Miklian, and Hoelscher, "Fortress India."
27. Evans and Reid, *Resilient Life*.
28. Million, *Therapeutic Nations*.

BIBLIOGRAPHY

Ahmed, Sara. *The Promise of Happiness*. Durham: Duke University Press, 2010.
Berlant, Lauren. *Cruel Optimism*. Durham: Duke University Press, 2011.
Brown, Jayna. "*Beasts of the Southern Wild*—The Romance of Precarity II." *Social Text*

(blog), September 27, 2012. https://socialtextjournal.org/beasts-of-the-southern
-wild-the-romance-of-precarity-i/.

Butler, Judith. *Frames of War: When Is Life Grievable?* London: Verso, 2009.

Carney, Scott, Jason Miklian, and Kristian Hoelscher. "Fortress India." *Foreign Policy*, June 20, 2011. http://foreignpolicy.com/2011/06/20/fortress-india/.

Derrida, Jacques. "No Apocalypse, Not Now." *Diacritics* 14, no. 2 (1984): 20–31.

Evans, Brad, and Julian Reid. *Resilient Life: The Art of Living Dangerously.* Cambridge: Polity Press, 2014.

Freud, Sigmund. *Beyond the Pleasure Principle.* Edited by James Strachey. 1920. London: Bantam Books, 1961.

Gosine, Andil. "Non-White Reproduction and Same-Sex Eroticism: Queer Acts against Nature." In *Queer Ecologies: Sex, Nature, Politics, Desire*, edited by Catriona Mortimer-Sandilands and Bruce Erickson, 149–57. Bloomington: Indiana University Press, 2010.

Hansen, Terri. "Biloxi-Chitimacha-Choctaw Get $48 Million to Move Off of Disappearing Louisiana Island." *Indian Country Media Network*, February 5, 2016. https://indiancountrymedianetwork.com/news/environment/biloxi-chitimacha -choctaw-get-48-million-to-move-off-of-disappearing-louisiana-island/.

hooks, bell. "No Love in the Wild." *NewBlackMan (in Exile)*, September 5, 2012. http:// www.newblackmaninexile.net/2012/09/bell-hooks-no-love-in-wild.html.

Ivakhiv, Adrian. "What Can a Film Do? Assessing *Avatar*'s Global Affects." In *Moving Environments: Affect, Emotion, Ecology, and Film*, edited by Alexa Weik von Mossner, 159–80. Waterloo ON: Wilfred Laurier University Press, 2014.

Million, Dian. *Therapeutic Nations: Healing in an Age of Indigenous Human Rights.* Tucson: University of Arizona Press, 2013.

Mirzoeff, Nicholas. "Becoming Wild." *Occupy 2012* (blog), September 30, 2012. http:// www.nicholasmirzoeff.com/O2012/2012/09/30/becoming-wild/.

Moser, Susanne C. "Getting Real about It: Meeting the Psychological and Social Needs of a World in Distress." In *Environmental Leadership: A Reference Handbook*, edited by Deborah Rigling Gallagher, 900–908. Thousand Oaks CA: SAGE, 2012.

Nyong'o, Tavia. "Little Monsters: Race, Sovereignty, and Queer Inhumanism in *Beasts of the Southern Wild*." *GLQ: A Journal of Lesbian and Gay Studies* 21, no. 2–3 (2015): 249–72.

Povinelli, Elizabeth. *Economies of Abandonment: Social Belonging and Endurance in Late Liberalism.* Durham: Duke University Press, 2011.

Schwab, Gabriele. "Haunting from the Future: Psychic Life in the Wake of Nuclear Necropolitics." *Undecidable Unconscious: A Journal of Deconstruction and Psychoanalysis* 1 (2014): 85–101.

Seymour, Nicole. *Strange Natures: Futurity, Empathy, and the Queer Ecological Imagination*. Urbana: University of Illinois Press, 2013.

Sharpe, Christina. "*Beasts of the Southern Wild*—The Romance of Precarity I." *Social Text* (blog), September 27, 2012. https://socialtextjournal.org/beasts-of-the -southern-wild-the-romance-of-precarity-ii/.

Spillers, Hortense. "Mama's Baby, Papa's Maybe: An American Grammar Book." In *Feminisms: An Anthology of Literary Theory and Criticism*, edited by Robyn R. Warhol and Diane Price Herndl, 384–405. New Brunswick NJ: Rutgers University Press, 1991.

Zeitlin, Benh, dir. *Beasts of the Southern Wild*. Los Angeles: 20th Century Fox, 2012. DVD.

PART 4

Environmentalist Killjoys

Politics and Pedagogy

11

The Queerness of Environmental Affect

NICOLE SEYMOUR

In the summer of 2016 I presented at a nonacademic conference for the first time: the Fab Planet Summit in San Francisco, hosted by the non-profit LGBTQ/environmental organization OUT for Sustainability.[1] In addition to having much better snacks than most academic conferences Fab Planet also had a different affective register. For instance, audience members snapped their fingers whenever the speaker made a point they found incisive or inspiring—"a less official, more spontaneous and impassioned in-the-moment response" than clapping, according to a *New York Times* article headlined, amusingly, "Why Snapping Is the New Clapping."[2] As the first speaker of the day, I was initially ruffled by the sound, until I looked up into the crowd and saw attentive smiles. Overall the mood of the conference was light-hearted and friendly, compared to the tension and formality of, say, an MLA convention—at which, as I always joke, you can feel the anxiety of job-market candidates (historically, myself included) in the air. My Fab Planet experience thus inspired me to consider one possible definition of queer environmental affect: the alternative forms of attachment, emotion, and response that emerge within the context of queer or non-normative spaces.

Less than two weeks later I woke up to the news of the mass shooting on Latin Night at Pulse, an LGBTQ nightclub in Orlando, Florida. After thirty minutes of panic before I heard from my close friend who lives in the area—safe and sound—the commentary began to pour in about the importance of the gay bar, the queer club. The journalist Richard Kim wrote a moving piece for *The Nation*, declaring that "gay bars are therapy for people who can't afford therapy; temples for people who lost their religion, or whose religion lost them; vacations for people who can't go on vacation; homes for folk without families; sanctuaries against aggression. They take sound and fabric and flesh from the ordinary world, and under cover of darkness and the influence of alcohol or drugs, transform it all into something that scrapes up against utopia."[3] The novelist Justin Torres wrote an ode in the *Washington Post* titled "In Praise of Latin Night at the Queer Club," describing how "a sense of safety *transforms the body, transforms the spirit.* So many of us walk through the world without it. So when you walk through the door and it's a salsa beat, and brown bodies, queer bodies, all writhing in some fake smoke and strobing lights, *no matter how cool, how detached, how over-it you think you are, Latin Night at the Queer Club breaks your cool. You can't help but smile.*"[4] Here we might find a slightly different definition of queer environmental affect: forms of attachment, emotion, and response *to* queer or non-normative spaces, including or perhaps especially those that cater to people of color. Indeed, Torres seems to understand Latin Night at the queer club as a time and space that combats (false) lack of affect, eliciting visceral, effusive reactions against one's conscious will: "*you can't help but smile.*"

This chapter sketches out these and other possible definitions of queer environmental affect. I begin by surveying extant work on affect from queer theorists. As I argue, queer theory is an essential resource for an affective ecocriticism, or any environmental humanities work engaged with affect, for two very different reasons. First, queer theory focuses on "bad," *as in negative,* affects such as shame, guilt, depression, and melancholia—the same affects that emerge in the context of environmental crisis. Second, queer theory also focuses on "bad," *as in inappropriate,* affects, including humor, camp, frivolity, and irony—affects that, as I argue elsewhere, are largely, and problematically, *missing* from the context of environmental crisis, especially from environmental art and scholarship.[5] I then explore the queerness *of* environmental affect, showing how any emotional investment in particular spaces or environments—be they gay bars or gardens—might be considered queer. To illustrate these claims I offer readings of two environmentally themed texts, looking first at the contemporary American artist Kim Anno's video projects and then at the American film director Douglas Trumbull's 1972 cult classic, *Silent Running*. I show how these texts both display and evoke a diverse range of affects, including "bad" ones, in response to environmental crisis.

Queer Theory, Affect, and Environment

Queer theory has had a long relationship with affect. As Michael Hardt states, "The two primary precursors to the affective turn I see in U.S. academic work are the focus on the body, which has been most extensively advanced in feminist theory, and the exploration of emotions, conducted predominantly in queer theory."[6] And indeed we might find that many if not most foundational queer theory scholars have been concerned with affect in some way or another. For example, Patricia Ticineto Clough has observed that "Judith Butler . . . introduced queer theory with her notion of 'melancholic heterosexuality,'" in which the possibility of homosexuality is foreclosed, becoming unmournable and thus lingering in the form of melancholia.[7] And Ann Cvetkovich points out that important queer theory figures such as Lauren Berlant, Butler, and Eve Sedgwick have built on their earlier work on sexuality with more explicit explorations of affect; Cvetkovich finds that, "as scholarship on affect flourishes, I no longer think of it as a minor spin-off from work on sexuality; instead, it extends the reach of studies of sexuality and enhances its status as a broadly intersectional category."[8]

As the invocation of Butler's melancholia might suggest, queer theorists have been particularly interested in *bad*, as in negative, affects. Heather Love observes broadly that "bad feelings have been central to the history of queer experience and queer feeling."[9] More specifically, Cvetkovich claims that "queer theory's critique of the normal" has inspired "discussions of the politics of negative affects, such as melancholy and shame."[10] We might also note that, when queer theorists do consider positive affects, they often find them to have negative implications. Take, for instance, Berlant's concept of "cruel optimism," a "relation [that] exists when something you desire is actually an obstacle to your flourishing"—as with, say, continued striving for the American Dream in a neoliberal era of precarity and downward mobility.[11]

Knowing that queer theory is a particularly rich site—perhaps even the richest—for thinking through affect, how can we employ queer theories of affect in ecocriticism and/or environmentalist work? First, and most obviously, we can use them to think through the bad-as-in-negative emotions associated with environmental crisis. Catriona Sandilands, for one, has taken up this possibility. She first observes that "recent queer scholarship on melancholia . . . much of it propelled by the enormity of AIDS and the omnipresence of . . . loss—in the midst, as Judith Butler points out, of a homophobic culture that barely tolerates, let alone values, homosexual attachments—is focused . . . on the condition of grieving the ungrievable: how does one mourn in the midst of a culture that finds it almost impossible to recognize the value of what has been lost?"[12] Sandilands uses that queer scholarship to diagnose a pervasive cultural condition, arguing that we contemporary humans suffer from "*melancholia*, a state of suspended mourning in which the object of loss is very real but psychically 'ungrievable' within the confines of a society that cannot acknowledge nonhuman beings, natural environments, and ecological processes as appropriate objects for genuine grief."[13] Sandilands is careful to note that this state is not apolitical: "melancholia is not only a denial of the loss of a beloved object but also a potentially politicized way of preserving that object."[14] In this sense we might define queer environmental affect as a socially "inappropriate" attachment to the nonhuman, the natural, and/or the ecological, one that honors those entities. I explore this definition further in my reading of *Silent Running*, below.

Second, and perhaps paradoxically, we might use queer theory's focus on bad-as-in-inappropriate affects such as humor, camp, frivolity, and irony to challenge debilitating and tiresome discourses of gloom and doom. Indeed, while I appreciate Sandilands's point about melancholia's politicism, I fear that the very invocation of melancholia replicates those discourses—and, more specifically, furthers environmentalism's off-putting reputation for gloominess and doominess. More pointedly, while Sandilands's application of Butler to environmental crisis may be novel, the image of melancholic environmentalists is quite a familiar one. My forthcoming book, *Bad Environmentalism: Irony and Irreverence in the Ecological Age*, responds to this paradigm, looking at artworks that employ humor, camp, frivolity, irony, and other alternative affective modes to speak to environmental concerns.

Here, then, I am inspired by how queer theorists of affect, along with activists, have insisted on the latter modes *alongside* modes such as melancholia and depression. For example, Cvetkovich describes how Feel Tank Chicago, a "cell" of the Public Feelings project spearheaded by herself, Berlant, and others, focuses on

> "political depression," the sense that customary forms of political response, including direct action and critical analysis, are no longer working either to change the world or to make us feel better. The concept of political depression is not, however, meant to be wholly depressing; indeed, Feel Tank has operated with the camp humor one might expect from a group of seasoned queer activists, organizing an International Day of the Politically Depressed in which participants were invited to show up in their bathrobes to indicate their fatigue with traditional forms of protest and distributing T-shirts and refrigerator magnets carrying the slogan "Depressed? It Might Be Political!" The goal is to depathologize negative affects so that they can be seen as a possible resource for political action rather than as its antithesis.[15]

Love has made similar points, showing how the "backward," negative feelings that define modern queer existence—shame, regret, bitterness, nostalgia—also produce merry cultural forms. As she argues, "Camp . . . with its tender concern for outmoded elements of popular culture and its refusal to get over childhood pleasures and traumas, is a backward art."[16] As we can see, queer affect theorists "promote a third way to crippling cynicism and stultifying optimism" in their synthesis of bad-as-in-negative and bad-as-in-inappropriate affects.[17] Put another way, such theorists can help us undertake a much-needed queering of today's dominant environmental affect.

We might also note that, while queer theory has been largely uninterested in environmental questions, it has always been interested in relationships, especially those that cross boundaries or break taboos.[18] And of course affect itself is understood as a question of interrelationality and interconnectivity; most affect theorists define affect as something that does not exist separately on its own and that is not interior to an individual. It is instead that which is generated between—between two bodies, between a person and an object, and so forth—or transferred across, in a kind of "contagion."[19] Consider, for instance, Berlant's concept of "the social potential of queerness, in which what counts is not one's 'object choice' as such but rather one's sustaining attachments, which are only sometimes also one's social relations."[20] Or consider José Esteban Muñoz's definition of affect as "the receptors we use to hear each other and the frequencies on which certain subalterns speak and are heard or, more importantly, felt."[21] Muñoz modifies Gayatri Spivak's well-known question "Can the subaltern speak?" to ask, "How does the subaltern feel? How might subalterns feel each other?" As he concludes, "Modified theories of object relations can potentially translate into productive ways in which to consider relationality within a larger social sphere."[22] Berlant and Muñoz both imagine queerness expansively, not as an issue of sexuality but as an issue of "sociality," as in relationality. Here I see potential for queer theory and ecocriticism to mutually inform one another: queer theorists allow us to see how affective attachments to nature or the ecological might be considered inherently queer, insofar as they vastly expand the scope of the social and the relational—just as they might see that one's "sustaining attachments," "subalterns," and the "larger social sphere" include nonhuman ecosystems and animals.

We must remember, however, that interrelationship is not always positive or inspirational—as mainstream environmentalist discourse so often has it, with slogans about how we are all connected in a web of life. And in this, queer theory and its interest in the negative can help us yet again. As Mel Y. Chen has observed, "Queer theory is an apt home for the consideration of toxicity, for I believe the two—queerness and toxicity—have an affinity. They truck with negativity, marginality, and subject-object confusions; they have, arguably, an affective intensity; they challenge heteronormative understandings of intimacy. Both have gotten under the skin. Yet queer theory's attachment to certain human bodies and other human objects elides from its view the queer socialities that certain other, nonhuman intimacies portend."[23]

Even as Chen acknowledges, again, that queer theory has been largely uninterested in environmental questions—"elid[ing] . . . nonhuman intimacies"—we see that queer theories of affect may nonetheless be important to those questions. Indeed Chen suggests that it is perhaps in the queerest moments—in which borders and boundaries are most troubled, and in which *we* might be most troubled—that we can see our interrelationship and interconnectivity with the environment and the nonhuman most clearly. Chen thus reminds us that queer environmental affect is a complex, ambivalent phenomenon.

Finally, I suggest that, especially in the wake of the Orlando mass shooting, we mine queer theory's work on attachment to places like the gay bar in order to further expand ecocriticism's purview beyond pristine and picturesque places such as "wilderness." While of course such expansion has been ongoing in ecocriticism for several years, and while several scholars have attended to queer spaces from an environmental standpoint and vice versa, affect has rarely been an explicit part of the conversation.[24] We might begin with Muñoz's work on subcultural spaces. Examining a Kevin McCarty photograph of the empty stage at Jewel's Catch One, a now-defunct black queer disco in Los Angeles, Muñoz observes that "the utopian performative charge of this image allows one to see the past, the moment before an actual performance, the moment of potentiality; and the viewer gains access to the affective particularity of that moment of hope and potential transformation that is also the temporality of performance."[25] Muñoz's work helps us think about the joys of *transitory* and *ephemeral* spaces—say, a bar you only go to on Latin Night, or a dance floor scene that only exists in the wee hours—spaces that ecocriticism, with its implicit focus on preservation, sustainability, and the material, has largely ignored.

While the transitory and/or ephemeral is sometimes a bad thing—a club closes because a neighborhood is gentrified, or one can only visit the bar in the wee hours because one works two jobs—it is, as Kim, Torres, and Muñoz suggest, part of the pleasure, as one savors a space's temporary respite all the more passionately.

We might note that odes to the gay bar have been particularly charged, even before the Orlando shooting, by the fact of its slow decline since a peak era in the 1970s. This decline *seems* to have a positive cause: increased acceptance of homosexuality and thus less need for separate spaces.[26] But we should recall how theorist Love, in asking us to "look backward"—to attach ourselves emotionally to a troubled queer past rather than an idealized queer future—reminds us of what has been lost in the march to mainstream acceptance. How has forward-leaning "progress" endangered or even destroyed queer spaces? Alternatively, how might affective attachments to a troubled queer past help preserve queer spaces? Or, perhaps, a more complicated set of questions: In remembering certain spaces, which others are forgotten? How do emotional attachments to the past inform which spaces are deemed worthy of protection and preservation and which are not? And, as Darren J. Patrick has put it in his work on the "gay and green gentrification" of New York's High Line, "What must be displaced in order to affirm the emergence of [a] particular space?"[27] These are questions of queer environmental affect. And they seem particularly important to consider, not just in a post-Orlando era but in an era when the U.S. National Park Service has recently declared the Stonewall Inn, site of a galvanizing rebellion in 1969, a national monument. Stonewall, the first LGBTQ space to receive such an honor, has a history that is contested to this very moment.[28]

Queer Environmental Affect in Visual Culture

KIM ANNO'S WATER CITIES

The Japanese American/Native American artist Kim Anno, with whom I was lucky to be paired for a Fab Planet panel, takes up in her work many of the aforementioned issues, including ephemerality, transitoriness, change, and cultural progress. Based in San Francisco, Anno has spent the last several years working on a series of short, non-narrative video films that, as she states, focus on "post sea level rise society for people in port cities."[29] These short films, including *Men and Women in Water Cities* (2011), *Water City, Berkeley* (2013), and *90 Miles from Paradise: Key West/Havana* (in progress), depict societies that are multiracial, gender diverse, and centered on cultural and aesthetic practices. In *Water City, Berkeley*, for instance, a black transgender woman in a bright yellow dress and blonde wig recites passages from classical Greek literature next to a bay; in all of the films in the series we see humans reading, singing, throwing parties, dancing, playing games, and playing sports. These films are not overtly queer in any obvious sense. However, as Anno states, "like the notion of the human not being at the center of nature but in the arena of nature, I also like to think of queerness in this way, not always at the center but in the milieu that I am creating. I want to create ecosystems, or ecologically focused images that are also queer images, [in which] the layers of these identities are presented without explanations but are present as something vital."[30] Like many queer theorists, Anno insists on a definition of "queer" that cannot be reduced to, say, same-sex object choice. In my brief reading below I locate the queerness of Anno's work in three aesthetic/affective features: disorienting visual form and sound; the ambivalent fusion of conflicting affects; and the insistence on cultural, and not just environmental, sustainability.

The visual form and sound of *Men and Women in Water Cities* disorient the viewer, perhaps highlighting the difference of this new future society. Just before the three-minute mark, for example, the film switches from its customary two-part split screen to a four-part split screen, with the first and third images rotated ninety degrees counterclockwise and the second and fourth rotated ninety degrees clockwise. The relatively normal image in question—a white, apparently heterosexual couple frolicking in the surf—has gone off-kilter. Soon after, a voice-over from Anno starts; it begins as audible, complete sentences but then fragments into overlapping tracks. The viewer struggles to hear the repeated phrase, "The boundary between sea and land is the most fleeting and transitory feature of the earth." While

Charlie Clark in Kim Anno's 90 *Miles from Paradise: Key West/Havana*. Courtesy of Kim Anno.

Lauren Marsden in Kim Anno's *Men and Women in Water Cities*. Courtesy of Kim Anno.

disorienting, the visual form and sound are not quite *disturbing*; they leave us in an emotional state somewhere between the normal and the unbearable.

In terms of visual content Anno's films present absurd images that evoke both pathos and amusement—again, an ambivalent emotional state. In *Men and Women in Water Cities* a young white boy, doubled by a mirroring split screen, reads a book intently as waves crash behind him, eventually soaking and spinning him but never breaking his attention. We might read this image as queer in a particular, though arguably stereotypical sense: the young man seems to personify the aesthete for whom a book is just as important, if not more so, than the "real world." But while his actions might therefore be interpreted as denialist—ignorant of the environmental processes that threaten him—they might also be described as resilient, refusing to accept defeat in the face of change. Later in the film a man wearing a suit and carrying a briefcase walks directly into the surf. A woman floats down an estuary on a mattress while casually reading a magazine. A group holds what looks like a business meeting at the bottom of a pool; others play basketball. Some people cry while others laugh and smile. The film concludes with nearly identical split-screen shots of a man who sinks to the bottom of the pool but then begins rising back up. The film freeze-frames and ends with him suspended in the water.

As a viewer, I don't quite know how to feel about these images. Does the last shot represent desperate crisis, as the man has not yet reached the surface, and perhaps never will? Does it depict resilience, as he is rising back up? Is it a charmingly absurd image, what with its juxtaposition of formal, adult attire (full suit and tie) and the pleasure, play, and immaturity we associate with a space like the swimming pool? Perhaps it is all of the above. The artist's statement that accompanies *Men and Women in Water Cities*—"Adaptation is a complex thing, sometimes pragmatic, sometimes light, sometime[s] dark"—captures its ambivalence, as does her own voice-over in the film: "This evidence of a rising sea is an interesting *and even an exciting thing* because it is rare that in the short span of human life we can actually observe and measure the progress of one of the great Earth rhythms."[31] From a traditional environmentalist standpoint this is an inappropriate affective response: one should not be "excite[d]" about sea level rise. But Anno, or at least the voice-over figure, nonetheless finds joy in a troubling development. She thereby articulates the queer affective complexity described by scholars such as Berlant and Cvetkovich.

Culture and aesthetics, as I have suggested above, are key to Anno's work. As the postcolonial scholar Kathy-Ann Tan has observed of *Water City, Berkeley*, "The reading of Oedipus' *Sophocles Rex* in the chorus-like chant of Greek tragedy heightens the solemnity and sense of slow catastrophe that impinge on the lives of the citizens of Water City, Berkeley, yet the sense of environmental crisis is somewhat staved off by the inhabitants' 'adaptation' to their new watery environment, *even if* this acclimatization is clearly also a highly performative and aestheticized act."[32] Tan captures the way that Anno's films never really slide into tragedy, finding (sometimes literal) buoyancy in images of adaptation. But we might take issue here with Tan's phrase "even if"—for, I would argue, Anno's work frames culture, aesthetics, and performance as *central to* survival in a time of crisis. Her films do not resemble the all-too-common bleak postapocalyptic narratives in which humans' needs are reduced to food, shelter, and self-defense; humans in her films cling to books, songs, clothes, and other cultural objects and practices. As Anno declared in her Fab Planet presentation, "I [locate] my projects at the intersection of multi-layered experiences such as environmental justice and cultural resiliency. . . . Cultural resiliency is something that I want to draw a line around, in order to fundamentally contest environmental deterioration. Culture is itself worth defining as a political act."[33] In addition to the obvious categories of literature, music, and fashion, which are well represented in her films, Anno insists that "queerness and LGBT identities are culture."[34] In a world in which queer people *and* queer spaces are still threatened—just as natural spaces are—Anno offers us affectively complex images of queer human and aesthetic survival.

SILENT RUNNING'S QUEER OVERINVESTMENTS

Released in 1972, two years after the first Earth Day, Douglas Trumbull's *Silent Running* is, I argue, first and foremost a film about human affective "overinvestment" in the nonhuman. This overinvestment, as I show, takes on queer dimensions both diegetically and extradiegetically; thus, while certainly more conventional than Anno's work in formal and narratological terms, *Silent Running* shares the latter's queer concerns. But first a brief plot summary: set entirely on a spaceship, *Silent Running* focuses on the ecologist Freeman Lowell (Bruce Dern), who has spent eight years tending to several geodesic domes that contain plant and animal specimens. Because such life has gone extinct on Earth, the ostensible hope is that these specimens can be reintroduced in the future. However, Lowell and his three fellow crew members receive sudden and inexplicable orders from the U.S. government to destroy the domes and return home. An outraged Lowell goes berserk, murdering his crew members as they attempt to fulfill the orders. After training a trio of robot drones to tend to the last remaining dome, Lowell sets it free—thus confirming its inherent value, outside of human use or appreciation—and commits suicide. The last shot shows the dome orbiting in space, perhaps to find a more welcoming reception elsewhere in the universe.

While Lowell's excessive affect is my main interest here, it is important to establish that the film's own affect is excessive—sentimental to the point of cheesiness. Consider the title sequence: the film opens on gauzy close-ups of nature, much like one might find on human faces in melodrama, backed by a slow, contemplative instrumental track (a version of the Joan Baez song "Rejoice in the Sun," which plays in original form later). The camera glides over foliage, flowers, a snail, turtle, and frogs, all kissed by dew. After two long minutes the sequence shifts from the gauzy close-up style and shows Lowell bathing in a pond filled with lily pads. The first words of the movie are spoken thereafter, and notably they're directed to a nonhuman. "How are you today, hmm?" Lowell sweetly inquires of a bunny. "Feeling good? Awww. I bet you'd like something to eat, wouldn't you?" The idyllic pastoralism of this first scene is finally broken by the entrance of Lowell's crass crewmates, recklessly running their ATVs through the dome—thus establishing early on that Lowell's position is, in the larger scheme of things, threatened and minoritarian. That is, the film both establishes Lowell's social queerness and frames it sympathetically.

Lowell's excessive affect takes center stage in three early, consecutive scenes. First, before the receipt of orders to destroy, an optimistic Lowell predicts that the United States will eventually reinstate the "parks and forest system" and that he will be picked to head it. Crew member Marty Barker (Ron Rifkin) scoffs, "Hey, Lowell, you're dreaming." We cut to a medium close-up shot of Lowell, who delivers an effusive diatribe: "And you don't think it's time somebody had a dream again, huh? You don't think that it's time that somebody cared enough to have a dream? What about the forests? You don't think anyone should care about these forests? What's gonna happen if these forests and all this incredible beauty is lost for all time?" Seemingly embarrassed for Lowell, crew member Andy Wolf (Jesse Vint) mumbles, "It's been too long, Lowell. People got other things to do now." In another scene shortly thereafter the men accept a radio transmission. "Anderson" (voice of Joseph Campanella) reports, "We have just received orders to abandon and nuclear-destruct all the forests and return our ships to commercial service." Meanwhile the camera zooms in closer and closer on Lowell's face, his jaw tight, eyes wide and glistening with tears. "It's insane," he whispers, consumed with rage and grief. The third scene in question finds crew members Barker, Wolf, and John Keenan (Cliff Potts) in the kitchen during dinnertime, joking about the dome destruction: "How far out do they go before they blow up?" Another answers, "About six miles. We should feel a hefty jolt," which prompts the comment, "I want a front-row seat when these babies go!" The men then turn their cruel attention to Lowell, who is eating a cantaloupe—which Wolf insists "stinks." "This happens to be nature's greatest gift," Lowell replies, incredulous. "To a celibate, maybe," Wolf scoffs, insisting that he doesn't see a difference between the synthetic food the three crew members are enjoying and the cantaloupe. This derision inspires yet another outburst from Lowell:

> You don't see the difference? The difference is that I grew it! That's what the difference is! That I picked it and I fixed it! It has a taste, and it has some color! And it has a smell! It calls back a time when there were flowers all over the earth! And there were valleys! And there were plains of tall, green grass that you could lie down in, that you could go to sleep in! And there were blue skies, and there was fresh air! And there were things growing all over the place, not just in domed enclosures blasted some millions of miles out into space!

Keenan, the most sympathetic of the three crew members, confides quietly, "The fact is, Lowell, if people were interested [in nature], something would have been done a long time ago."

Lowell's affect is everything Love describes in her queer concept of "feeling backward": nostalgic, bitter, regretful. Indeed in addition to the above verbal reminiscences ("there were blue skies"), he seems to have frequent visual flashbacks, such as when he runs down the ship's hallway in a panic over the dome and the film intercuts images of redwood forests. And even Lowell's personal aesthetic is "backward": he wears a traditional monk's robe in the opening sequence and, in later scenes, a jumpsuit adorned with patches of the U.S. national parks—which, within the film's diegesis, no longer exist.[35] We might note that Lowell's affect also bears qualities that have been specifically associated with the queer: it is excessive, unreasonable, inappropriate, immature, awkward, and embarrassing.[36] And perhaps even more explicitly, the crew members queer him through their bullying, particularly the "celibate" jab. As this jab implies, Lowell has invested all of his energy and emotion into something that's not only not a woman but not even human.[37] In the fictional but ultimately realistic world of *Silent Running*—which is, to paraphrase Sandilands, a social context that cannot acknowledge nonhuman beings or natural environments as worthy of emotional attachment, much less "grievable"—any investment in the nonhuman constitutes *over*investment. In such a context, the film suggests, emotional attachment to the nonhuman is, by definition, queer.

But I want to consider the queerness of the film not just in terms of the social, political, and material dynamics it depicts but also in terms of the extradiegetic: the dynamics of audience reception. We might begin by positing the queerness of *Silent Running's* cult classic status. Just as Lowell "overinvests" in the nonhuman, rabid fans "overinvest" in this marginal film, to the extent that they design, buy, and/or assemble models of the spaceship and the robot drones.[38] Here we might be reminded of "the value frequently given to the unexpected object" that Cvetkovich claims is central to both queer culture and theory.[39]

More specifically, I'm interested in returning to the concept of camp in order to read the film through that queer tradition of appreciation—a kind of "overinvestment" of its own.[40] Key to this reading is Dern's over-the-top, scenery-chewing performance—which, I would propose, belongs in the pantheon of camp performance, along with, say, Joan Crawford in *Queen Bee* (dir. Ranald MacDougall, 1955) or Faye Dunaway *as* Joan Crawford in *Mommie Dearest* (dir. Frank Perry, 1981). The blogger Scott Ashlin pronounces Dern's performance "ridiculous," stating that "[his] acting here is simply beyond belief. He's really just doing the same shtick as he had in all those drugs-and-bikers movies he made for Roger Corman starting in 1966."[41] We might consider how closely Ashlin's comment resonates with one of Susan Sontag's classic explanations of camp: "When something is just bad (rather than Camp), it's often because it is too mediocre in its ambition. The artist hasn't attempted to do anything really outlandish. ('It's too much' […] '*It's not to be believed*' are standard phrases of Camp enthusiasm.)"[42] As Sontag puts it more simply, camp is "the love of the exaggerated, the 'off.'"[43] To appreciate a camp film or performance is to recognize its "exaggerated," "beyond belief" qualities and thus its inadvertent ridiculousness—and to love it *not in spite of but because of* those qualities. Thus we might say that the queerness of *Silent Running*'s environmental affect can be located not just in the film itself but also in cult audiences' embrace of it and of Dern's performance in particular—thus further demonstrating the mobile qualities of affect. Importantly, then, Sontag reminds us that "Camp taste *identifies* with what it is enjoying. People who share this sensibility are not laughing at the thing they label as 'a camp,' they're enjoying it. Camp is a *tender* feeling."[44] To recognize *Silent Running*'s ridiculousness is thus not (necessarily) to deride it, the way Lowell's crew members deride him. One can both identify with *and* make fun of the text, both laugh at Lowell and identify with his predicament.

Above I have described the intellectual import of attending to queer environmental affect—from widening ecocritical lenses to critiquing the gloom and doom of environmental rhetoric to probing discourses of historic preservation. But perhaps the more quotidian question remains, What does such affect mean for environmental relations? First, as the Public Feelings project and my visual texts demonstrate, modes such as camp and humor cannot, and should not, be divorced from negative modes such as melancholia, grief, or rage. Thus, we might not only accept but also draw strength from the diversity of feelings that environmental change can invoke in us. Indeed, as Anno suggests, even our own ambivalence has much to tell us. Second, and more specifically, I propose "inappropriateness," "overinvestment," and "excessiveness" not as traits to be disavowed but rather as rallying points for environmental activists—a particularly significant move in the face of *both* mainstream environmentalism's calls for austerity *and* certain conservative administrations' recent rollbacks on environmental protection. Perhaps then this is the most important definition of queer environmental affect: all of the messy, contradictory, utterly sad, and deeply joyous dimensions of human life lived in connection to the nonhuman, in a social, political, and material context deeply hostile to both.

I wish to thank Kathy-Ann Tan for originally alerting me to Kim Anno's work and Kim herself for the inspiring conversation and help with images.

1. For more on the Fab Planet Summit and its sponsor see OUT for Sustainability, http://out4s.org/.

2. Katherine Rosman, "Why Snapping Is the New Clapping," *New York Times*, November 21, 2015, https://www.nytimes.com/2015/11/22/fashion/snapping -new-clapping.html.

3. Richard Kim, "Please Don't Stop the Music," *The Nation*, June 12, 2016, https:// www.thenation.com/article/please-dont-stop-the-music/.

4. Justin Torres, "In Praise of Latin Night at the Queer Club," *Washington Post*, June 13, 2016, https://www.washingtonpost.com/opinions/in-praise-of-latin-night-at -the-queer-club/2016/06/13/e841867e-317b-11e6-95c0-2a6873031302_story .html (emphasis added).

5. See Seymour, "Toward an Irreverent Ecocriticism"; and Seymour, *Bad Environmentalism* (forthcoming).

6. Hardt, "Foreword," ix.

7. Clough, introduction to *Affective Turn*, 7.

8. Cvetkovich, "Public Feelings," 462.

9. Love, *Feeling Backward*, 26.

10. Cvetkovich, *Depression*, Kindle location 131. For a discussion of queer theory's larger "negative turn"—which is not necessarily limited to affect—see Seymour, *Strange Natures*. The trend of attention to negative affect can be found in nonqueer work as well, as in Ngai's *Ugly Feelings*.

11. Berlant, *Cruel Optimism*, 1.

12. Sandilands, "Melancholy Natures," 333.

13. Sandilands, "Melancholy Natures," 333.

14. Sandilands, "Melancholy Natures," 333.

15. Cvetkovich, "Public Feelings," 460.

16. Love, *Feeling Backward*, 7.

17. Houser, *Ecosickness in Contemporary U.S. Fiction*, 221.

18. On queer theory and environmental questions see, among others, Azzarello, *Queer Environmentality*.

19. Sara Ahmed, for example, states, "I do not assume there is something called affect that stands apart or has autonomy." She observes further that a "number of scholars have recently taken up the idea of affects as contagious"; doing so "challenge[s] an 'inside out' model of affect by showing how affects pass between bodies." Ahmed, "Happy Objects," 30, 36.

20. Berlant, *Cruel Optimism*, 123.

21. Muñoz, "Feeling Brown," 677.

22. Muñoz, "Feeling Brown," 677.

23. Chen, *Animacies*, 207.

24. Scholars attending to queer spaces from an environmental standpoint and vice versa include Gordon Brent Ingram, Petra Doan, and others.

25. Muñoz, *Cruising Utopia*, 103.

26. One journalist has observed that "in major cities, the number of gay bars has declined [since] the 1970s" by as much as 50 percent and goes on to surmise that "the decline . . . may be attributable to how welcome gays are everywhere; as [interviewee Gina] Gatta, who lives in the Bay Area, put it, 'Every bar in San Francisco is a gay bar.'" We should ask of course who can afford to live in a place like San Francisco at this point, though I do not have room here to discussion the connection between gay "acceptance" and gentrification. June Thomas, "The Gay Bar: Can It Survive?," *Slate*, July 1, 2011, http://www.slate.com/articles/life/the_gay_bar/2011/06/the_gay_bar.html.

27. Patrick, "Matter of Displacement," 921, 937.

28. The director Roland Emmerich was recently excoriated for "whitewashing" history with his fiction film *Stonewall* (2015). See, for example, Leela Ginelle, "The New Stonewall Film Is Just as Whitewashed as We Feared," *Bitch Media*, September 24, 2015, https://bitchmedia.org/article/new-stonewall-film-just-whitewashed-we-feared. Meanwhile scholars and activists have been critical of the fetishistic focus on Stonewall at the expense of other locations and events and of how that focus enables the normalization of queer history. See, for example, Grace Dunham and Toshio Meronek, "How the United States' First LGBT National Memorial Gets It Wrong" (editorial), *Truthout*, July 2, 2016, http://www.truth-out.org/news/item/36678-how-lgbt-national-memorial-gets-it-wrong.

29. Anno, *Men and Women in Water Cities*, artist's description accompanying video.

30. Anno, "Queer Eco Aesthetics," 2.

31. Anno, *Men and Women in Water Cities*, artist's description accompanying video and voice-over narration.

32. Tan, "Queer Ecologies and the Postnational," 5–6 (emphasis added).

33. Anno, "Queer Eco Aesthetics," 2.

34. Anno, "Queer Eco Aesthetics," 2.

35. While Love wants to reclaim "feeling backward" from a queer standpoint, such feeling is actually de rigueur in many environmental contexts—and often problematically so. See, for example, critiques of pastoralism and environmental nostalgia in Sandilands, "Melancholy Natures." However, scholars such as Jennifer Ladino recognize the (limited) potential of nostalgia for environmental politics; as she notes, "It is not difficult to find conservative, reactionary examples of nostalgia.

But . . . nostalgia often transcends its stigmatized role, and in surprising ways." Ladino, *Reclaiming Nostalgia*, xii–xiii. Following Ladino, I would argue that Lowell's backward feelings have radically posthumanist implications here, especially considering how "the future" in *Silent Running* has even less room for the nonhuman than our present day.

36. Queer theoretical work on these qualities is too numerous to detail here, but to offer one example, Jack Halberstam's *In a Queer Time and Place: Transgender Bodies, Subcultural Lives* (2005) discusses the connection between queerness and immaturity.

37. We might note here that certain environmentalist practices, such as vegetarianism, have been associated with effeminacy and queerness. See, for example, Hall, "Queer Vegetarian."

38. See the ad at Monsters in Motion, http://www.monstersinmotion.com/cart/sci -fi-model-kits-other-c-271_274_299/silent-running-valley-forge-49-inch-1–650 -scale-p-18938 and at Destiny Models, http://www.destinymodels.co.uk/.

39. Cvetkovich, "Public Feelings," 463.

40. Sontag, cited below, is the most obvious touchstone for such a reading. Much work also exists on the specific phenomena of camp appreciation of melodrama by gay male audiences; see, for example, Mercer and Shingler, *Melodrama*.

41. Ashlin, "Review of *Silent Running*," n.p.

42. Sontag, "Notes on Camp," 283 (emphasis added).

43. Sontag, "Notes on Camp," 279.

44. Sontag, "Notes on Camp," 291–92.

BIBLIOGRAPHY

Ahmed, Sara. "Happy Objects." In *The Affect Theory Reader*, edited by Melissa Gregg and Gregory J. Seigworth, 29–51. Durham: Duke University Press, 2010.

Anno, Kim. *Men and Women in Water Cities*. YouTube video, posted September 17, 2011. https://www.youtube.com/watch?v=V7nsmuqlIu4.

———. "Queer Eco Aesthetics." Paper presented at the Fab Planet Summit, San Francisco, June 4, 2016.

———. *Water City, Berkeley*. Internet Movie Database video, 2013. Accessed May 24, 2017. http://www.imdb.com/video/wab/vi1125035289.

Ashlin, Scott. Review of *Silent Running*. *1000 Misspent Hours and Counting* (blog). Accessed May 23, 2017. http://www.1000misspenthours.com/reviews/reviewsn -z/silentrunning.htm.

Azzarello, Robert. *Queer Environmentality: Ecology, Evolution, and Sexuality in American Literature*. Burlington VT: Ashgate, 2012.

Berlant, Lauren. *Cruel Optimism*. Durham: Duke University Press, 2011.

Chen, Mel Y. *Animacies: Biopolitics, Racial Mattering, and Queer Affect*. Durham: Duke University Press, 2012.

Clough, Patricia Ticineto. Introduction to *The Affective Turn: Theorizing the Social*, edited by Patricia Ticineto Clough with Jean Halley, 1–33. Durham: Duke University Press, 2007.

Cvetkovich, Anne. "Public Feelings." *South Atlantic Quarterly* 106, no. 3 (2007): 459–68.

———. *Depression: A Public Feeling*. Durham: Duke University Press, 2012. Kindle.

Hall, Lauren Rae. "The Queer Vegetarian: Understanding Alimentary Activism." In *International Perspectives in Feminist Ecocriticism*, edited by Greta Gaard, Simon C. Estok, and Serpil Oppermann, 166–83. London: Routledge, 2013.

Hardt, Michael. "Foreword: What Affects Are Good For." In *The Affective Turn: Theorizing the Social*, edited by Patricia Ticineto Clough with Jean Halley, ix–xiii. Durham: Duke University Press, 2007.

Houser, Heather. *Ecosickness in Contemporary U.S. Fiction: Environment and Affect*. New York: Columbia University Press, 2014.

Ladino, Jennifer. *Reclaiming Nostalgia: Longing for Nature in American Literature*. Charlottesville: University of Virginia Press, 2012.

Love, Heather. *Feeling Backward: Loss and the Politics of Queer History*. Cambridge MA: Harvard University Press, 2009.

Mercer, John, and Martin Shingler. *Melodrama: Genre, Style, and Sensibility*. London: Wallflower, 2004.

Muñoz, José Esteban. *Cruising Utopia: The Then and There of Queer Futurity*. New York: New York University Press, 2009.

———. "Feeling Brown, Feeling Down: Latina Affect, the Performativity of Race, and the Depressive Position." *Signs* 31, no. 3 (2006): 675–88.

Ngai, Sianne. *Ugly Feelings*. Cambridge MA: Harvard University Press, 2005.

Patrick, Darren J. "The Matter of Displacement: A Queer Urban Ecology of New York City's High Line." *Social and Cultural Geography* 15, no. 8 (2014): 920–41.

Sandilands, Catriona. "Melancholy Natures, Queer Ecologies." In *Queer Ecologies: Sex, Politics, Nature, Desire*, edited by Catriona Sandilands and Bruce Erickson, 331–58. Bloomington: Indiana University Press, 2010.

Seymour, Nicole. *Bad Environmentalism: Irony and Irreverence in the Ecological Age*. Minneapolis: University of Minnesota Press, 2018.

———. *Strange Natures: Futurity, Empathy, and the Queer Ecological Imagination*. Urbana: University of Illinois Press, 2013.

———. "Toward an Irreverent Ecocriticism." *Journal of Ecocriticism* 4, no. 2 (2012): 56–71.

Sontag, Susan. "Notes on 'Camp.'" In *Against Interpretation and Other Essays*, 275–92. London: Penguin, 1966.

Tan, Kathy-Ann. "Queer Ecologies and the Postnational." Paper presented at the Nation in the Age of Environmental Crisis workshop, Augsburg, Germany, July 18, 2015.

Trumbull, Douglas, dir. *Silent Running*. 1972. Universal City CA: Universal, 2002. DVD.

12

Feeling Let Down

Affect, Environmentalism, and the Power of Negative Thinking

LISA OTTUM

Among the most famous instances of disappointment in Romantic literature is William Wordsworth's account of crossing the Alps in Book VI of *The Prelude* (1805). In this part of the text the poet recounts his ambivalent encounter with Mont Blanc as well as the much-analyzed Simplon Pass incident, in which he and his friend Robert Jones cross the Alps without realizing they have done so. The episode goes this way. Having departed from France in early August 1790, Wordsworth and Jones enter Switzerland on foot, resolutely focused on their goal of reaching the mountains. Passing "from Province to Province" at "military speed," they hurry through the Swiss countryside, "Keen hunters in a chace of fourteen weeks / Eager as birds of prey."[1] Once they finally reach the mountains, however, Wordsworth finds himself not dazzled, but rather discomfited. Upon beholding the acclaimed summit of Mont Blanc, he "griev[es] / To have a soulless image on the eye / Which had usurped upon a living thought / That never more could be."[2] While the "wond'rous Vale / of Chamouny" manages to make up for this first event, further letdown follows when the travelers lose their way and wander haplessly down the Gordo Ravine.[3] "By fortunate chance" they come across a peasant who offers directions.[4] Wordsworth recalls his own incredulous response to their exchange:

Hard of belief we questioned him again,
And all the answers which the Man returned
To our enquiries in their sense and substance,
Translated by the feeling which we had,
Ended in this, that we had crossed the Alps.[5]

Much has been written on this moment in *The Prelude*, in part because of what follows: a lengthy and somewhat incongruous-seeming celebration of the imagination.[6] Just as striking as Wordsworth's alleged "writer's block," though, is his effort to capture disappointment, an emotion whose elements of surprise, dismay and momentary disorientation are difficult to describe.[7] The wandering indirectness of the above lines and the matter-of-fact flatness with which they end suggest some of disappointment's affective complexities. We *feel* disappointment before we process it as such; the instant between our affective response and an intellectualized one is fleeting. Disappointment arrests us; it is both a sensation and a perceptual disruption, an experience that seems to distort regular temporality. Vitally, it arises from something outside the feeling subject: we are disappointed *with* something or *about* something.

What does it mean to be disappointed by a landscape? That is, how precisely does this peculiar response to nature come about—and what are its personal and political consequences? Similar to regret, disappointment focuses the feeling subject's attention on counterfactuals—on outcomes that would have been better than the one at hand. Among social scientists, disappointment is seen as an obstacle to logical thinking. According to behavioral economists, for instance, disappointment aversion interferes with our decision-making mechanisms: so profound is our desire to avoid disappointment that we will often forgo opportunities that involve risk. Disappointment aversion thus complicates expected utility theory, a paradigmatic set of assumptions about how economic agents exercise choice.[8] Psychologists also tend to see disappointment as stultifying. Associated in laboratory settings with feelings such as powerlessness, disappointment causes people to "turn away from the [disappointing] event," leading to "goal abandonment" and similarly dire-sounding behaviors.[9]

Cultural critics meanwhile have long seen disappointment as an inevitable consequence of postmodern capitalism. Faced with a paralyzing number of consumer choices, we are almost certainly disappointed by the choices we *do* make; we become trapped in a stultifying loop of counterfactual thinking, second-guessing even our most carefully considered decisions. Worse, as purveyors of pop psychology such as Daniel Gilbert and Barry Schwartz have argued, the "problem of adaptation" ensures that even initially satisfactory decisions become disappointing over time.[10] For the theorist Sara Ahmed, disappointment belies the cognitive and affective work necessary to sustain the dominant cultural conception of "happiness." Happiness, she argues, "is attributed to certain social objects," such as marriage or the heteronormative family, which in turn "circulate as social goods."[11] When we are properly aligned with the community, we experience proximity to such objects as happy. However, when we *fail* to experience this pleasure, the ensuing gap "between the affective value of an object and how we experience it" leads to disappointment.[12] Disappointment thus signals something much more pernicious than a temporary dismay. Disappointed subjects are alienated from their culture's notion of what makes life meaningful. Their only options are to will themselves to become happy or to descend into a morass of self-doubt, anxiety, or even anger.

Given the consensus that disappointment is a "bad" affect—or an "ugly feeling," to borrow Sianne Ngai's term for noncathartic states such as a boredom and paranoia—it might seem an unlikely vehicle for green thinking, green action, or prosocial action of any kind.[13] Yet, as it is represented in literature, disappointment is seldom the paralyzing affect described by its many detractors. In *The Prelude*, for example, Wordsworth's disappointment with particular settings is figured as the catalyst for reflection, both at the instant of disappointment and at quite some distance in the future. The peculiar temporality of disappointment leads the poet to greater self-awareness about the mediating role of culture in his encounters with nature—and ultimately to a more nuanced and, I argue, politically useful attitude toward the natural world. As I explain, the potential value of disappointment for ecocriticism lies in its unique properties as an affect, that is, as an embodied response to sensory stimuli that is subsequently shaped by memory, language, and other facets of cognition. Similar to its inverse—elation—disappointment reveals a disjuncture between something we expected to feel and something that we actually feel. In order to transpire in the first place, disappointment must be preceded by memory; to arrive at the physical experience of feeling disappointed, we must have first formed expectations. Thus, it is no coincidence that a trend in people writing about their disappointment with particular settings corresponds to the rise of mass media and modern tourism in the eighteenth and nineteenth centuries.

Below I offer two case studies of disappointment, one drawn from this moment when modern tourism emerged and one from the present, when tourism has become more commercialized and hypermediated than ever before. In *The Prelude* Wordsworth grapples with touristic disappointment, an affect made newly available in the Romantic era by the mass circulation of mediated natures. As a practice founded on prior expectations, tourism engenders disappointment; however, built into tourism from the outset was the notion that one's affective responses to nature could be managed. I contend that Wordsworth learned to recognize his initial responses to landscape as affects and in turn to channel these responses toward a conscious affection for nature. In our own moment the travel writer Geoff Dyer offers a more ambivalent take on touristic disappointment. For Dyer storied places are almost always disappointing, yet disappointment is complicatedly intertwined with interest and volition: at certain times disappointment with a place propels Dyer toward curiosity, while at others, it leads elsewhere. While Dyer's representation of disappointment is less obviously "green" than Wordsworth's, it nevertheless points to a matter of ecocritical urgency—namely, in Heather Houser's words, how affect "lends phenomena relevance, organizes individuals' perceptions, and converts awareness into an ethic."[14] Can being let down by nature serve environmentalist ends? Wordsworth's and Dyer's texts tentatively suggest yes, though as I explain at the end of this chapter, disappointment and other "negative" affects demand further attention.

Disappointment Defined

To begin, some further exploration of how disappointment works is in order. Similar to other affects, disappointment is registered initially by the body—the telltale sting of "letdown" with which we are all familiar: a momentary catch in the breath or instant of disorientation that signals we have come into contact with something unexpected in our environment. From there disappointment can proceed in any number of directions—the initial moment of affective intensity exhausted, one might, if disappointed by a visual scene, turn again toward the scene to confirm its disappointingness. While affect theorists disagree on the extent to which affects are separate from "emotions," "feelings," or cognition, it is clear that affects undergo some amount of processing by our brains. We sense disappointment somatically; we only later arrive at the thought *I am disappointed*. The process by which feeling let down becomes internalized and articulated through language is usefully illuminated by William Reddy's account of emotions as "navigatory." Reddy contends that the "awake body" generates a "flow of coded messages" or available "thought material" that arrives through our five senses, as well as our memory, and other systems.[15] This diverse thought material must be "translated" across systems of the body in order to become "emotion"; moreover we can only pay attention to a fraction of this information at a time. Thus emotions—like any translation—capture affect imperfectly. More important, though, expressions of emotion, or what Reddy refers to as "emotives," can be "self-exploratory" and "self-altering."[16] This means they have the ability to confirm or disconfirm the emotion claim and/or "intensify or attenuate the state claimed."[17] For example, a "person whose current state includes an element of confusion may say 'I love you' in order to find out if it is true, and the 'truth' or 'falsehood' of the statement depends on its effects on the speaker."[18] In this way expressions of an emotion are experiments; they can essentially change the feelings they "test."

Emotional expressions are thus similar to performative utterances in that they can, in Reddy's words, "do something in the world."[19] This account of how emotions relate to reality is quite different from the account offered by many literary critics, who, especially prior to the so-called affective turn, have tended to view emotions skeptically. More recent work by scholars in various literature subfields has changed the conversation about affect and emotion. However, disappointment is among affects that remain underexamined, perhaps because it seems overdetermined compared to other, less clearly culturally inflected emotions. What little work exists on disappointment tends to emphasize writers' efforts to resolve or move past disappointment. Nicola Trott examines Wordsworth's response to disappointing landscapes (including Mont Blanc), noting that the poet often seeks to neutralize disappointment by insisting that subsequent experiences "make amends" for the disappointing event. For Trott this maneuver is an act of Kantian "substitution" through which "the mind decides to accept its relation to Nature as an approximation of its own, *un*attainable ideas."[20] Laura Quinney meanwhile explores disappointment through a psychoanalytic lens, reading the disappointment expressed in Romantic and post-Romantic poetry as "an erosion within the self such that it cannot recover the empowering inaccuracy of self-idealization."[21] On Wordsworth and the representation of nature specifically, Quinney offers this assessment: "The psychological dilemma of his critical lyrics [including "Tintern Abbey"] is that he feels the loss of glamour in Nature as a loss within himself. He therefore makes a desperate attempt to reconstruct the benevolence of Nature, who is clearly figured as the good mother."[22] Wordsworth responds to disappointment—in his own idealized conception of himself and nature—through an act of evasion, one that not only sublimates his own anxieties but also substitutes an anthropomorphized Mother Nature for nature. As in Trott's schema, Quinney's reading suggests that disappointment inevitably leads us away from reality and into the sort of anthropocentric, egocentric territory usually shunned by ecocriticism.

How then do we begin to understand expressions of disappointment with nature as useful? To be sure, in Wordsworth's poetry and elsewhere, disappointment—with nature or with something else—is almost always situated within a larger narrative of healing, compensation, or amends, wherein the feeling subjects see themselves as changed by disappointment and very often discover some remedy for the initial shock of disappointment. Yet if we embrace Reddy's notion of emotions as "navigatory," then authors' efforts to articulate disappointment and its aftermath are not simply acts of evasion. As Reddy and other theorists contend, affects are not determinate; they position us to act but do not engender any particular course of action. This brings me to another important point about disappointment as an affect. While theorists agree, as Megan Watkins notes, that "individuals are innately predisposed to affective response, much of what we respond to, and how we respond, is a consequence of learning: the repeated experience of similar affects accumulating into a dispositional tendency."[23] Affect, in other words, is subject to training: people can (and do) learn to direct disappointment into a productive state such as interest, especially if we are armed with conceptual templates that help us to channel activated thought material in a particular direction.

Confronting Disappointment: Wordsworth and Gilpin

Brief as it is, Wordsworth's description of accidentally crossing the Alps reveals traces of his affective experience as well as his subsequent effort to render this experience as poetry. Like any tourist of his Romantic milieu, Wordsworth had been primed to expect the mere sight of the Alps—especially Mont Blanc—as well as his ascent over them, to be revelatory. Thus, discovering that he and Brown have bumbled across them is disappointing: they are first shocked and disoriented, then cognizant of their loss, and then self-consciously regretful about what this loss means. Questioning the peasant they accost, Wordsworth and Brown are "hard of belief"—incredulous. Notably, comprehending the peasant's reply is an act of *feeling* rather than thinking: the peasant's words, "in their sense and substance" are "translated by the feelings which we had," and only then arrange themselves into meaning in the poet's mind. A "dull and heavy slackening [. . .] ensue[s]" in which the travelers pause before heading down into the ravine.[24] These lines subtly capture the somatic dimensions of disappointment specifically, as well as the "navigatory" nature of affect generally. That the peasant's words have both a "substance" and a "sense" suggests that in the moment his speech had a physical effect on the poet—a "sense" or sensation that was simultaneously a "sense" or meaning. Wordsworth's use of the word "slackening" is suggestive, too: similar to "sense," "slackening" conveys, according to the *Oxford English Dictionary*, the dual meaning of a physical slowing, as well as a figurative relaxing or slowing. These ambiguities, along with the lines' grammatical structure, convey something of the "self-exploring" nature of emotives: here Wordsworth tries to recapture the instantaneous working-through of affective intensity that precedes emotion.

As a retrospective work, *The Prelude* also captures Wordsworth's processing of disappointment after the fact: Book VI and subsequent books chart the long-term effects of feeling disappointed, including the role this affect later plays in the poet's environmental ethic. First, with further reflection, Wordsworth comes to recognize his disappointment with the Alps as *affect*—as a sensory response to the landscape that preceded any conscious ethical commitment to nature. The Wordsworth writing *The Prelude* realizes that his response was driven by sight—by what he terms in Book XI the "tyranny" of the eye.[25] Rather than attending to "the spirit of the place," he responded only to what he saw—to "superficial things" such as "colour or proportion."[26] Reflecting on disappointment also helps Wordsworth to articulate the properties of affect, especially the ways that affects can combine or accrue over time—sometimes in surprising ways—to create memories and beliefs. Musing on his travels, the poet summarizes his experience this way:

> whate'er
> I saw, or heard, or felt was but a stream
> That flowed into a kindred stream, a gale
> That helped me forwards, did administer
> To grandeur and to tenderness, to the one
> Directly but to tender thoughts by means
> Less often instantaneous in effect,
> Conducted me to these along a path
> Which in the main was more circuitous.[27]

Wordsworth differentiates between the immediate and lingering influence of sensory impressions and the affects they create. In the short term, affects fostered his sense of nature's "grandeur"; in the longer term they somehow led him to a feeling of tenderness, or caring, toward nature. If the social science accounts are correct, then repeated exposure to disappointing scenery would have actually *diminished* Wordsworth's attraction to nature. However, disappointment seems to have prompted a different response: for

Wordsworth, feeling let down by nature was a vital catalyst for reflection and in turn for the development of an ethic that James McKusick, Jonathan Bate, and other ecocritics have hailed as protoecological.[28]

I would argue that what we witness in *The Prelude* is the training of affective response over time. As Megan Watkins points out, many psychologists see affect as "accumulative"; similar affects accrete over time and eventually "predispose one to act and react in particular ways."[29] That affective responses to nature could accumulate and be trained was a commonplace in Wordsworth's era, as exemplified by the eighteenth-century vogue in "picturesque" theory. Partly because of Wordsworth's professed contempt for this "infection of the age," ecocritics have tended to dismiss the picturesque aesthetic as a pernicious, anthropocentric way of interacting with landscapes.[30] Yet in some of its iterations, picturesque theory actually encouraged people to cultivate an affective stance that, if not "green" on its surface, nonetheless positioned its practitioners to experience delight and curiosity in response to ordinary natural phenomena.

One of the more popular purveyors of picturesque guidebooks, William Gilpin, embraced the notion that being disappointed by nature was surmountable with the right set of emotional and intellectual resources. For Gilpin a "picturesque" eye is important because it allows the traveler to work through disappointment: armed with a set of strategies for seeing, he is trained to channel disappointment directly into appreciation, and even affection.[31] In his *Three Essays on Picturesque Beauty* (1792) Gilpin describes the picturesque traveler's emotional regimen—the process by which he converts an initial affective response into a positive emotional response and, later, into a pleasing representation of that response. The "first source of amusement to the picturesque traveler, is the *pursuit* of his object," Gilpin explains, likening the search for picturesque settings to "the pleasures of the chase."[32] Propelled forward by excitement, the traveler hesitates in a state of "agreeable suspense," his "every human faculty... dilated with joy."[33] Of course such intensely felt anticipation has a downside: it sets the traveler up for disappointment once he at last attains his object. Most scenes require intellectual effort to become pleasurable. Hence, the picturesque traveler sets about "examin[ing] what would amend the composition; how little is wanting to reduce it to rules of [picturesque theory]; what a trifling circumstance sometimes forms the limit between beauty, and deformity."[34] His "next amusement arises from inlarging, and correcting [his] general stock of ideas."[35] Notably, this step not only helps the viewer recover from disappointment but also prepares him to see nature more accurately: "The variety of nature is such, that *new objects*, and new combinations of them, are continually adding something to our fund, and inlarging our collection: while the *same kind of object* occurring frequently, is seen under various shapes; and makes us, if I may so speak, more learned in nature. We get it more by heart."[36] In other words we gain a "more complete idea" of natural objects, such as particular kinds of trees. With this "correct knowledge of objects," the traveler is finally ready to sketch or write about what he has seen so that he can later remember what he saw and experience "pleasure in recollecting" his experience.[37] Gilpin thus models a process by which disappointment can be habitually trained toward reflection. This reflection leads the viewer to more accurately "see" nature; in turn he receives pleasure at a later time by thinking back on this process of reflection.

The picturesque emerged alongside, and in dialogue with, modern scenic tourism, and while Gilpin and others were disparaged even in their own day for the programmatic nature of "proper" landscape appreciation, treatises and guidebooks such as Gilpin's served an important, and overlooked, function: imparting tools for disappointment management, consisting of a set of strategies for teaching oneself to turn less-than-ideal encounters with nature into opportunities for personal growth. With practice, the tourist might teach himself to convert the feeling of disappointment into pleasure and even incorporate this pleasure—as Wordsworth does—into a larger narrative of identity. To be sure, there remains a wide leap from warm feelings of personal satisfaction to consciously held principles; developing people's moral imagination was not among Gilpin's aims. It is worth noticing, however, that in at least some circumstances the affect of disappointment orients feeling subjects toward interest, a state more clearly congenial to ethical action.

Disappointment Overcome? Dyer's *White Sands*

In our own moment, when tourism is implicated in quite a few ethical dilemmas, including a number of obvious environmental ones, it is more urgent than ever before to explore how touristic affects dispose travelers emotionally. One intriguing starting point for such an inquiry is Geoff Dyer's *White Sands: Experiences from the Outside World*, a text that thematizes uncomfortable affects. *White Sands* comprises ten loosely related essays, most of which chronicle Dyer's journey to a famous work of public art (such as Robert Smithson's *Spiral Jetty*) or a setting closely associated with a famous figure (e.g., the artist Paul Gauguin, musician Don Cherry, philosopher Theodor Adorno). Although Dyer's stated aim is to "work out what a certain place—a certain way of marking the landscape—means; what it's trying to tell us; what we go to it for," the collection is in many respects a study of touristic disappointment.[38] Most of the places Dyer visits prove underwhelming—some comedically so. Such is the case with his visit to Norway, to which he and his wife travel from London to see the Northern Lights. Shocked by the cold and perpetual darkness of January above the Arctic Circle, the pair descend into a state of despair as, night after night, the aurora fails to appear. Eventually they depart from the region "empty-handed and empty-eyed." "We had had the experience of a lifetime," Dyer writes, "but it was not the experience we had hoped for; it was like a lifetime of disappointment compressed into less than a week, which actually felt like it had lasted the best—in the sense of worst—part of a lifetime."[39] The essay "Northern Dark" offers no concessions to the landscape's sublimity and no gesture toward the Arctic as an ecosystem. The affects of boredom, irritation, and disappointment turn Dyer inward rather outward; in a striking reversal of much current writing about the Arctic, there is no trace of concern for, or even acknowledgment of, climate change there.

Other parts of the book, however, raise the possibility that disappointment might serve as a conduit toward more outward-facing states. In "Where? What? Where?" Dyer recounts a trip to French Polynesia to visit sites where Paul Gauguin lived and worked in the 1890s.[40] Framed by an irreverent biographical sketch of the artist, Dyer's account begins with his own arrival on Tahiti, where he adopts a stance of ironic distance from the landscape and its people. The island's tradition of gifting leis to visitors is "soul-destroying"—so "thoroughly commodified and packaged that even though . . . the flowers were fresh and wild and lovely they might as well have been plastic."[41] His hotel room meanwhile features "a magnificent view as long as you didn't turn your head to the right and see the other balconies gawping and Gurskying out to sea."[42] It might at first seem that Polynesia disappoints Dyer because it is not what he expected; however, Dyer insists that Polynesia was always already disappointing, even in the era of empire. The capital Papeete "would have been wonderful . . . at the tail end of the nineteenth century, when Gauguin first arrived—or so we think," he writes. "But Gauguin himself arrived too late. . . . Only in Gauguin's art would it become paradise regained and reinvented."[43] What conflicts Dyer is something else: he discovers that certain aspects of Polynesia actually *excite* him and involve him in affectively appealing ways, despite his best effort to inhabit what he supposes was Gauguin's initial disappointment.

For example, Dyer visits the island of Hiva Oa to see several of the famed *tiki*, and at first he is bored by "a few blackened stones that the guide sought to render interesting by nattering on about human sacrifice."[44] Just as Dyer is "bracing [himself] for some climactic letdown, for disappointment of such purity that [he] would not even realize it was being experienced," he arrives at a site that utterly arrests him: "The jungle had been cleared, the air swarmed with mosquitoes and, as soon as we approached, I felt the gravitational pull of the place. I mean that literally. The main *tiki*—the largest in Polynesia—is squat, rounded, strong. There is an unmistakable power here. Even the leaves are conscious of it, can feel it, are part of it."[45] What Dyer describes here is affect: a physical response to his surroundings so powerful that it momentarily breaks down the boundaries of his own subjectivity and he feels a force connecting himself, the landscape, and the *tiki*. He continues: "I wanted to stay put . . . to give this god his due and bask in the simplest emotions (though it is more than that): I was glad I came."[46] Thus disappointment primes Dyer for further disappointment, which in turn renders him vulnerable to a sudden instant of radical connection to his surroundings, ending in contentment.

One theme that emerges from Dyer's writing is the notion of disappointment as a necessary prelude to interest, an affective state linked in Silvan Tomkins's schema to surprise—and more vitally to learning.[47] For Dyer disappointment is indeed a vehicle for curiosity: it is an affect that moves him time and again toward further engagement with his surroundings. In one passage of "Where? What? Where?" he recalls an epiphany he had while exploring a neighborhood where Gauguin painted some of his most famous works. His mind, he explains, "was completely blank," and try as he might he "could not think [himself] into Gauguin's shoes, couldn't see the world through his eyes." However, while standing and "seeing what [Gauguin] had seen without even coming close to what he had seen," Dyer realizes that his frustration may actually be liberating—that his "enormous capacity for disappointment [is] actually an achievement, a victory." "The devastating scale and frequency of my disappointment," he declares, "was proof of how much I still expected and wanted from the world, of what high hopes I still had of it. When I am no longer capable of disappointment the romance will be gone: I may as well be dead."[48] This is hardly a moment of radical ecocentric awakening: Dyer and his own desires are firmly at the center of the affect, emotion, and subsequent expression captured by this passage of the text. At the same time, however, *White Sands* offers suggestive insights for ecocritics. Disappointment leads Dyer to a stance of openness, an attitude that balances vulnerability with hope. What is more, he reaches this state not through a "pure" unmediated encounter with nature but because of his ambivalent engagements with Gauguin's art.

Coping with Disappointment

I offer Dyer's experience not as a postmodern corrective to Wordsworth but as one example of how media, affect, and landscape intersect in the context of travel. In fact, contemporary though it may be, Dyer's account of touristic disappointment is prefigured in any number of earlier texts, including travel writing from the 1800s. Consider briefly Frances Trollope's *Domestic Manners of the Americans* (1832), a volume that chronicles Trollope's journey from England, up the Mississippi to the Ohio River, and later to upstate New York. Widely read in its time, Trollope's travelogue is best remembered for its biting social commentary. Less often noted are the volume's detailed descriptions of American landscapes, which brim with emotions ranging from disgust to delight. Primed by travel literature and fiction set in the United States, Trollope arrived in the country eager to see the settings she had read about. Indeed many of her responses to the landscape, such as this one, explicitly invoke her prior expectations: "On the 30th of May we set off for Niagara. I had heard so much of the surpassing beauty of the North river, that I expected to be disappointed, and to find reality flat after description. But it is not in the power of man to paint with the strength exceeding that of nature, in such scenes as the Hudson presents. Every mile shows some new and startling effect of the combination of rocks, trees, and water."[49] Like other parts of *Domestic Manners*, this passage reveals the extent to which media had already—even in the 1820s—come to determine how tourists approached, and experienced, the settings they visited. Rather than simply raising Trollope's excitement, circulating descriptions of the Niagara region heightened her anticipation of possible disappointment. Thus, when she actually encounters the area, the pleasure she receives is intensified by realizing that she has, in fact, *not* been disappointed, as she had planned to be. A similar moment occurs in her account of confronting Niagara Falls, "an object which, for years, [she] had languished to look upon":

> I can only say that wonder, terror, and delight completely overwhelmed me. I wept with a strange mixture of pleasure and pain, and certainly was, for some time, too violently affected in the *physique* to be capable of much pleasure; but when this emotion of the senses subsided, and I had recovered some degree of composure, my enjoyment was very great indeed. . . .
>
> To say that I was not disappointed is but a weak expression to convey the surprise and astonishment which this long dreamed of scene produced.[50]

To be sure, this description draws on the discourse of the sublime and on the representational tropes associated with it. Yet to dismiss Trollope's remarks as merely rhetorical misses something important. Mediated natures set the terms upon which Trollope's affective response to Niagara Falls unfolded: the initial somatic shock she feels is the shock of elation, of prior expectations suddenly and dramatically exceeded. Once again her self-conscious sense that reading about and imagining the falls might lead to disappointment heightens her joy: it is a joy that comes from the grandeur of the landscape *and* from her interaction with so many simulacra of the landscape, so many textual or visual representations that failed to convey the true affective force of the falls.

Writing a little more than a decade later, Margaret Fuller offers an equally striking account of touristic affects in her *Summer on the Lakes, in 1843.* For Fuller—who had read Trollope—Niagara Falls proves disappointing because the spectacle merely meets her expectations. "When I first came [to the falls]," she writes, "I felt nothing but a quiet satisfaction. I found that drawings, the panorama, &c. had given me a clear notion of the position and proportions of all objects here; I knew where to look for everything, and everything looked as I thought it would."[51] Thus underwhelmed, Fuller quickly becomes bored. Yet her initial ambivalence evolves into something more complicated. As she later confesses, she *did* have a strong affective response to the landscape—but this response was provoked by the Niagara River, not the celebrated falls. Fuller describes standing on a footbridge: "When I stood upon this frail support, and saw a quarter mile of tumbling, rushing rapids, and heard their everlasting roar, my emotions overpowered me, a choking sensation rose to my throat, a thrill rushed through my veins, 'my blood ran rippling to my finger's [*sic*] ends.' This was the climax of the effect which the falls produced upon me—neither the American nor the British fall moved me as did these rapids."[52] The rapids plunge Fuller into an intense physiological response, one that overwhelms her in its suddenness. The rapids themselves are important here, but so too is Fuller's surprise. "For the magnificence, the sublimity [of the falls]," she explains, "I was prepared by descriptions and by paintings. When I arrived in sight of them I merely felt, 'ah, yes, here is the fall, just as I have seen it in picture.'"[53] She was not, however, "prepared" for the rapids, having never encountered them in mediated form.

In a humorous moment of self-deprecation, Fuller laments her "stupidity in feeling most moved in the wrong place." When she turns from the falls "with almost a feeling of disappointment," she feels let down by the landscape, as well as by her own failure to experience the "correct" emotions, correctly timed. Such ironic self-awareness might seem postmodern—a pose we would expect from Dyer rather than his Victorian forerunners. Yet Fuller herself looks backward, yearning for an always-already lost moment of unmediated wonder. After her disappointing visit to the falls, she returns at night to the Niagara River. "It was grand," she recalls, and "the yellow rays of the moon made the broken waves appear like auburn tresses twining around the black rocks." This time, she feels not "inspire[d] . . . as before"; instead there comes "a mightier emotion to rise up and swallow all others." As in Trollope's account, the sublime surfaces here, with Fuller awed into "humble adoration of the Being who was the architect of this all."[54] Ultimately, though, Fuller arrives at something more like wistfulness: "Happy were the first discoverers of Niagara," she writes, "those who could come unawares upon this view and upon that, whose feelings were entirely their own."[55] Affect theory tells us that affects are in fact *never* entirely our own: the dream of a "pure" affect is unrealizable. Still, Fuller's desire is worth contemplating. Disappointment has led her, eventually, to imagine the landscape otherwise, to suspend it mentally in a moment of contingency. That turn toward the distant "otherwise" might seem dubious, yet it is also a skill essential to envisioning positive change.

There is no evidence I can find to suggest that travel led Trollope or Fuller to actions we would characterize as "ecocentric," "green," or even protoenvironmentalist. Still, their work provides lessons for our moment. Today globalization and digital technology make it difficult to encounter any setting, including the most quotidian places, without prior expectations. Added to this dilemma is the increasingly wide chasm between reality and the hyperidealized images of nature made possible by technology: as Photoshop and similar technologies improve, environmental degradation accelerates. Thus on our screens high-def nature grows ever more colorful and resplendent, while out the window, pollution, a changing climate, and other problems make "Kodak moments" ever more elusive. If the research about disappointment is accurate, then the possibility of being disappointed by nature—by animals that fail to look as majestic in real life as on camera or by sunsets that do not live up to the ones on TV—must be increasing. Of course we are also increasingly confronted with images of nature that are upsetting. Forests ablaze and starving polar bears stumbling across thawing permafrost are frightening. Such images are difficult to watch or to read about; they may engender apathy or ambivalence instead of the action they are intended to promote. Although disappointment aversion is seldom invoked in discussions about environmental communication, it is likely that this phenomenon plays a role in the collective inaction on climate change and other problems. In our moment nature feels like a risky investment: Why donate some of our scarce emotional resources to loving or caring about something that might—that probably will—disappoint us with its continued decline?

Still, many people do invest despite the risk. There are a number of archaic meanings attached to "cope," a word that referred originally to battlefield scenarios (one would "cope with" an opponent as in "strike" or "meet in the shock of battle or tournament" [OED]). Only later did cope acquire its more familiar meanings: "to face, encounter (dangers, difficulties, etc.)" or "to manage, deal (competently) with, a situation or problem" (OED). Fundamentally, "coping" entails encounter—"to meet with; come into contact, touch, or relation with" in Early Modern English. Thus, coping with disappointment means embracing disappointment, learning in a sense to "strike back" against the feeling of shattered expectations. Timothy Morton has identified melancholy as a useful stance, arguing in *Ecology without Nature* and elsewhere that melancholy not only guards us against false optimism but also helps us to see ourselves as "radically involved in [our] world, and thus responsible for it."[56] For Morton coping is proactive; we cope by never allowing ourselves to forget the "dark, depressing quality of life in the shadow of ecological catastrophe" in the first place.[57] Perhaps such an attitude can help us to confront the current crisis. I think we need something else, too, something that makes more room for surprise. As we have seen, disappointment contains the seeds of its inverse: within every opportunity for disappointment lies the possibility for expectations exceeded, for the elation that Trollope feels, or the thrill that seizes Fuller.

Postmodern nature might disappoint, but it might also transport us, especially if we can train affect toward interest and reflection. We would do well to cultivate a radical openness to good surprises, to affects such as delight and interest, even in the midst of melancholy.

NOTES

1. Wordsworth, *Wordsworth's Poetry and Prose*, 251 (VI.433, 428, 434–35). All citations for *The Prelude* include page number(s), followed by book and line number(s).
2. Wordsworth, *Wordsworth's Poetry and Prose*, 251 (VI.453–56).
3. Wordsworth, *Wordsworth's Poetry and Prose*, 251 (VI.456–57).
4. Wordsworth, *Wordsworth's Poetry and Prose*, 253 (VI.511).
5. Wordsworth, *Wordsworth's Poetry and Prose*, 253 (VI.520–24).
6. The scholarship on this portion of *The Prelude* is too voluminous to list; for an overview of some major claims about the Simplon Pass incident, see Miall, "Alps Deferred."
7. The "writer's block" is mentioned in Owen, "Crossing the Alps," 101.
8. Loomes and Sugden, "Disappointment and Dynamic Consistency," 524. Research since the mid-1980s has tried to explain "illogical" deviations from expected utility theory, which assumes that decision makers dispassionately weigh the possible outcomes of particular actions and assign a utility to them. "Regret theory" suggests that this process is complicated by anticipated disappointment or regret. For a foundational study on disappointment and decision-making, see Bell, "Disappointment in Decision Making."
9. Zeelenberg et al., "On Bad Decisions and Disconfirmed Expectancies," 528. Zeelenberg and his team also find that disappointment aversion may cause people to "simply avoid making decisions," to "delay their decision making," or to avoid receiving feedback on their decisions for fear of discovering positive information about a forgone option (534).
10. See Gilbert's best-selling *Stumbling on Happiness*; see also Schwartz's popular *Paradox of Choice* and related TED talk at https://www.ted.com/talks/barry _schwartz_on_the_paradox_of_choice.
11. Ahmed, *Promise of Happiness*, 41–42.
12. Ahmed, *Promise of Happiness*, 41.
13. Ngai, *Ugly Feelings*.
14. Houser, *Ecosickness in Contemporary U.S. Fiction*, 16.
15. Reddy, *Navigation of Feeling*, 110.
16. "Emotives," as Reddy terms them, are "utterances aimed at briefly characterizing the current state of activated thought material that exceeds the current capacity

of attention." Reddy, *Navigation of Feeling*, 111. For further explanation, see Reddy, *Navigation of Feeling*, chap. 3, "Emotional Expression as a Type of Speech Act."

17. Reddy, *Navigation of Feeling*, 103.
18. Reddy, *Navigation of Feeling*, 102. This is because emotives not only reflect whatever "activated thought material" gave rise to them in the first place: they can also *change* that thought material and/or activate other thought material, including information from our memories.
19. Reddy, *Navigation of Feeling*, 111.
20. Trott, "Wordsworth Making Amends," 29.
21. Quinney, *Poetics of Disappointment*, 19.
22. Quinney, *Poetics of Disappointment*, 18.
23. Watkins, "Desiring Recognition," 233.
24. Wordsworth, *Wordsworth's Poetry and Prose*, 254 (VI.549).
25. Wordsworth, *Wordsworth's Poetry and Prose*, 351 (XI.180).
26. Wordsworth, *Wordsworth's Poetry and Prose*, 351 (XI.163), 350–51 (XI.159, 161).
27. Wordsworth, *Wordsworth's Poetry and Prose*, 257 (VI.672–80).
28. See Bate, *Romantic Ecology*; and McKusick, *Green Writing*.
29. Watkins, "Desiring Recognition," 278.
30. Wordsworth, *Wordsworth's Poetry and Prose*, 350 (XI.156). See Miall, "Alps Deferred." For more recent critiques see Hess, *William Wordsworth and the Ecology of Authorship*; and Broglio, *Technologies of the Picturesque*.
31. The pronouns here are gendered male, as Gilpin intended.
32. Gilpin, *Three Essays*, 48.
33. Gilpin, *Three Essays*, 48.
34. Gilpin, *Three Essays*, 49.
35. Gilpin, *Three Essays*, 49.
36. Gilpin, *Three Essays*, 50 (original emphases).
37. Gilpin, *Three Essays*, 51.
38. Dyer, *White Sands*, 84.
39. Dyer, *White Sands*, 120–21.
40. The essay's title echoes Gauguin's famous painting *Where Do We Come From? What Are We? Where Are We Going?* (1897).
41. Dyer, *White Sands*, 7.
42. Dyer, *White Sands*, 8.
43. Dyer, *White Sands*, 9.
44. Dyer, *White Sands*, 26.
45. Dyer, *White Sands*, 27.
46. Dyer, *White Sands*, 28.
47. See Tomkins, *Affect, Imagery, and Consciousness*.

48. Dyer, *White Sands*, 14–15.
49. Trollope, *Domestic Manners*, 202.
50. Trollope, *Domestic Manners*, 225–26 (original emphasis).
51. Fuller, *Summer on the Lakes*, 6.
52. Fuller, *Summer on the Lakes*, 8. Fuller refers here to the American Falls and the Horseshoe Falls.
53. Fuller, *Summer on the Lakes*, 8.
54. Fuller, *Summer on the Lakes*, 8.
55. Fuller, *Summer on the Lakes*, 9.
56. Morton, *Ecology without Nature*, 187.
57. Morton, *Ecology without Nature*, 187.

BIBLIOGRAPHY

Ahmed, Sara. *The Promise of Happiness*. Durham: Duke University Press, 2010.

Bate, Jonathan. *Romantic Ecology: Wordsworth and the Environmental Tradition*. New York: Routledge, 1991.

Bell, David E. "Disappointment in Decision Making Under Uncertainty." *Operations Research* 33, no.1 (January–February 1985): 1–27.

Broglio, Ron. *Technologies of the Picturesque: British Art, Poetry, and Instruments, 1750–1830*. Lewisburg PA: Bucknell University Press, 2008.

Dyer, Geoff. *White Sands: Experiences from the Outside World*. New York: Pantheon Books, 2016.

Fuller, Margaret. *Summer on the Lakes, in 1843*. 1844. Champaign: University of Illinois Press, 1991.

Gilbert, Daniel. *Stumbling on Happiness*. New York: Knopf, 2006.

Gilpin, William. *Three Essays on Picturesque Beauty*. London: R. Blamire, 1792.

Hess, Scott. *William Wordsworth and the Ecology of Authorship*. Charlottesville: University of Virginia Press, 2012.

Houser, Heather. *Ecosickness in Contemporary U.S. Fiction: Affect and Environment*. New York: Columbia University Press, 2014.

Loomes, Graham, and Robert Sugden. "Disappointment and Dynamic Consistency in Choice under Uncertainty." *Review of Economic Studies* 53, no. 2 (April 1986): 271–82.

McKusick, James. *Green Writing: Romanticism and Ecology*. New York: Palgrave, 2000.

Miall, David. "The Alps Deferred: Wordsworth at the Simplon Pass," *European Romantic Review* 9, no. 1 (Winter 1998): 87–102.

Morton, Timothy. *Ecology without Nature*. Cambridge MA: Harvard University Press, 2007.

Ngai, Sianne. *Ugly Feelings*. Cambridge MA: Harvard University Press, 2005.

Owen, W. J. B. "Crossing the Alps Again." *Wordsworth Circle* 25, no. 2 (Spring 1994): 100–107.

Quinney, Laura. *The Poetics of Disappointment: Wordsworth to Ashbery.* Charlottesville: University of Virginia Press, 1999.

Reddy, William M. *The Navigation of Feeling: A Framework for the History of Emotions.* New York: Cambridge University Press, 2001.

Schwartz, Barry. *The Paradox of Choice: Why More Is Less.* New York: Harper Perennial, 2005.

Tomkins, Silvan. *Affect, Imagery, and Consciousness: Volume I, The Positive Affects.* New York: Springer, 1962.

Trollope, Frances. *Domestic Manners of the Americans.* New York: Whittaker, Treacher, & Co., 1832.

Trott, Nicola. "Wordsworth Making Amends." *Wordsworth Circle* 21, no. 1 (Winter 1990): 27–34.

Watkins, Megan. "Desiring Recognition, Accumulating Affect." In *The Affect Theory Reader,* edited by Gregory J. Seigworth and Melissa Gregg, 269–85. Durham: Duke University Press, 2010.

Wordsworth, William. *Wordsworth's Poetry and Prose.* Edited by Nicholas Halmi. New York: Norton, 2013.

Zeelenberg, Marcel, et al. "On Bad Decisions and Disconfirmed Expectancies: The Psychology of Regret and Disappointment." *Cognition and Emotion* 14, no. 4 (2000): 521–41.

13

Feeling Depleted
Ecocinema and the Atmospherics of Affect

GRAIG UHLIN

> I think that if one is faced by inevitable destruction—if a house is falling down
> upon you, for instance—one must feel a great longing to sit down, close one's
> eyes and wait, come what may.
> –Fyodor Dostoyevsky, *The Idiot*

Feeling is a feature of the world as much as it is a feature of the self. In distinguishing between affect and emotion Brian Massumi understands the latter as "subjective content," the capturing and domestication of affect's free-floating intensity.[1] Emotion is personal and embodied, tied to a subject, whereas affect resists the stability of structure and narrativization. Continually overspilling the forms that attempt to capture it, affect for Massumi is transpersonal and "infrastructural": although affect is virtual, its discernible effects make it no less "a real condition, an intrinsic variable of the late-capitalist system, as infrastructural as a factory."[2] In *The Transmission of Affect* Teresa Brennan similarly emphasizes affect's transpersonal nature, arguing that it is not the case that it goes "no farther than the skin."[3] The concept of the autonomous individual, Brennan contends, confined emotion to an internal state, both psychological and physiological, and suppressed the acknowledgment of the social dimensions of feeling, readily noted by any person who has sensed the mood of a room they've entered or a situation they've encountered. "There is no secure distinction," she writes, "between the 'individual' and the 'environment.'"[4] In her book *Ugly Feelings* Sianne Ngai likewise notes that "feelings are as fundamentally 'social' as the institutions and collective practices that have been the more traditional objects of historicist criticism," and it is this social aspect that makes affect amenable to ideological analysis in ways that the more privatized experience of emotion is not.[5]

The "environmentality" of feeling indicates more than the observation that our surroundings shape our moods. Rather, environments are best apprehended through feeling. Ngai comments, for instance, "how entirely appropriate emotive or affective qualities seem, as compressed assessments of complex 'situations,' for indicating the *total* web of relations."[6] As surround or background, an environment is difficult to perceive, since taking it as an object of attention means it no longer functions as background. An environment is not a thing, and the totality of its relations outruns any descriptive account. As Ngai notes, though, feeling provides a holistic impression of this totality, condensing and unifying its "web of relations" into a singular affective quality. An individual registers an environmental surround through affect, which generalizes and abstracts from a given totality. An affective quality emerges out of all of the elements that compose the environment, while remaining relatively autonomous from each of them—which is to say, it is not localizable in any of its particular elements. As such, affect resists any analysis that aims to break it down into component parts, as this runs counter to its "virtual, diffused, but also immanent character."[7] However, this holistic aspect means that affect renders the surround perceptible and intelligible without relinquishing its background status.

Ngai is referring to the literary concept of tone, which characterizes the mood of an artwork, but ecocriticism is likely better served by the related term "atmosphere." Atmosphere entails a dual perspective that describes both the mood of an artistic production and the experience of an environment, whether natural or built. That is to say, atmosphere characterizes the affective quality of environments both internal and external to a text, and the possible relations between them. Hans Ulrich Gumbrecht, for instance, has recently observed that *Stimmung*, as an object of literary analysis, encompasses both subjective "mood" and objective "climate," especially insofar as atmosphere points to the indiscernibility between the two. He compares the atmosphere of a text to the act of hearing sounds or music, insofar as the auditory minimizes the difference between the internal and the external: "every tone we perceive is, of course, a form of physical reality (if an invisible one) that 'happens' to our body and, at the same time, 'surrounds' it."[8] Like the idea of tone, the affective quality of atmosphere refers neither to the emotions represented in a text nor to the emotional response of a spectator or reader to the text. Its diffuse nature slides across or simply envelops the assembled elements, eliding the difference between subject and object since it opens a porous relation between them. As understood by Mikel Dufrenne, whose phenomenological aesthetics have been influential to this line of thought, atmosphere describes the feeling of the text's "expressed world," which exceeds its represented elements as a type of "emanation" or "radiation." Following Dufrenne, Ben Anderson, in discussing "affective atmospheres," stresses this "constitutive openness" of atmosphere, which in resisting the "stability of form" names a quality that is at once impersonal and "intensely personal."[9]

Emphasizing atmosphere as opposed to tone or mood demonstrates that affective responses to aesthetic works are often modeled on similar responses to the natural environment. For instance, in addition to music Gumbrecht analogizes literary atmosphere to the experience of weather, in that it is both "out there" and registers as an inner feeling. Anderson stresses that, in Gilles Deleuze's definition of affect, feeling assumes the "dynamic, kinetic qualities" of atmospheric phenomena, such as rain, wind, or meteors.[10] Comparisons of atmosphere to Walter Benjamin's concept of aura similarly emphasize that Benjamin's primary example involves a view of nature. An artwork's aura, as the "unique appearance of distance, however near it may be," is likened to the apprehension of "a mountain chain on the horizon" while "resting on a summer evening."[11] For Gernot Böhme, as "aura is clearly something which flows forth spatially, almost something like a breath or a haze—precisely an atmosphere," it is therefore not simply restricted to artworks but also can be extended to natural objects.[12] Moreover, as Ngai notes, nature features prominently in Theodor Adorno's reconsideration of Benjamin's aura. What Adorno refers to as "the atmosphere of an artwork" can be likened to the appearance of a distance in nature "when it is not seen as an object of action."[13] Finally, in defining tone, Ngai references Otto Baensch's 1923 essay "Art and Feeling," itself an important influence for Susanne Langer's notion of "significant form," where Baensch writes, "The mood of a landscape appears to us as objectively given with it as one of its attributes, belonging to it just like any other attribute we perceive it to have. . . . The landscape does not express the mood, but *has* it; the mood surrounds, fills, and permeates it."[14] These examples underline the homologous relation between spectatorial responses to art and nature, encompassed by the concept of atmosphere, and the central role of feeling in the subjective apprehension of aesthetic and natural environments.

As Benjamin's bucolic example attests, this homologous relation often appears as a virtuous circle, where atmosphere (whether of art or nature) sustains and enlivens the subject. However, the relevance of atmosphere for ecocriticism, and for ecocinema specifically, is perhaps most pointed when it concerns representations of environmental degradation. If, as Benjamin notes, one "breathes the aura" of the mountain chain, what affective qualities characterize the experience when the atmosphere turns toxic? What feelings attend situations where the natural environment is experienced as hostile, inhospitable not just to quality of life but also to life itself? This chapter considers environmental crisis as productive of a range of negative affects, which constellate around feelings of sorrow, depression, and exhaustion. In this way, resource depletion is linked to feeling depleted; ecological collapse prefigures emotional collapse. Environmental crisis registers as an atmospheric shift where a restorative or life-sustaining atmosphere turns suffocating and draining. In films pertaining to environmental crisis—and thus received as aesthetic experiences of depleted environments—the mood created can be dispassionate, even resignation, stemming from recognition of the unavoidable consequences of some environmental harm that has already taken place and is therefore beyond redress. To be clear, feeling depleted is not the same as indifference to or the absence of feeling toward environmental despoliation. Rather, the stifling atmospheres of these films express a palpable sense that there is nothing to be done in the face of catastrophe.

In Kelly Reichardt's 2006 film *Old Joy*, for instance, atmospheric shift makes discernible the unspoken tension between two old friends on a weekend camping trip, and the film formally links their broken relationship to the ecological destruction of the Oregon wilderness. Kurt (Will Oldham) proposes the trip to the Bagby Hot Springs, located in the Pacific Northwest, in order to revive his friendship with Mark (Daniel London), now married and with a child on the way. While Mark has settled down, Kurt remains committed to an itinerant lifestyle, always with a temporary residence and unstable employment ("I've never gotten myself into anything that I couldn't get myself out of"). The trip to the hot springs offers an opportunity for reconciliation, but it serves only to confirm the distance between them. The film thus concludes on an ambiguous note, and it seems likely that they will not see each other often, if at all. Nothing dramatically significant happens during their expedition that might confirm this; there is no definitive breaking point, only the barely perceptible shifting of attitudes between two old friends. The ground of their relationship has seemingly shifted beneath their feet. Kurt senses this is the case and attempts to address the issue, to bring it out of the background: he says, "I miss you, Mark. I miss you really, really bad. I want us to be real friends again. There's something between us, and I don't like it. I want it to go away." The "something" that Kurt cannot name but nonetheless feels is the affective atmosphere between them, the indescribable yet perceptible surround. The awkwardness of their interactions is evident in their stilted conversation, which seems at once familiar and forced. Mark especially makes repeated assurances to Kurt that everything is fine between them, but these gestures seem merely polite, and he subtly contradicts them when talking to his wife on his cell phone—for instance, after telling Kurt that he trusts him to find the springs, he then complains to his wife about being lost.

This inability to reclaim their friendship indicates how Reichardt renders ambiguous the conventional trope of nature's restorative effect. As David Ingram argues in his book *Green Screen*, depictions of pristine wilderness

Trashed wilderness in Kelly Reichardt's *Old Joy.*

are typically constructed around an "aesthetic of exclusion" that removes "all signs of human intervention in nature."[15] He contends that the purity of wilderness is maintained because it functions as "a psychological safety valve for anxieties over modern development" and contributes to the "spiritual redemption" of an alienated humanity.[16] Reichardt does gesture, at least partially, in this direction: Mark comments that they are entering "a whole other zone" the closer they get to the hot springs, and once they are there Reichardt cuts away repeatedly to close-up images of nature (a slug slowly gliding across moss, birds in the trees, water dripping from branches, etc.). More generally, though, the film blurs the boundaries between industrialized and natural spaces. In the film's first scene, when Mark receives a phone call from Kurt, Reichardt similarly cuts away to close-ups of his front yard that feature the co-presence of the natural and technological, eschewing Ingram's aesthetics of exclusion: ants crawling around a water hose and birds perched near electrical wires. When they arrive at a campsite for the night, the clearing is filled with debris, including an abandoned couch. As Kurt notes later that night, "It's not like there is any big difference between the forest and the city though, you know what I mean? It's all one huge thing now. There's trees in the city and garbage in the forest. What's the big difference, you know?" The trashed landscape not only disrupts the restorative effect of nature but also signals a particular feeling of loss that the environmental philosopher Glenn Albrecht terms "solastalgia," which describes the psychological distress that results when one's home or familiar environs are subject to transformation or devastation.[17] Distinguished from nostalgia, which names a homesickness stemming from dislocation, solastalgia involves the harm in losing a homeland one nonetheless cannot leave. The familiar sites revisited by Kurt and Mark no longer ground their friendship, and these newly strange spaces produce the film's sorrowful central atmosphere.

The feeling of sorrow is linked to the film's title, which is taken from a story Kurt tells at the hot springs. He describes an uncanny experience of repeatedly encountering an elderly man while running errands. Having nearly collided with the man earlier, Kurt feels each new accidental meeting reviving his guilt, which subsides each time he thinks he has finally shaken the man ("I can finally move on with my life and not have this guy"). On the final encounter Kurt suddenly remembers a dream from that morning that anticipated these events. In the dream a woman comforts him by saying, "Sorrow is just worn-out joy." In other words joy is subject to depletion. The man who reappears symbolizes Kurt's unwillingness to relinquish the past, that is, his earlier happiness with Mark. In the atmospheric shift from joy to sorrow, though, Kurt faces the improbability of their reunion. As he earnestly tells Mark at the campfire, "The entire universe is in the shape of a tear falling down through space. I don't know how it happened, but it's just the way that it works. It's this tear that's been dropping down forever, and it just doesn't stop." A tear forever falling suggests a universal sorrow, from a joy that is running out, and provides an image of a friendship and a natural environment beyond restoration.

Reichardt subtly references the clear-cutting of Oregon's old-growth forests as a visual marker for the atmospheric shift that has undermined their friendship. At one point, having gotten lost because Kurt is unable to remember the way, they stop on the roadside to consult a map. Reichardt stages the scene at a dividing line between the forest and a clear-cut area, contrasting the plenitude of the past with the barrenness of the future. A blank road sign fails to point them in the right direction, creating a sense of disorientation in a once familiar space. Earlier, as they drove out of Portland, Reichardt's traveling shots from the car window capture the increasingly industrialized landscape of the city and, most pointedly, depict a semi rig carrying timber. The hot springs might be an exceptional space, but it is steadily encroached upon by development and natural resource extraction; depletion seems inevitable. The references to logging point to the film's ambiguous politics, which is no less charged with the same sense of inaction and disaffection that characterizes the mood of the film's other elements. The immediate context of the film's release was the reelection of President George W. Bush, which left progressive and environmental groups dispirited. For instance, when Mark drives to meet up with Kurt prior to their trip, he listens to a call-in radio show on Air America, the now-defunct liberal alternative to conservative talk radio. The callers on the program complain about the minority status of the Democratic Party, suggestive of the pessimistic mood of the political landscape, in parallel with the film's central personal relationship. The historical moment of the narrative follows in the wake of pro–logging industry reforms made by the Bush administration in March 2004. The Northwest Forest Plan, which went into effect in 1994 under the Clinton administration, protected old-growth forests in western Oregon from logging interests in order to preserve the habitats of certain rare species, such as the spotted owl, and to conserve the integrity of regional watersheds. Bush officials amended the regulations so that proposed logging sites were no longer required to "survey and manage" the prospective areas for species protection, nor did each individual project have to assess its environmental impact on local waterways. These loosened regulations vastly expanded the reach of the logging industry into the old-growth forests of western Oregon. *Old Joy* makes no explicit reference to these developments, nor does it contain conventional pro-environment messages. Its depictions of clear-cutting do not inspire passionate feelings, leading to decisive action; rather, its

A divide between forest and clear-cut in Kelly Reichardt's *Old Joy*.

negative affective register results only in an "unsatisfying" conclusion of stalled agency, of nothing to be done but letting go.

The negative affects produced by certain films related to environmental crisis are therefore not easily enlisted for an environmentalist agenda and may in fact aggravate or disturb the standard assumptions that depictions of environmental harm compel action for the protection of nature. The dispassionate moods or sapped energies of these cinematic atmospheres often run counter to the rhetorical demand made by environmentalist film that the natural world should be an object of our care. As Ngai notes, referencing the psychologist Silvan Tomkins, affect facilitates our concern for the world. For Tomkins it performs this function through a process of "amplification," which describes affect's relation to the physiological systems that serve as its source: affect "increas[es] the urgency of anything with which it is co-assembled."[18] The pain mechanism exemplifies the process: "If we cut our hand, saw it bleeding, but had no innate pain receptors, we would know we had done something which needed repair, but there would be no urgency to it. . . . But the pain mechanism, like the affect mechanism, so amplifies our awareness of the injury which activates it that we are forced to be concerned, and concerned immediately."[19] As Ngai observes, the "echolalic effect" of affect's amplification—its extension and intensification of its originating physiological impulse—underlines its significance in "making things matter to us."[20]

Emotional appeals made by pro-environment media rely on this production of urgency; environmental crisis demands that something be done now. In an essay on the environmental documentaries *The Cove* (2009) and *Darwin's Nightmare* (2004), for instance, Belinda Smaill argues that these films establish a "sentimental contract" with their audiences, utilizing emotion in order to advance their environmental advocacy.[21] This is characteristic of studies of affect and emotion in cinema that tend to focus on the film's effect on a spectator. David Ingram, for instance, offers a comprehensive model of spectatorship that combines cognitive and phenomenological approaches to examine how "eco-films" solicit viewer identification and provoke embodied responses in order to promote environmental causes. His discussion of *Local Hero* (Bill Forsyth, 1983), in which oil executives are convinced to protect the pristine natural landscape of a Scottish island by relocating a new refinery offshore, emphasizes how the film "celebrates the environmentalist values of place attachment and ecological connectedness" by facilitating the spectator's sympathetic identification with the executive's conversion and appealing to the natural beauty of the landscape to align the viewer with the film's conservationist message.[22]

The production of a negative affective atmosphere, however, breaks or disrupts what Ngai calls the "imaginary circuit of sympathy" between reader and text, which involves "how feeling can make a work of art become an object of our concern *by the production of immediacy*."[23] If feeling is a motor for action, its depletion is the symptomatic response when the possibility for immediate action is foreclosed, primarily because the situation has already reached a point beyond remediation. Films with atmospheres marked by sorrow, melancholy, or exhaustion therefore feature minimal action, and these de-dramatized narratives create a palpable sense of inertia. This stifled mobility finds its expression in the slow or suspended movements of the film's form. The range of negative affects generates what Ngai refers to as a "noncathartic aesthetic," defined by the "failure of emotional release."[24] Insofar as the "ugly feelings" she describes are "less object- or goal-oriented," they are not easily mobilized for political action, even as "the unsuitability of these weakly intentional feelings for forceful or unambiguous action is precisely what amplifies their power to diagnose situations, and situations marked by blocked or thwarted action in particular."[25] The difficulty of action around environmental crisis, especially on the scale of climate change, can thus generate any number of ugly feelings, and the atmospheres of ecocinema, which transmit these feelings as part of the film's expressive form, can register this stalled action as a barometer of our pessimism or resignation.

Consider as another example a film about the unavoidable destruction of Earth—Lars von Trier's apocalyptic *Melancholia* (2011)—caused by its collision with another planet, named Melancholia, its arrival having gone unnoticed as it was "hiding behind the sun." The film is divided into two parts, with an introductory prologue consisting of surreal or fantastical imagery that foretells the coming disaster. The first part takes place at the wedding of Justine (Kirsten Dunst) at the country estate of her brother-in-law, John (Kiefer Sutherland); the second part occurs later, following the discovery of Melancholia, as Justine and her sister Claire (Charlotte Gainsbourg) await its arrival. Justine suffers from depression throughout the film, the causes of which are not specified or even able to be specified. The relation of her pronounced melancholy to the imminent apocalypse is left ambiguous, but in its depiction of ecological devastation and emotional collapse *Melancholia* underlines atmosphere's overriding of the difference between the internal and external, between the subjective and objective.

It is possible to interpret the world-ending planetary collision as an allegory for the experience of depression, as the exteriorizing of a psychological state. Christopher Peterson, though, has argued against understanding the film's apocalyptic scenario as an allegorical depiction of the melancholic, in part because doing so means avoiding having to confront the actual obliteration of Earth depicted in the film.[26] Relatedly, Nicole Merola points to von Trier's film as a means of conceptualizing an "environmental melancholy," which "extend[s] grief to encompass nonhumans and ecological processes," thereby emphasizing our affective relationship to the earth.[27] As these scholars highlight, *Melancholia* connects the subjective experience of emotional collapse to the objective experience of ecological collapse, but the destruction of the earth is not an outward expression of a psychological condition, nor is the persistent state of depression caused by the imminent disaster. Atmosphere, rooted in the film's formal construction, elides the difference between these two perspectives. It encompasses both a personal feeling of depression (feeling down) and an impersonal sense of depression (pressing down)—on the one hand, the experience of grief, and on the other, the interplay of gravitational forces.

As Brennan notes, "depression is marked by inertia," and throughout the film, Justine cannot perform the actions expected of her, whether personal or professional. Characteristic of Freud's identification of melancholia with the "inhibition of all activity" and "cessation of interest in the outside world," she appears unhappy and withdrawn at her wedding, inviting frustrated or aggressive responses from those around her, a hostility that Brennan argues is typical of reactions to depression.[28] Repeatedly Justine resists the rituals of the wedding. She arrives two hours late to the reception; she delays the cutting of the cake by lying down for a nap in a child's bed and then taking a bath; she declines to consummate the marriage (though she engages in a quick fling on the golf course with another man); and she impassively holds her bouquet as guests expectantly wait for it to be thrown, necessitating that Claire do it for her. Justine's emotional withdrawal only causes those around her to insist that she be grateful: "You better be goddamn happy," John says. Her husband takes a more sympathetic approach, presenting her with a photo of an orchard, on land that he has purchased for their home: "If there are times that you are sad, I think that will make you happy again." She uncaringly leaves the photo behind when she leaves the room. Brennan notes that the social aspect of affect means that individuals orient themselves in response to a particular mood. For example, depression and hostility are often paired, since aggression is a common response to depression's deflated feeling. The internalized anger that constitutes depression only invites more aggression from others, causing a "secondary depression" resulting from these external pressures: the depressed person induces negative moods in others.[29] As Claire says to Justine, "Sometimes I hate you so much." It is her depression's tendency toward inaction that provokes the most hostile responses. As the film transitions to its second half, Justine's inertness worsens. Seemingly unable to get into the cab provided, she has difficulty arriving at the country estate. Once there, she is put immediately to bed, as she barely utters, "I'm so tired." Claire prepares a bath for her, but Justine is unable to even lift her foot to get in the tub. Her depression has nearly immobilized her.

In *Melancholia* Justine's withdrawal of affection for others and for the world is matched by the world's indifference to her, as the imminent destruction of Earth cares nothing for its inhabitants. She voices at one point a nihilistic perspective, typical of von Trier, that "the earth is evil" and thus deserving of its fate: "We don't need to grieve for it. Nobody will miss it." Yet Justine's bodily disposition suggests that she is already grieving its loss. In *The Forms of the Affects* Eugenie Brinkema observes that grief, which she cites to displace the Freudian opposition between mourning and melancholia, "is derived from *grever* (afflict, burden, oppress), from the Latin *gravare* (to cause grief, make heavy)—hence, the etymological intimacy of *grief* and *gravity*, both from *gravis* (weighty)."[30] The experience of grief is characterized by "a pressure on the body, a dragging the body down to earth like gravity, a vector of invisible force pulling down and down further still."[31] Grief here is not a subjective emotion but an objectified affect, acting on and through the body, bending it to its force. Depression is "environmental" then, insofar as the atmosphere lacks breathing room ("the felt experience of heaviness . . . as on one's sternum in sighing, choking breaths that do not fully arrive," writes Brinkema).[32] *Melancholia* restricts its characters to confined spaces, underlining their sense of entrapment when faced with an unavoidable catastrophe: when the whole earth is threatened, there is nowhere left to escape. Justine's horse, for instance, refuses to pass over a bridge on the estate, and later a golf cart mysteriously breaks down at the same point, setting an invisible boundary to the action. When Melancholia approaches Earth, John offers an explanation to lessen the panic: "It's taking a part of our atmosphere. For a little while, it'll make us winded."

What Ngai refers to as the "de-animating effect" of depression is evident in the formal heaviness of von Trier's film—specifically, the use of exaggerated slow motion.[33] In the introductory sequence von Trier stages a prophetic vision of the apocalypse to come. In one shot in extreme slow motion Claire runs across a golf course while holding her young son, barely progressing forward over the duration of the shot. In another Justine runs through a wooded area in her wedding dress, all the while wrapped and tangled in what she later calls "gray woolly yarn" when describing a dream she had. "It's really heavy to drag along," she says. Another shot depicts these three characters walking forward, again in slow motion, on the lawn of the country estate as three planets or moons hover in the sky behind them. Von Trier also includes several images of planetary motion, scaled so that it is not possible to determine how close each of the planets is to each other or how fast they are moving. Through this play with scale, the slowed movements of people on Earth resemble the balletic motion of planets, linking, as the rest of the film will do, the personal to the cosmic: grief and gravity operate as twinned forces pulling down whatever falls within their respective fields. This sequence prepares the spectator for the film's inevitable conclusion: the destruction of Earth. Justine rejects Claire's attempt to make their final hours "nice," just as she rejected the empty propriety of the wedding, and instead opts for passive resignation. The final (in)action of the characters is to sit down on the lawn and await the arrival of their end and the film's.

As evidenced by the enervating effects of depression in *Melancholia*, affect can be considered a type of energy modulation. According to Brennan, affects are "carriers of energy."[34] They are thus equally capable of enhancement and depletion, just as Massumi's characterization of affect as intensity suggests greater or lesser force. In Brennan's understanding, negative affects such as depression deplete energy, since depression's inwardly directed aggression requires persistent applications of pressure (repression), while positive affects such as love energize individuals. Enhancement of affects occurs, she notes, when they are "projected outward"; individuals invest in objects outside themselves and are thus relieved of the blocked energy. Brennan refers to this process as "dumping."[35] Negative affects tend toward the depletion of energy since this blocked energy accumulates, leaving the subject feeling drained. Gus Van Sant's film *Gerry* (2002) makes this steady erosion of energy its main focus. The first film in the director's "death trilogy," which includes *Elephant* (2003) and *Last Days* (2005), it centers on the slow exhaustion of two friends (Matt Damon and Casey Affleck) who get lost while hiking. For days they are stranded, wandering around the desert without knowing where they are, subsisting without food or water. Finally, fatigued and dehydrated, they collapse, and with barely a gesture Affleck's character asks Damon's (they refer to each other only as "Gerry," a catch-all term that serves as noun, verb, and proper name alike) to end his misery. After this mercy killing and facing his own likely end, Damon's character at last spots rescue in the form of a distant highway, where he is soon picked up by a passing car.

If *Melancholia* created a suffocating atmosphere that weighed down the body, stressing its heavy materiality, the hostile and indifferent environment of *Gerry*, with its overwhelming heat and barren landscapes, causes a progressive wearing down of the body, a metaphorical evaporation of its corporeality into the atmosphere. The slow wasting away of energy corresponds to the formal austerity of the film. Making extensive use of the empty frame, Van Sant stages his actors in extremely long shots against an open landscape. Their bodies are significantly diminished, reduced to graphic elements within the shot or blurred in the distance, as the oppressive heat and abundant sunlight steadily impede their ability to continue moving. As their search for rescue progresses, the range of their actions becomes more restricted. Severely exhausted and feeling hopeless, the Gerrys move more slowly, their heads bowed and covered to protect them from the sun. Through Van Sant's strategic use of blurred focus or hiding their faces in dwindling light, their bodily presence seemingly evaporates, as the boundaries between self and environment are visually obscured. The surrounding environment assumes an increasingly central place within the frame, as their presence within it diminishes, shuttled to the margins or placed in the extreme distance. As their dehydration worsens, the landscape takes on dreamlike qualities, as when Affleck's character hallucinates a conversation with Damon's, who in actuality appears as a blurred figure in the distance walking toward the camera. In these extreme circumstances what

Exhausted bodies in Gus Van Sant's *Gerry*.

is internal versus what is external is harder to distinguish, as the physical and the psychological commingle.

Given the dissipative energies of the film, as character is subordinated to landscape and bodies are nearly immobilized by dehydration and exhaustion, *Gerry* tends to privilege silence over speech, especially as the film develops. There is little dialogue overall, though it is more prevalent near the beginning than by the end. The dialogue that is spoken is often of little consequence, as with the recounting of a *Wheel of Fortune* episode. The more exhausted the Gerrys get, the less they speak. By their third night around a campfire they say nothing to each other. Despite the gravity of their situation, then, the Gerrys rarely voice their anxieties. At one point Affleck's character starts to cry, out of fright and desperation, but this expression of emotion is immediately stifled by Damon's character: "Stop crying, man." The oppressive and overheated atmosphere of the film flattens affect and dampens its articulation. The physical exhaustion of the Gerrys, their bodies literally laid flat by their ordeal, corresponds to this "evaporation" of feeling. The stifling atmosphere incapacitates their ability to act, such that even the film's mercy killing is a labored process, with barely any words passing between the two longtime friends. Faced with an indifferent and hostile environment, the two Gerrys make the choice to succumb to the elements. On the part of Affleck's character the choice is a resignation to the nearly unavoidable consequence of past decisions, the moment when they elected to depart from the marked route of the trail, taking them past the point when any action could save them both from their fate.

As indicated by the films discussed, the atmospherics of affect recognize that feeling cannot be separated from the influence of our surroundings, including the natural environment and its despoliation by industrial processes or transformation by climate change. Affect in this sense was always "environmental." Regarding ecocinema, the atmosphere created by a particular film, as an aesthetic experience, expresses a perceptible mood that encompasses the emotional state of the characters, the "feel" of the work produced by its formal construction, and ultimately the spectatorial response. This chapter has emphasized that environmental crisis provokes a diverse range of affective responses, not all of which align with the environmentalist media's investment in converting emotional urgency into decisive action. Rather than saving the environment, these films depict resigned acts of letting go. This is especially the case, it was emphasized, because their narrative situations are such that the opportunity for decisive action has passed. This is not to recommend despondency in the face of environmental crisis. Instead the broader range of affective responses to environmental harm can function as diagnostic (in Ngai's sense) of our situation, as a barometer of our feelings toward our possible destruction.

NOTES

1. Massumi, "Autonomy of Affect," 88.
2. Massumi, "Autonomy of Affect," 106.
3. Brennan, *Transmission of Affect*, 2.
4. Brennan, *Transmission of Affect*, 6.
5. Ngai, *Ugly Feelings*, 25.
6. Ngai, *Ugly Feelings*, 42 (original emphasis).
7. Ngai, *Ugly Feelings*, 47.
8. Gumbrecht, *Atmosphere, Mood, Stimmung*, 4.
9. Anderson, "Affective Atmospheres," 80.
10. Anderson, "Affective Atmospheres," 80.
11. Benjamin quoted in Böhme, "Atmosphere as the Fundamental Concept," 117.
12. Böhme, "Atmosphere as the Fundamental Concept," 117.
13. Adorno quoted in Ngai, *Ugly Feelings*, 87.

14. Baensch quoted in Ngai, *Ugly Feelings*, 44.
15. Ingram, *Green Screen*, 26.
16. Ingram, *Green Screen*, 25.
17. See, for example, Albrecht, "'Solastalgia,'" 41–55.
18. Tomkins quoted in Ngai, *Ugly Feelings*, 53.
19. Tomkins quoted in Ngai, *Ugly Feelings*, 54.
20. Ngai, *Ugly Feelings*, 55.
21. Smaill, "Emotion, Argumentation, and Documentary," 104.
22. Ingram, "Emotion and Affect in Eco-Films," 32.
23. Ngai, *Ugly Feelings*, 82, 83 (original emphasis).
24. Ngai, *Ugly Feelings*, 9.
25. Ngai, *Ugly Feelings*, 26, 27.
26. Peterson, "Magic Cave of Allegory," 400–422.
27. Merola, "Mediating Anthropocene Planetary Attachments," 253.
28. Freud, "Mourning and Melancholia," 244.
29. Freud, "Mourning and Melancholia," 44.
30. Brinkema, *Forms of the Affects*, 73.
31. Brinkema, *Forms of the Affects*, 73.
32. Brinkema, *Forms of the Affects*, 73.
33. Ngai, *Ugly Feelings*, 31.
34. Brennan, *Transmission of Affect*, 34.
35. Brennan, *Transmission of Affect*, 6.

BIBLIOGRAPHY

Albrecht, Glenn. "'Solastalgia': A New Concept in Health and Identity." PAN: *Philosophy Activism Nature*, no. 3 (2005): 41–55.

Anderson, Ben. "Affective Atmospheres." *Emotion, Space and Society* 2 (2009): 77–81.

Böhme, Gernot. "Atmosphere as the Fundamental Concept of a New Aesthetics." *Thesis Eleven* 36, no. 1 (August 1993): 113–26.

Brennan, Teresa. *The Transmission of Affect*. Ithaca: Cornell University Press, 2004.

Brinkema, Eugenie. *The Forms of the Affects*. Durham: Duke University Press, 2014.

Freud, Sigmund. "Mourning and Melancholia." In *The Complete Psychological Works of Sigmund Freud*, vol. 14, translated by James Strachey, 243–58. London: Hogarth Press, 1957.

Gumbrecht, Hans Ulrich. *Atmosphere, Mood, Stimmung: On a Hidden Potential of Literature*. Translated by Erik Butler. Stanford: Stanford University Press, 2012.

Ingram, David. "Emotion and Affect in Eco-Films: Cognitive and Phenomenological Approaches." In *Moving Environments: Affect, Emotion, Ecology, and Film*, edited by Alexa Weik von Mossner, 23–40. Waterloo ON: Wilfrid Laurier University Press, 2014.

———. *Green Screen: Environmentalism and Hollywood Cinema*. Exeter: University of Exeter Press, 2000.

Massumi, Brian. "The Autonomy of Affect." *Cultural Critique* 31 (Autumn 1995): 83–109.

Merola, Nicole. "Mediating Anthropocene Planetary Attachments: Lars von Trier's *Melancholia*." In *Design, Mediation, and the Posthuman*, edited by Dennis M. Weiss, Amy D. Propen, and Colbey Emmerson Reid, 249–68. Lanham MD: Lexington Books, 2014.

Ngai, Sianne. *Ugly Feelings*. Cambridge MA: Harvard University Press, 2005.

Peterson, Christopher. "The Magic Cave of Allegory: Lars von Trier's *Melancholia*." *Discourse* 35, no. 3 (Fall 2013): 400–422.

Smaill, Belinda. "Emotion, Argumentation, and Documentary Traditions: *Darwin's Nightmare* and *The Cove*." In *Moving Environments: Affect, Emotion, Ecology, and Film*, edited by Alexa Weik von Mossner, 103–20. Waterloo ON: Wilfrid Laurier University Press, 2014.

14

Coming of Age at the End of the World

The Affective Arc of Undergraduate Environmental Studies Curricula

SARAH JAQUETTE RAY

A recent Facebook video shows a boy, perhaps eight or nine years old, weeping hysterically because he has become aware that animals are dying, air is polluted, and humans are destroying the planet. On the Environmental Studies Club (ENST) Facebook page that I manage for the program I lead at Humboldt State University (HSU), students post comments identifying with the boy and even blaming my classes for causing their own similar meltdowns. I often feel like a parent whose job it is to facilitate my students' awakening to a world whose grim future stands in stark contrast to their precollege idealism. Other times I think that the ENST degree is some kind of twelve-step program, with its own arc of affects, moving in stages from idealism, to lost innocence, shame, denial, grief, apathy, optimism, and then, I can only hope, agency to work against diminution. At the same time, I feel guilty about the world we are leaving the next generation, and I wonder how to manage students' worries. Are millennials so sheltered, privileged, or delicate that they cannot "take" the reality of environmental crisis or social injustice? Is it just cool to be down? Does my students' despair inhibit their ability to learn, much less become "engaged citizens and leaders," as our catalog promises?

In what follows I argue that attending to the "affective arc" of environmental studies and sciences (ESS) curricula is crucial both for liberatory pedagogy and for climate justice and that an uncritical "arc of hope," as I call it, does students a disservice. This chapter is part love letter to my students, part proposal for ESS curricula, part strategy to save the planet through pedagogy, and part guide for how to save our own selves from the demands that students in this challenging field make on us. This is not a study of depression in higher education; like bell hooks, I believe that "teachers are not therapists."[1] We should direct students to experts when they are in crisis, but, as Catherine Savini writes, there is "much we can do" to attend to students' emotional lives in the classroom "without positioning ourselves as therapists or saviors."[2] I am convinced that it is important to take my students' emotions into account as part of curriculum design, but I also feel a need to draw boundaries and protect myself as a person—and as a female—who has her own scholarly and nonacademic commitments. I know that "processing" my students' existential crises both compels and depletes me and that female faculty are disproportionately sought by students for this kind of emotional care. Moreover, cultural taxation makes female faculty of color even more in demand as higher education diversifies. How can attending to the affective experiences of students in ESS curricula do triple duty: cultivate resilience in our students, protect faculty from burnout, and contribute to planetary salvation?

Affect in the Classroom

Taking emotion seriously means valuing lived experiences with and responses to the material. Scholarship on educational psychology avers that "emotion plays a central part in so many aspects of the teaching and learning system," and effective teachers and advisors "need to be aware of their own and their students' emotional lives."[3] Turning toward affect, particularly in climate science classrooms, is also a focus of current pedagogical discussions.[4] All my classes travel an intensely affective arc, even when I try to avoid it. How students *feel* about the material saturates our time together. Trying to limit this by maintaining a reason/emotion dichotomy in my classes does not work, as affect scholars such as Sara Ahmed and Teresa Brennan similarly argue.[5] Anguish in response to the material we teach belongs in the classroom, as uncomfortable as it is, and as untrained we might feel to manage it. Students' deep engagement with that material is a sign of success, and our task is to politicize and direct those emotions in ways that give them a sense that they are improving the world. As Kari Norgaard notes, emotion is central to "public life and social movements."[6] Emotions "are tied to the moral values" that "shape social movement goals, provide motivation for potential participants . . . and form the basis of solidarity among movement participants."[7] Making affect a focus of our work together helps students connect their inner lives to the broader context of politics and its possibilities. In what follows I trace the affective arc of ESS curricula, explore how issues of power and justice help us navigate that arc, and scrutinize the value of the affect of hope as a means of addressing students'—and our own—emotional experiences with the material.

Environmental Affect in the Classroom

Several aspects of the ESS curriculum produce strong affective responses. There is a growing scholarship on the mental health consequences of climate change, such as literature on "solastalgia"—the distress caused by environmental degradation.[8] Some of this work focuses on the impacts on those most likely to experience climate change's effects (e.g., "disaster mental health").[9] Others address the privileged who can, at least for now, distance themselves from the effects (e.g., Norgaard's *Living in Denial*). ESS students come to college idealistic and optimistic but become despairing and even apathetic when they learn how difficult and entrenched our environmental crises are. Internalizing the eco-mantras to "leave no impact" or, worse, to "save the planet, kill yourself," many ESS students are seduced into a kind of self-erasing, misanthropic eco-nihilism. They are further depressed by the stories and analyses they encounter daily in their courses. An "environmental grief" emerges; faced with the enormity of Earth's devastation, students are given few tools to address their mourning in classrooms.[10] Faculty consider their jobs "done" when they have convinced students that these problems exist and are not just Chinese hoaxes. Students also learn that their individual efforts cannot address these challenges, and they become pessimistic about the ability of existing institutions and systems to act in anything but the short-term interests of capitalist growth. They thought they were going to college to learn how to save the world, but instead they are asked to deconstruct cherished beliefs—in their own moral righteousness, in the capacity of science and technology to solve all of these problems, in the belief that nature can be saved, and in their concept of nature itself. Without curricula that attends to affect, students are likely to leave college not as the well-trained, problem-solving leaders that ESS programs promise on their websites but deflated, aimless, angry, or apathetic.

To be clear: neither the scope of this chapter nor the ability of any one program leader or professor can address all of the reasons today's college students experience higher rates of mental health issues and depression.[11] Debates about the "coddling" of millennials notwithstanding, this generation faces serious economic, political, environmental, and cultural challenges.[12] College students come from more diverse environments and face the stress of higher costs. HSU, for example, recently became a designated Hispanic-Serving Institution, and approximately half of those enrolled are first-generation college students. Many of them are in precarious circumstances—they face food insecurity and/or homelessness, are veterans, have been exposed to toxins and drug abuse, are navigating intergenerational trauma, or feel homesick and alienated by being so far from their communities.[13] Funding cuts and increased student body size have shifted some of the responsibility for addressing student mental health needs onto faculty and staff. A structural analysis of our students' depression is relevant but is not the focus of this chapter.

Scholarship about affective responses of students to ESS programs is limited. It focuses on whether students become more aware of environmental problems or engage in more pro-environment behavior, while the dominant literature about affective responses to climate change focuses on the impact of associated traumas on the underprivileged. Here I draw on my own experience teaching undergraduates to fill gaps in this literature, focusing on the specific nature of ESS-*related* anguish and offering some thoughts on how to address it. ESS majors have already drunk the dying-polar-bears–eco-apocalypse Kool-Aid, so assessing how well our program converts students to a sustainability mindset is not important, and it reinforces troubling assumptions about the ultimate purpose of an ESS degree.[14] My students are relatively privileged—they attend a North American college and are generally sheltered from the everyday disasters of climate change, though this region increasingly experiences a range of effects, from wildfires (e.g., in Sonoma and Santa Rosa) to long-standing salmon crises along the Klamath, to name only two. Scholarship on teaching sustainability and on disaster mental health thus does not help much with my problems, so I have sought resources in the growing scholarship on environmental affect, hope, and liberatory pedagogy.

ESS classes put students on an affective roller coaster as they learn not only about the complexity of environmental crises but also about the intersections between social justice and the environment. The material challenges their beliefs in positivism, in objective truth, and in the nature of knowledge. For many, it challenges their own "white-savior industrial complex."[15] As they learn more about the seriousness of the climate change crisis, students gain new insights: they are complicit in the crises; their moral and political energies are often misguided, even oppressive; environmental problems are too entrenched, structural, and complicated to be addressed by their green lifestyle choices; and the experts in technology and science may not have all the answers. "This 'urgency + inability' equation," Michael Maniates writes, "can overwhelm students with a sense of hopelessness and despair."[16] In addition, they may learn that the wilderness and nature are socially constructed.[17] That realization undermines their notion of what nature is, undermines their love of "being in nature," and dissolves their fantasies of "protecting" it. These insights shake their epistemological foundations and emotional armor.[18]

But it gets worse. ENST courses are not just about the urgency of *environmental* problems; they are also about power and privilege. "Save the whale" millennials are not expecting this next level of humbling, which is hard on those who, as Stacy Alaimo suggests, may pursue ESS precisely to *avoid* self-reflection, politics, discomfort, analysis, and complexity. For them "nature" may seem a "tamer topic" than politics or sociology, for example, "a refuge from the political morass of identity politics."[19] Deconstructing assumptions about nature is alarming to students because "nature is so firmly articulated to notions of the transcendent, the sublime, the enlightening that it has become, well, natural, to exult rather than to examine."[20] Students often seek ESS as an escape from the "uncomfortably agonistic and political" world and prefer the solace of exultation.[21] Students who choose ESS because they think it will be a safe, feel-good, and easy major are thus upset when they learn that addressing environmental problems will require uncomfortable self-reflection, not just learning how to argue better from established normative positions. My students are stunned how hard this work is, and I am stunned they expected anything different.

In both content and method ENST courses draw connections between systems of social injustice and systems of environmental degradation. Students report to me that their downward spiral begins on the first day of a required lower-division course: Power, Privilege, and the Environment. The assignment that day is to complete an "environmental privilege knapsack" questionnaire. Drawing on Peggy McIntosh's "white privilege knapsack," this exercise exposes privileges underlying dominant environmental beliefs. Students are asked to answer yes or no to statements like "My sense of intimacy with the land does not entail spending a hot day in the sun picking strawberries or tending someone else's lawn."[22] Many students who are not Native American are appalled when they realize that their love of national parks, for instance, is shaped by a privilege that makes it possible for them to be unaware of the history of genocide in these landscapes. These students reel from becoming aware of their myriad cognitive dissonances, and they struggle to reconcile their love of nature with their ostensibly progressive social ideals. Perhaps we could see these responses as a stage of "eco-white fragility."

We begin to connect the discomfort caused by newly recognized privileges and the anguish of planetary destruction. Critical concepts like "coercive conservation" and "green imperialism" reveal how conserving wilderness can occur at the expense of indigenous rights and is often not even ecologically sound. Julie Guthman's *Weighing In* similarly unmoors students' zealous passion for the contemporary food movement. Arguing that the commercialization of food production externalizes the costs of capitalist growth onto the bodies of the poor and showing how obesity is part of a broader structure of injustice, Guthman shatters students' righteousness about the links between an individual's health and the environment. These critiques of cherished politics leave students wondering what to do with themselves.

In contrast, students who respond "no" to many of the statements in this exercise are already politicized about social injustice. Such students constitute the minority of ENST majors, though the demographics are changing quickly. Nonwhite students, white first-generation or working-class students, or those who are already engaged in liberation struggles often report *positive* affects in response to the content in ENST courses, because it centers their experiences. Attending to the heterogeneity of these affective responses can create conditions for underrepresented minorities (URMs) to thrive.[23] URMs may realize that their nonmainstream environmental attitudes are valid and that there is more than one way to be an environmentalist. For example, a group of ENST Latinx students led several workshops "deconstructing" an environmental center on campus as a "white space," and two ENST students received a grant to study the gaps between Latinxs and sustainability on campus. Tying identity politics to environmental concerns becomes central to many students' pursuits. These examples attest to the need for an environmental *justice* approach—as opposed to either mainstream environmental or strictly natural science approaches—at an increasingly diverse institution. They attest to the effectiveness of directing students' affective responses toward intellectual passions.

While some students find momentum through their sense of purpose and identity, others start to lose faith that ENST is a good fit for them. In the next required course, Research and Analysis in Environmental Studies, students critique positivism and the myth of objectivity. We read Peter Bowler's preface to *The Norton History of the Environmental Sciences*, Ted Toadvine's "Six Myths of Interdisciplinarity," Jason Corburn's *Street Science*, and Linda Smith's *Decolonizing Methodologies*, for example, to learn about identity, power, and the production of knowledge in different disciplines, as well as to challenge conventional ecological studies.[24] We learn that even the most objective knowledge is situated and that "expert" knowledge cannot always address issues of social justice and environmental degradation. Scrutinizing environmental truths from the perspectives of social justice strips some students of tools—epistemological (Why were they taught wrong all along, and how can they trust what they're being taught now?) and professional (What jobs will they get if they question existing truths?)—that they had been taking for granted. The affects and conversations that emerge from putting politicized, empowered URM students into dialogue with anguished students from dominant positionalities are a challenge to navigate, to be sure, but I am convinced that they represent the potential of ESS to be the problem-solving, real-world discipline for our collective future.

The Importance of Negative Affects

Like most ESS instructors, I initially turned to the affect of hope for my solution to problems of despair in the classroom. In researching this chapter, however, I realize that hope is not a good strategy in itself. Anguish, discomfort, shame, guilt, and even apathy are all productive affects for decolonizing environmental studies. The affective arc is different for different students, and this creates tension as well. But the tension is productive, for *both* social justice *and* ecological health.[25] I have come to realize that, for ESS programs that prioritize analyses of power, privilege, justice, and interdisciplinarity, challenging mainstream environmental assumptions is an important outcome, one that creates both positive and negative affects among different students, and even within the same student at different points in the curriculum.

In "The Educational Power of Discomfort" Irina Popescu argues that we should not shelter our students from failure and suffering or avoid content that could "make students feel uncomfortable or unsettled." "History is unsettling," she writes. "The present is unsettling. . . . There should be more being said about the power of discomfort."[26] When students who are unaware of the scope of historical injustice realize that depressing things have been happening for a long time, they are less shocked by our current and future crises. Affect theory is also helpful for these students because it further challenges the middle-class conceit that the point of life is "happiness," as it can gloss over historical injustice and prohibit resilience. Ahmed rejects the notion that "bad feelings are backward and conservative and good feelings are forward and progressive"—an assumption that "allows historical forms of injustice to disappear" from our memories.[27] Students never imagine that seeking happiness can, ironically, get in the way of their well-being and rarely question whether it is effective for the long-term work of social change.

Discomfort is not inconsistent with meaningful hope. In their controversial *Atlantic* article Greg Lukianoff and Jonathan Haidt suggest that "vindictive protectiveness" of students reflects a larger problem of the millennials' "flight to safety."[28] For these authors, though, students exposed to ideas that make them uncomfortable acquire skills that will be needed in relationships in work and life: "Would they not be better prepared to flourish if we taught them to question their emotional reactions?"[29] Maniates too thinks that ESS programs in particular "fail to acclimate students to contentious environments" and therefore do not prepare them to navigate the "turbulence" of working among conflicting stakeholders, communicating across interests and backgrounds, and challenging dominant thinking.[30] That is, it seems that students find the material in the ENST program existentially challenging to the extent that they have thus far been sheltered from the contingencies of social and environmental injustice and the relationship between power and knowledge.

Exploring their negative affects also helps students resist the brainwashing effects of green capitalism, which has convinced them that their individual actions will save the planet. We read Derrick Jensen's polemical "Forget Shorter Showers," which shows students that personal change is not the same as social change, while John Meyer's *Engaging the Everyday* gives students a way to see the implications of their personal choices in politicized terms. As Maniates notes, the "'easy ways to save the planet' narrative quickly fills: buy green, initiate a few lifestyle changes, spread the word, and wait for the totality of these small changes to sum into fundamental social change."[31] The green consumer approach is individualistic, and it distracts us from thinking about our collective identities, those "networks of obligation to which we all belong."[32] Individuals cannot solve climate change on their own, but they often see other forms of civic engagement as "too diffuse."[33] They need to think more broadly about how social change happens.

The environmental justice approach shifts students' frames of "the problem" away from a blaming-the-victim approach toward an understanding of structural injustice. They learn that they each exist within structures that attenuate their "choices" while making it more difficult for them to imagine and seek collective solutions. Getting uncomfortable shows students the limits of individualism. As Janet Fiskio explains, it is difficult to get students in ESS courses "to articulate *collective* responses outside of a market economy," because "the doctrine of human selfishness and the privatization of public life have subjugated our minds and desires."[34] Once students realize that "'reduce, recycle, reuse' is a form of neoliberal, individualist consumer behavior," they struggle to "think of collective, non-consumer actions they can take to confront climate change."[35] Dwelling in negative affect plugs students into networks of obligation: "on an affective level, what this means is that I hold students in the presence of the unbearable grief of climate change," Fiskio concludes.[36] Grappling with affect helps students get out of the urgency + inability trap, and the "clichéd dichotomy of hope/despair that dominates the usual discussions of climate change."[37]

Do students have to choose between ignorant bliss and depressing knowledge? The end point of ESS curricula should be neither naïve optimism nor informed despair. We must help students accept the affective journey of exploring difficult material. My experience tells me that we cannot teach critical environmental studies to privileged students without some discomfort, risk, and unhappiness and that liberatory pedagogy requires that we center underrepresented perspectives. Both of these approaches make classrooms more emotional than students expect. Tom Bristow and colleagues argue that the "best work in the humanities, even if it is about grim or uncomfortable subjects, inspires people to change their thinking, to want to learn more, to want to avoid faults of the past, to address the legacy of injustice, to talk and organize and act."[38] Norgaard adds that "pressures to be optimistic limit open discussion of the seriousness of the problem" of climate change.[39] We want our students to be hopeful and empowered, but not for the wrong reasons, and we want them to dwell in the grief, but not too much. Discomfort about their own privileges and a more complex understanding of their role in environmental issues can inspire students to *desire* more just social change. When ESS courses accept such discussions and link environmental issues to privilege, white students' shame and defensiveness can be translated into solidarity.[40] It is better that those students get more comfortable with the messiness of being or working with allies rather than settling into the "cruel optimism" of techno-optimist, consumer-based green futures.[41]

Against Hope? Senior Capstone

Students report in evaluations that course material is "so depressing" and ask that we "give them more solutions." Would that we could! Giving students what they ask for—more hope and more prescriptive solutions—may temporarily boost their mood, but it will not sustain their lives' work. Although hope is often seen as a basis for action, in this concluding section I argue *against* hope or at least for a *critical* hope, linking positive prospects for the future with social change, following Maniates: ESS programs "that leave students with an emaciated theory of social change and that fuel a politics of guilt and crisis do little to foster the creativity and compassion that sustains personal and collective transformation."[42] So, what affect can furnish students a vision of the possible?

Because I am in the fortunate position of being able to build the ENST classes around a coherent narrative, thereby guiding students' "affective arc" over the course of their time in the program, I designed the senior capstone course with the intention of concluding the bildungsroman of their degree with goals of fostering confidence in their skills, a critical hope, a broad idea of how social change works, and some sense of how they will join in those efforts.[43] I believe the answer is to design a capstone experience that achieves hope through *agency* and through a *sense of collectivity*.

Most instructors simply end their classes on a note of hope, balancing, as Norgaard observes, their "personal doubts and deep feelings of powerlessness with the task of sending a hopeful message to their students."[44] The fact that concern for our environmental future causes anxiety, apathy, and nihilism has spawned a genre on apathy and "hope."[45] Doom-and-gloom apocalypticism, as exemplified by Al Gore's pronouncements in the documentary film *An Inconvenient Truth*, is increasingly regarded as having done more harm than good. "The sense of the world as threatening and hostile . . .

produces a fraying of citizenship and democracy, as well as a vulnerability to the politics of self-interest and fear," writes Richard Eckersley.[46] The dramatic imagery of apocalypse is a dystopian story that overplays what humanity is facing and actually "hinders the development of particular responses," especially ones that might be gradual rather than urgent.[47] As Greg Garrard observes, it polarizes "responses, prodding skeptics towards scoffing dismissal and potentially inciting believers to confrontation and even violence."[48] Apocalyptic rhetoric also "fosters a delusive search for culprits and causes."[49] In the classroom we can ask, "What do these narratives make us feel, how do those feelings affect our ability to act, connect, and empathize, and why is it easier for us to imagine apocalypse than it is for us to imagine society transitioning away from carbon?" ESS classes should address the cultural work of apocalyptic rhetoric and the problems with the oversimplified hero/villain narrative of "crisis" narratives.

Norgaard concludes that hope is a kind of denial. Similarly, Bristow and colleagues proclaim that "hope can too readily become a form of denial or distraction."[50] Thom van Dooren rejects hope: it is a "passive abdication that says everything is okay, our consciences are assuaged, there's no need to think about responsibility, someone else has it covered."[51] Hope "eschews reality" and "becomes self-censorship" that "serves the status quo."[52] Jeff Duncan-Andrade calls for a "critical hope" that gives students new "resources to deal with the forces that affect their lives" and acknowledges that the "painful path *is* the hopeful path."[53] Heather Houser criticizes the American penchant for "positive thinking" and, echoing Timothy Morton's distaste for "bright greenness," counts the problems with this green version of what Barbara Ehrenreich has called "bright-sidedness": "First, optimism prevents us from recognizing signs of adversity for which we could prepare." Second, it supports "the capitalist mandate to grow at all costs" and "obfuscates 'the crueler aspects of the market economy' in favor of 'a harsh insistence on personal responsibility.'"[54] Critically examining "hope" in these ways allows students to develop a broad range of alternatives.

Rebecca Solnit's work on how social change happens and the evidence of community utopias is crucial at this stage, as students evaluate the personal and collective trauma of doom-and-gloom narratives and consider how they will personally intervene in social change.[55] In addition to reading widely on "hope," then, we broaden our ideas of what counts as social change. We cultivate hopefulness by seeing social change in the work we are already doing, as well as in "actions" we may not have thought of as valuable because of narratives of urgency and myths of individualism. As we read Solnit, we ask what counts as social change and how we can measure it. Is "activism" standing on a picket line protesting something? Is changing somebody's mind a form of activism? Is changing your own mind a form of social change? Is theory a form of social change? Is sitting in a classroom reframing environmental problems a crucial step toward solving them? To my impatient millennials, who only see social change happening in spectacles of tidy resolution, Solnit's writing on the slow, messy, collective work of social change is buoying. Howard Zinn concurs: "Revolutionary change does not come as one cataclysmic moment (beware of such moments!) but as an endless succession of surprises, moving zigzag toward a more decent society. We don't have to engage in grand, heroic actions to participate in the process of change."[56] Teaching students that change is everywhere and hard to measure, as well as that spectacular, triumphant moments are only the result of the invisible work of a lot of faceless idealists, is crucial to giving students critical hope. Seeing positive changes as an accumulation of lots of "small" things tempers students' impatience.

Students feel despair in all the critical, theoretical work we do in the classroom, too. They proclaim, "We're doing so much deconstructing. What about constructing something?" And so I ask them to consider the possibility that critiquing "wilderness" and "nature" is the best way to love those ideas. Van Dooren helps me make this case. Critique is an act of optimistic caring, "the assertion that things might have been, and so still might be, otherwise." A careful hope is understood as "a practice of 'care for the future.'"[57] Morton similarly argues for the ecological value of deconstruction because it shows us our networks of obligation: "deconstruction is the cure for postmodern cynicism" and results in "a painful awareness of our intimacy with others."[58] Students can really get in touch with the earth, not by "rubbing their noses in the soil" but by "rubbing their noses in their minds."[59] Reading Morton's ideas about how "reflection is a form of ecological action" challenges students' valuing of action over theory, activism over academia, oral over written communication, practice over thought.[60]

These readings lead students to seek out narratives of social change from sources other than dominant media, so they can see their own way. It leads them to recognize the power they already have. Solnit cautions against our "narratives of powerlessness," because they "let us off the hook."[61] All of this helps students to learn that feelings like desire or pleasure are important for generating social change, leading them to appreciate that the arts not only "give expression to those affects, but innovatively deploy them."[62] Working through their emotional responses, considering and responding to the emotions of others, and conversing, thinking, and reflecting all build community and cultivate the ecological imagination; I contend that these are all *actions*.

Students do not need to be field biologists gathering data or legislators who can make structural change from the top down; they don't have to wait around for, or become themselves, that "one magical politician" that Solnit warns against. They can put aside their science envy when they realize that the ways they can affect the world are limitless: "Reframing our world, our problems, and ourselves is part of the ecological project. This is what praxis means—action that is thoughtful and thought that is active."[63] Ecological thought—awareness of connection—as Morton defines it, can "call us from within the grief."[64] The ability to critique existing narratives and create new ones is key to cultivating critical hope and gives students power over information overload and imagining options for political action.[65]

It is not our duty to take care of students' psychic lives. Given the myriad stresses that impinge on them, as well as the greater pressure on teachers in this field—and especially on women—to meet students' emotional demands, I am not arguing that we should do more care work than we already do.[66] But there are steps ESS instructors and program developers can take. ESS curricula can trouble students' assumptions about happiness, provide them tools to critically analyze the effects of environmental narratives on their energies, challenge their views of what "counts" as social change, and deconstruct their attachments to binaries that limit imaginations and sap motivation to act. These skills are needed in order to avoid slipping into paralysis, for destabilizing existing power relations, and for creating the affective conditions for sustaining mind and body in the face of crisis. We cannot deny that our very syllabi "set into motion messy emotions," but these can "direct our [students'] energies toward planetary threats" and action.[67] Greater attention to the affective experiences of ESS students within ESS curricula is crucial to developing the generation of environmental leaders able to absorb this information and still act effectively.

This is not only a matter of meeting our designated outcomes; it is a pedagogical concern: it is unethical to expect students to devote themselves to saving the planet but then fail to prepare them affectively for this challenge. To the extent that we can help them understand their anguish in the context of broader structures, be self-reflexive about their emotional responses to narratives of urgency, and recognize the simultaneous humility and power that comes with being part of a network of obligation, we will turn their impotence into agency. The future I would wish for them attenuates desire with witness and embraces critique as a form of active care.

Moreover, as we address the increasing diversification of student bodies, the "narrative affect" (to use Houser's term) of our curricula is all the more important. An ESS curriculum should show how environmental problems are part of students' lives, not something happening far away. If, through thoughtful pedagogy, we can help students be resilient in the face of crisis, we would find ourselves *less*, not *more*, in the role of therapists. We can devote class time, not office hours and midnight emails, to processing the affective trajectory that students will inevitably experience. This approach is win-win-win—for diverse student learning, planetary environmental justice, and our own self-preservation as loving instructors.

NOTES

1. hooks, *Teaching Community*.
2. Savini, "Are You Being Rigorous."
3. Robertson, "Thriving in Academe," 8.
4. Koballa, "Framework for the Affective."
5. Ahmed, "Happy Objects."
6. Norgaard, *Living in Denial*, 8.
7. Norgaard, *Living in Denial*, 9.

8. Albrecht et al., "Solastalgia."

9. Fritze et al., "Hope, Despair, and Transformation."

10. Eaton, "Environmental Trauma and Grief."

11. According to one study, "rates of mental illness in young adults have been rising, both on campus and off," and that study cites a 2014 survey reporting that 54 percent of college students said that they had "felt overwhelming anxiety" in the past twelve months, up from 49 percent five years earlier. Lukianoff and Haidt, "Coddling of the American Mind," 9. See also Weaver, "High Anxiety." While the need for student mental health services is increasing, campuses are not keeping up with the demand for such services.

12. On the "coddling" of millennials see Heller, *Big Uneasy*.

13. Carlson, "On the Path to Graduation, Life Intervenes." Scott Carlson commends HSU's efforts to address food security. The environmental humanities can say much more about why the future seems so uncertain; from the "risk society" to scholarship on dystopian cli-fi to debates about whether we have entered the Anthropocene, future studies is growing.

14. Researching this chapter led me to focus on the challenge of answering the question, What is the end goal of students' training in our program? Literature on "teaching sustainability" is vapid on issues of justice and uncritical about the eco-governmentality implications of "training environmental leaders." We might ask whether trying to manage ESS graduates' affect is a kind of Foucauldian biopower disciplining, designed to produce productive eco-subjects. Timothy Luke's "Eco-Managerialism: Environmental Studies as Power/Knowledge Formation" defines ESS as a breeding ground for "resource managers," an approach that depresses students because it dismisses their passion to save the world as just another form of brainwashing green capitalism. But it raises an important question: What kinds of eco-subjects should we be cultivating?

15. Cole, "White-Savior Industrial Complex."

16. Maniates, "Teaching for Turbulence," 257.

17. As Stacy Alaimo attests, "For students who are only just beginning to embrace an environmentalist stance," like my ENST majors, recognizing that "even the most 'wild' of places is, in part, culturally constructed, may be a bit deflating." Alaimo, "Trouble with Texts," 375. Regarding how to ask students to embrace the ecological value of this argument, in addition to all of the environmental justice reasons, I recommend using if not teaching Timothy Morton's "Practising Deconstruction in the Age of Ecological Emergency," in which he provides "ecological thought" as a way out of students' anguish caused by the crisis of learning that nature is a social construction.

18. I assign Maniates's "Teaching for Turbulence" so students can see how the affective

arc is a common trend in ESS programs. His argument aligns with my observations that ESS programs frequently make the mistake of following the "trend toward urgency and alarm, coupled with a focus on the inability of prevailing systems of economic accounting and political decision-making to address looming environmental ills" (257).

19. Alaimo, "Trouble with Texts," 369.
20. Alaimo, "Trouble with Texts," 369.
21. Alaimo, "Trouble with Texts," 369.
22. Mengel, "Race and Class Privilege in the Environmental Movement."
23. URM is the term HSU uses to describe nonwhite and first-generation students, who self-identify as such in their application.
24. For more details about my approach to this class, see a write-up about it on the teaching resources link on the website of the Association for the Study of Literature and Environment, http://www.asle.org/features/interdisciplinary-matters-questions-environmental-studies/.
25. For example, Timothy Morton argues that "uncertainty" and "melancholy" are actually *good* for the environment. Morton, *Ecological Thought*, 17.
26. Popescu, "Educational Power of Discomfort."
27. Ahmed, "Happy Objects," 50.
28. Lukianoff and Haidt, "Coddling of the American Mind."
29. Lukianoff and Haidt, "Coddling of the American Mind."
30. Maniates, "Teaching for Turbulence," 265.
31. Maniates, "Teaching for Turbulence," 265.
32. Houser, *Ecosickness in Contemporary U.S. Fiction*, 223.
33. Norgaard, *Living in Denial*, 259.
34. Fiskio, "Building Paradise in the Classroom," 104 (emphasis added).
35. Fiskio, "Building Paradise in the Classroom," 101.
36. Fiskio, "Building Paradise in the Classroom," 102.
37. Fiskio, "Building Paradise in the Classroom," 104.
38. Bristow, van Dooren, and Muir, "Hope in a Time of Crisis," 5.
39. Norgaard, *Living in Denial*, 101.
40. hooks, *Teaching Community*, 63.
41. Utt, "True Solidarity"; Berlant, *Cruel Optimism*; Luke, "Eco-Managerialism."
42. Maniates, "Teaching for Turbulence," 267.
43. In spring 2015 students wrote reflections on their views on hope, social change, and their own agency in a blog we called *Critical Hope*, http://enst490.blogspot.com.
44. Norgaard, *Living in Denial*, 101.
45. For example, Solnit's *Hope in the Dark*, McKibben's *Hope, Human and Wild*, Al Gore's TED talk and *Rolling Stone* article on optimism, Naomi Klein's film and

book *This Changes Everything*, Paul Hawken's *The Blessed Unrest*, and Josh Fox's 2016 documentary *How to Let Go and Love All the Things Climate Can't Change*.

46. Eckersley, "Nihilism, Fundamentalism, or Activism," 37.
47. Reidy, "Interior Transformation," 44.
48. Garrard, *Ecocriticism*, 114.
49. Garrard, *Ecocriticism*, 115.
50. Bristow, van Dooren, and Muir, "Hope in a Time of Crisis," 4.
51. Bristow, van Dooren, and Muir, "Hope in a Time of Crisis," 4.
52. Bristow, van Dooren, and Muir, "Hope in a Time of Crisis," 4.
53. Duncan-Andrade, "Note to Educators."
54. Houser, *Ecosickness in Contemporary U.S. Fiction*, 220, 221.
55. Solnit's *A Paradise Built in Hell* is exemplary in this regard.
56. Zinn, "Optimism of Uncertainty," 85–86.
57. Bristow, van Dooren, and Muir, "Hope in a Time of Crisis," 3.
58. Morton, "Practising Deconstruction," 157.
59. Morton, "Practising Deconstruction," 158.
60. Morton, "Practising Deconstruction," 160.
61. Rebecca Solnit, "One Magical Politician Won't Stop Climate Change: It's Up to All of Us," *The Guardian*, May 15, 2015, 2–3, https://www.theguardian.com/commentisfree/2015/may/15/one-magical-politician-wont-stop-climate-change-its-up-us.
62. Houser, *Ecosickness in Contemporary U.S. Fiction*, 228.
63. Morton, *Ecological Thought*, 9.
64. Morton, *Ecological Thought*, 2.
65. To explore this point, I teach William Cronon's "A Place for Stories: Nature, History, Narrative," which gives students tools to recognize the affective implications of declensionist versus progressive narratives about the environment.
66. Mountz et al., "For Slow Scholarship."
67. Houser, *Ecosickness in Contemporary U.S. Fiction*, 223.

BIBLIOGRAPHY

Ahmed, Sara. "Happy Objects." In *The Affect Theory Reader*, edited by Melissa Gregg and Gregory J. Seigworth, 29–51. Durham: Duke University Press, 2010.

Alaimo, Stacy. *Exposed: Environmental Politics and Pleasures in Posthuman Times*. Minneapolis: University of Minnesota Press, 2016.

———. "The Trouble with Texts; or, Green Cultural Studies in Texas." *Teaching North American Environmental Literature*, edited by Laird Christensen, Mark C. Long, and Fred Waage, 369–76. New York: Modern Languages Association of America, 2008.

Albrecht, G., G-M. Sartore, L. Connor, N. Higginbotham, S. Freeman, B. Kelly, H. Stain, A. Tonna, and G. Pollard. "Solastalgia: The Distress Caused by Environmental Change." *Australasian Psychiatry* 12, no. 10 (2007): 95–98.

Berlant, Lauren. "Cruel Optimism." In *The Affect Theory Reader*, edited by Melissa Gregg and Gregory J. Seigworth, 93–117. Durham: Duke University Press, 2010.

Bowler, Peter J. *The Norton History of the Environmental Sciences.* New York: Norton, 1993.

Bristow, Tom, Thom van Dooren, and Cameron Muir. "Hope in a Time of Crisis: Environmental Humanities and Histories of Emotions." *Histories of Emotions*, November 6, 2015. https://historiesofemotion.com/2015/11/06/hope-in-a-time-of-crisis-environmental-humanities-and-histories-of-emotions/.

Carlson, Scott. "On the Path to Graduation, Life Intervenes." *Chronicle of Higher Education Online*, March 6, 2016. http://www.chronicle.com/article/On-the-Path-to-Graduation/235603.

Cole, Teju. "White-Savior Industrial Complex." *The Atlantic*, March 21, 2012. Accessed at https://www.theatlantic.com/international/archive/2012/03/the-white-savior-industrial-complex/254843/.

Corburn, Jason. *Street Science: Community Knowledge and Environmental Health Justice.* Cambridge MA: MIT Press, 2005.

Cronon, William. "A Place for Stories: Nature, History, Narrative." *Journal of American History* 78, no. 4 (1992): 1347–76.

Duncan-Andrade, Jeff. "Note to Educators: Hope Required When Growing Roses in Concrete." *Harvard Educational Review* 79, no. 2 (2009): 181–94.

Eaton, Marie. "Environmental Trauma and Grief." 2012. Manuscript provided by the author.

Eckersley, Richard. "Nihilism, Fundamentalism, or Activism: Three Responses to Fears of the Apocalypse." *The Futurist* 42, no. 1 (2008): 35–39.

Fiskio, Janet. "Building Paradise in the Classroom." In *Teaching Climate Change in the Humanities*, edited by Stephen Siperstein, Stephanie Lemenager, and Shane Hall, 101–9. New York: Routledge, 2017.

Fox, Josh, dir. *How to Let Go of the World and Love the Things Climate Can't Change.* 2016; Brooklyn NY: International WOW Company, 2016. DVD.

Fritze, Jessica, Grant Blashki, Susie Burke, and John Wiseman. "Hope, Despair, and Transformation: Climate Change and the Promotion of Mental Health and Wellbeing." *International Journal of Mental Health Systems* 2, no. 13 (September 2008): 1–10.

Garrard, Greg. *Ecocriticism.* 2nd ed. New York: Routledge, 2012.

Gore, Al. "The Case for Optimism on Climate Change." TED.com, May 10, 2016. https://www.ted.com/talks/al_gore_the_case_for_optimism_on_climate_change.

———. "The Turning Point: New Hope for the Climate." *Rolling Stone*, June 18, 2014.

http://www.rollingstone.com/politics/news/the-turning-point-new-hope-for
-the-climate-20140618.

Guggenheim, Davis, dir. *An Inconvenient Truth*. 2006; Beverly Hill CA: Lawrence
Bender Productions, 2006. DVD.

Guthman, Julie. *Weighing In: Obesity, Food Justice, and the Limits of Capitalism*. Berkeley:
University of California Press, 2011.

Hawken, Paul. *The Blessed Unrest: How the Largest Movement in the World Came into
Being and Why No One Saw It Coming*. New York: Viking, 2007.

Heller, Nathan. "The Big Uneasy." *New Yorker Online*, May 30, 2016. http://www
.newyorker.com/magazine/2016/05/30/the-new-activism-of-liberal-arts-colleges.

hooks, bell. *Teaching Community: A Pedagogy of Hope*. New York: Routledge, 2003.

Houser, Heather. *Ecosickness in Contemporary U.S. Fiction: Environment and Affect*.
New York: Columbia University Press, 2014.

Jensen, Derrick. "Forget Shorter Showers." *Orion Magazine Online*, July 7, 2009. https://
orionmagazine.org/article/forget-shorter-showers/.

Klein, Naomi. *This Changes Everything: Capitalism vs. the Climate*. New York: Simon
and Schuster, 2014.

Koballa, Thomas. "Framework for the Affective Domain in Science Education." Teach
the Earth, September 12, 2016. http://serc.carleton.edu/NAGTWorkshops
/affective/framework.html.

Luke, Timothy W. "Eco-Managerialism: Environmental Studies as Power/Knowledge
Formation." In *Living with Nature: Environmental Politics as Cultural Discourse*, edited
by Frank Fischer and Maarten Hajer, 103–20. Oxford: Oxford University Press, 1999.

Lukianoff, Greg, and Jonathan Haidt. "The Coddling of the American Mind: How
Trigger Warnings are Hurting Mental Health on Campus." *The Atlantic*, September
2015. https://www.theatlantic.com/magazine/archive/2015/09/the-coddling
-of-the-american-mind/399356/.

Maniates, Michael. "Teaching for Turbulence." *State of the World 2013: Is Sustainability
Still Possible?*, 255–68. Washington DC: Worldwatch Institute and Island Press,
2013. https://link.springer.com/chapter/10.5822%2F978-1-61091-458-1_24.

McKibben, Bill. *Hope, Human and Wild: True Stories of Living Lightly on the Earth*.
Minneapolis: Milkweed Editions, 2007.

Mengel, Gregory. "Race and Class Privilege in the Environmental Movement."
Pachamama.org, May 10, 2016. https://www.pachamama.org/news/race-and
-class-privilege-in-the-environmental-movement.

Meyer, John. *Engaging the Everyday: Environmental Social Criticism and the Resonance
Dilemma*. Cambridge MA: MIT Press, 2015.

Morton, Timothy. *The Ecological Thought*. Cambridge MA: Harvard University
Press, 2010.

————. "Practising Deconstruction in the Age of Ecological Emergency." In *Teaching Ecocriticism and Green Cultural Studies*, edited by Greg Garrard, 156–66. London: Palgrave Macmillan, 2012.

Mountz, Alison, Anne Bonds, Becky Mansfield, Jenna Loyd, Jennifer Hyndman, Margaret Walton-Roberts, Ranu Basu, Risa Whitson, Roberta Hawkins, Trina Hamilton, and Winifred Curran. "For Slow Scholarship: A Feminist Politics of Resistance through Collective Action in the Neoliberal University." *ACME: An International E-Journal for Critical Geographies* 14, no. 4 (2015): 1235–59.

Norgaard, Kari. *Living in Denial: Climate Change, Emotions, and Everyday Life.* Cambridge MA: MIT Press, 2011.

Popescu, Irina. "The Educational Power of Discomfort." *Chronicle of Higher Education Online*, April 17, 2016. http://www.chronicle.com/article/The-Educational-Power-of/236136.

Reidy, Chris. "Interior Transformation on the Pathway to a Viable Future." *Journal of Futures Studies* 20, no. 3 (March 2016): 35–54.

Robertson, Douglas L. "Thriving in Academe: Reflections on Helping Students Learn." *NEA Higher Education Advocate* 34, no. 3 (May 2016): 6–9.

Savini, Catherine. "Are You Being Rigorous or Just Intolerant? How to Promote Mental Health in the College Classroom." *Chronicle of Higher Education Online*, May 10, 2016. http://www.chronicle.com/article/Are-You-Being-Rigorous-or-Just/236341.

Smith, Linda Tuhiwai. *Decolonizing Methodologies: Research and Indigenous Peoples.* New York: Zed Books, 2012.

Solnit, Rebecca. "Acts of Hope: Challenging Empire on the World Stage." *TomDispatch.com*, June 11, 2016. http://www.tomdispatch.com/post/677/rebecca_solnit_on_hope_in_dark_times.

————. *Hope in the Dark: Untold Histories, Wild Possibilities.* New York: Nation Books, 2005.

————. *A Paradise Built in Hell: The Extraordinary Communities That Arise in Disaster.* New York: Viking, 2009.

Toadvine, Ted. "Six Myths of Interdisciplinarity." *Thinking Nature* 1, no. 1 (2011).

Utt, Jamie. "True Solidarity: Moving Past Privilege Guilt." *Everyday Feminism Online Magazine*, March 26, 2014. http://everydayfeminism.com/2014/03/moving-past-privilege-guilt/.

Weaver, Sandra Long. "High Anxiety: Colleges Are Seeing an Increase in the Number of Students with Diagnosable Mental Illness, Anxiety, and Depression." *Chronicle of Higher Education*, March 18, 2016, 25–26.

Zinn, Howard. "The Optimism of Uncertainty." In *The Impossible Will Take a Little While: Perseverance and Hope in Troubled Times*, edited by Paul Rogat Loeb, 78–86. New York: Basic Books, 2014.

CONTRIBUTORS

Jobb Arnold is assistant professor in the Department of Conflict Resolution Studies at Menno Simons College, a joint program of the University of Winnipeg and Canadian Mennonite University. His work focuses on community building and creative cultural approaches to conflict during periods of social transition.

Robert Azzarello is associate professor of English at Southern University at New Orleans. He is the author of *Queer Environmentality: Ecology, Evolution, and Sexuality in American Literature* (2012).

Kyle Bladow is assistant professor of Native American studies at Northland College, with teaching and research interests in ecocriticism, environmental justice, and gender and sexuality studies. His work appears in *Studies in American Indian Literatures, Green Letters, Gastronomica,* and *New International Voices in Ecocriticism.*

Neil Campbell is emeritus professor of American studies at the University of Derby, in the UK. His major research project has been an interdisciplinary trilogy of books on the post–World War II American West: *The Cultures of the American New West* (2000), *The Rhizomatic West,* and the final part,

Post-Westerns: Cinema, Region, West (2008, 2013). He is co-editor of the book series Place, Memory, Affect with Rowman and Littlefield International and has a volume within it, *Affective Critical Regionality* (2016). He has also edited a collection of essays on the fiction and music of Willy Vlautin for the University of Nevada Press (2017).

Brian Deyo is assistant professor of English at Grand Valley State University, Allendale, Michigan. His main areas of research are in the fields of postcolonial ecocriticism and animal/animality studies.

Ryan Hediger is associate professor of English at Kent State University, where he teaches U.S. literature, ecocriticism, and animal studies. His publications treat such subjects as animals and war, violence and sympathy in Hemingway's work, and sports and recreation.

Tom Hertweck is lecturer of English at the University of Nevada, Reno. He is the editor of *Food on Film: Bringing Something New to the Table*, author of pieces on American literature and culture, and is editor (with Iker Arranz) for the series Cultural Ecologies of Food in the 21st Century for the University of Nevada Press.

Allyse Knox-Russell is PhD candidate in women's, gender, and sexuality studies at Stony Brook University. Her research and teaching interests include feminist and queer theory, feminist science studies, decolonial and indigenous studies, environmental justice, and ideas of wellness, resilience, and sustainability.

Jennifer Ladino is associate professor of English at the University of Idaho. In addition to her first book, *Reclaiming Nostalgia: Longing for Nature in American Literature* (2012), she has published on various issues in the environmental humanities, including topics in ecocinema, animal studies, the American West, and affect theory.

William Major is professor of English at Hillyer College of the University of Hartford, where he teaches classes in American literature, environmental literature, and writing. He is the author of *Grounded Vision: New Agrarianism and the Academy* (2011), as well as numerous articles and essays.

He is currently working on a book investigating the relationship between empathy, reading, and teaching.

Nicole M. Merola is professor of environmental humanities and American literatures at the Rhode Island School of Design. She teaches and writes about the Anthropocene, biodiversity and extinction studies, climate change cultures, critical animal studies, and theories of naturecultures.

Lisa Ottum is associate professor of English at Xavier University in Cincinnati, Ohio, where she teaches British literature, literature and the environment, and rhetoric, among other subjects. She has published essays on William Wordsworth, Charlotte Smith, and Mary Shelley and is the co-editor of *Wordsworth and the Green Romantics: Affect and Ecology in the Nineteenth Century* (2016).

Sarah Jaquette Ray is associate professor of environmental studies at Humboldt State University, where she also serves as leader of the bachelor of arts program in environmental studies. Ray is the author of *The Ecological Other: Environmental Exclusion in American Culture* (2013) and works in the fields of environmental justice, cultural studies, and the environmental humanities.

Nicole Seymour's first book, *Strange Natures: Futurity, Empathy, and the Queer Ecological Imagination*, won the 2015 Book Award for Ecocriticism from the Association for the Study of Literature and Environment. She is currently associate professor of English at California State University, Fullerton.

Graig Uhlin is assistant professor of screen studies at Oklahoma State University. His scholarship appears in *Cinema Journal*, *Quarterly Review of Film & Video*, *Spectator*, *Games and Culture*, and several edited collections. His research focuses on modernist film and environmental aesthetics.

Alexa Weik von Mossner is associate professor of American studies at the University of Klagenfurt in Austria. She is the author of *Cosmopolitan Minds: Literature, Emotion, and the Transnational Imagination* (2014) and *Affective Ecologies: Empathy, Emotion, and Environmental Narrative* (2017).

INDEX

affect (*continued*)

206–7, 260; and form, 30–32; navigatory nature of, 263; in non-human animals, 180–83; ontological importance of, 103–4; ordinary affects, 73, 82, 87, 100–101; political impacts of, 85–86, 102, 106; potential of, 43, 108–9; processing of, 261; "pure" affect myth, 272; relationship with queer theory, 237–41; relation to drive system, 139–40; relation to emotion, 5, 18n22, 279; role in education, 300–301; social aspect of, 279–80, 290; subject to training, 263, 265–66; transmission of, 5, 252n19; transpersonal nature of, 240–41, 279. *See also* emotions; *specific affects*

affect theory: affective turn, 4–5, 117–18, 127–28, 130n3; cognitive ecocritical approach to, 12; cultural studies approach to, 12; and ecocriticism, 3–4, 8–9; ecological nature of, 158; formalist approaches to, 11; interdisciplinary approaches to, 4–10, 11, 12; materialist approaches to, 6–8; potential of, 3, 16–17; understanding change, 157–58

The Affect Theory Reader (Gregg and Seigworth), 4

Against Empathy (Bloom), 130n5

agency: of affect, 206–7; and ecophobia, 201–2; hope through, 309; of literary forms, 30; of nature, 7–8; in warfare, 158

The Age of Empathy (de Waal), 129n1

Ahmed, Sara, 6, 19n39, 96, 98, 105–6, 141, 144, 252n19, 259, 300, 306–7

Alaimo, Stacy, 7, 303, 314n17

Albrecht, Glenn, 52–53, 59, 65, 156, 285

Alps, 257–58, 263

ambivalence: in awareness of animality, 199–200; in *Beasts of the Southern Wild*, 222–23; in *Men and Women in Water Cities*, 245–46

American Tobacco Company, 122

Anderson, Ben, 5, 281

animality: awareness of, 195–96, 199–200, 205; and ecophobia, 200, 202, 203–4; as path to empathy, 221–23. *See also* nonhuman species

animals. *See* nonhuman species

Anno, Kim, 242–47, 251; *Men and Women in Water Cities* (film), 243–46; *90 Miles from Paradise* (film), 243, 244; *Water City, Berkeley* (film), 243, 246–47

Ansted, David Thomas, 44n4

Anthropocene: advent of, 27; cruel optimism in, 42–43; definitions of, 25, 52; features of, 26–27, 43n1; psychoterratic dis-eases in, 59–61; relevance of tragedy in, 209; role of narratives, 56–57; shift from Holocene to, 28–29; unpredictability in, 157–58

Anthropocene affects: captured through literary forms, 28–29; potential of, 43; types of, 31–32

Anthropocene anxiety: asymptotic nature of, 41; in "December 2, 2002" poem, 29; defined, 11, 27; embodiment of, 34, 38–41; enacted through contrary forms, 33–34; enacted through metric-stanzic forms, 35–39; indicated by breathing, 29, 33, 34, 39–40; role of scientific technologies in, 27–28

anthropocentrism: affective dynamics behind, 207–9; in Descartes's works, 200–204; and ecophobia, 202; origins of, 199–200

Brennan, Teresa, 5, 19n24, 142, 143–44, 279–80, 290, 292, 300
Brillat-Savarin, Jean Anthelme, 150n4
Brinkema, Eugenie, 30–31, 291
Bristow, Tom, 308, 310
Brown, Jayna, 218
Buell, Lawrence, 8
Bush, George W., 286
Butler, Judith, 214, 237, 238

camp humor, 239, 250, 250–51
capitalism: affective disconnection facilitating, 107; and affective economies, 124; and consumption, 134, 137–38, 146, 148–49; and cruel optimism, 42–43; cultural capitalism, 137–38; disappointment as consequence of, 259; green capitalism, 307–8; impact of veterans' experiences on, 157; impacts of climate change on, 171n8; impersonal nature of, 122; and Indigenous-led movements, 109–10; and mental ecosophy, 73, 77; and obesity, 304; role of hope in, 310; Spahr's critiques of, 33; and start of the Anthropocene, 27
Cariou, Warren, 104
Carnal Appetites (Probyn), 141
Casey, Edward, 60
Chen, Mel Y., 240–41
Chow, Rey, 107
Civilization and Its Discontents (Freud), 188–89
Clark, Charlie, 244
Clark, Timothy, 18n6, 33, 43
climate change: and affective impasses, 99–100; apparent apathy regarding, 2–3; approaches to grieving, 213–15;

and disappointment aversion, 273; empathic responses to, 130n10; for ENST students, 303–5; impact on emotions, 52; importance of negative affect to, 307–8; and Indigenous-led movements, 109–10; and land affect, 99, 102, 106, 109–10; linear film approaches to, 215–16; lives disproportionately affected by, 227–29; mental health consequences of, 301–2; nonlinear film approaches to, 216–18; ontological barriers to awareness of, 199–204; popular affective responses to, 14–15; possible impacts on capitalism, 171n8; relevance of tragedy to, 199. *See also* environmental crises
climate grief, 2, 11, 17n6
Clinton, Bill, 286
Clough, Patricia Ticineto, 4, 130n3, 237
Clover, Joshua, 25
Coetzee, J. M., 204–5
colonialism: and the Canadian tar sands, 101; and Indigenous rights, 101, 103, 109–10, 228; portrayed in *Beasts of the Southern Wild*, 226–27; through affective disconnection, 107; through appropriation of Indigenous worldviews, 110n7
commodity paratext (food labeling), 135–37, 144–45, 146, 150n8
conatus concept, 184
Connolly, William, 199
consciousness: and affective awareness, 111n11, 143; and anthropocentrism, 208; and desire, 183; and empathetic experiences, 119; and fictocriticism,

contagion, 125–26; emotion elicitation modalities, 58–59; Hogan's perceptual account of, 54–55; as navigatory, 261, 262, 263; in nonhuman animals, 180–83; relationship to affect, 5, 18n22, 261, 279; role in education, 300–301; role of environment in, 19n23, 51–52; translation of, 261; William James's theories on, 38–39. *See also* affects

emotives, 261, 263–64, 274n16, 275n18

empathic realism, 119, 129

empathy: animality as path to, 221–23; in Berry's ethical economy, 120–21, 128; compared to sympathy, 120–21; and consciousness, 126–27; definitions of, 13, 120; and emotional contagion, 125–26; as imagined ideal, 117–18; as innate in humans, 129n1; and issues of scale, 122–24, 128; political role of, 118–19, 124; referenced by President Obama, 117, 128, 129n2; in self/other differentiation, 118–19, 121, 124–28; and social change, 130n10

Endeavor (space shuttle), 28–29

Engaging the Everyday (Meyer), 307

Enlightenment period, 199, 200–207

Ensor, Sarah, 8–9

ENST programs. *See* Environmental Studies programs (ENST)

environmental affects, 15; amplification of, 28; in environmental studies programs, 301–6; melancholy, 289–90. *See also* queer environmental affects

environmental crises: affective responses to, 2, 282–83, 287–89, 295; atmosphere representing, 282–83; in environmental studies curricula, 303–5; inappropriate affects in,

236–37; linear film approaches to, 215–16; lives disproportionately affected by, 214, 228–29; narratives of, 1–2; negative affects associated with, 238–41; nonlinear film approaches to, 216–18; ontological barriers to awareness of, 199–204; privileges underlying, 304; related to food consumption, 147–48; relevance of tragedy to, 199, 201–2. *See also* climate change

environmentalism: and disappointment, 259–60, 272–74; environmental ethic, 264–65; environmental justice, 3, 12–15; and queer affects, 251; and tourism, 267

environmental killjoy, 15, 19n38

Environmental Studies programs (ENST): affective arc in, 299–300; environmental affect in, 301–6; environmental justice approach, 307–8; goals of, 308, 314n14; importance of negative affects in, 306–9; potential of, 306; required courses and readings in, 304, 305–6, 314n18, 316n65; role of faculty in, 312–13; senior capstone course in, 309; underrepresented minority students in, 305; use of critical hope in, 309–12

environments: in affect theory, 8–9, 17; agency of, 7–8; apprehended through affect, 280–82; atmosphere describing, 280–82, 295; atmospheric shifts in *Old Joy*, 283–86; connectivity of, 158; and cultural conditioning, 157; definitions of, 155; of ephemeral nature, 241–42; in *Gerry*, 293–95; in *Love in the Anthropocene*, 55–65; in material

Indigenous peoples: American racialized erasure of, 226–27; connections to the land, 97, 98, 102, 103–5, 111n24; disproportionately impacted by climate change, 228; impact of colonialism on, 101, 103, 110n7; impact of tar sands on, 101–2, 104–5; opposing tar sands extraction, 95–96; political movements of, 109–10
individualism, 161, 307–8
industrialism: and ethical economies, 122–28; and food production, 136; impersonal nature of, 122. *See also* capitalism
Ingram, David, 283–84, 288
"In Praise of Latin Night at the Queer Club" (Torres), 236
"Instincts and Their Vicissitudes" (Freud), 186
International Geological Congress, 65
Iovino, Serenella, 7
Isle de Jean Charles (LA), 227, 230n22
"It All Turns on Affection" (lecture), 119–20
Ivakhiv, Adrian, 225
ivory, 76–77

James, Erin, 53, 54
James, William, 31, 38–39, 41
Jameson, Frederic, 156
Jamieson, Dale, 52, 56
Jefferson Lecture in the Humanities, 119–21
Jensen, Derrick, 307
Jones, Robert, 257–58
Junger, Sebastian, 158, 159–60, 161, 167, 170, 172n25
Jurafsky, Dan, 145

Keeling Curve, 27–28
Keen, Suzanne, 54, 127

Kim, Richard, 236
King Lear (Shakespeare), 196, 197–98, 202
Klay, Phil, 156, 161–70
Klein, Naomi, 171n8
Krznaric, Roman, 121, 122, 124, 130n10

Ladino, Jennifer, 60, 65, 253n35
Lamb (Nadzam), 59
land: embodied experiences with, 109; energy of, 96; Indigenous connections to, 97, 98, 111n24; as mode of reciprocal relationship, 110; ontological importance of, 103–4. *See also* environments; nature
land affect: as counterpoint to affective economies, 98–99, 105–6; definitions of, 12–13, 97–98; experienced through extreme weather events, 96–97, 106, 108–9; grounded conceptions of, 98–99; negation of, 104; potentials of, 102, 105, 109–10; transmission of, 98; two modalities of, 108–10
The Land of Oil (documentary), 104
Langer, Susanne, 282
Larsen, Nella, 142
learning: affective responses, 263; disappointment enacting, 269; role of emotion in, 300–301
LeMenager, Stephanie, 32
Leys, Ruth, 111n11, 130n3
The Lives of Animals (Coetzee), 205
local economies: Berry's vision for, 119–21, 123–24, 128–29; compared to global, 118, 123–24, 128; connections to the land, 127; empathy in, 120–21; imagination as foundation for, 119–20; impacts of industrialism on, 122–24; self/other differentiation in, 124–25
Local Hero (film), 288

logging industry, 286

loss: affective turn originating in, 118; from climate change, 213–14; in disappointment, 262; grieving of, 238, 291; portrayed in *Beasts of the Southern Wild*, 221; portrayed in *Old Joy*, 285

love: defined, 51; impact of impoverished environments on, 62–63; as part of nature, 52; relationship to environment, 51–52

Love, Heather, 237, 239, 242, 249, 253n35

Love in the Anthropocene (Jamieson and Nadzam), 52; anticipatory nostalgia in, 65; environments described in, 55–56, 62–63; "Flyfishing," 57–61, 62–63, 64; "Holiday," 61–63, 64; psychoterratic dis-eases in, 55–65; purpose of, 56–57; "Zoo," 63–64

Luke, Timothy, 314n14

Lukianoff, Greg, 307

Lyons, H. A., 159–60

Macondo well, 34, 35–38

Maniates, Michael, 303, 307, 309, 314n18

Mar, Raymond, 53

marketplace: commodity paratext in, 137–38; control in, 143–44; establishing tastiness in, 146; and food options, 135; food's discursive reality in, 134. *See also* capitalism; food

Marsden, Lauren, 245

mass shootings, 235–36

Massumi, Brian, 5, 18n18, 30–31, 141, 145, 155, 157, 158, 162, 279, 292

material ecocriticism, 7–8, 19n24

Material Ecocriticism (Iovino and Oppermann), 7–8

Material Feminisms (Alaimo and Hekman), 7

material turn, 4, 6–8

Matless, David, 86

Mayr, Ernst, 185

McCarty, Kevin, 241

McIntosh, Peggy, 304

McKibben, Bill, 19n38

media: affective disconnection through, 107–8; amplifying Anthropocene anxiety, 28; covering environmental crises, 1–2, 288, 295; embodied processing of narratives, 2; impact on expectations, 272–73; impact on tourism, 270–72; narratives creating affective impasse, 99; narratives establishing affective economies, 96; tar sands narratives, 95–96, 99. *See also* films

melancholia, 237, 238–39

Melancholia (film), 289–92

melancholy, 237, 273–74, 288–92

memory, 2, 58–60, 259–60, 261, 264, 275n18

Men and Women in Water Cities (film), 243–46

mental ecosophy (Guattari's), 73, 77

Meredith, Jenna, 130n10

Merola, Nicole, 289–90

Messer, Sarah, 83–84

Mettler, Peter, 107–8

Meyer, John, 307

Million, Dian, 228

Milton, Kay, 51–52

Mirzoeff, Nicholas, 217

#Misanthropocene (Spahr and Clover), 25–26

Montaigne, Michel de, 196, 207–8

Morton, Timothy, 195–96, 273, 310, 311–12, 314n17, 315n25

Moser, Susanne C., 213, 214

Moss, Michael, 145, 152n26

Norgaard, Kari, 301, 308, 309, 310
"Northern Dark" (Dyer), 267
Northwest Forest Plan, 286
Norway, 267
nostalgia: defined, 285; in embodied
    encounters, 63–64; in homesickness,
    156; in *Love in the Anthropocene*,
    59–61, 63–64; motivational power
    of, 65; political potential of, 253n35;
    positive affects from, 68n71; in *Silent
    Running*, 249; and subjectivity, 170
Nussbaum, Martha, 51
Nyong'o, Tavia, 226–27

Oatley, Keith, 53, 54
Obama, Barack, 117, 124, 128, 129, 129n2
obesity, 141, 152n29, 304
objects: happiness attributed to, 259;
    relational networks of, 75–77, 80–82
O'Brien, Tim, 165
oil industry: connections to the land,
    96; and national sacrifice zones,
    103–4; portrayed in "Dynamic
    Positioning," 34–38. *See also* tar
    sands (Canada)
Old Joy (film), 283–87
The Omnivore's Dilemma (Pollan), 135–36
On the Origin of Species (Darwin), 183–85
ontologies: affective ontologies, 98–99,
    104, 105, 109–10; destruction of,
    103–4; of Indigenous peoples, 97,
    98, 102; place-based, 97, 98, 103–5;
    resurgence of, 104–5
Oppermann, Serpil, 7
optimism: in climate containment
    films, 216; "cruel optimism,"
    42–43, 118–19, 126, 128–29, 238; film
    portrayals of, 218–19; lack of in

Beasts of the Southern Wild, 218, 221,
    223–25, 229
Orbis Spike, 27
ordinary affects, 73, 82, 87, 100–101
Oregon, 283, 285–86
organic foods, 138, 150n8
the "Other": desiring, 177–78; "out"
    groups, 121; self/other differentia-
    tion, 118–19, 121, 124–28, 131n25
Otto, Eric, 57
Our Aesthetic Categories (Ngai), 142
OUT for Sustainability, 235
Outside magazine, 1
overburden (stripping process), 104
overconsumption, 146–47, 152n29

Packer, George, 172n39
Parables for the Virtual (Massumi),
    18n18
A Paradise Built in Hell (Solnit), 159
Paris Agreement (2015), 3, 100
Park, Ondine, 157
The Passions of the Soul (Descartes),
    200, 204
Patrick, Darren J., 242
perception, 38–39, 54–60, 160
Peterson, Christopher, 289
Petropolis (film), 107–8
Physiologie du goût (Brillat-Savarin),
    150n4
picturesque theory, 265–66
pleasure principle (Freud), 190
Plumwood, Val, 196
"Poem Written after September 11,
    2001" (Spahr), 33
"Poem Written from November 30,
    2002 to March 27, 2003" (Spahr), 33
Political Emotions (Nussbaum), 51

regionality: dialogical nature of, 79; and fictocriticism, 72, 78–79; and Guattari's three ecologies, 82–84; and mental ecology, 74–75; new gentleness of, 84–85. *See also* affective critical regionality; local economies

regret theory, 274n8

Reichardt, Kelly, 283–87

Reid, Julian, 228

religious experiences, 131n25

resignation, 294–95

resilience: neoliberal ideology of, 228–29; as trope in climate disaster films, 215–16

Resilient Life (Evans and Reid), 228

"Road Registers" (Stewart), 80, 81–82, 84

Robinson, Marilynne, 129n2

Rodriguez, Ramiro, 163–64

Romanticism, 257–58, 260, 262, 263

Rooney, Ellen, 30

Rosetta (film), 218–19

sacrifice zones (oil industry), 103–4

Salt Sugar Fat (Moss), 152n26

Sandilands, Catriona, 8, 238–39, 250

Savini, Catherine, 300

Scarry, Elaine, 54

Schmidt, Laura, 17n6

Schwab, Gabriele, 215, 216

Schwartz, Barry, 259

Scott, A. O., 217–18

Scranton, Roy, 164–65, 172n39

Sedgwick, Eve Kosofsky, 4, 237

Seigworth, Gregory J., 118

self/other differentiation, 118–19, 121, 124–28, 131n25

sexual desire (Freud), 186–87

sexual selection (Darwin), 179, 185

Seymour, Nicole, 9, 220

Shakespeare, William, 196, 197, 202

Sharpe, Christina, 218, 219

Shields, Rob, 104, 108, 157

significant form, 282

Silent Running (film), 247–51

Slow Violence and the Environmentalism of the Poor (Nixon), 172n45

Smaill, Belinda, 288

Smith, Andrea, 18n13, 103

Smithson, Robert, 109

social change: addressing underlying privileges, 303–4; affect theory's potential for, 3; and food choices, 137–38; and Guattari's expanded ecology, 71–72, 85–86; role of critical hope in, 309–12; role of emotion in, 301; role of negative affect in, 307–8

solastalgia: defined, 301; in homesickness, 53, 156; portrayed in *Old Joy*, 285; as a psychoterratic dis-ease, 65; solastalgic distress, 53, 60

soldiers. *See* veterans

Solnit, Rebecca, 159, 310–11, 312

Sontag, Susan, 250–51

sorrow, 282, 285, 288–89

Spahr, Juliana, 11, 25–26, 31–32, 41–43; "December 2, 2002," 28–29; "Dynamic Positioning," 34–42; *#Misanthropocene*, 25–26; "Poem Written after September 11, 2001," 33; "Poem Written from November 30, 2002 to March 27, 2003," 33; *That Winter the Wolf Came*, 25–26, 34; *this connection of everyone with lungs*, 25–26, 28–29, 33, 42, 43n3; *The Transformation*, 25–26, 32–33, 43n3, 46n63; "Unnamed Dragonfly Species," 33–34; *well then there now*, 25–26

touristic disappointment: of Frances
Trollope, 269–71; of Geoff Dyer,
260, 267–69; of Margaret Fuller,
271–72; in *The Prelude*, 260
tragedy: affective power of, 196, 202;
question of agency in, 201–2;
relevance to environmental crises, 199,
209; temporal disruption in, 198–99
The Transformation (Spahr), 25–26,
32–33, 43n3, 46n63
transmedial capture, 107–8
The Transmission of Affect (Brennan),
143, 279–80
trauma: as consequence of war, 157;
experiences defining, 160–61; homesickness resulting from, 169–70;
impacts on social behaviors, 159–61;
reshaping perspectives, 172n25
"The Trauma Hero" (Scranton), 164–65
Tribe (Junger), 159–60, 172n25
Trollope, Frances, 269–71
Trott, Nicola, 262
Trumbull, Douglas, 247
Trump, Donald, 2–3, 117
Truth and Reconciliation Commission
(TRC), 103
Tsing, Anna Lowenhaupt, 88n21
Tuan, Yi-Fu, 8

Ugly Feelings (Ngai), 9, 142, 280
unheimlich (uncanny), 156
"Unnamed Dragonfly Species" (Spahr),
33–34

van Dooren, Thom, 310, 311
Van Sant, Gus, 293–95
veterans: challenges of reintegration,
156, 161–62, 166–70, 171.; complex
affective state of, 169; disorientation

experienced by, 161, 166–70;
experiences defining, 160; extreme
affective openness of, 156, 157,
170; guilt felt by, 165; impact of
homesickness on, 156–57; new
perspectives forced on, 163–64, 167–
68. *See also* wartime environments
Vibrant Matter (Bennett), 6, 150n3
von Trier, Lars, 289–92
vulnerability: exposed through disappointment, 269; exposed through
nature, 197–99; human awareness
of, 205–6; portrayed in *Beasts of the
Southern Wild*, 220; in war, 155–56

Waal, Frans, de, 129n1
war: agency in, 158; disorientation of,
164; experiencing change in, 157–58;
homesickness in, 156, 170; impacts
of, 155, 159–60; new perspectives
forced by, 163–64, 167–68; openness
and vulnerability in, 155–56; trauma
caused by, 157. *See also* veterans
"War and Representation" (Jameson), 156
wartime environments: disorientation of,
164; extreme nature of, 161–62; forcing
new perspectives, 164; human-created
affectivity in, 155–56; potentials of,
168; processing of experiences in,
162–63. *See also* veterans
Water City, Berkeley (film), 243, 246–47
Watkins, Megan, 263, 265
Weighing In (Guthman), 304
Weik von Mossner, Alexa, 9, 10
well then there now (Spahr), 25–26
"What Are Affects" (Tomkins), 183
"What Is an Emotion?" (James), 38
"Where? What? Where?" (Dyer),
267–69

Lightning Source UK Ltd.
Milton Keynes UK
UKHW012023160820
368239UK00012B/45